MODERATE PURITANS AND THE
ELIZABETHAN CHURCH

Moderate puritans
and the
Elizabethan church

PETER LAKE

Lecturer in History, Bedford College, London

CAMBRIDGE UNIVERSITY PRESS

CAMBRIDGE

LONDON   NEW YORK   NEW ROCHELLE

MELBOURNE   SYDNEY

FOR JOY AND ANN

Moderate puritans and the Elizabethan church

PETER LAKE

Lecturer in History, Bedford College, London

CAMBRIDGE UNIVERSITY PRESS

CAMBRIDGE

LONDON   NEW YORK   NEW ROCHELLE

MELBOURNE   SYDNEY

PUBLISHED BY THE PRESS SYNDICATE OF THE UNIVERSITY OF CAMBRIDGE
The Pitt Building, Trumpington Street, Cambridge, United Kingdom

CAMBRIDGE UNIVERSITY PRESS
The Edinburgh Building, Cambridge CB2 2RU, UK
40 West 20th Street, New York NY 10011–4211, USA
477 Williamstown Road, Port Melbourne, VIC 3207, Australia
Ruiz de Alarcón 13, 28014 Madrid, Spain
Dock House, The Waterfront, Cape Town 8001, South Africa

http://www.cambridge.org

First published 1982
First paperback edition 2004

A catalogue record for this book is available from the British Library

Library of Congress catalogue card number: 81–17052

ISBN 0 521 24010 7 hardback
ISBN 0 521 61187 3 paperback

Contents

FOR JOY AND ANN

Preface

During the protracted preparation of this book I have incurred many debts. Of these the greatest is to Professor Gordon Rupp who first suggested moderate puritanism as a subject and who supervised my Ph.D. thesis. Without his kindness and encouragement my research would never have even started. Professor Geoffrey Elton has also been an unfailing source of help and encouragement. Professor Patrick Collinson has always shown remarkable patience and kindness in the face of the persistent queries of a novice in a field of which he is the undoubted master. I owe a great deal to the members of the Tudor seminar at the Institute of Historical Research who first taught me what a friendly place the scholarly world can be. Professor Conrad Russell was a source of great encouragement when it was most needed, as were Ann Hughes, Richard Cust, Gerry Bowler, John Nichols, Ron Fritze, Patricia Croot, David Hebb, David Thomas and Alan Thomas. I am extremely grateful to all of them. I have also had the benefit of discussions with Dr H. C. Porter, who stood in as my supervisor when Professor Rupp was on sabbatical, and Dr N. R. N. Tyacke. Latterly, Andrew Foster, Simon Adams and Bill Sheils have all provided stimulation and advice. I owe a debt to two books which no amount of citation in notes can properly convey. Professor Collinson's *The Elizabethan puritan movement* and Dr Porter's *Reformation and reaction in Tudor Cambridge* provided the starting point and constant guidelines for my research. This study stands in the relation of an extended footnote to these two seminal works. I should also like to thank my parents for putting up with the oldest student in Ilford. My research was first financed by a three-year studentship from the D.E.S. and then by a research fellowship at Clare College, Cambridge. I should like to thank the Master and Fellows of Clare for thus allowing me to finish my thesis and complete the reworked and rewritten version which has become this book. I have used material in Emmanuel College, Cambridge; Trinity College, Cambridge; and Pembroke College, Cambridge; Lambeth Palace Library; the Chetham Library; the North Yorkshire Record Office; the British Library; the Public Record Office, and Cambridge University Library. I should like to thank those concerned for permission to use the material discussed below and to acknowledge the unfailing courtesy and helpfulness of the staff in all those libraries as well as the Institute of Historical Research. My colleagues at Bedford College have been a source of great encouragement in providing so congenial an atmosphere in which to work and I should like to acknowledge a special debt to the patience and kindness of Miss Sheelagh Taylor who typed the final version of the manuscript with exemplary accuracy and care. I will conclude by thanking Kevin Watson, Richard Cust and Ann Hughes whose friendship and support were of crucial importance at a most difficult time.

In what follows the dates are in the old style, with the year taken to begin on 1 January. Extended passages of Latin have been paraphrased or translated. The translations are my own except where otherwise stated.

Introduction: Laurence Chaderton and the problem of puritanism

Puritanism is normally defined in negative terms. Puritans were people who, with varying degrees of intensity, disliked the Elizabethan settlement. Puritanism was a series of negative gestures directed against that settlement and the church it created. Those gestures could, at the simplest level, express a refusal to become implicated in the allegedly corrupt and corrupting elements in that settlement. Clerical non-conformity can be construed as such a gesture of disassociation from the supposedly popish remnants in the liturgy. These negative gestures, these drives to disassociate the godly elements in the English church from popish corruption, reached their most polemically developed and coherent form in the presbyterian platform. This summed up previous criticisms of the liturgy and polity of the church in terms of a fully developed and supposedly entirely scriptural vision of an alternative church polity. But presbyterianism was not merely a polemical gesture, a significant escalation in the confrontation between defenders of the ecclesiastical status quo and their opponents, it also provided the basis for the classis movement of the 1580s.[1] As Professor Collinson has shown, that movement constituted an attempt to take over the English church by constructing within the existing corrupt and popish shell the very model of a true church. This attempt to set up 'presbytery within episcopacy' allowed the members of the classis movement to conceive of themselves as, in some sense, the true representatives of the protestant English church.

There is in all this a logical progression of rejection and withdrawal from the established church; a progression which reached its logical conclusion in separation. It was no accident that the final collapse of the classis movement in 1589/90 was accompanied by a resurgence of separatist activity in London, or that when asked, in 1593, what had prompted them to become separatists, many of the members of Francis Johnson's London church replied that, through listening to presbyterian sermons, they had become convinced of the complete corruption of the English church.[2] Any account of puritanism in the Elizabethan period must centre itself on this phenomenon. In so far as there was a coherent puritan movement during this period it was forced, by its own failure to capture the commanding heights of ecclesiastical power, to define itself against the ecclesiastical status quo. The key texts for any study of puritanism are hence polemics directed against that status quo, in which the authors are concerned to emphasise the points of difference and dispute which separated them from their conformist opponents. It is thus the emergence of presbyterianism, both as an ideology in the 1570s and as an underground movement in the 1580s, that stands at the centre of Professor Collinson's book on *The Elizabethan puritan movement.*

But puritanism, even in its most overt gestures of refusal and rejection (most notably the refusal to *conform* to the ceremonies and liturgical forms of the established church which is conventionally regarded as the first expression of the puritan impulse),[3] cannot be convinced in primarily negative terms. For the refusal to conform was justified and motivated by the need to avoid the offence of the godly and the delusion of the weak in faith. The ceremonies involved were conceived to be so associated with popery in the popular consciousness that while those truly affected to the gospel would be, perhaps irredeemably, offended and alienated by their use, the ignorant and crypto-popish majority would be deluded into thinking that nothing in the church had really changed, and so confirmed in their popish errors. In short, rejection of conformity was justified in terms of 'edification', that process through which a true community of godly and properly self-conscious true believers was called together and sustained within the church.[4] That was the positive goal that prompted the puritan critique of the established church. For that critique, in all its forms, was designed to identify the liturgical and institutional faults in a church which hindered or altogether prevented such a process. Hence, while it is possible and legitimate to regard the puritan critique of the established church as the product of

a precise, even pettifogging legalism and to characterise presbyterianism as a product of a literal-minded scripturalism, that is
far from the whole truth. For behind all these diverse phenomena
lay an intense vision of the reality and mutuality of the community of the godly and of the way in which that community could
and should be called together through the word, particularly the
word preached. Presbyterianism can thus be characterised simply
as a developed analysis of the inadequacies of the English church
as a proselytising institution. Admittedly it was justified and, in
part, prompted by a certain set of attitudes to scripture and its
authority. Yet the highly arcane and academic disputes that it
produced between its clerical proponents and conformist apologists (notably in the Admonition controversy) should not blind
us to the intensely evangelical impulse that had prompted the
whole affair in the first place.

But as soon as the historian's attention is shifted to the positive
evangelical protestant aims that lay behind puritan attacks on,
and rejections of, the established church, the whole issue of
puritanism takes on a different aspect. For while the English
church might be a defective proselytising institution, while it
might hinder that process whereby the community of the godly
were called together, it did not altogether prevent it or render it
impossible. Their own presence in the English church, the strong
links of thought and feeling that bound together puritan ministers,
their clerical colleagues and their lay followers and patrons,
provided a powerful reminder of the extent to which the corrupt
forms and structures provided by the English church could be
infused with the values of true religion. Hence, the very aims and
values that had first prompted the puritan assault on the church
also served to attach puritan loyalties to that church. When conformists sought to make continuance in the ministry conditional
on acceptance of what puritans took to be the corrupt elements
in the structure of the English church, puritan ministers were
forced to confront a choice between their puritan principles, the
public, polemical commitments that their vision of true religion
had led them to make, and their practical capacity to pursue
those same edificational, evangelical aims as ministers of the
word.

This study seeks to examine how a certain group of divines
sought to negotiate that choice and still retain both their self-

image as 'puritans', principled members of the most godly and committed section of English protestant opinion, and their active role within the established church. These men, in fact, hoped to enjoy the best of both worlds. The present study is intended to demonstrate the extent to which they succeeded in achieving that aim and the practical and ideological means they used to achieve it. It started as an examination of the career of Laurence Chaderton. Chaderton was a noted puritan divine, whose career covered the entire span of Elizabeth's reign and beyond. First as a fellow of Christ's College, Cambridge, and from 1584 as the first Master of the new puritan foundation, Emmanuel College, Chaderton stood at the very centre of Cambridge puritanism from the 1560s until his retirement in 1622. He was a noted presbyterian and closely involved in the classic movement. Yet his career in the university proceeded without let or hindrance from the authorities. However, by the end of the century he can be found defending the puritan position before King James at the Hampton Court Conference in the most moderate terms. Chaderton's career seemed to raise a number of interesting questions about English puritanism. How could the different roles, that of presbyterian radical and that of university divine and administrator, be so easily combined in one career? Even if Chaderton himself experienced no sense of strain in reconciling the two roles, why did the authorities allow him the luxury of doing so for so long unmolested? What happened to his puritanism after the final collapse of the classis movement in 1590? Was Chaderton merely a young radical turned ageing conservative? If not, what did his fellow puritans make of his performance at Hampton Court and his subsequent espousal of ceremonial conformity?

In short, Chaderton's career raised the issue of the existence and nature of a continuous puritan tradition during the half century after 1559. If Chaderton did indeed represent the personification of just such a tradition, how did he manage to negotiate the potential clash between his puritan principles and the commitment to the national church represented by his position in the power structure of the university? And if a career like his could be used to demonstrate just such a continuous puritan tradition running throughout the period, what was it about that tradition that rendered it distinctively 'puritan'? That last question took on a particular urgency since Chaderton's attitude to the supposedly central issues of conformity and church polity shifted as his career progressed.

These, then, were the issues and considerations which prompted my research. The extent to which they are subject to coherent or satisfactory answers is, as ever, a function of the nature of the available sources. For Chaderton himself these are interesting without being comprehensive. They comprise two printed sermons, some draft letters and lectures from the period immediately after Hampton Court, some notes taken from lectures delivered in 1590 and some rather scanty material from Emmanuel College itself. A study of Chaderton based on these alone, while feasible, would be of limited significance. However, his central position in the university, together with his longevity, rendered Chaderton an ideal focus for a more general study. The sources available permitted a relatively full, if rather patchy, analysis of Chaderton's style of divinity, in terms of both formal theology and practical preaching, as well as an account of his attitudes to the issues of conformity and church polity between roughly 1580 and 1605. To broaden the scope of this study I have attempted to arrange a similar analysis of other men prominent in the university and the wider puritan movement. As well as the broad resemblances between their career structures and concerns, all these men enjoyed demonstrable personal links with Chaderton. And in addition to providing the central point of ideological reference, the touchstone of 'moderate puritanism', Chaderton's career and contacts also provide a 'prosopographical' point of reference for this study. All the men discussed below were either friends, colleagues or protégés of Chaderton.

Hence this study starts not with Chaderton but with Edward Dering. A fellow of Christ's College, Cambridge, during the 1560s, Dering was perhaps the leading puritan scholar of his generation. His career serves to tie this study into the earliest years of Elizabethan puritanism, when the lines of ideological dispute and division of later decades had barely been laid down. Dering helped to establish the style of evangelical protestantism into which the young Chaderton was inducted at Christ's during the 1560s. His continuing loyalty to that style of protestantism provided a central unifying theme throughout his career and it is thus through Dering that its essential characteristics may be established at the outset. As a leading scholar and a man with friends in high places, Dering also provides the model of the moderate puritan divine's social position and career structure. His struggle to reconcile his attachment to protestant or puritan principle with his own relatively exalted position in the church and university likewise serves to establish a central theme of this study.

However, of these other men, introduced to supplement and extend the material on Chaderton himself, the most prominent is William Whitaker. Whitaker was a leading defender of the English church against Rome during the 1580s and early 1590s. A university divine, first as a fellow of Trinity College and then as Master of St John's, he provides an interesting contrast and complement to Chaderton. There can be no doubting the closeness of the ties between them, related as they were by friendship and then by marriage (the two men were brothers-in-law). Yet Whitaker was neither a presbyterian nor a non-conformist. In what, then, did his puritanism consist, what ideological considerations, if any, underwrote the closeness of his links with Chaderton, and the undoubted perception of Whitaker, by contemporaries, as a puritan? This leads directly to a consideration of the activity that dominated Whitaker's career – the production of anti-papal polemic. Taking up the cudgels against Rome had a dual significance for the puritan divine. It was at once an expression of protestant zeal and an implicit gesture of loyalty to a national church, the protestantism of whose doctrine was generally acknowledged. To underline this point the role of anti-papal polemic in the careers of both Thomas Cartwright and Walter Travers is examined.[5] For both of these men were university-trained divines of the same stamp as Chaderton and Whitaker and both enjoyed demonstrable links with Chaderton. It is one of the basic contentions of this study that Cartwright's position during the 1580s can be assimilated to that occupied by men like Chaderton and Whitaker, and that Cartwright's enlistment as a major polemicist against Rome represents an attempt to advertise and exploit that common front for polemical anti-conformist purposes.

Indeed, it might be argued that the moderate puritan position as it is described here was virtually invented by Cartwright. In so far as that position represented an attempt to vindicate puritan claims to occupy the middle ground of protestant orthodoxy against conformist counterclaims of puritan subversion, it is best approached as it sought to define itself against the spectre of popery. The sources for this section of the analysis are provided by some letters in the Lansdowne Manuscripts in the British Library and the State Papers Domestic, and by the massive corpus of printed polemic produced by Whitaker and Cartwright.

But if one end of the spectrum of religious opinion against which moderate puritans sought to define their position was provided by popery, the other extreme was provided by separatism. Separatism, however, was a considerably less comfortable subject for the puritan divine than popery. For separation represented the unacceptable face of puritan radicalism, the logical extension of puritan and presbyterian positions past the point of no return. Certainly conformists claimed that this was the case and most puritan divines gave implicit force to their allegations by rigorously avoiding the subject. Yet it was in the face of separation, the ultimate gesture of criticism of and disillusion with the status quo, that the ambiguities of the moderate puritan position best reveal themselves. Hence, Cartwright's response to the separatist challenge in two letters, one to Anne Stubbe and the other to Robert Harrison (edited and published by Albert Peel and Leland Carlson in their *Cartwrightiana*), provides a crucial source for the position adopted by conforming presbyterians such as Chaderton or Cartwright himself.

While the simple production of anti-papal polemic was a gesture which in itself carried a considerable ideological charge, the polemics produced by both Whitaker and Cartwright can also be used to establish the theological content of the moderate puritan position. But there was more at stake here than a formal doctrinal consensus, important though that was. Of crucial significance here was the way in which certain doctrines were applied and used in the course of puritan practical divinity. While it is possible to say something about the internal logical and emotional structure of puritan divinity from the formal doctrinal treatises themselves, by far the best source is provided by puritan practical divinity as produced from the pulpit. For puritan preaching was simply the attempt to apply the truths of right doctrine to the spiritual condition and varying situations of the godly.

Unfortunately, William Whitaker himself printed no such practical sermons and no manuscript notes survive. There is, however, one such sermon by Chaderton extant in print. This can be augmented by a series of notes taken from lectures given by Chaderton in 1590. In addition there is the commonplace book of Abdias Ashton, Whitaker's protégé and eventual biographer. Using these sources, chapter 7 attempts an analysis of the nature and internal structure of puritan practical divinity during the 1580s and 1590s.

However, the men under dicussion here were not only theologians, academics and preachers, they were also men of affairs who, within the closed world of the university, were magistrates and administrators in their own right. Moreover, it is in their attempts to convert their 'puritan' principles into practical guidelines for the conduct of affairs that the distinctive nature of their puritanism, and the differences that separated it from other, more conformist styles of protestantism, show most clearly. Here the paradigm of a puritan institution is provided by that godly seminary Emmanuel College. However, more interesting because more contentious and therefore better documented, is the history of St John's College under Whitaker's mastership. For Whitaker's attempt to convert St John's into a godly seminary on the same lines as Chaderton's Emmanuel provoked bitter opposition within the college. The resulting controversies generated considerable documentation both in the Cambridge University archives and in the Lansdowne Manuscripts, and it is on this basis that the account included below is constructed.

A parallel instance of an attempt to turn a basically puritan set of assumptions (this time about the nature and content of right doctrine) into the informing principle of university administration is provided by the theological disputes of 1595/6. Here again the account centres around the subtle but essential difference between a doctrinal consensus and the puritan and conformist visions of the implications of that consensus. The disputes are approached from the perspective provided by the moderate puritan position outlined thus far, and they are seen as revolving around the moderate puritan Heads' attempt to enforce their own view of the nature of right doctrine and its role in the determination of true membership of the English church. In short, the disputes are seen as a product of the Heads' attempt to give practical force to the sort of attitudes and assumptions already analysed in terms of theory and formal polemic in the sections on anti-papal polemic. The account of these disputes is based on a letter book in Trinity College, Cambridge, and owes much to Dr Porter's brilliant treatment of the same events in his *Reformation and reaction in Tudor Cambridge*. If my emphasis differs slightly from that of Dr Porter, it is largely because I wish to use the disputes to address a slightly different set of issues. My concern is not mainly with the disputes as a series of exercises in formal theology. For a more detailed interpretation of that aspect of the affair I can do no better than refer the reader to Dr Porter.

The final sections of this study deal with the issue of subscription and conformity in the immediate aftermath of Hampton Court. The first part deals with the response of Laurence Chaderton. It is based on a series of manuscript lecture notes and draft letters in the Chaderton Manuscripts in Lambeth Palace Library, and seeks to see Chaderton's position as a logical extension of the moderate position as it had emerged during the 1580s. A central element in the argument here concerns the continued links of respect and practical co-operation that still joined Chaderton to his younger and more radical brethren in the ministry. Moderation in matters ceremonial was no bar to the acceptance of a man like Chaderton as a friend and colleague. Here a key example is provided by the nature of Chaderton's contact with Thomas Brightman, as evidenced by their correspondence after Hampton Court. A more detailed examination of the same theme is essayed in the concluding section of this study through the life and opinions of William Bradshaw. This chapter is based largely on Bradshaw's published tracts, with biographical details supplied from the life in Clarke's *A general martyrologie*. Bradshaw's radicalism, on the issues of church polity and conformity, can hardly be doubted. Yet he was also a protégé of Chaderton. This section attempts to locate Bradshaw within the mainstream puritan tradition personified by Chaderton. The point is not simply to assimilate his position to that of Chaderton. It is to suggest that Bradshaw's position can as easily and legitimately be set in the context provided by the preceding analysis of the moderate puritan tradition, as in that provided by the subsequent history of 'non-separating congregationalism' or Independency. This in turn sheds an interesting sidelight onto the nature of that mainstream tradition. For if it was necessary, in order to preserve the self-image, the polemical and personal cutting edge of 'English puritanism', for Bradshaw to adopt the position that he did, and if, having adopted it, he was not irrevocably cut off from the puritan mainstream, what does that say for the 'moderation' of moderate puritanism? If Chaderton's most obvious successors in the university were conformist and careerist divines like Samuel Ward,[6] it does no harm to recall that Bradshaw could advance just as good a claim to be the true heir of the moderate puritan tradition as formulated and transmitted by Laurence Chaderton and William Whitaker.

Finally, having attempted briefly to explain the contents of this study, I ought perhaps to attempt to justify an omission. It could be argued that if anybody belonged in a study of 'moderate puritans and the Elizabethan church' it would be William Perkins. Certainly, I would argue that Perkins has to be seen as a product of precisely the moderate puritan tradition with which this study is concerned. A friend and pupil of Chaderton, he was in many ways the inheritor of the Dering/Chaderton tradition of puritan divinity. But Perkins is a vast subject in himself. In the compass of the present study it would not have been possible to add anything of note to the brilliant portrait to be found in Dr Porter's book, or the more extended analysis by Dr Breward. While the present study can be taken as an attempt to outline the intellectual milieu or context which produced Perkins' thought, the attempt to set Perkins within that context has been left for another occasion. In the meantime the reader is referred to the work of Dr Porter and Dr Breward.[7]

It may be as well to conclude these introductory remarks by making the rather crude methodological assumptions implicit in the preceding account somewhat more explicit. To begin with, it might be objected that in taking moderate puritanism as a subject certain central questions of definition have been begged. Apart from the perennially difficult question of defining puritanism, we now have the equally problematical question of defining moderation. In the sixteenth century, as now, 'moderate' was a much prized label of great polemical value. The use of the term 'puritan' or 'precisian' was similarly an extremely highly charged polemical activity. What then were to be the criteria for inclusion in such a study?

The difficulties involved in defining 'puritanism' are easier to identify than solve and I really have nothing original to say on that subject. To do so at the outset of an enquiry which is, in a sense, an extended exercise in definition would perhaps be inappropriate. It seemed to me that any attempt to define my terms too closely at the start would be to indulge in a circular process whereby the results of the entire enterprise would be determined by its initial terms of reference. Certainly, the history of puritanism has been bedevilled by just this sort of solecistic procedure. At the outset the existence of something called 'puritanism' is assumed. The particular examples of this entity are then amassed and arranged under different headings, as specimens of the 'puritan' attitude to this or that. The tendency is to attribute almost a higher reality to the general phenomenon than to its particular embodiments in individual men or texts. Certainly, such an approach needs to be subjected to a 'nominalist' critique.[8] This is not to challenge the need for any concept of 'puritanism' as a coherent, logically and emotionally related, set of opinions and attitudes. But it is to remark that such a concept should only emerge from a study of the activities of particular men, in particular contexts, acting and reacting to events over a period. It is also to point out that the resulting general picture of the 'puritan world-view' will be a heuristic device constructed by the historian, not necessarily conforming precisely to the opinions of any one man, or group of men. For the position thus constructed will contain many elements or strains, some of which will be given greater prominence by some men rather than others, or by the same man at different stages of his career.

By concentrating on Chaderton and limiting myself to men closely related to him, both in their careers and in their opinions, I have attempted to root my analysis in the ideological and social practice of a specific group of men. Chaderton was a man who by any definition has to be accepted as a puritan. By taking him as a central point of reference and arranging the others who figure in this study around him, I have attempted to establish a certain spectrum of opinion, stretching from the most committed and well known proponent of presbyterianism, Thomas Cartwright, on the left, to the entirely conformable Dr Whitaker on the right.

Now that this spectrum has been delineated the central concerns which united these men as proponents of the same world-view have to be identified. Here an attempt has been made to see the different aspects of their commitment to true religion as a unity and hence to establish the interconnections between their various activities. Central to this enterprise was an attempt to distinguish between the essential and inessential elements in a man's puritanism. Given that some men were presbyterians and that others were not, what were the principal areas of agreement that underwrote their status, both in their own eyes and in the eyes of their contemporaries, as proponents of basically the same case, as adherents of the same 'puritan' position?

To answer that question it was necessary to analyse firstly the contents of these men's views. But the formal analysis of set positions on key issues like conformity or presbyterianism was not in itself sufficient. Perhaps even more crucial for this sort of enquiry than what was said was when it was said, and to whom, and in what terms it was expressed. Hence, Chaderton's advocacy of conformity in 1605 was not construed by the godly as apostasy precisely because of the ideological credit he had built up throughout his long career and because of the polite and brotherly terms in which it was expressed, and further because it was circulated in private letters and sermons and not printed in some public gesture of recantation and reconciliation towards the conformists.[9] The same thing could be said of Thomas Cartwright's dealings with the separatists. The reputation of the author, his brotherly, comradely tone, and the form used (again Cartwright had chosen to express himself in private letters, not printed public polemic) saved Cartwright from charges of backsliding and conformity.[10]

This, of course, raises the issue of the contemporary reputation of the men discussed here. To an extent puritans were men who were regarded by their contemporaries as 'puritans'. Certainly, the capacity of the godly to recognise one another in the face of a corrupt and potentially hostile world was a central part of puritan divinity.[11] But while the godly recognised one another as simply zealous protestants, the 'leaven that leavened the whole lump' of the English church, their opponents and critics saw them as 'puritans', using that term as an insult and an accusation. What from the inside of godly opinion looking out appeared to be personal godliness and a proper zeal for God's cause seemed, from the outside looking in, to be an over-precise hypocrisy and subversive radicalism. Clearly, the term 'puritan' was a loaded one, its use charged with ambiguity and polemical edge. Equally clearly, the nature and extent of a man's recognition of his contemporaries as true professors would vary according to the individual's ideological presuppositions and polemical situation. Conformist perceptions of the nature and extent of precisian radicalism and subversion would similarly vary, according to the perspective and situation of the viewer. Obviously, contemporaries did not use the term as a value-free category for social analysis. But this does not mean that when they did use the word they were referring to nothing in particular or indeed everything in general. To take an example, in some lectures given in 1590 Laurence Chaderton lamented that the most godly and zealous of preachers were incessantly labelled with the hateful name of 'puritan', an occurrence he attributed entirely to the jealousy and malice of the ungodly. At first sight Chaderton would appear to be repudiating the use of the term altogether. It was, we are often told, simply a term of abuse, devoid of positive meaning, and Chaderton's attitude appears to confirm that. Yet it is a necessary consequence of Chaderton's remarks that those people against whom the word was employed as an insult were to be equated with the most zealous and godly elements in the English church, and that those who used it as a term of abuse were to be regarded as having condemned themselves out of their own mouths as profane and ungodly. From here it was but a short distance to the positive use of the term by Chaderton's protégé, William Bradshaw, who flaunted and gloried in the word, using it to denote simply the most godly and zealous of English protestants, as opposed to their corrupt and careerist conformist opponents.[12] To conclude, as Professor Collinson has recently observed: 'if we share with contemporaries a sense of Puritanism which is at once polemical and nominalistic then far from circumscribing its meaning we should regard the incidence of the term in contemporary discourse as indicative of theological, moral and social tension which should be the prime object of our investigations'.[13]

With these remarks in mind, if we look at William Whitaker and observe that his closest links were with men like Chaderton of undoubted 'puritan' persuasion, that his opponents consistently condemned him as a 'puritan', and that his actions were consistently seen to favour the 'puritan' side in any dispute, it becomes impossible to sustain any definition of the word which does not allow its application to Whitaker, whatever the nature of his formal attitude to conformity or the polity of the church. Similarly, in 1605, the fact that outright non-conformists like Walter Jones or Thomas Brightman could readily accept Chaderton as a colleague and even a mentor, despite his known and longstanding attitude to conformity, must mean that any definition of puritanism which would include Brightman and Jones and exclude Chaderton must be defective. In short, rather than attempt formally to define the term at the outset I have instead allowed the structure of the argument, the demonstrable links of thought and feeling, of friendship and co-operation, that bound the men under discussion here together, to define it as the analysis progresses.

That progress is, it must be admitted, episodic and rather uneven. This is deliberate. It is a function of the nature of the sources upon which it is based. While quite full, these are incomplete and patchy. They do not allow the sort of smooth chronological account, giving a fully rounded analysis of puritan attitudes to a wide range of subjects, for which one might wish. To take the example of Chaderton, the major sources used below for the reconstruction of his attitudes are all very different, the product of different situations, the need to appeal to different types of audience, and structured by differences in his own situation and in the situation in the church at large. Each, then, has to be treated in its own right.

Clearly, such a 'nominalist' approach can be taken too far, and the analysis conducted below is written on the assumption that the writings and activities of any one man can be usefully juxtaposed and compared, and that through that comparison certain basic structures and tendencies will emerge. Indeed, it is written on the further assumption that if this man has friends and colleagues all engaged in the same intellectual, social and emotional project, their various works and activities can be likewise compared, with like results. The analysis conducted below thus rests on a calculated risk on the gamble that the assumption that the various texts and events discussed here have some bearing on each other is sufficiently balanced by the sensitivity of the treatment of each particular nexus of sources, thus avoiding the crudest sort of confusion between the general phenomenon of puritanism and its particular embodiments. Clearly, no study of this subject can avoid such confusions. This present study rests on certain assumptions about puritanism brought to the sources from outside, of which the most glaring is that Laurence Chaderton, because of his presbyterianism, his contemporary reputation and contacts, can indeed be accepted as a puritan. It aims to justify that assumption through its treatment of the sources used below. The success with which it does so is, of course, a matter for the reader to judge.

2

Moderate beginnings: the case of Edward Dering

In any account of moderate puritanism, in particular of moderate puritanism in the University of Cambridge, the obvious place to start is Christ's College and the obvious person to start with is Edward Dering. For it was with Dering, a fellow of Christ's College throughout the 1560s, that the foundations of the moderate puritan tradition were laid. Writing of Dering Professor Patrick Collinson has identified, as 'the obsessive theme' which 'necessarily dominates any account of the man', 'the intense evangelical experience by a first generation protestant of justification and union with Christ through the renunciation of "will works" and of the world and the exercise of a lively faith'. It was this, together with a 'consuming desire to convey this experience to others', that produce Dering's 'puritanism'. This, as Collinson concluded, 'should serve as a reminder that much of what we call puritanism at this time was nothing but authentic protestantism and that the reign of Elizabeth was not conspicuously a post-reformation age...but the age of the English reformation par excellence when protestantism was for the first time taking a strong hold on families of the country gentry and the urban middle classes'. The passage is the basic text upon which this study is but an extended commentary.[1]

Certainly Dering himself was well aware that he was living in no post-reformation era; that, in his own words, 'scarce one of a great many can give an account of their faith'.[2] For Dering there was only one means to put this situation to rights – the incessant preaching of God's word. For 'we cannot believe except we hear no we cannot hear without a preacher'.[3] 'Thus God hath appointed it to make his power known that by the foolishness of preaching he might confound the wisdom of the world with the weak strength of the sound of words overthrow the fear of the heart of man. . . All other fear it is but little and we may either withstand it or fly from it but the power of the word is such as shall pass through all stops and hindrances; every mountain shall be brought low and every valley shall be filled, crooked things shall be made straight and rough ways shall be made smooth that the law may pass out of Sion.'[4]

The necessary concomitant of this view was an extremely exalted vision of the ministry which preached this all-powerful word of God. True ministers were 'the dispensers of the mysteries of God' 'by whom the people do believe'.[5] 'The minister is but the mouth of God in whose person Christ himself is either refused or received before whom to exalt a man is to set up the clay above the potter and make a difference of persons before whom there is neither Jew nor gentile, bond nor free, prince nor subject.' It followed 'that if this function were supplied with dutiful officers the sword of the spirit which God hath given them would vanquish Satan and destroy the power of darkness, till the knowledge of God were plentiful upon earth and all the joys of heart were sealed unto men in perfect beauty'.[6]

That such a happy state of affairs had not come into being Dering attributed to the fact that 'this function' was patently not supplied with 'dutiful officers'. 'Scarce one parish of an hundred' could claim to have a properly trained and pious incumbent.[7] For that Dering laid the blame firmly at the door of the authorities. Hence, during the period 1569/70 Dering set out to do something about the parlous state of the church. He attempted singlehanded to transform the church by 'converting' perhaps the three most powerful figures in the ecclesiastical hierarchy – Parker, Cecil (Lord Burghley after 1571) and the Queen – to his own brand of evangelical protestant religion.[8] Casting himself in the role of the Old Testament prophet, Dering set himself to awaken a true protestant zeal in the hearts of these three august personages. In each case Dering's theme was the present state of the church, devoid of godly preachers, afflicted by dumb dogs, non-residence, pluralism and a faulty form of ecclesiastical discipline. In addition, Cecil incurred his particular displeasure for sponsoring the new, anti-precisian statutes for the University of Cambridge, while Parker was rebuked for personal lapses, ranging from his own excessive swearing and the ostentatiously large size of his household to the gaudy dress of his sons.

In each case Dering's appeal was essentially a moral and personal one; an attempt to awaken a personal sense of sin and responsibility to God for the charges vouchsafed to them as magistrates. By the unaided force of the word Dering was attempting to achieve a basic reorientation of the personalities of these three magistrates and through them, at a stroke, to reform the whole church. Hence, his basic theme was the integral link between the individual's internal spiritual condition and his external conduct – in this instance summed up in the magistrates' stewardship of God's church. He remarked to Cecil that 'I would you had seen the horror of sin, I am sure you would also be afraid of the shadow. Because you have not felt it as you should if you think it but a trifle and spare not to grieve the weak conscience of others your case is such that it were better for you that a mill stone were tied about your neck and you thrown in the bottom of the sea.'⁹ Likewise he wrote to Parker, 'you know not (my Lord), you know not what pleasing cogitations these are in a life so instituted there are no miscarriages shall vex them, no discommodities shall break thy heart, no misfortunes shall hurt thee, no cares shall molest thee, no fear of sickness or death shall afflict thee; so the world shall by little and little seem vile unto you, so heavenly desires shall be of esteem that you might often cry out with the Apostle "I desire to be dissolved". Get unto yourself these abundant riches of the mind and you shall accomplish great felicity; if yee shall suffer yourself to be deprived of this prize, you shall (my Lord), be of all men most unfortunate.'¹⁰

Here, then, is that intense evangelical experience of justification as Dering tried to communicate it to Parker and Cecil, and even to the Queen. For it was from the essence of that experience that the zeal for the further reformation which Dering was trying to engender in the heart of the magistrate sprang. By working a sudden change in the individual, protestant conversion produced an intense feeling of isolation in the regenerate man, newly won to the kingdom of heaven but still surrounded by the iniquities of an unregenerate world. That stark contrast produced by the failure of the external world to mirror the spiritual metamorphosis undergone by the individual generated great tension. Puritan zeal, as a drive to bring external reality into line with the subjective experience undergone by the individual believer, was the direct expression of that tension. It was, therefore, the doctrine and experience of justification by faith, and the sense of election it engendered, that lay behind the puritan drive to further reformation.

Certainly, Dering conducted his campaign for reform almost entirely in such general ethical terms. He did not indulge in detailed analyses of the faults and institutional failings of the church and at no time directly denounced episcopacy as unlawful. His relationship with 'iure divino' presbyterianism seems fairly straightforward. 'I have never', he told Cecil, 'broken the peace of the church neither for cap nor surplice, for Archbishop nor bishop, if those that should be the light of the world do think me fantastical, these are my fancies that I have told of their common swearing the name of God in vain; that I have misliked their covetousness; that I have complained of papists...; that I have said this courtly apparel is not meet for such as should be more sober.' Hence, while Dering appealed to Cecil 'for your own sake and for the church of God stand favourable to Mr Cartwright', he did so without endorsing Cartwright's opinions. Cecil was to 'exhort him [Cartwright] to use Christian liberty and to bear with the time' but not to punish him 'because he is afraid of the shadow of sin. We have a common saying he that hath been stricken with the sword is afraid of the scabbard. I would you had seen the horror of sin, I am sure you would also be afraid of the shadow.'[11] Once again Dering's emphasis was on the spiritual reality of sin, not its external forms. Faced with a choice between Cartwright's over-zealous confusion of the two, and Cecil's conformist insensitivity to them both, there was no doubt where Dering stood. But he had not yet aligned himself with Cartwright's presbyterianism.

By 1573, however, things had changed. Dering's attempt to reform single-handed the entire church through his personal influence with its leaders can perhaps be seen as a last attempt to exploit and perpetuate the broad-based protestant consensus of the 1560s in order to force the church into more fully reformed courses. When that failed (as it had to) Dering was forced into the arms of the nascent presbyterian party. In the crisis of 1573 Dering aligned himself quite clearly on the presbyterian side. He wrote once more to Burghley on Cartwright's behalf and visited Field and Wilcox in Newgate.[12] Evidently the suspicions of the authorities were now well and truly aroused, for on 29 May Dering (along with others who had visited the two radicals in prison) was called before Star Chamber and asked to comment on a series of articles taken from Cartwright's book.[13]

Dering's answers are instructive. They reveal avowedly presbyterian opinion, veiled behind what were to become the distinctive features of the moderate puritan position. Hence, Dering allowed an area of adiaphora in externals and spoke as though the issues raised by the continuing use of the prayer book could usefully be discussed under that heading. However, his endorsement of the liturgy was limited to a grudging acceptance of the basic legal requirement as he saw it. At present the prayer book was too similar to popery and too lax in its allowance of a mere reading ministry to allow him to subscribe without qualification. Remarking on the seeming triviality of many puritan objections Dering explained that 'the weight of sin is not in substance of matter but in the majesty of God that is offended and be the thing never so little yet the breach of his commandment deserveth death'. In short, while he accepted the inherent indifference of the ceremonies in question, he remained obstinately committed to the fine details of the puritan critique of the liturgy and reserved the right to criticise the present liturgical arrangements most severely on the grounds of expediency and edification. This nicely balanced piece of equivocation became typical of the stance adopted by moderate puritans and presbyterians who were unwilling to allow themselves to be deprived over mere externals but who yet refused simply to conform.

Such sentiments left room for presbyterian principles. Certainly, the admission that the ceremonies in question were inherently indifferent and not, in themselves, worth the loss of the ministry did not preclude a full espousal of the presbyterian platform as both Thomas Cartwright and Laurence Chaderton were to prove. Moreover, Dering's replies to specific questions seem to have been calculated to leave room for presbyterian scruples. Challenged on the power of the prince in causes ecclesiastical Dering acknowledged that 'princes have full authority over all ecclesiastical and civil persons and equally over both to punish the offenders or give praise to the well doers'. But he added significantly, 'in the church there is no lawgiver but Christ Jesus'. Hence, the 'prince ruleth in the commonwealth herself and in the church of God seeth that

be ruled of the Lord'.[14] Dering did not venture an opinion as to
what laws Christ the lawgiver may have handed down for the
government of his church. Nevertheless, he had effectively divided
church and state leaving, as he remarked in a letter to Burghley,
jurisdiction over the natural man to the prince but reserving for
the ministers of God alone the spiritual sphere 'where the worldly
power of the prince hath no place'.[15] Moreover, Dering did imply
that questions of church government were part of this spiritual
sphere. 'The Lordship of the bishop hath been even a plague sore
in the state of a kingdom and is at this day a swelling wound of
corruption in the body of a commonwealth... Yet if the state did
require it the voice of the Lord must be obeyed though all the
kingdoms in the earth did fall before it. God is not a man that
we may countervail his honor.'[16] Hence, in admitting that 'the
articles of faith and sacraments are good', Dering explicitly
excepted 'that one which is of consecration of Archbishops and
bishops'. 'Let him allow of it', he wrote, 'that hath profit by it
and he that liketh not of it, let him have no bishopric'.[17]

Dering was similarly circumspect in all his answers in Star
Chamber. In reply to the question whether he held that every
parish should have pastors, elders and deacons chosen by popular
election Dering distinguished carefully between the manner of
election and the offices themselves. While the former was a matter
indifferent which could be safely left to the discretion of human
authority, the offices themselves were a very different matter.
'For the order to be had it is manifest in the apostles' time and
in the primitive church it was the use. Neither any man I think,
will deny it. After long time in some places this order ceased as
St Ambrose sayeth "superbia doctorum qui soli videbant regere
ecclesiam" (Ambrose I Tim.cap.5) and therefore I know now there
ought to be elders as at the first and as in Tertullian's time.' Similarly, he held that 'a minister may be no more without a charge than
a king without a kingdom for exercising civil government',[18] and
that between such properly constituted ministers there should be
equality: 'That all ministers are equally called to the preaching
of the word and the ministry of the sacraments no man I think
will deny.' While he admitted that some ministers are 'worthy
of double honour', 'of singular love', 'of great reverence', he
denied that there should be any lordship in the ministry.[19]
Professor Collinson has assumed that by these ministers 'worthy

of double honour' Dering meant bishops. But there is no reason
to suppose that he did. For in a letter to Burghley of November
1573 Dering had assured his erstwhile patron that Christ had
been opposed not only to the evil rule of one minister over another
but to all superiority or pre-eminence of order amongst the
ministers of the word. Those who claimed such lordship should
remember the honour of our Archbishop, Jesus Christ, whose lot
had been poverty and death on the cross. Hence, Dering concluded, 'the lordship or civil government of a bishop is utterly
unlawful in the church of God'. 'Bishops' kingdoms' were derived
from the 'Pope's monarchy'. 'It stands with the Pope, it reigns
with the Pope, it falls with the Pope, it is shamed with the Pope
and is it not of the Pope?'[20]

Certainly, Dering admitted that both Ambrose and Augustine
had been 'bishops' but they had not been lords as the present
prelates were. He listed twelve differences between these bishops
of the primitive church and the present bishops in the English
church. They had been merely ministers of the word, administering a purely spiritual discipline and preaching in only one cure
of souls. In short they had been totally unlike the present bishops
who ruled over whole counties, exercising a civil jurisdiction as
well as a spiritual one.[21] Hence, when he was asked 'whether
there be any right ministry or ecclesiastical government at this
time in the church of England or no?', Dering replied, 'if you
mean right having such a calling as the word of God requireth
I am sure you will confess it is not right. If you mean a right
ministration as concerning sacraments and doctrine I humbly
confess and think that no man ought to separate himself from
the church which God hath given us in this land.'[22] There could
be no clearer statement of that dual allegiance to godly principle
and the national church that was so typical of Elizabethan
puritanism.

But the question remains – was Dering a presbyterian? I would
contend, on the basis of the evidence marshalled above, that by
1573 he was. For we have to remember the situation in which
the statements cited above were made. Given his extremely exalted
conception of the ministry, his belief 'that no man ought to
separate himself from the church which God hath given us in
this land' and his admission that the ceremonies raised by subscription were in themselves indifferent, it seems safe to conclude

that Dering did not want to be deprived or suspended. It would, therefore, be entirely unreasonable to expect an explicit avowal of the presbyterian platform. He might visit Field and Wilcox in prison, but he had no wish to join them there. What we have in Dering's replies is a constant sense of tension as Dering struggled to maintain both his place in the ministry and the integrity of his conscience. Even so the promptings of conscience led him to the very edge of an avowedly presbyterian position. As for what lay behind his carefully calculated responses to the questions put to him, we can surely conclude that in other, freer circumstances Dering would have gone the whole hog and espoused the presbyterian platform.[23]

The significance of all this is that here, as early as 1573, we have present in the person and principles of Edward Dering all the major elements that were to comprise the moderate puritan position taken up by Laurence Chaderton and many others. But the figure of Dering serves another function; it serves to remind us that there was no great gap or discontinuity between the ethical puritanism of a Dering and the 'doctrinaire' presbyterianism of a Cartwright or even a Field. Of course, the presbyterian platform, with its clear-cut division between lawful and unlawful, godly and ungodly, Christian and Antichristian, constituted a very definite escalation of the continuing confrontation between conformist and precisian. Dering's views had been shaped during the 1560s when the memory of popery was still fresh and English religious opinion still characterised by a broad protestant agreement. There can be little doubt that Dering would have preferred to avoid further polarisation. It was his fervent desire to preserve the unity of the English church that had prompted his frenetic proselytising efforts of 1569/70. But when that failed to produce the desired changes Dering's position, based on a purely ethical appeal to shared protestant principles, was bankrupt. Dering accepted the logic of his situation and raised the stakes. By 1573 he was in substantial agreement with the presbyterian platform. But this change, significant though it was, represented no transformation. Presbyterianism for Dering was not the same aggressive, polemical gesture it was for Field.[24] Moreover, all the major elements in the presbyterian platform had been present in Dering's puritanism well before 1573. The central protestant concern with the word of God and its concomitant exalted view of the ministry, the principle of parity amongst ministers, the drive to a proper spiritual discipline in the church and the demand for a more scriptural liturgy, were all contained in the presbyterian platform. But these elements had remained disparate, diffuse, united only by the zeal of men like Dering. Now they were united in a logically coherent and polemically effective whole. The difference was one of tone and presentation, of form not of content. The classis movement and its ideology constituted an organisational and theoretical superstructure, built for polemical purposes but based firmly on the spiritual and ethical commitment that had characterised Dering's puritanism.

3

Chaderton's puritanism

We can find precisely the same links between Dering's style of
evangelical protestantism and presbyterianism in the career of
Laurence Chaderton. Having come up to Christ's College in
1562 Chaderton was to spend the rest of his active career in the
university, first at Christ's and then at the new puritan foundation, Emmanuel. In many ways he can be regarded as Dering's
successor. Of his two printed works one was a piece of presbyterian
propaganda printed at the height of the subscription crisis of
1583/4. It is this that forms the basis of the present chapter. But
his first printed sermon was preached at St Paul's Cross in 1578
and published in 1580. This is dealt with below in the section on
puritan practical divinity. For our present purpose it is sufficient
to note that its main theme – the need for good works as a validating sign of true faith – came straight from the heart of Dering's
style of moral exhortation. Chaderton was concerned with the
hypocritical and purely formal profession of many English protestants and attempted in the sermon to awaken his audience to a
true zeal and a lively faith through the power of the word
preached.[1]

Chaderton's presbyterianism represented the transfer of these
attitudes from the realm of personal belief and behaviour to the
external sphere of church government. Just as the individual was
to leave his old life of sin behind and gradually free himself from
the toils of the world, so the English church was to free itself
from its popish and Antichristian past. In the process, the proper
institutional structure for the control and suppression of those
very sins that he had denounced from the pulpit was to be set
up.

Chaderton's involvement with the classis movement is known from a number of sources. He is mentioned several times in the depositions taken from a number of presbyterian divines in 1590 as a regular attender at presbyterian synods, sometimes even taking the chair as moderator. His involvement shows no signs of having tailed off – he was present at the last national synod held at St John's College, Cambridge, in 1589. As the corresponding secretary for the movement in Cambridge and the leading presbyterian figure in the university Chaderton was a figure of some significance in the movement.[2] In the 'acta' of a formal synod held at Cambridge in 1587 (which he attended as the official Cambridge representative) Chaderton, along with Edward Gellibrand of Magdalen College, Oxford, was named as one of the two experts to be consulted about any doubts or difficulties arising from Cartwright's books on the discipline.[3]

But perhaps the most conspicuous example of Chaderton's presbyterian commitment was contained in a sermon on Romans 12.3–8. However, when the sermon was published in 1584 by Robert Waldegrave, the famous radical printer, it appeared anonymously. The ascription of the sermon to Chaderton must, therefore, rest on indirect, inferential evidence. In 1593 in some depositions taken from members of Francis Johnson's London separatist congregation, when asked what had first set him on the road to separation, a certain Christopher Bowman twice mentioned a sermon on the twelfth chapter of Romans by Laurence Chaderton.[4] Similarly, in his book published in 1606 entitled *The recantation of a brownist or a reformed puritan*, Peter Fairlambe likewise cited Chaderton as the author of the sermon.[5] Now Fairlambe's book, although printed in 1606, revealed a separatist career in London (notably in the parish of Stepney) dating back to the 1580s. There was, therefore, a tradition in London separatist circles that held Chaderton to be the author of the sermon in question. In many ways this was what one would have expected. Published by Waldegrave, a prominent figure in radical circles, the sermon formed part of a concerted presbyterian campaign; a campaign orchestrated, no doubt, by John Field and his radical colleagues in the London classis. It is, therefore, in the London protestant underground amongst the radicals that one might expect to find such information.

In addition, the fact of Chaderton's authorship fits perfectly with what is known about presbyterian intentions in 1584. The same spate of publishing activity that produced Chaderton's sermon also saw the publication for the first time of William Fulke's presbyterian treatise *A brief and full declaration concerning the decrees of all those faithful ministers that have and do seek for the discipline and the reformation of the church of England*. That work had been written in 1572, and in the interim Fulke had somewhat moderated his opinions and started to make a name for himself as an anti-papal polemicist.[6] It was published now not by Fulke but by John Field, acting, it seems, without the author's permission.[7] It would appear that Fulke's name and reputation as a defender of the English church against popery was being invoked to lend an aura of respectability and moderation to the presbyterian cause that it had previously lacked. As Dudley Fenner observed in 1587, the book had been published because 'we had it in reverent regard for the learning of the man acknowledged of both parties; and because we thought it would appear to be most void of partiality which was not written upon the occasion of these late grievances'.[8] But if this determination to present the movement's most respectable aspect to lay opinion did indeed lie behind presbyterian intentions in 1584, who better to foster that image than Laurence Chaderton? Certainly the terms in which the sermon was couched fit this view perfectly. But if this was the intention behind the sermon, why did Chaderton choose to remain anonymous? As the newly appointed Master of Emmanuel College, an institution that already enjoyed a strongly puritan reputation, Chaderton had a lot to lose by a misplaced gesture of this sort. Should events take the wrong turn, Chaderton's name on an avowedly presbyterian work would not only threaten his own position as Master, it could endanger the whole existence of the new college. Chaderton owed it to himself, the college and its founder, Sir Walter Mildmay, to be discreet. In conclusion, it is worth noting that the actual text of the sermon corresponds almost exactly with Chaderton's other known attitudes and in fact provides a beautiful example of the moderate, respectable puritan attitude to presbyterianism.

The interesting point about the sermon is not its basic contention that there was a perpetual law for the government of the church, set out by God in scripture, upon obedience to which depended our eternal salvation. That was the central premise of the presbyterian case and as such a commonplace. The interesting and significant point about Chaderton's formulation of the presbyterian case is the context in which he sets the basic issue of church polity. That context is provided by the theme of order and hierarchy. Chaderton maintained that over and above its application to church polity, his text contained a general injunction to all men 'truly to understand, soberly to esteem, soundly to judge and modestly to use the gifts he hath received of God being fully contented and satisfied therewith'.[9] For what, asked Chaderton, can 'be more excellent than for every member of the mystical body of Christ truly to know his proper gifts and wisely and soberly to esteem and use them?'

What can be more profitable for the church of Christ our mother, than that all her children, according to their age, strength, gifts and place and calling should be without hate, envy, disdain, swelling contempt and neglect of duty, love, succour, relieve and maintain everyone another as becometh the dearly beloved children of God.[10]

Citing Old and New Testament examples Chaderton outlined the doctrine of callings, which saw society as an interdependent whole with each person given a finite social role to which he ought assiduously to keep. For both the role and the gifts necessary to fulfil it came directly from God. As soldiers in war should keep to their ranks, said Chaderton, so Christians at all times should keep to their callings. To do otherwise 'must needs tumble and endanger themselves, vex and grieve others, hurt and disquiet the church'.[11] Such breaches of this general law for the regulation of human society Chaderton attributed to the sins of pride and ambition:

From these two pestilent fountains flow envying of the good, bitter contention and striving with equal, disdain and contempt of the inferiors. Hence, it is that the governors of the church think too well of themselves, not humbly begging the direction of God's spirit but expound the word to their own fancies; that they desire to rule as they list; devise new offices, confound those which the Lord hath wisely distinguished; challenge unto themselves new titles, new names, princely prerogatives and unlawful jurisdiction over their brethren.[12]

It was attitudes such as these that had prompted the pharisees to condemn Christ and which had started the corruption of the Roman church. Unless they were now plucked out 'by the roots' they would destroy all 'by the poison of their corruption'. Similarly, in the commonwealth 'it is the light head and aspiring mind which through pride and ambition flieth into the Prince's palace'.[13]

It was the magistrate's task to restrain all such tendencies in the name of order:

Above all things it behoveth you that be the Lord's servants in magistracy to establish everyone within his charge and jurisdiction, this general law providing that every man have wherein to occupy himself and his gifts according to the tenor of this law in his own standing, place and vocation; and that he do discharge it according to the measure and proportion of his gifts which he hath received for that purpose.[14]

Such arguments, of course, were quietist in tendency as long as there were no basic structural faults in the hierarchy of callings that made up the social order as a whole. Chaderton implied that this was indeed the case in lay society, where all that was needed was constant vigilance on the part of the authorities to preserve the principles of balance and order inherent in the social organism. This was not true in the spiritual sphere. In the church there was a basic structural fault which had to be repaired before anything approaching good order could be achieved. 'None in the Church and house of God', wrote Chaderton, 'must want his office, none must walk inordinately; none must be idle in his calling, or unprofitable.' At present, however, the ministry was full of 'many ignorant men, not only void of all skill in the Hebrew, Greek and Latin tongues, in logic, rhetoric and other arts; but also (which I am ashamed to speak) both void of the knowledge of the doctrine of repentance and also wicked and lewd in life'.[15]

Chaderton condemned all those who connived at this situation:

Oh covetous patrons that for gain present such unworthy men to the bishops; oh foolish men that will commend them for whom they ought to dispraise; oh miserable bishops, that by laying on to their hands lift up those into Moses' chair who ought rather to be thrust to the tail of the plough. What doth more dishonour God, discredit the Gospel, confirm the adversaries of the truth and encourage the rebel in his treason than this ignorance and impiety of the ministers?[16]

Chaderton was trying to counter the oft-repeated conformist charge that presbyterianism was subversive because it infringed the Royal Supremacy. He sought to do so by assimilating the problem of right order in the church to the problem of order and hierarchy in society as a whole. Good order could never be preserved on the basis of an inherently disordered structure. But that was precisely what the church of England, in its unreformed state, amounted to:

She wanteth her pastors, teachers, elders, deacons and her attenders upon the poor...As she is grieved for the lack of those parts which are wanting; so she abhorreth and loatheth such as are abounding; as namely the callings of Archbishop, Bishop, Deans, Archdeacons, Deacons, Chancellors, Commissaries, Officials and all such as be rather members and parts of the whore and strumpet of Rome.[17]

Just as these corruptions first came into the church through the agency of human ambition and greed, so they were sustained in the contemporary church by similar motives. Chaderton was appealing, in this sermon, over the heads of the proud and lordly prelates, the greedy and lax clergy and the corrupt lay patrons who presided over the ruin of the church, to all those 'that are in higher places and have access unto her majesty...that they would send for the preachers of the word, inquire what is lacking and what is too much and so impair and build up the walls of Jerusalem'.[18]

In his earlier sermon preached at St Paul's Cross and published in 1580 Chaderton had envisaged the sanctification of the social order through the conversion to true religion of the dominant groups.[19] Here was that same theme applied in presbyterian terms to the very pinnacle of the social hierarchy. And once established the presbyterian eldership would have involved even the most local of magistrates.

Chaderton's central assertion here was that the presbyterian polity was more conducive to good order, more congruent with the contemporary social hierarchy, than any other rival pattern of church government. It was this that produced his angry denial of the name of 'the devilish sect of puritans' and the concomitant charge of disloyalty to the Queen. 'I persuade myself moreover', he said, 'that if her majesty should hear and know the grounds of this doctrine we should not pray long for the reformation of the Church.'[20]

At first Chaderton made the point theoretically. Since the hierarchy of callings in church and state came directly from God both must be ordered down to the last detail according to God's will. 'God hath given us in great mercy pastors and doctors to be our eyes, to lead and direct us in the ways of truth and holiness, elders and deacons to be our hands to keep us and hold us in the way and also to reach unto us those things we want.'[21] These various offices were perfectly suited to man's spiritual condition. For 'by the fall of Adam there is in the mind darkness and ignorance of the will of God; in the heart there is nothing but rebellion and enmity against him so that scripture hath judged us to be by nature the children of darkness and the sons of rebellion'.[22] Hence, without these officers to guide, enlighten and discipline us, disorder and corruption must inevitably follow. But as things stood, all was chaos.

The deacon encroacheth upon the office of the pastor (for he prayeth openly and ministreth the sacraments); women upon the office of men (for they baptise); private men upon the office of the public persons (for one man doth suspend from the sacraments and excommunicate); the doctor upon the office of the pastor (for both indifferently teach, exhort and minister the sacraments); the ecclesiastical person upon the office of the civil magistrate; and contrarily the civil upon the ecclesiastical (for they interchangeably handle and decide civil and ecclesiastical controversies).[23]

No good could come from such chaos. And, indeed, Chaderton maintained all the 'evils that are perpetually in our church' could be attributed to the deficiencies of the polity of that church.

For if it be demanded why there is in this land such gross ignorance of God? The answer is at hand – we want doctors and teachers. Whence come such swarms of atheists and papists, erroneous and heretical sectaries of the family of love and such like? There are no doctors to teach, nor pastors to exhort. How cometh it to pass that in a Christian church professing newness of life and the doctrine of regeneration there should be such a huge mass of old and stinking works, of conjuring, witchcraft, sorcery, charming, blaspheming the holy name of God, swearing and forswearing, profaning of the Lord's sabbaths, disobedience to superiors, contempt to inferiors, murder, manslaughter, robberies, adultery, fornication, covenant breakers, false witness-bearing, liars with all kinds of unmerciful dealing with one another? Is not the cause evident? We lack elders and governors of every congregation to admonish, correct, suspend and excommunicate such noisome, hurtful and monstrous beasts out of the house of God, without respect of persons.[24]

Passages such as this recall Chaderton's earlier condemnation of English social mores in 1578. Then he had blamed the 'shameless conversation' of English protestants for the prevalence both of popery and 'the erroneous doctrine of H.N. and his family, falsely termed the family of love'.[25] Now that same point was merely being transferred into institutional terms as the outrageous behaviour of the mass of English protestants was attributed to the lack of any proper disciplinary machinery in the church. Whereas before Chaderton had put his faith in the influence of the word on the dominant social groups working itself down through the normal means of social control to the mass of the population, now in 1584 he advocated the insertion into those traditional channels of social power and influence of a parallel system of spiritual discipline with its own officers in every parish. Only thus, he argued, could the cause of true religion be properly safeguarded, the godly encouraged and the ungodly controlled and repressed. There was, of course, no sharp disjunction between the two positions. The second was merely a logical extension of the first and there remained many elements of continuity. Hence the preacher still stood at the centre of the presbyterian system. The word of God, mediated to the people by a learned ministry, still provided the dynamic element in the process of further reformation. Certainly, according to Chaderton, the preacher was superior even to the doctor. For while the doctor was concerned only with the rational part of the mind 'therein to plant true knowledge and sound doctrine', the pastor was 'occupied about that part wherein the affections have their abode, to bring the heart and will to continual obedience of the truth, which is so much more necessary than the other, by how much the Lord is more delighted with obedience than with naked and bare knowledge'.[26]

A pastor is a prophet that upon sound doctrine grounded upon the sincere interpretation of the scripture continueth in exhortation wisely applied to the present use, necessity and edification of his people and in the administration of the sacraments; all the parts whereof may appear in this sort. Doctrine is the ground, every exhortation not builded thereon is fruitless and weak and vanisheth away as smoke in the wind, though it be zealous, yet it is blind and without knowledge. As the scriptures are able to instruct the doctor with all knowledge in teaching so the pastor in exhorting and improving and correcting. It is certain that obedience is the end of exhortation and faith is the mother of obedience and that faith leaneth only upon the word.[27]

As the capacities and temperaments of the auditory varied so the pastor should vary his style of exhortation.

The Lord's children are not all of one age and strength, therefore their spiritual father must feed some with milk and some with stronger meat...He exhorteth the weak ones to take comfort by the sweet mercies and promises of God; the good he exhorteth to proceed partly by the fear of God's judgements and partly by the love of his mercies. The wicked he exhorteth to repentance by laying before them the eternal and severe judgements and curses of God and the multitude and greatness of their sins.[28]

There was, therefore, the need for a close and permanent relationship between the pastor and the flock.

The spiritual enemies of our soul are many, strong, mighty, malicious, vigilant, subtle and full of deceit, the sheep of the great pasture few, weak, feeble, simple, dull, unwise, therefore their keeper and defender had need always to be among them, to know their ways, to see their going out and their coming in, that he may the better going before them in all sound doctrine and godliness keep them to Christ and defend them from their enemies he must harken unto the voice of Christ 'feed, feed, feed'.[29]

There could be no clearer statement of the evangelical core of the puritan impulse than that. The minister, through his skill as a scholar, preacher and practical divine, was the mediator between the pages of scripture and the spiritual predicament of his flock; he was the channel through which the word was to be brought to the people. It was through his constant vigilance in that role that the cause of further reformation was to be advanced. In many ways the rest of the presbyterian platform was merely the context, the necessary framework within which the preacher's work was to be carried out. It was necessary first because God had willed it, and second because it rendered the ministry of the word that much more effective.

Pastors and doctors should, having a true relation from their seniors touching the estate of their flock be much more fruitfully occupied in teaching and exhorting for they might with all knowledge and wisdom deliver unto everyone that which were most fit to draw him to God and his eternal salvation.[30]

Chaderton saw the discipline as a perfectly integrated organism, with each part assigned its own unique and essential role in the functioning of the whole. 'As it is in the body so in the Church, keep all, preserve all, keep some, preserve some, keep none, preserve none, change one, some or all then you break the Lord's decree and ordinances established in his Church.'[31] At present the church was like a maimed boy;[32] but once set the preacher in the midst of a properly ordered polity and all manner of benefits would accrue to both the church and the commonwealth. For so perfect was the divinely created mechanism that once restored to its original form all would immediately be well. 'Hereby all godly laws ecclesiastical and civil should either universally be kept of all or else the breakers come under such civil and ecclesiastical punishments as they should deserve.'[33] A genuinely close relationship between ecclesiastical officers and their charges in each congregation in the country would act as a sort of intelligence service for the government.

For hereby her gracious majesty and her honourable council might truly know within a short time by name who and how many enemies there are (a very few subtle hypocrites excepted) to religion and the commonwealth. How many obstinate, malicious and traiterous papists? How many Anabaptists, libertines of the family of love? How many atheists? How many unruly and inordinate walkers which then might be punished according to their faults; whereas now Archbishops, Bishops, Archdeacons, Deans, Commissioners, Officials having (contrary to the word of God) pulled the reins of government from the elders, ruin and destruction is feared but not avoided. Not one enemy of an hundred is known of the greater part and yet there be more secret enemies than the wisest and most provident can think of. Hereby all secret mischievous devices against her majesty's person, religion and the whole state might easily be tried and searched out by the diligent and wise search of the elders in every Church; whereas now did not the Lord sometimes most wonderfully for the singular care he hath over her counsel bring them to light, we should have been often ere now swallowed up by the secret undermining of the common peace and state.[34]

Here, then, is the core of Chaderton's refutation of the conformist claim that presbyterianism was subversive. His sermon can be seen as an attempt, on behalf of the learned preachers of England, to outbid the episcopal hierarchy as defenders of the status quo. According to Chaderton there was a hierarchy of callings in both the church and state underwritten by God. The only threat to that hierarchy lay in human pride and ambition. Through its popish origins and continual usurpation of authority, the episcopal hierarchy was itself a product of those very sins of pride and ambition and was hence inherently inimical to all good order. On the other hand a church polity based not on the usurped jurisdiction of the bishops but on the zeal and learning of the proper ministry of the word would not only conform to the divine schema for church government but would also provide a more effective discipline of morals, opinion and behaviour for the ruling class than anything that had preceded it.

Chaderton, therefore, ended with a picture of the godly commonwealth purging itself, in an orderly but thorough way, of the Antichristian dress and superfluous human inventions that plagued it.

Seeing then these things are so as hath been set forth out of the word of God, that this is his order to which all ought to bow their backs, everyone keeping his proper place and none intruding upon the right and interest of another; seeing superfluous things ought to be cut off and such offices as are from Antichrist ought to be abandoned; let us everyone in our places, pray to our good God... that truth and righteousness may kiss each other, that his sceptre may flourish that the stiff necks of the obstinate and the iron sinews of the rebellious may be bowed and broken; to the end [of] these confusions that appear everywhere; this pompous pride and cursed ambition, enemy to all sincerity, good order and true religion may cease and only the glory and victory of Christ our only King, Prophet and Priest may be established.[35]

HIS ROLE IN THE UNIVERSITY

The protestant insistence on the need for learned preaching ministers to bring true religion to the unregenerate mass of the people placed the universities at the forefront of the campaign for further reformation. Chaderton himself had a fervent belief in the value of preaching. In the preface to one of his own printed sermons he warned the reader:

Let no man think that the reading of this can be half so effectual

and profitable to him as the hearing was or might be. For it wanteth
the zeal of the speaker, the attention of the hearer, the promise of
God to the ordinary preaching of his word, the mighty and inward
working of his holy spirit and many other things which the Lord
worketh most mercifully by the preaching of his glorious Gospel
which are not to be hoped for by reading the written sermons of
his ministers.[36]

Chaderton himself was a prolific preacher. He was the lecturer
at St Clement's in Cambridge for about fifty years, resigning
that post only in his eighties. Dillingham, his biographer, relates
that he used to preach on his visits home to Lancashire and also
mentions a sermon preached at Debden in Essex. But due to his
position in the university Chaderton's effectiveness as a preacher
was magnified many times over. For Chaderton was not only a
preacher himself, he was also a trainer of preachers. When he
finally retired from St Clement's 'he received about forty letters
from ministers of the word begging him not to do so and alleging
among other arguments that by his ministry God had brought
them knowledge of the truth'.[37]

At one point Chaderton committed himself to paper concerning the scholarly attainments necessary for a properly trained
minister of the word. It was essential, he argued, for every minister
'to teach sound doctrine by the true interpretation of the word
and to confute all contrary errors by unanswerable arguments
and reasons'. In order to acquire the requisite skills to allow him
to do this Chaderton recommended 'mutual conference of such
as being very studious and of good towardness in learning have
purposed only the profession of divinity'. The intention was to
form a class for the intensive study of scripture, the aim being
to cover the entire corpus of God's word once every ten years.
Chaderton then listed the gifts necessary for the successful completion of the operation:

The first hereof is the knowledge of the tongues especially of the
Hebrew and Greek wherein God hath revealed and written his will
and Testament by his prophets and Apostles and therefore hath
given this gift to his Church for the better understanding of the
etymology, true construction, proper signification, phrase and use
of all words, wherein his will is expressed.

The second is the art of rhetoric which teacheth truly to discern
proper speeches from those which are tropical and figurative.

The third is the art of reasoning called logic; which teacheth to find out the matter and the whole sense that is expressed in the words and to frame and gather necessary arguments and conclusions, as well as for the proof of true as for the disproof of false doctrines and that by the diligent searching and judging every argument by itself and the right disposition thereof in propositions in syllogisms, in method and due order, which serveth not only for the directing of judgement and...of the understanding touching the interpretation of the word, but also for the helping and preserving of memory.

The fourth is a wise comparing together of the same or like places of the Scripture which agree in words, propriety of speech, circumstance or matter.

The fifth is the reading of the learned commentaries of the old and new writers and of the ancient Councils with due examination of their interpretations and judgements; not differing from them but upon just occasion, whereof good reason may be rendered by the means aforesaid.

The sixth and last is the knowledge of Greek and Latin histories and chronologies, for the better understanding of the histories in the scriptures and the reconciling of many places which otherwise might seem doubtful.

At the end some sort of collective judgement about the meaning of the passage under discussion was to be arrived at, either through the natural emergence of a consensus, or, failing that, through a formal disputation 'as in questions of doctrine'. Indeed, parallel to these collaborative exercises in scriptural exegesis there was to run a series of disputations in which, during the same two-year period, 'all the principal questions in controversy between us and the papists and the other heretics shall be handled and determined'.[38] Chaderton is mentioned in two separate passages from Clarke's *A general martyrologie* as holding such meetings to expound the scripture with various of his contemporaries; in one instance with William Fulke and William Whitaker, and in another with Lancelot Andrewes, John Knewstubb, Ezekiel Culverwell and some others. But in both instances it is clear that aspiring puritan scholars and ministers like the young Dod and John Carter were present.[39] This serves to underline the point that this ferocious list of requirements was being proffered not merely for university divines but also for ordinary ministers of the word. Here Chaderton's protestant biblicism can be seen integrating the most arcane linguistic and grammatical skills into a vision of true religion. For in an age denied all prospect of further direct revelation the only way to protect the corpus of right doctrine and extend the progressive revelation of God's will was through the application of the greatest possible scholarly rigour to the minutiae of scriptural exegesis. There could be no clearer example of the central role to be played by the university in the propagation of true religion and the dissemination of those skills so necessary to its progress throughout the main body of the people.

Hence, for Chaderton the pursuit of learning at the university had the intensely practical aim of training young men in the ministry. But this involved Chaderton in administrative as well as scholarly activity. Chaderton, it would seem, was at the centre of a considerable web of contacts through which suitable young men were channelled into the university. Apparently, once his reputation had been established amongst the godly, he took no pupils himself but concentrated on co-ordinating the machinery of godly education, thus ensuring that suitable pupils were placed under properly pious tutors.[40] Hence in 1578 John Ireton can be found writing to Anthony Gilby, assuring him that although 'Mr Chaderton taketh none to his tuition' yet he (Chaderton) had successfully placed Gilby's son Nathaniel under 'Mr Dickinson, a Lancashire Man, a young man, very godly and learned'. Here it is worth noting that young Nathaniel Gilby became one of the first fellows of Emmanuel College. To take another example from later in the century, in 1600 Lord Zouche wrote to Chaderton from Guernsey recommending to him one Peter Painsacke, a poor young scholar. 'Persuading myself of your zeal to God's church', wrote Zouche, 'I have undertaken to write as earnestly as I can to you that you will take some care of this young man.' Chaderton was to ensure that 'he may so mix his studies as he may be not altogether unfit for the service of God in his church in this place whensoever he shall be called thereunto'.[41]

But as well as attracting promising or deserving young scholars to the university Chaderton also sought to 'place' his protégés within the church at large. He was not only running a clerical training college, he was also, it seems, running a sort of employment exchange for would-be ministers. Hence, Professor Collinson has found Chaderton cited as a referee for John Ward of Haverhill in his application to become town lecturer at Ipswich in 1592.[42] He was also involved in a puritan attempt to get a puritan nominee appointed as schoolmaster at Colchester School in 1588.[43] Chaderton, it seems, was continually approached by well-affected lay patrons for advice on likely candidates for the ministry. It was by means of one such approach from Sir Anthony Cope that John Dod obtained his first benefice.[44] But the most detailed information concerning Chaderton's activities as a manipulator of patronage comes from his dealings on behalf of William Bradshaw.[45] Bradshaw, a protégé of Sir Francis Hastings and Arthur Hildersham (the famous puritan radical), came up to Emmanuel in 1589. He swiftly established himself as one of Chaderton's favourite pupils. However, due to the statute which limited each English county to only one fellowship, Chaderton was unable to prefer Bradshaw within Emmanuel since Joseph Hall, who came, like Bradshaw, from Leicestershire, already had a fellowship there. He therefore turned to the new puritan foundation – Sidney Sussex College. On Chaderton's recommendation Bradshaw obtained a fellowship there, but due to the unfinished nature of the college buildings Bradshaw was unable to take up residence straight away.

Thomas Cartwright was in Guernsey at this time and the governor, Sir Thomas Leighton, asked him to write to Chaderton to obtain a suitable tutor for his children. There followed a bout of correspondence involving Cartwright, Chaderton, Montague (the Master of Sidney Sussex) and Bradshaw's old patron Sir Francis Hastings, the end result of which was Bradshaw's appointment as tutor to Leighton's children. On his return to Sidney Sussex Bradshaw seemed set for a bright future, but he was a man of radical opinions and after a scrape with Bancroft over the merits of the puritan exorcist John Darell, he found himself dismissed from the university and without a living to which to retire. The problem of course, given 'the tenderness of his conscience and scruple of things that he stuck at which were like to be tendered unto him', was how to avoid the official demand for subscription and yet find a settled place in the church in which to exercise his ministry. Once again Chaderton came to the rescue. In Kent to marry William Whitaker's widow to Josiah Nichols (the Kentish puritan minister),[46] Chaderton was approached concerning a vacancy in the ministry at Chatham.

In Gataker's words 'the business of supplying them with an able and faithful teacher was by general consent referred to Master Chaderton'. Chaderton gave such a glowing report of Bradshaw's attainments that the parishioners determined to accept no one 'but him whom he had already propounded'. Chaderton acted as a go-between during the negotiations between Bradshaw and his future parishioners, informing Bradshaw of the situation at Chatham and arranging for him to go there for a trial period, at the end of which Bradshaw was 'by joint consent' chosen as minister. However, Bradshaw's radical proclivities reasserted themselves and although he survived a series of scrapes with the authorities through the good offices of Sir Francis Hastings, he was at last asked to subscribe. Having refused, he was banned from preaching and bound over. Again Chaderton tried to help. 'Going up to London upon occasion of some college affairs' Chaderton promised to 'deal in Master Bradshaw's behalf'.

As it happens that attempt at intercession was a failure and Bradshaw was deprived. However, if nothing else the whole affair gives a fascinating glimpse of Chaderton's role as the focal point of a network of patronage and influence that included fellow divines like Cartwright, godly laymen like Sir Francis Hastings or Sir Anthony Cope, radical parishes like Chatham where the minister was apparently elected (albeit only by 'those of any note or repute in the place') and even, though in this instance unsuccessfully, Richard Bancroft. It is, of course, worthy of note that it was Chaderton, the respectable moderate, whom Bradshaw and his parishioners asked to intercede on their behalf with Bancroft. There could hardly be a greater tribute to his mediating role between the puritan impulse and the ecclesiastical establishment.

From 1568 Chaderton had carried on his many activities as a fellow of Christ's College. But his career in the university found its perfect expression in his appointment as the first Master of Emmanuel College. The college personified the extent to which puritan attitudes had penetrated to the centre of the Elizabethan establishment. It was founded by Sir Walter Mildmay, himself a proponent, as Professor Collinson has observed, 'of that philosophy that lies like bedrock under many of the policies and events of the high Elizabethan period; at home a desire to promote preaching, to reform the ministry and discipline of the church; and abroad a protestant ideological approach to problems of foreign relations'.[47] Mildmay's foundation provided a focus for the generosity of wealthy and powerful men of a puritan persuasion. Sir Henry Killigrew the diplomat contributed £140 for the purchase of a house for the master. Sir Francis Walsingham gave the college the advowson of Thurcaston, Leicestershire, while advowsons at Brompton Regis and Winsford, Somerset, came from Henry Neal, and others at Loughborough, Leicestershire, and North Cadbury and Allerton in Somerset were donated by the Third Earl of Huntingdon.[48] Huntingdon's nephew, Sir Henry Hastings, endowed the college with some books. Sir Wolfstan Dixie, one-time Lord Mayor of London, endowed the new foundation with £650 for new buildings while his wife Mary also endowed a college lectureship in Greek and Hebrew; in addition they both donated books. Godly families like the Lewknors and the Jermyns and the Culverwells also figured in the list of benefactors. That staunch presbyterian Walter Travers left the college £100 for the endowment of a scholarship,[49] while Thomas Cartwright left twenty marks for distribution in the university by Chaderton and Montague (the first Master of that other puritan foundation, Sidney Sussex) for the upkeep of poor scholars.[50] Provincial urban elites also sought to further the fortunes of the new college. In 1595 one John Titley, a wealthy town-merchant and former mayor of Kings Lynn, left the town corporation £130 with which to endow two scholarships for local scholars at Emmanuel.[51] Neither were such bequests limited to the influential or wealthy. In 1590 we find Chaderton and John Richardson (another fellow of the college) involved in a legal battle to prove the will of a certain Philip Harris of Brickley in Essex, who had left £3 6s. 8d. to the college for the upkeep of the poor.[52]

Here we have representatives of all the important strands in godly opinion – Privy Councillors and courtiers like Walsingham or Mildmay, families of the gentry like the Lewknors or the Jermyns, metropolitan and provincial merchants, and presbyterian divines like Cartwright and Travers, all united behind Mildmay's and Chaderton's vision of Emmanuel as a godly seminary dedicated to the training of ministers of the word. For that had been Mildmay's aim from the first: 'In establishing this college we have set before us this one aim of rendering as many persons as possible fit for the sacred ministry of the word and sacraments; so that from this seminary the Church of England might have men whom it might call forth to instruct the people and undertake the duty of pastors.'[53] The college was to be 'a seed plot' where 'these most noble plants of theology and right good learning' might be tended and 'from which such as had grown to maturity might be transplanted to all parts of the Church that she, being watered by their labours and increased by the gift of God might come at last to a flourishing and most blessed estate'.[54]

By an interesting coincidence, in the very year that Mildmay had founded Emmanuel Chaderton had published his presbyterian sermon[55] on the twelfth chapter of Romans. The juxtaposition of the two events reveals quite clearly the completely complementary nature of Chaderton's presbyterian commitment and his more respectable activities in the university; for Chaderton (and presumably for Mildmay) there was no contradiction between these two facets of his career. As Master of Emmanuel Chaderton had to

swear by God that I will sincerely embrace the true Christian religion contrary to popery and all other heresies; that I will set the authority of scripture before the judgement of even the best of men; that other matters which may in no wise be proved from the word of God I will hold as of men; but I will regard the King's authority as supreme over all men under his rule and in no wise subject to the jurisdiction of foreign Bishops, Princes and powers; that I will refute all opinions that be contrary to the word of God and I will in the cause of religion always set what is true before what is customary, what is written before what is not written.[56]

Here was the hierarchy of allegiances and values that underlay the protestantism of both Chaderton and Mildmay; scripture above all, a zealous defence of right doctrine against popery and other heresy, and loyalty to the prince. It was the completely complementary quality (indeed they were perceived as virtually synonymous) of these three imperatives that underwrote Mildmay's career as a loyal servant of the Queen and a staunch protestant, and Chaderton's career as a pastor, academic, administrator and presbyterian. If any tension did appear between the various parts of this ordered hierarchy of values it was to be attributed not to any fundamental incompatibility or conflict between the will of God and that of the Queen and the social order of which she was the head. On the contrary, such a clash was an aberration, an illusion produced by human perversity and sin (on the issue of church polity specifically, the perversity and sin of the bishops).

Some idea of the way in which the puritan or presbyterian tone of Chaderton's world-view influenced the atmosphere in the college can be gained from the outline for a prophesying drawn up by Chaderton and approved by the fellows in 1588.[57] They started, of course, with scripture (1 Cor. 14.19). The Apostle, they wrote, having attempted to persuade the Corinthians of the value 'of a greater estimation and more diligent use of the gifts of prophecy, as a thing most profitable to the edification of the church', proceeded to set out 'a very good and profitable course for the right use of this gift to the greater benefit of themselves and of the Church'. The meeting was to be a meeting of 'prophets' or ministers where, one or two having spoken, the doctrine thus propounded was to be subjected to discussion and mutual criticism 'to the end that if it were sound they might give the doctrine their allowance, that so it might be of more authority; if not that the speaker might brotherly be admonished of it and the church take no hurt thereby'. For this to work effectively each 'prophet' 'should in his course be admitted to speak, as order and the Church's good would permit' and all those present 'should willingly submit themselves and doctrine to the judgement and censure of the whole company of prophets; and be content to be advised or reformed (if need were) by their discreet and brotherly censure'. The meeting was evidently intended to embody the collective will of the college and hence to give formal expression to the basic protestant consensus and spiritual unity on which the college was founded.

The fellows claimed the general warrant of scripture for their enterprise, such prophesyings 'being generally set down and not appropriated to that Church or time, no more than the calling of prophets; and having a good and necessary use wheresoever there is (as was in Corinth) a number of prophets or sons of the prophets together; we think it layeth hold on us; if not in every circumstance, yet in the substance of the action'. For since the time of the Apostles the gift of 'immediate revelation' had ceased and it was imperative that a check should be placed on the zeal of the individual minister. Such a check could only come from the judgement of his fellow ministers so that 'if need require' the speaker should 'be content upon good ground and reason rendered either to reform his opinion or at least to cease from further publishing of it until it pleased God to reveal more clearly the truth in such matters'. For it was only by 'being admonished of their several faults and taught how to amend them they may grow daily unto a greater ripeness and perfection in that honourable calling wherein they serve the Lord'. There followed a classic definition of that doctrine of edification which Coolidge has identified as typical of the puritan world-view.[58]

Moreover St Paul I Cor. 12.7 having showed that there be divers gifts of the spirit in the church of God doth set down why the spirit doth so plenteously bestow his graces which is...for the good and benefit of the whole body and every member thereof. And verse 25 after he had showed how as in the body so in the church, those who had the best gifts should not condemn others which had the meanest; he requireth this of all the members that they all have a mutual care for the good of the whole church and every member therein; according as in the body every member is careful to procure the good and benefit of the rest of the members. Wherein this duty is laid on every one of us that we do not every one look to himself and neglect others but all bestow our care and study in furthering the good of another even in that kind wherein his goodness doth consist.

Applied to the ministry this meant that

having received any gifts of the spirit, profitable for the whole church or any member thereof whether it be the gift of judgement to judge of sound doctrine; or of discretion to discern of the manner of delivery; or of interpretation to find out the true sense and meaning of the scriptures; we are by the Apostles rule to use these gifts to the good of others.

All of which they concluded was 'sufficient ground out of the word for that which we have taken in hand; which may both warrant our own consciences and afford a just defence of our doings unto all'.

Hence the fellows agreed that 'all of us do meet together at seven of the clock the same day that any exercise hath been' so that the doctrine there propounded could be discussed. Each should have his say, although in strict order of seniority, and at the end the master was to 'signify the judgement of the company in their hearing unto him that hath spoken'. All personal animosities were to be laid aside. No one was to 'reveal unto the party censured who it was that found fault with him; because the judgement is the judgement of all and not of any one alone'. Finally, all this was to be kept firmly within the walls of the college. 'No man which is not of the company be made privy of that which is done amongst us.'

Although very specific in intention, this document is general enough in its form and tone to allow something to be said concerning the underlying assumptions of those involved. As we have seen, the idea of a closed body of doctrine, which could only grow by the painstaking work of co-operative biblical scholarship envisaged in the prophesying, was central to Chaderton's career. But the great insistence on the need for direct scriptural warrant for contemporary ecclesiastical and academic practice was very reminiscent of the presbyterian position. Similarly, the doctrine of distinct callings or spiritual gifts within the ministry and the comparison of the church with a living organism with mutually dependent organs or limbs also recalled the presbyterian position.[59] Here it is worth noting that on 10 December 1588 'all the society' agreed that Chaderton and Mr Jones would 'principally endeavour by exhortation to apply the doctrine of religion to the present state of the College and to administer the sacraments. And that Mr Chadwick, Mr Pickering and Mr Cork would especially endeavour to teach sound doctrine and confute error at other times than only when they are bound by Statute of the University and of the College so to do.'[60]

There was, of course, a marked similarity between this division of labour amongst the four senior fellows of the college and the distinction between the office of pastor and that of the teacher or doctor under the presbyterian dispensation. Certainly, the structure of the prophesying implied some concept of ministerial parity, with the individual subject only to the spiritual authority lodged in the collective judgement of his peers. Moreover, the very attempt to set up and sustain an unofficial body with such sweeping powers to define right doctrine was in itself impressive testimony to the degree of ideological agreement that could be expected to subsist amongst the fellows. Further evidence for the puritan consensus in the college comes from the remarkable degree of ceremonial non-conformity that Chaderton was able to sustain there. According to Samuel Ward the surplice did not make an appearance in the college until January 1605.[61] An anonymous observer of 1603 noted, amongst other irregularities, that in Emmanuel 'they do follow a private course of public prayer after their own fashion both Sundays, Holy days and week days' and receive the communion 'sitting upon forms about the Communion Table'.[62]

In short, Emmanuel was a puritan enclave at the heart of the university. The college was a monument in bricks and mortar to the penetration of puritan attitudes to the very centre of the Elizabethan establishment and Chaderton's position as Master a tribute to the extent to which commitment to true religion could be combined with membership of that establishment.

THE BALANCE OF THE MODERATE POSITION

Thus far we have stressed the internal consistency and coherence of the moderate puritan position. Our emphasis has been placed on the continuities linking the evangelical protestantism of Edward Dering with 'iure divino' presbyterianism; on the ease with which that presbyterianism could be integrated with conventional notions of hierarchy and degree; and on the way in which Chaderton's activities in the university dovetailed with his wider puritan commitment. But this happy state of coherence and consistency did not pass uncontested. The whole thrust of the conformist case was designed to disrupt the coherence of the puritan position and deny the compatibility between the godly divine's commitment to puritan principle and his commitment to the national church. The cutting edge of the conformist offensive was provided by the issue of subscription. This raised in an acute form the most pressing question facing the presbyterian divine – how, if both the liturgy and polity of the church were thoroughly Antichristian, was it possible to justify continued membership of that church?

We have already seen the rudiments of the moderate response to this dilemma formulated in 1573 by Edward Dering. By 1576 no less a figure than Thomas Cartwright was recommending such a means to the wider puritan movement as the best way of negotiating the issue of conformity and subscription.

For in 1576 Cartwright was asked the question 'whether the ministry be for certain ceremonies that are the dregs of popery (namely the cope, the surplice, the cross in baptism and other like) laid upon them under pretence of church policy only and not with any opinion of worship or religion to be forsaken or no?'. Since the enquiry came not from the authorities but from his fellow ministers confronted with the threat of deprivation, Cartwright could hardly dodge the issue.

His reply asserted that the ceremonies in themselves were inherently indifferent, that is they were neither explicitly commanded nor condemned by scripture. However, he denied that this meant, as the conformists appeared to claim, that they should be left 'to the beck and pleasure of men'. On the contrary, they should be judged according to the law of expediency as set out by the Apostle. This comprised a series of general considerations which should always be regarded in deciding questions concerning things which were in themselves indifferent. Of these the effect of one's actions on others, either one's fellow professors of true religion or the ignorant and the weak in faith, was perhaps the most important.[63] For what, asked Cartwright, could possibly outweigh the offence of the brethren (which, it was argued, would inevitably follow the acceptance of the offending popish ceremonies)? Cartwright's response was immediate: 'it is the perpetual and constant commandment of God whereby such a necessity of preaching the Gospel is laid upon them that woe is to them if they preach not the Gospel'. In view of that Cartwright concluded 'in respect of offences the ministry is not to be forsaken'. That, however, was as far as he would go. He vigorously denied 'it to be lawful either by scribing or subscribing to allow them as fit and agreeable to the doctrine of the Gospel, yea and I affirm that the discommodity of them is to be taught in due and convenient time'.[64]

Cartwright's pronouncements were the necessary product of the presbyterian platform's failure to carry the day at its first proclamation. For, given that failure, some accommodation had to be reached between the puritan minister and the sadly unregenerate church of which he was still a member. Cartwright's position went some way to achieving such an accommodation. Certainly it allowed the main thrust of the conformist case to be turned aside. The minister's duty to preach was placed above all other considerations; it was the one single imperative to which all else should be subordinated. In the short term therefore it provided the impulse for a compromise settlement with the authorities, perhaps on the basis of some modified form of subscription. But at the same time it provided a frame of reference which enabled the subscribing puritan not to construe his subscription as a full acceptance of the status quo. On the contrary, this position expressly allowed for the continuation of the puritan campaign for further change, pursued in terms of edification and the law of expedience. In short, this position allowed the puritan minister to maintain both his membership of the national church and his identity as a member of the godly party within that church. As such it turned aside the construction put forward by both conformists and radical puritans, both of whom construed subscription as a once and for all choice between puritan principle and the minister's calling inside the national church.

Such a position perfectly suited men like Chaderton and his fellow divines in the university – among others William Whitaker and William Fulke. During the course of the 1580s all three became heads of houses. For them the price of influence became moderation in matters of conformity. Moreover, since their entire careers in the university were dedicated to the infusion of the English church with properly trained ministers, any full-scale confrontation with authority over subscription which led to large scale deprivations would effectively destroy a lifetime's work.[65]

This was in marked contrast to the radicals who, driven on by the considerations of ideological and polemical consistency, almost welcomed the confrontation with the conformists, and instead of seeking to limit and turn aside the conformist case tried rather to up the stakes and press for a final show-down with the bishops. For them the great risks involved in such an approach were worth taking if in the process influential lay opinion could once and for all be alienated from the bishops and their tyrannical rule finally removed from the English church.[66]

Many of the radicals like Field and his colleagues in London were sustained by their own supporters and hence enjoyed a position outside the conventional ecclesiastical hierarchies. This was not true of the mass of puritan ministers. As Professor Collinson has observed, the pressure to conform was 'felt especially by the beneficed, family man who depended not on salaries, gifts and subscriptions such as sustained the other doctors; but upon livings which could be sequestered or even, in the last resort, taken away'.[67] There was, therefore, a natural alliance between the moderate divines in the universities and the mass of puritan ministers. I have argued elsewhere that it was this natural alliance of interest and outlook that caused the moderate position to prevail amongst the godly during the subscription crisis of 1583/4, and that it is the moderate position that provides the key to puritan tactics during that crucial year.[68]

For the moment, however, let us confine ourselves to the consideration of the accusation, often levelled by the radicals, that the moderate position allowed the initiative entirely to pass to the conformists. Chaderton, for one, might in certain situations advocate conformity, but he never became a conformist. Conformity was merely the price that had sometimes to be paid for the infusion of the existing forms of the church and state with a puritan content. The subtle but all-pervading influence of his puritanism on Emmanuel College has already been noted. To that can be added the evidence of a series of lectures on St John's Gospel. These are discussed at length below. However, the subject matter for much of these lectures was provided by a clash between Christ and the pharisees over the healing of a blind man, an act which the pharisees refused to acknowledge as a true miracle. This provided Chaderton with an opportunity to discuss the nature of true spiritual authority and its relation with high office in the church. As such it allows us an interesting glimpse of the nature of Chaderton's puritanism in the very year of the final collapse of the classis movement, and provides an example of the puritan view of true religion used as a basis for an implicit critique of the English church while yet avoiding any mention of those issues of polity and ceremony that are usually taken as characteristic of puritan opinion.

For true religion, Chaderton claimed, had

many adversaries, yea even among the learned and those that are of great authority in the church. For we see that although these pharisees could find no fault with our saviour Christ yet they would oppose themselves against him. And this hath been the lot of Christ and his apostles and will be of his ministers and therefore this instructeth the ministers that they should not fear but prepare their minds to suffer this particular cross of Christ.[69]

The pharisees, added Chaderton, were 'the most learned men of all the earth and had most skill of all the others in the scripture'.[70] Yet they had made 'a decree clean contrary to the word of God'. But if that was the case, why had men continued to obey and fear them? 'The cause is', answered Chaderton, 'because the Lord hath given to the governors the spirit of boldness and to the subject a more timorous spirit of subjection. But if they [the subjects] fear otherwise than they ought this doth proceed from their own corruption.' The implication was, of course, that such ungodly decrees ought not to be obeyed. Chaderton did not shirk the logic of his own argument. There were, he said, 'two sorts of constitutions, some to be obeyed and some disobeyed; these constitutions which be good and for the glory of God, they ought to be obeyed, but such as be wicked they ought not to be obeyed'.[71] That, of course, left rather a lot of questions unanswered. Who was to judge the status of such constitutions and by what criteria? Chaderton was clear about the criteria. For if these pharisees, greatly learned as they were, could err so seriously, 'others may err as they did, and therefore this teacheth us not to lie or trust upon the constitutions of man and therefore that we ought so to be conversant in the scriptures that we may by them judge of what sort they be'.[72] Scripture, then, was to provide the criteria. But who was to judge? Here Chaderton was less than specific. Certainly he denied that we should passively accept the verdict of those in authority. That was a popish habit and could only lead to an enormity of error. But, suggestively enough, Chaderton continually emphasised the stark contrast between the self-love and ambition of the pharisees and the humble and truthful testimony of the poor, blind man on Christ's behalf.

And this example is to be imitated of us true Christians for although this man had been blind from his birth and thereof ignorant yet he according to the measure of knowledge that he had received he speaketh. Therefore this little spark of knowledge which he had did make him so bold then how much more will the greater measure of knowledge make a man bold.[73]

Chaderton immediately applied the lesson to contemporary

affairs: 'If this poor man to whom the Lord had given such small talent was not daunted to defend his cause before such great men of authority as the pharisees were what shall we say of many men in our time which have great gifts and yet will not defend the truth so boldly?'[74]

But there was 'another extremity' current 'in these our days' that the blind man's example condemned. 'They refuse [who precisely 'they' referred to Chaderton left to the imagination of his audience] to confer with those that have the gifts of God's Spirit. But the children of God they must not disdain to learn of the simplest.'[75] Similarly, Chaderton denounced the pharisees as false Christs because 'they did intrude themselves as divines in the church of God and was not sent...they assumed to themselves the regiment of the whole church... thirdly these men also did challenge to themselves the title of a great pastor [yet] they denied the habit of the sheep'.[76]

If these two passages are juxtaposed, we can see quite clearly that Chaderton had provided a rationale for a biting attack on the established church. Even if the passages just quoted were aimed exclusively at Rome, with no hint of even a passing reference to Canterbury, as general statements they remained sufficiently ambiguous to allow certain elements in the audience to apply them directly to the contemporary puritan experience. Hence, when Chaderton assured his hearers that 'wheresoever we be whether wrongfully cast forth of the church or whether we be led forth into the wilderness yet our shepherd he goeth always before us and hath a care to save us',[77] are we to believe that no one saw behind that statement the heroic figure of a deprived, imprisoned or exiled puritan minister? In 1590, to take just one example, no less a figure than Thomas Cartwright was in the Fleet.

But how did Chaderton intend his arguments to be taken? To an extent, I think, we have to assume that the ambiguity of his remarks was intentional, a shield with which to conceal or at least camouflage the decidedly precisian bent of his doctrine. In one notable example, however, Chaderton went out of his way to qualify the radical implications of his remarks. This involved his position on the issue of subscription. As we have seen, he had denounced the reliance on the mere institutions of men in the church, remarking 'how dangerous a thing it is for a tradition to continue long in the church of God',[78] and generally pointed out 'the difference between the commandment of God and the commandment of men'. (For the one 'spiritual obedience' was requisite, for the other mere 'civil obedience'.)[79] All of which appeared to argue powerfully for the refusal of subscription, at least on Whitgift's terms. But Chaderton would have none of that. Citing the example of Christ in lawfully observing a feast of human origin, he asserted that 'this teacheth us wisely to keep and to use the institutions of men. It is not for us straightway to cast off the institutions of man only because it is the ordinance of man.'[80] 'Let us', he concluded, 'only learn to behave ourselves religiously in all such institutions seeking the glory of God and the edification of the church.'[81] Certainly Chaderton would have no truck with those that held that by his mere presence Christ did 'allow the whole ceremonies that was in the temple'. On the contrary, Chaderton contended,

he did allow none but that which he did, namely the lauding of God. He took occasion here to confer with the Jews and thereby to deliver unto them the word of life and thus must the ministers of our land assemble themselves to such places and this condemneth the schismatics of our years which for some corruptions [have left the ministry or church].[82]

The key to Chaderton's position, as ever, stemmed from his attitude to scripture. Only where the will of God, as revealed in his word, was crystal clear should people finally commit themselves. 'If every one would compromit their judgements til such time as the Lord hath revealed then there would not be such dissension amongst us as there is.'[83] Certainly there would have been no great demand for conformity of the sort master-minded by Whitgift.

Chaderton's view of the godly commonwealth rested firmly on scripture. Here he cited Christ's example in seeking to confute the pharisees by means of the word of God. 'Here he noteth the original of this erroneous judgement of the pharisees that it is their ignorance or contempt of God's institution, for indeed the ignorance of God's holy scripture is the source of errors in the church and commonwealth',[84] 'whereas our Saviour for the decision of the controversies doth call them to the written word.'[85] When men alleged merely human traditions, we were always to reply from scripture. In the immediate context Chaderton applied the lesson of the church of Rome. But taken generally the passage fitted perfectly with Chaderton's presbyterianism, with its insistence that many of the 'present errors in the church and commonwealth' would disappear were we but to decide all our controversies by the 'written word of God'. Moreover Chaderton's claim, maintained elsewhere in the same discourse, that failure to accept or understood the dictates of scripture could only proceed from personal sin and hardness of heart, and his present castigation of the pharisees (learned men all and leaders of the church) as riven with 'pride and self-love',[86] correspond perfectly with the presbyterian picture of the bishops. There too the prelates' perverse and self-interested opposition provided the only real obstacle to the triumph of further reformation. Of course, that Chaderton himself did not spell out the comparison is hardly to be wondered at. As Master of Emmanuel he had a position to protect, and 1590 was hardly a propitious year in which to broach such inflammatory topics.

But to Chaderton, as we have seen above, such issues were hardly dangerous. A careful reading of these lectures can go some way to telling us what assumptions enabled him to sustain his belief in the inherent congruence of the presbyterian platform and the contemporary status quo. For Chaderton had what is best described as a pluralist view of authority in a Christian commonwealth. Since the final arbiter in questions of importance was scripture, the real question became how best to interpret the word. And this, according to Chaderton, was a co-operative work. Hence he asserted the value in the resolution of doubts of 'conferences of the children of God'. In another passage he asserted the value of 'counsel'.

In the natural body there are many parts having divers functions yet they are so bound together that they make but one body, even so every politic society by counsel is holden together, and that bond broken all falleth asunder. When counsel is the eye of our life and the guider of our actions how can we but needs fall if it be wanting.

Now this process of giving counsel was a collective activity, the product of a reciprocal giving and taking, of advice. Hence, wrote Chaderton, 'if the husband or the wife cannot counsel one another they must needs perish. Therefore it behoveth magistrates to be men of wisdom and to have the spirit of counsel.' But two heads were better than one and therefore 'where many councillors are there is health'.

And this is most true in the Church of God for when there be many to give counsel to the conscience there the church flourisheth. And therefore our Saviour Christ when as he saw the people as sheep without a shepherd he prayed unto his father to thrust out his labourers into his harvest and with that he sent forth 70 at once and took twelve to himself so that there [was] never such a flourishing church in the world. And we have experience of this in our land. What is the cause that the kingdom flourisheth so nowadays like it never did? The cause is because the number of councillors are augmented, let us therefore never let the Lord to rest but desire him send forth more wise and great councillors.[87]

This of course applied, as Chaderton said, with equal force to both the contemporary church and the state: in the state where councillors like Huntingdon, Leicester or Burghley had stood for many years four-square behind the cause of true religion; and in the church where men like Chaderton, Whitaker and their puritan brethren, as well as the more protestant of the bishops, likewise upheld the same cause. In a situation like that, for Chaderton, all that was necessary for the cause of true religion and further reformation to prevail was that the artificial and corrupt obstacles (and here the merely human institution of episcopacy would bulk large for Chaderton the presbyterian) be removed to allow this plethora of 'good counsel' to take effect. Then Chaderton's extremely exalted view of the magistrate (they were 'gods', he said, 'because they are advanced into higher places than others are')[88] would naturally fall into place alongside his attitude to the supremacy of scripture, and the spiritual authority of the ministry and the 'clear right of the Lord' 'that his word be preached and that the Sabbath day be kept'[89] would at last be fully respected and enforced by the magistrate.

4

The moderate puritan divine as anti-papal polemicist

Hitherto, this study has concentrated on capturing the harmonies and dissonances inherent in the puritanism of Laurence Chaderton. In the process it has discussed the concerns and issues that traditionally stand at the centre of any definition of puritanism. Certainly Chaderton was a presbyterian. But in this present section I want to discuss the career of another moderate – William Whitaker – who possessed none of the distinguishing marks normally assumed to be characteristic of precisian opposition to the status quo but who, I shall argue, must be seen as a puritan if that term is to retain any real meaning or significance for an analysis of Elizabethan religious opinion. Central to this argument will be a discussion of the links of thought and feeling, of personal friendship and ideological solidarity that bound Whitaker to the mainstream of puritan thought. In order to do so it will prove necessary to deal with committed presbyterians like Walter Travers and Thomas Cartwright and, by means of a comparison between their attitudes and those of Whitaker, to arrive at a view of the moderate puritan middle ground.

Central to this analysis is the protestant perception of the threat from Rome. For it was that which underwrote and sustained the consciousness shared by both precisians and conformists of their common identity in the face of the Romish Antichrist. This chapter will be concerned in the main with that common identity and the ways in which it could be invoked for personal and 'party' advantage, in short with its role in the maintenance of the moderate puritan world-view. Hence, it is Whitaker as an anti-papal polemicist, and, similarly, Cartwright and Travers as opponents of Rome rather than Canterbury, who will concern us here. For these men were not only – perhaps not even primarily – presbyterians. Only by taking the other elements in their careers and printed works into full consideration can any rounded appreciation of their overall position be achieved.

As Dr Hill has pointed out, virtually all sections of English, indeed European, protestant opinion were united in the belief that the pope was Antichrist.[1] It was a distinguishing mark of the precisian opposition to the established church that it held that the English church contained too many remnants of the rule of Antichrist to qualify as a properly reformed church. But that was not the end of the story. For while it was perfectly possible for polemical, anti-conformist purposes to emphasise that aspect of the puritan position, such an emphasis remained simply the particular application of a more general doctrine – the identification of the pope with Antichrist. This conviction of the Antichristian nature of popery served to bolster the Elizabethan church. The greater and more terrible the threat from Rome, the greater the achievement in effecting a definitive break with the popish past. Of course, puritans also held that that break had not been definitive enough. Nevertheless, it remained true that the same obsession with popery that prompted and shaped their critique of the national church also served to underwrite their allegiance to it. It was the hallmark of moderate puritanism that it retained, indeed was sustained by, a creative tension between those contrary tendencies.

The relative significance or prominence granted to these two divergent aspects of the protestant world-view provides perhaps the best guide to the precise nature of any man's puritanism. The most moderate concentrated almost exclusively on the straightforwardly anti-papal implications of this outlook. Others sought to combine the two in a dynamic synthesis. The most radical, while they undoubtedly hated Rome and paid lip-service to a common protestant front against Rome, in practice concentrated on a precisian critique of the Antichristian remnants in the English church.[2]

Certainly, anti-papal polemic retained a compelling attraction for the godly divine. For there were few areas of interest to the protestant scholar that were not centrally involved in the confrontation with Rome. William Whitaker outlined 'the greatest and most principal controversies' that divided papist from protestant. These involved 'grace, predestination, free will, justification, the Scripture, the Law, the Gospel, sin, good works, sacraments and the Church'.[3] He might have added patristic studies and church history for both were essential tools for the zealous opponent of Rome who wished to refute papist claims of protestant novelty and to validate his identification of the pope with Antichrist. Given this almost unlimited sphere of competence, the role of the anti-papal polemicist provided, perhaps, the perfect vehicle for that zealously committed pedantry that was the hallmark of the godly divine. Moreover, in the absence of any works of English systematic theology dating from this period, it is to these works of polemic that we must turn if we wish to gain some idea of the sort of divinity that passed for orthodoxy in the English church during the last two decades of the sixteenth century. Here, surely, is the main expression of that doctrinal consensus that provided the necessary background for the puritan drive for further reformation.

But this was far from the limit of its usefulness to the puritan scholar. For anti-papal polemic embodied perfectly that combination of loyalty to the Elizabethan church and commitment to the cause of further reformation that typified the moderate puritan position. To attack Rome was at once an avowal of loyalty to the church of England and the Royal Supremacy, and a defence of the cause of true religion. In terms of this confrontation between Christ and Antichrist the issues that separated precisians from conformists melted into insignificance and the tensions that usually beset the puritan position simply faded away. In short, the role of anti-papal polemicist managed to combine respectability with ideological rectitude to an extent unrivalled by any other single activity open to the godly scholar.

Dr Bauckham has shown the mediating role played by this switch of perspective, from the Antichristian remnants in the English church to the full reality of Antichrist in the church of Rome, in the career of that erstwhile radical William Fulke. Fulke's progress from young firebrand to middle-aged moderate may be unexceptional enough in itself. But it is significant that in making that transition he managed to retain the respect of his former radical colleagues. His self-appointed role as an opponent of Rome not only prompted him to moderate his opinions but also attracted the support of the Earl of Leicester and eased his preferment to the mastership of Pembroke College; it also ensured that, in the process, he lost none of his reputation for zeal and integrity amongst the godly.[4]

The other leading exponent of the art of anti-papal polemic during the 1580s was William Whitaker. But unlike Fulke, Whitaker had never been a presbyterian. However, like the older man he too contrived to remain on friendly terms with virtually all shades of English protestant opinion. Whitaker came from a fairly well-to-do family in Lancashire. His parents were stubborn papists and at the age of twelve Whitaker was taken away to London by his uncle Alexander Nowell, Dean of St Paul's, lest he be infected by the popery of his native county. Once in London Whitaker attended St Paul's school until at the age of fifteen he went up to Trinity College, Cambridge. As a young man Whitaker seems to have shown none of the conventional marks of precisian disaffection with the established church.[5] His first published work was a translation into Greek of the Book of Common Prayer in 1569.[6] He followed that with a Latin translation of the longer and shorter catechisms by his uncle, Dean Nowell, published in 1574 and 1578 respectively.[7] As his biographer somewhat grandiloquently put it, Whitaker was here 'giving an unfeigned specimen how great an honour and ornament he would afterwards prove to the kingdom of England'.[8] Certainly, Whitaker was anxious to prove his zeal and reliability as a defender of the English church.

In 1578 he published a Latin translation of Jewel's attack on Harding. This he dedicated to Archbishops Grindal and Sandys, and Bishops Aylmer, Whitgift, Freake and his uncle Dean Nowell, 'viri omni doctrina atque virtute praecellentes'. They had all, he wrote, been friends of the great Jewel in life and now, cherishing his memory in death, would surely welcome this translation of his magnum opus as a monument to his memory. The book, he claimed, was intended as a token of 'meam bene de ecclesia nostra merendi voluntatem'.[9] Although he expressly denied angling for patronage there can be no doubt that in attempting to set himself in the tradition of Jewel as a champion of the protestant cause Whitaker was, as it were, issuing a prospectus to potential patrons.

Certainly, Whitaker seems to have committed himself to a

life of scholarship, with the need to defend the English church against Rome uppermost in his mind. Ashton tells us that he set himself 'in a few years' to examine 'almost all the founder fathers as well Greek as Latin. All of whom he was reported to have drunk in so greedily that, when I was a boy, fame reported that if on any occasion, either by the visits of friends or by due relaxation, any part of the time he had allotted for the reading of divines was lost he was wont to watch till very late at night till he had accomplished the work of the whole day.[10] All of which can safely be taken as a self-conscious preparation on Whitaker's part for the task ahead.

By 1581 Whitaker's efforts had reaped their reward. For in that year he seems to have gained the pseudo-official position as champion of the English church against Rome that remained the backbone of his career for the rest of his life. In 1581 he published his reply to Campion's *Ten reasons*. It had, he claimed in the dedicatory epistle (it was dedicated to Burghley), been undertaken at the express request of the Archbishop of Canterbury and the leading men in the university.[11] This came hard on his appointment in 1579, at the unusually young age of thirty-one, to the Regius chair of divinity.[12] By the early 1580s, then, Whitaker was a coming man.

His efforts against Rome certainly seem to have won him the backing of influential men. Whitgift, it appears, had fostered Whitaker's career since his days as an undergraduate at Trinity, when Whitgift had been Master. In a dedicatory epistle of 1594 Whitaker paid tribute to the help and encouragement he had received from the Archbishop throughout his career. Whitgift fully reciprocated Whitaker's regard. As he wrote to Nevile, the Master of Trinity, in 1595.

Mr Whitaker's death doth affect me exceedingly in many respects; he being a man whom I love very well and had purposed to have employed him in matters of great importance. At his last being with me he signified unto me what things he had in hand touching Stapleton. And therefore I am very desirous to have his notes and writings as well concerning that matter as other thing. And therefore I pray you procure them unto me if you can.[13]

It was Whitaker's activities against Rome, therefore, that had won the Archbishop's respect.

But Whitaker also enjoyed a similarly close relationship with Burghley. At some point in the early 1590s he became Burghley's university chaplain, and of the six major works of polemic that Whitaker produced before his premature death in 1595, five were dedicated to Burghley and one to Whitgift.[14] Such illustrious patrons allowed Whitaker to claim almost official 'confessional' status for his works. Hence, in his *Disputation of holy scripture* of 1588, while he took great care to acknowledge his debt to the Archbishop, Whitaker dedicated it to Burghley:

I did nothing without the approbation of the most reverend father the archbishop of Canterbury...who having read and thoroughly considered the whole controversy declared it worthy of publication. Now it is published I dedicate it to you most worthy Cecil whom I have ever to esteem the greatest patron and Maecenas of my studies.[15]

Such influential support was the foundation upon which Whitaker's career was built. As one would expect of a man from Whitaker's background, he had little time for that upsurge of radical presbyterianism that threatened to disrupt the peace of the English church in the early 1570s. Hence Bancroft, as part of his later attempt to isolate the hard core of the classis movement from their moderate colleagues, quoted Whitaker's opinion of the second part of Cartwright's second reply. It was hardly complimentary:

I have read a great part of that book which master Cartwright hath lately published...I pray God I live not if ever I say anything more loosely written and almost more childishly. It is true that for words he hath great store and those both fine and new; but for matter as far as I can judge, he is altogether barren. Moreover, he doth not only think perversely of the authority of Princes in causes ecclesiastical, but also flyeth into the papists holds, from whom he would be thought to dissent with a mortal hatred. But in this point he is not to be endured; and in other parts also he borroweth his arguments from the papists.[16]

These remarks amount almost to a 'review' of Cartwright's book. Since they do not come from any of Whitaker's published works they can probably be seen as an extract from a private letter (perhaps to Whitgift) occasioned by the publication of Cartwright's book and Whitgift's failure to answer it. (Whitaker closed the review with the opinion that Cartwright's concluding volume 'is altogether unworthy to be confuted by any man of learning'.) It is perhaps significant that the only occasion at which Whitaker moved from a criticism of the particular deficiencies of Cartwright's own personal exposition of the presbyterian case to a substantive criticism of the whole case itself, was over the issue of the Royal Supremacy. And here his comparison of Cartwright's position with that of the papists can be taken as the reaction of a man whose attention was fixed firmly on the protestant conflict with Rome and for whom the Royal Supremacy provided the only effective defence against that threat.

But it is doubly significant that Bancroft had to go outside the corpus of Whitaker's printed works to find a suitably explicit rejection of the presbyterian case. All Whitaker's public pronouncements were notable for their lack of reference to any of the disputes or disagreements that beset the church of England. Certainly, his polemical works could be construed as pseudo-official defences of the national church. This, indeed, was an impression that Whitaker did his best to foster in many of his prefaced and dedicatory epistles. But in practice, while Whitaker might pose as a defender of the English church, he was in fact defending a nebulous protestant world-view to which the church of England was assumed to belong but which in truth was not exclusively attached to any one visible church. It was this that enabled Whitaker to remain largely uncommitted on issues which, at this date, are usually taken to have sharply divided conformists from precisians. And it was this central ambiguity of attitude that underlay Whitaker's links with avowed presbyterians like Laurence Chaderton.

For Whitaker did indeed enjoy many links with puritan circles. In 1577 he had married Susan Culverwell, the daughter of Nicholas Culverwell the London merchant haberdasher and a noted lay puritan.[17] Susan's sister Cecilia was married to none other than Laurence Chaderton. Now related by 'marriage and friendship the two men for a time set up home together in the same house'.[18] Whitaker also figured in the will of Richard Culverwell, his uncle by marriage. Culverwell remembered each one of the members of John Field's London classis in his will. In addition Whitaker, Chaderton, Richard Greenham, William

Charke and Walter Travers were all made trustees of a sum of £150 for distribution to the poor.[19]

Nor was this precisian connection a mere accident occasioned by Whitaker's marriage. In 1589 his wife Susan died only to be replaced in Whitaker's affections by Joan Fenner, widow of the leading puritan divine Dudley Fenner.[20] Moreover, even after the death of his first wife Whitaker continued to refer to Chaderton as 'my brother Chaderton', most notably in a letter to Burghley of 1590 defending them both from charges of puritanism. Similarly, in 1595 Samuel Ward recorded that Whitaker, on his departure for London and the meeting that culminated in the Lambeth Articles, had 'promised Mr Chaderton and thereupon given him his hand that he would stand to God's cause against the Lutherans'.[21] Hence, whatever the ambiguities of Whitaker's relations with mainstream puritan or presbyterian opinion, there can be no doubt that his reputation stood high amongst the godly. Samuel Ward bewailed his premature death in 1595 as a body-blow to the puritan cause in the university,[22] while, in a letter to Sir Robert Sidney, Robert Beale lamented 'the deaths of the Earl of Huntingdon, Doctor Whitaker in Cambridge and Sir Roger Williams here; "all three worthy men in their callings and hardly to be seconded again"'.[23] Now, Beale's letter was mainly concerned with the conduct of foreign policy and ended with a lament that 'for lack of countenance the cause of religion goeth to wrack. The Lord amend all.' It provided, therefore, a perfect illustration of the nexus of concerns – theological, political and diplomatic – that centred around the work of ideologues like Whitaker and their identification of the pope as Antichrist. In this context Whitaker's ability to engage on his side in a college dispute both Leicester and Essex – both of whom were proponents of a forward, anti-Catholic foreign policy – takes on considerable significance.[24]

Of course Whitaker's puritan contacts were not lost on his contemporaries. Andrew Perne for one reacted very adversely to them. Indeed, Perne went so far as to intrigue against Whitaker's proposed election to the Mastership of St John's College. Since Whitaker was Burghley's chosen candidate for the place this earned Perne a stinging rebuke from the Lord Treasurer. Faced with an angry Burghley Perne denied everything but could not resist a Parthian shot at Whitaker's precisian sympathies. Three or four years previously Whitaker had been extremely eager to take his doctorate before he had reached the age required by statute. He had petitioned Perne as Vice-Chancellor for special permission to take the degree early. Perne had acceded to the request but suddenly Whitaker's enthusiasm had evaporated and even as Perne wrote Whitaker had yet to take the degree. To the presbyterians any office of doctor save that outlined in scripture as the pedagogic counterpart of the preaching minister was anathema. Perne, therefore, interpreted Whitaker's unlooked-for modesty as a sign of precisian leanings:

Ever since that time that he might have proceeded without any dispensation and since the time of his marriage for that by none of the persuasions of the heads of colleges at Cambridge he could be induced to proceed it is feared that he hath been alienated by the persuasion of some that be very near unto him which are thought not to like well of that degree nor of other good orders in the university. Which fantastical humours daily given to dangerous innovations if any such should take root in the university as they do in other places both the church and consequently the commonwealth shall soon come to ruin thereby if he principally and all the governors of colleges shall not study and labour to bridle and restrain the licentious affections of the youth of the university at this day. Wherein if either he or we should want your honourable assistance all good exercises of learning and good order in the said university would shortly be overthrown. To the maintenance whereof Mr Whitaker by his good example in that great college shall do more good than a great many other to God's glory, the peace of his church, her Majesty's good liking, your honour's great comfort and his singular commendation.[25]

Despite the conciliatory tone of these concluding remarks there can be no doubt of Perne's basic intention. He was denouncing Whitaker as a precisian and sharply reminding Burghley of his responsibilities as a major bulwark of the Elizabethan church settlement.

But knowing that Whitaker had puritan leanings and connections was one thing – proving it was quite another. Whitaker had been nothing if not cautious and in the face of the considerable opposition to his appointment at St John's Whitaker had only to fall back upon his unimpeachable record as a servant and defender of the English church. Hence, in a letter to Burghley of 1585 Whitaker protested his suitability for the post. He well understood the qualities of prudence and moderation necessary amongst men of such varied dispositions and temperaments. He undertook to avoid all occasions of faction and give no fair observer any opportunity to accuse him of partiality. He would, he claimed, behave as the laws and the nature of the position demanded, and as authority required. If he failed in that regard he could easily be removed. What, he asked, were the qualities in which he was thought to be wanting? What was it that rendered him unfit for the post? After all, if he was unfit for the mastership was he not also unworthy to hold the divinity chair that he now held and had held for several years? Burghley well knew how he had lived, how great his labours in the service and defence of the church had been. The accusations of his enemies were better answered by those labours than by any mere words. For he had dedicated his life to study, the better to engage the adversary in polemical warfare. With that Whitaker threw himself on Burghley's mercy; only he could now save him from the malicious rumours circulated by his enemies.[26]

Whitaker's appeal did not fall on deaf ears. In 1587, in the face of considerable opposition from within the college, the Ecclesiastical Commissioners (Whitgift and Burghley amongst them), acting as the college visitors in the absence of a bishop of Ely, forced through Whitaker's election as Master of St John's. It was an appointment they justified in terms of Whitaker's services to the church and university. Whitaker they described as

a man of long time conversant among you and of gravity and learning, discretion and zeal to the furtherance of godliness, well known unto us all, to be a person meet for such a charge as any other we know there; and besides in respect he is her Majesty's reader in divinity is rather to be preferred than any other for his better countenance in the University.[27]

It was, therefore, Whitaker's activity against Rome that had once again ensured his preferment. But ironically it was precisely the need to oppose popery in all its forms that forced Whitaker into his most overtly puritan public gestures. It was, for instance, the ineffectiveness of the English church in the fight against popular popery that led Whitaker to exhort Burghley to take the present state of the church to heart and sponsor reform. Whitaker began by observing that many men wondered at the popish relics ('reliquas papistarum') that remained amongst the English despite their long enjoyment of the gospel. The cause was easily enough perceived by any one who cared to examine the state of the church. Many churches were altogether devoid of a preaching ministry. Yet without that true religion could never flourish and popery and ignorance would continue to predominate. But if the word of God were once established in a properly organised and qualified ministry it would soon inflict a signal defeat on popular superstition and ignorance and dispel the dark clouds at present hanging over the English church. The experience of many other churches proved that.[28] Similarly, it was the need to oppose popery that caused Whitaker to compare unfavourably the severe treatment meted out to precisians with the comparatively lenient attitude to papists current in some circles, and on that basis to petition Burghley for the relief of Cartwright and the other presbyterians imprisoned in 1590.[29]

But just as this zeal against popery pushed Whitaker towards the precisians, so the precisians' own recognition of the need to preserve a common front against Rome served equally to push them towards the moderates like Whitaker. For it was a basic premise of the presbyterian position that what was at stake in the puritan campaign was but the completion of the English reformation, a process, which, while it had been carried to fruition in the realm of doctrine, was still sadly lagging behind in the realm of discipline. Hence Walter Travers compared them to two twins, so close that the health of one was directly dependent on that of the other. 'True doctrine as the elder sister is recovered let us not hinder her to affect also discipline with her health; that as it began to be sick together with doctrine, it may be also recovered together with it.'[30]

What is significant here is the primacy of place accorded to doctrine. That was a point central to the puritan position and one which tended to be obscured in the purely polemical presbyterian works produced by puritan ideologues like Cartwright and Travers. Concerned there to argue the necessity of the changes they desired, they were hardly likely to labour the

primacy of doctrine over discipline and thus appear to undermine the very 'iure divino' claims of which their case consisted.
For, as that passage from Travers reveals, it was a central
assumption of their case that the doctrine of the church of
England was entirely sound.

However, when they were called upon to defend the English
church against Rome it was precisely this aspect of their position
that came to the fore. Indeed, if the protestant unity of the
church of England were to be preserved, it was the normal
concerns and principles of the presbyterian position that had to
be suppressed in the face of the doctrinal consensus of the English
church.

An excellent example of the sort of protean change that
could befall an avowed presbyterian once he took up the cudgels
against Rome is provided by Walter Travers' *An answere to a
supplicatorie epistle of G.T. for the pretended catholiques* of
1583. The book was intended, according to Travers, to refute
the 'unworthy slanders wherewith the enemy chargeth the sacred
truth of God and lawful authority in this land'.[31] In so doing
Travers presented England as the very paragon of a godly
commonwealth: 'What can be more wise and honourable than
a Prince and state by whom true religion is zealously and sincerely
advanced, justice uprightly administered, the royal oath, word
and promise of a Prince inviolably observed, virtue rewarded,
vice punished, good laws wisely made.'[32] Travers catalogued the
blessings of the English with eulogistic fervour. Almost alone
amongst the peoples of Europe, in the midst of popish plots and
wars, England was at peace. The Queen had called back the
exiled ministers of the gospel, brought succour to the persecuted
people of Christ and cast out popery:

Instead whereof her Majesty hath brought in prayers in our own
tongue, the holy word of God to be read and truly expounded unto
us. The sacraments which are the seals of the Gospel duly administered, the pure clean and undefiled water of baptism, the
Lord's Table furnished as the royal table of a king at the marriage
of his son with the sweet bread of the finest wheat and with wine
of a grape of a most noble kind that is with the most precious body
and blood of our Saviour Christ Jesu.[33]

Of course Travers could not continue in that vein indefinitely
and intermittently throughout the book he appealed to the

Queen and her councillors to 'increase God's favour to her and her country'[34] by establishing 'all the order of the house of God in every point'.[35] In view of his presbyterianism Travers was obliged to admit that the English church was a good deal less than perfect: 'It is indeed to be admitted that our ministry in many places is greatly unprovided, contrary to the command-ment of God and to the just cause of fear of his indignation against us for it, if it be not some way in time relieved.'[36] But even here Travers was careful to put the blame for this not on the bishops or their conformist acolytes, but on the papists: 'But this especially ariseth of the spoil which they made by impropri-ating the livings of many particular churches to the maintenance of their cloisters or nests of their superstitious corruptions for remedy whereof we are most humble and continual suitors to God and the authority he hath set over us.'[37]

Similarly, in meeting the papist allegation that the protestants lacked proper means to bring the laity to a good and godly life, Travers was forced to raise the issue of a proper church dis-cipline:

For as the discipline of Christ is the special means next to the true preaching of the word, of all godliness and honesty both to be preserved amongst men and also to be restored after a declination and decay, so that Antichristian disorder and confusion in all the chief parts thereof is, next to their false and heretical doctrine the greatest cause that all impiety and wickedness both first entered into the Church and yet cannot be driven out, that the ancient estate of the Church may be recovered and restored again.[38]

But having said as much Travers had to admit that the English church was far from perfect in that regard. However, it did possess 'the living word of God that striketh deep to the parting between the soul and the spirit'. And such churches where the gospel

is truly taught, as by the grace of God it is amongst us are not without not only the chiefest and most principal means to keep the people in due obedience to him. For further means of discipline we acknowledge what the right order is which God hath commanded and both see and heartily grieved to see in so noble a part of the Church as this is and after so long continuance of the Gospel preached amongst us, great abuses contrary to it; so we cease not to be most humble and continual suitors to God and to the authority he hath set over us that we may enjoy it. Which being in the use thereof and in the ordinance of our Saviour Christ so necessary for the service of God and the salvation of men that we sue for being thoroughly understood the Lord will dispose the hearts of so Christian authority as we are subject unto most willingly to grant it.[39]

Having thus put his cards on the table Travers proceeded to invoke the threat of popery to convince the Privy Council of the need for a properly reformed church discipline to act as a bulwark against the forces of Antichrist. But in the meantime, as Travers was forced to concede, 'the preaching of the Gospel by the blessing of God may be of power to those in whom God shall work by it to keep them in his fear'.[40]

In thus stressing the role of the 'gospel' Travers was implicitly ranking discipline behind doctrine as a mark of the true church, and hence making an admission that could only undermine the fundamental coherence of the presbyterian case. But while phrases like 'the living word of God' might sound vague and imprecise, they in fact denoted what was a very precise notion of doctrinal orthodoxy. The doctrinal consensus of the English church provided a major argument against the papists:

Now let us see with what dissension he can charge our church in England. Wherein if he would have proceeded soundly to the just charging of us he ought if he had been able to have brought out the public confession and articles of faith agreed upon in King Edward's time and have showed any in England that professing the Gospel dissenteth from them.[41]

Indeed, so confident was Travers of the doctrinal consensus of the English church that, charged with the name 'Calvinist' by the papists, he simply denied that the term could have any meaning in an English context. For, wrote Travers,

he is to understand we have no such custom nor the Christian church of God to name ourselves of any men. Christ is not divided with us, we all content ourselves with that honourable name of Christians. To be a Franciscan or a Dominican, a Thomist or a Scotist we leave to them who have divided and rent asunder both Christ's coat and body.[42]

Cartwright was to make precisely the same point in his *A Confutation of the Rhemists translations*,[43] and Whitaker too assumed the existence of both a doctrinal consensus within the English church and an essential congruence between that consensus and his own doctrinal position.[44]

Here, then, is a new perspective from which to view the erstwhile presbyterianism of men like Travers and Cartwright. This is not to argue that their position vis-à-vis Rome was somehow more truly representative of their ideas than their position vis-à-vis the English conformists. The two were expressions of the same protestant world-view and as such have to be seen as but two sides of the same coin. There might be a tension between them, but it was not a straightforward contradiction between mutually exclusive sets of values. Indeed, it was the essence of the moderate position to keep the one balanced against the other in a fruitful tension whereby the common front against Rome kept them safely and securely within the English church while their zeal against popery and the popish remnants yet remaining within the church of England saved them from a mere conformity.

Of course, this delicate balance was open to manipulation for polemical purposes. The entire conformist position, for instance, was expressly designed to force onto the puritan minister a definitive choice between puritan principle and loyalty to the national church. The puritans for their part could invoke the popish threat and their own central role in repelling it in order to stress their own basic reliability as defenders of the protestant order and hence vindicate their claim to represent the vanguard of English protestantism.

Here the central example is provided by the campaign to enlist Cartwright to the anti-papal cause in the early 1580s. For in 1583 a group of puritan divines wrote to Cartwright, then in exile in the Low Countries, urging him to confute the translation of the New Testament recently published by the papists at Rheims. The terms in which this appeal was couched are themselves instructive. Ordinarily, they claimed, they would not seek to burden Cartwright with tasks more onerous than those inherent in the ordinary exercise of his ministry. But 'it is not now sufficient for us to build the Temple of the Lord; but we must also, with the other hand, fight against the frequent armies of heretics'. Their earlier ploys having failed the papists had 'of late enterprised a new course whereby they might persuade unskilful men that the divine Scriptures and heavenly oracles stand on their side'. The danger was great, for not only were the papists endowed with diabolical cunning but, typically, the protestants were pictured as a beleaguered minority surrounded by a sea of popular ignorance and apathy. 'For though a few of the learned sort see that all things are by them overwhelmed with blind darkness and thick mists yet are there manifold snares laid for weak minds and the wavering in religion beaten upon by divers waves of doubtings.' Cartwright, they continued, was eminently suited to refute this latest popish subterfuge:

It is not for every man workmanlike to frame God's tabernacle but for Basaleel and Aboliah; neither is every one to be rashly thrust forth into the Lord's battles but such captains are to be chosen from amongst David's worthies. Of which as we acknowledge you to be the former battles undergone by the walls of our city the Church we doubt not if you will enter into this war, which truly you ought according to the zeal and piety you bear to your country and religion but that you (fighting for conscience and country, yea even for the very inmost holy place of the temple) will be able to tread underfoot the forces of the Jesuits which set themselves to assault the tower of David. Moreover (which marvellously serveth to the sharpening of your courage) you are not now to fight with any brother or fellow of the same religion (which maketh the conflict more faint) but with the most inveterate enemies of the Church of Christ, far more cruel than ever was any Philistine or Ammonite.

Hence, they concluded, 'you see to what an honourable fight we invite you. Christ's business shall be undertaken against Satan's champions, we stir you up to fight the battles of our Lord where the victory is certain which the triumph and applause of the angels will ensue.'[45]

This letter was signed by Roger Goad, William Fulke, William Whitaker, William Charke, John Field, Nicholas Crane, Giles Saintloe and Richard Gardiner. It was printed as part of the preface of the 1618 edition of Cartwright's *A confutation*, and since the names of those signatories still alive at that date were 'by the advice of our most reverend friends of the present concealed' it seems likely that the original was also signed by Laurence Chaderton and Walter Travers. Certainly, apart from them, the signatories represent an interesting and almost complete roll-call of John Field's London classis and the moderate puritan divines of Cambridge University. Coinciding with this commission from the puritan 'high command' Cartwright received a similar appeal from the Dedham classis 'to despatch this monster that is come out of the camp of the uncircumcised'. In his reply to that letter Cartwright mentioned still more messages of encouragement from the godly in England.[46] While none of these is extant there is a remarkable letter from Sir Francis Walsingham to Cartwright again exhorting him to undertake the task and promising him an income of £100 a year until such time as the book should be finished.[47] Here, then, we have the notable spectacle of virtually all sections of English protestant opinion uniting in the face of the popish threat, and uniting, moreover, behind the figurehead of Thomas Cartwright, the most notorious precisian of his generation.

The full significance of this for the puritan movement as a whole has perhaps not been fully appreciated. At this date, of course, Cartwright was in exile at Middelburg and had just been informed by an apologetic Walsingham that the Queen was insisting that he should leave his post there as the minister of the English congregation.[48] But Cartwright was in many ways still the representative puritan, the figurehead of the movement.[49] His exile, therefore, was very much a symbol of the entire puritan movement's exclusion from the pale of respectable religious opinion in England. Any attempt to rehabilitate him was, therefore, an attempt to rehabilitate the entire 'left wing' of English protestant opinion.

One of the main arguments used by his colleagues in the ministry and by Walsingham to induce Cartwright to undertake the task was that in so doing he might make his peace with Whitgift, convince the Queen of his reliability as a loyal servant of the English church and hence win his way back 'into the service of the church in some more high and open place'. This collective effort on the part of virtually all the strands of godly opinion to rehabilitate Cartwright's reputation must be seen as a conscious decision on the part of the puritan movement to put forward its most conciliatory and moderate aspect. That they conceived of the project in just these terms can be gleaned from the pseudo-public nature of the letters sent to 'persuade' Cartwright to undertake the task. Far from being purely private letters of advice or encouragement, these were demonstrations of support, designed for public consumption. (It was no accident that the one from London was printed in 1618.) Cartwright's *A confutation* was to be no private gesture, but a clear embodiment of the 'official' policy of the puritan party. As such, if the book received a favourable reception from the Magistrate, this would represent a victory not merely for Cartwright but for the entire body of puritan opinion in England.

But Cartwright had to pay the price of moderation for the polemical advantages that his role as an opponent of Rome had brought him. This is not to say that *A confutation* does not contain presbyterian opinions. It does.[50] Since the nature of the task in hand required a virtual commentary on the entire corpus of the New Testament Cartwright could not ignore the more controversial elements in the puritan world-view. Neither could he ignore a whole series of popish ceremonies (many of them still in use in the English church) which were mentioned in the Rhemists' own marginal notes. But within these limits there can be no doubt that Cartwright did his best to avoid attracting attention to the avowedly precisian elements in the book and at no time did he seek to 'point' his remarks at the present imperfect state of the English church. As he himself wrote to Burghley in 1590:

In the care I have of not provoking and of covering our disagreement in that behalf I never come to any of those points but where they call me. And there I answer with as much brevity and as great generality as I can; without any application unto our church or any the governors in the same.[51]

Moreover, it appears that Cartwright was as good as his word. Hence, when answering the papist allegation that 'the protestants otherwise denying this pre-eminence of Peter yet to uphold their archbishop do avouch it against the puritans', Cartwright merely rehearsed the arguments against Peter's supremacy over the other Apostles without applying them to the English context at all.[52]

Professor Collinson has suggested that the meeting of the London classis that is 1583 dispatched the letter to Cartwright quoted above was, in fact, one and the same as that held at Roger Goad's house in London to condemn Peter Baro's doctrine and also the same as that cited by Thomas Rogers (Bancroft's chaplain) as deciding that, should conformity be enforced again, a limited form of subscription would be conceded by the godly party. 'The whole episode', wrote Professor Collinson, 'is characteristic of the church in Grindal's primacy; the co-operation of the extremists in Field's London group with learned Cambridge men and Privy Councillors in the defence of fundamental protestantism, against the false doctrine of Rheims and the heterodox theology of Peter Baro.'[53] Professor Collinson could be taken to imply here that the contact and co-operation between moderates and radicals, while typical of Grindal's primacy, ceased during that of Whitgift as the two wings of puritan opinion split apart under the pressure of the conformist challenge and radicals like Field increasingly came to dominate the councils of the godly. But this is to posit too hard and fast a distinction between radicals and moderates. For while the common front built around Cartwright's *A confutation* took shape during Grindal's period at Lambeth, it can, even so, be seen as a conscious preparation for a less congenial regime in the church, undertaken to emphasise puritan unity and present the expected conformist campaign with the movement's most moderate face.

Moreover, hard as they tried, conformists like Whitgift and Bancroft never succeeded in definitively splitting the classis movement and its members from the mainstream of moderate puritan thought. Merely to take Cartwright's *A confutation* as an example, while the decision to undertake the work was taken in 1583 the production of the text went on throughout the 1580s. Indeed, we have Cartwright's own testimony that he was still actively engaged on the book in 1586 and preoccupied with its eventual fate in 1590. Similarly, as the decision to sponsor the work had been a collective one, so the work on it was a co-operative effort. The satirist Thomas Nashe has left an account of the way in which the puritan divines of Cambridge University used to meet every week to monitor the progress of the work.

Were not all the elected in Cambridge assembled about the shaping of the confutation of the Rhemish Testament? O so devoutly they met every Friday at St Laurence his monastery [a reference to Laurence Chaderton's college, Emmanuel] where the councils and fathers were distributed amongst several companies and everyone of the reformed society sent there combined quotations week by week in a capcase to my brother Thomas yet wandering beyond sea.[54]

A confutation, therefore, was the result of the efforts of a virtual committee of puritan divines. Certainly, on this basis, we can posit continuing close co-operation between Cartwright and Cambridge scholars like Chaderton and Whitaker throughout the 1580s. Hence, in the 1618 edition of *A confutation* it was implied that William Fulke's own reply to the Rhemists had been intended only as a stop-gap until Cartwright's work should see the light of day.[55] In the preface of his own book (published in 1589) Fulke admitted as much:

It was reported that by other men of very good gifts it was already even at the first undertaken. But so many years having passed and the expectation of many godly men not being satisfied with a full and general answer being solicited by men of good judgement and qualities I have attempted to set forth that which I have long looked for and much rather desired to be performed by other men. Not meaning thereby to prejudice the more learned labours and longer studied commentaries of them that had taken the matter in hand before me, if they purpose at length to bring them to light.[56]

And that was as close as the now eminently respectable Dr Fulke could come to publicly lamenting the official bar on the publication of Cartwright's book.

Not that this concern for the fate of Cartwright's book was limited to moderate scholars like Fulke. At a national presbyterian synod held at Cambridge in September 1587 it was resolved 'de libro responsaris ad Rhemensis Testamenti translationem scribendum a D. Fen ad comitem Leicestransem et ad D. Fennerum'.[57] Similarly, Whitgift's opposition to the publication of *A confutation* figured amongst Martin Marprelate's list of complaints against the bishops.[58]

Now, this refusal by Whitgift was highly significant. He was, of course, as we have seen in the instance of Whitaker, perfectly prepared to sponsor the production of anti-papal polemic. His refusal to allow the publication of Cartwright's effort can, therefore, be taken as a recognition on his part of the veiled polemical purpose behind its production and a refusal to countenance the seal of official approval and respectability that its publication would inevitably bestow on the whole puritan movement. In this context it is worth remembering Cartwright's persistent refusal to allow the book to be clandestinely published, either in England or abroad. As he later explained, having been commissioned to produce the work by Walsingham and having completed 'a rude and first draught of a great part thereof', he had, on 'understanding from some in authority that I might not deal with it', ceased in his own efforts to get it into print and 'laboured by letters and friends here and in Scotland' to prevent the unlawful publication of certain extracts which 'had come into the hands of divers to whom I would never have let them come'.[59] Since the while project had been intended to win the approval of the authorities, to have confronted those very authorities with an unauthorised attempt at publication would have been utterly self-defeating. Hence, the book remained unpublished until after Cartwright's death.

We have been concerned in this chapter with the way in which the production of anti-papal polemic and the co-operative efforts it inspired came to symbolise the common ground of protestant commitment that united moderate and radical puritans and, more particularly, with the way in which this was used by the puritans to refute the conformist view of them as potential sectaries and subversives. But the conformists did not allow this covertly polemical manoeuvre to go unchallenged. Indeed, Bancroft, with his unerring polemical instinct, went straight to the heart of the matter and attempted to demonstrate a split between the presbyterians and the moderates by taking passages from the anti-papal works of the moderates and comparing them with the presbyterian platform. Certainly by this means he had no difficulty in demonstrating a theoretical disagreement on certain issues (most notably on the exact status of episcopacy).[60] But as this and the succeeding chapters seek to demonstrate, the links of thought and feeling which bound moderate scholars to presbyterian activists and which were rooted in their common evangelical protestant world-view, were more important than mere academic differences over the details of church polity.

Certainly, there is every reason to believe that the conformists failed in their attempt to drive a wedge between the radicals and the moderates of the puritan movement. Here the central role was played by the moderate puritan divines of the universities.

Their position as the virtual guardians of Elizabethan protestant orthodoxy was implicitly acknowledged by both precisians and conformists. Hence, Bancroft's attempts to disassociate respectable moderates like Whitaker or John Rainolds of Oxford from any hint of presbyterian sympathy were paralleled, indeed they were prompted, by the attempts of the radical pamphlet *M. Some laid open in his coulers* to claim the likes of Fulke, Whitaker, Chaderton and Rainolds, if not for the presbyterian cause itself, then certainly for that puritan style of divinity and evangelical protestant concern.[61] Claimed as their own by both presbyterians and conformists, these men undeniably stood at the centre of the spectrum of contemporary religious opinion. Moreover, from the fact that Bancroft's book was published as late as 1593 and the pamphlet against Some in 1589, it is clear that the intellectual and emotional links that bound together presbyterians and non-presbyterians were still very much alive at the end of the 1580s.

The personification of this common front was surely Laurence Chaderton. Both respectable university scholar and presbyterian activist, Chaderton combined in his own career all the diverse aspects of moderate puritan activity that form the subject of this study. Yet, despite the clear mention of Chaderton as a prominent member of the classis movement in the depositions of 1590, his name does not appear in any of Bancroft's printed accounts of the membership of the movement.[62] Why should this have been so? Chaderton's biographer tells a story of how Chaderton saved the young Bancroft's life in the course of a Cambridge town/gown brawl, thus laying the basis for a lifetime's friendship between the two men. It could be, therefore, that in thus omitting Chaderton's name Bancroft was merely protecting a friend.[63] There is, however, a more likely explanation. For the consistent and continuous involvement of Chaderton in the classis movement would have made Bancroft's portrait of a 'Scottizing' conspiracy even more difficult to sustain than the more intangible 'puritan' connections of a Whitaker or a Fulke. While the latter could be explained away, the former could only be ignored if Bancroft's picture of a radical puritan threat to the existing social order was to retain any credibility.

5

Thomas Cartwright: the search for the centre and the threat of separation

If one end of the spectrum of religious opinion was constituted by popery, then the other was provided by the threat of separation. Presbyterians were stretched in tension between the need to oppose both of these threats and yet retain their commitment to godly principle and the discipline intact. In fact, concentration on either of these opposite poles tended to emphasise the need for moderation; in the case of popery because it emphasised that community of interest and identity which bound together both conformists and precisians as protestants; in the case of separation because it threatened that very unity and called into question the carefully cultivated respectability of the whole puritan position.

Since the whole debate between conformists and precisians can be seen as a struggle for the middle ground, their respective polemical positions can in turn be seen as attempts to shift and modify the definition of 'true moderation' by the manipulation of the twin threats of popery and separation. For the exact location of the centre of the spectrum of religious opinion depended entirely on the attitude adopted towards the two extremes. Hence, a sure sign of a man's religious affiliations was provided by his attitude to the relative significance to be attached to the threat of separation as compared to popery. For, while the puritans put great emphasis on the threat of popery, conformist apologists like Whitgift and Bancroft adopted a far more sceptical, low-key approach to Rome and emphasised instead the threat of separation, seen as the inevitable consequence of basic precisian principles, however mildly stated.

Separation, therefore, was hardly one of the favourite themes of the puritan divine. There was, after all, an undeniable link between presbyterian principle and separation. The continuing allegiance of the committed presbyterian to the established church could be an ambiguous and volatile thing. Asked in later life at what point he had become a separatist Francis Johnson had replied that he did not know the precise date; the development of his views from presbyterian to separatist had been a gradual one, the result of a slow progression and not a sudden conversion. The links were as close as that.[1]

As for the laity, separation marked the breakdown of the check placed on the radical tendencies inherent in presbyterianism, indeed in protestantism as a whole, by the doctrine of callings. For while men like Chaderton professed to limit their appeals for further reformation to the ruling class, most notably to the Queen's most immediate advisers and councillors, they contradicted the moderation of their own professed intensions by making those appeals public, both from the pulpit and in print.[2] Not surprisingly there were those who, having heard the ministers preach or having read their published works, did not respect the minister's moderate intentions and applied the presbyterian message directly to their own experience. Hence, an attempt to form opinion, indeed a virtual call to action, that could be defended as perfectly respectable when addressed to the magistrate, took on a completely new and rather sinister significance when taken up by the lower orders. For instance, in the depositions taken from members of Francis Johnson's separatist congregation in London in 1593, we find fishmongers, shipwrights, haberdashers, feltmakers all admitting that they were first set on the path to separation not by the works of avowed separatists like Harrison or Browne, but by the sermons and tracts of mainstream presbyterians like Gardiner, Sparke, Egerton, or Chaderton himself.[3] This merely served to confirm the conformist gibe that presbyterianism was but separation writ small and that consequently all precisians, however moderate they might appear, were in practice little better than sectaries.

All this, of course, was profoundly embarrassing for mainstream puritans. For, while they deeply disapproved of schism, the subject of separatism remained fraught with difficulties for them. Certainly, they had little incentive to deal with the matter in print. To have done so would have meant openly repudiating men whose motives and principles were almost identical to their own, in the defence of a church which on their own admission

was far from perfect. In terms of theory this entailed the admission
that the corruptions and errors to which the church of England
was subject were but of secondary importance, an admission
which would have crippled the radical coherence of the presbyterian platform. Practically, it meant running the risk of alienating
the more zealous of their colleagues in the ministry and hence
driving even more of the godly over the edge into open schism.[4]
It was this potential split between the radical and moderate wings
of puritan opinion that conformist policy was expressly designed
to exploit.

From a purely polemical or tactical point of view, therefore,
the best course for the committed presbyterian confronted with
the spectre of separation was to ignore it. But polemical considerations were not the only ones that counted for a puritan
divine. There was also the minister's pastoral duty to rebuke,
advise and admonish both laymen and other ministers who had
wandered from the straight and narrow path of true religion.
Such considerations applied with particular force to Thomas
Cartwright. Due to his pre-eminent position as the figurehead
of the movement Cartwright was peculiarly vulnerable to the
pressures that afflicted the presbyterian position as a whole, both
because the authorities tended to seek him out for especially severe
treatment and because the less illustrious members of the puritan
movement tended to look to him for guidance, torn as they were
between their allegiance to the national church and their
allegiance to the discipline. It was the sensitivity of Cartwright
to such pressures that caused him virtually to invent all the major
characteristics of the moderate puritan position. Just as he had
done in the 1570s over the issue of subscription, and again in the
1580s in taking up the cudgels against Rome, so Cartwright once
more grasped the nettle and addressed himself directly to the
challenge of separatism.[5] Not that the initiative was entirely
Cartwright's. He was, after all, an obvious target for the zealous
separatist, eager to vindicate his claim to have taken over the
cause of true religion from a weak and temporising presbyterianism. Hence, on both occasions when Cartwright dealt with
the subject it appears to have been in response to a separatist
attack. But once approached Cartwright dealt with the matter
not in his 'public' role as the leading ideologue and polemicist
of the presbyterian movement, but in his 'private' capacity as a

practical pastor. Hence all his pronouncements on the subject of separatism are contained in two private letters, one to Robert Harrison, the separatist minister and Cartwright's fellow exile in Middelburg, the other to Cartwright's sister-in-law, Anne Stubbe.[6] This is in marked contrast to the performance of Robert Some who attacked the separatists in print in order to extract the maximum personal and party advantage from the exchange.[7] But in neither of these letters was Cartwright's avowed intention the public vindication of his position. His aim was simply to win over two misguided but well-intentioned zealots to the cause of true religion. His letter to Harrison seems to have been part of a continuing discussion between the two men, the aim of which, for Cartwright, was 'the reuniting of yourself [Harrison] with the rest of your company unto us'.[8] As for the letter to Anne Stubbe, it was prompted solely, he claimed, by 'my desire to do you good'.[9]

Since virtually all the evidence concerning Elizabethan presbyterianism is polemical in form there is a built-in tendency to overrate the radicalism of the classis movement.[10] For neither precisian nor conformist propagandists wished to admit the existance of the moderate position. A rationale for continued presbyterian allegiance to the church of England, even in its present unreformed state, had no place in a campaign to underline the absolute necessity of further reformation. Neither were conformists anxious to call attention to the success with which many moderates sustained their position in the church while yet retaining their identity as puritans. That is why 'off the record' statements like these are such invaluable sources. For here, in seeking to justify the mainstream puritan commitment to the national church Cartwright allowed himself to set out in unusual detail the normally unstated assumptions that underlay the presbyterianism of moderate scholars like Chaderton and Cartwright himself.

But now let us consider the actual arguments that Cartwright used to turn aside the remorseless logic of the separatist case. In the face of the separatists' stance, based on a stark choice between black and white – as Anne Stubbe remarked at one point, 'it must needs be Christ or Antichrist'[11] – Cartwright replied with shades of grey. Perhaps his basic point was that by definition all visible churches must remain imperfect. Since in this world it was impossible to distinguish even approximately between the elect and the reprobate – 'otherwise then every one is able to discern of himself by the fruits of the spirit, as first of adoption and secondly of sanctification' – the church was inevitably composed of a mixture of the two and hence could not but be subject to the frailties of man's fallen nature.[12] Hence the separatist search for a perfect 'separation' between the sheep and the goats, the godly and the ungodly, was doomed to failure, at least in this life. 'As if your unity with Christ and separation from all that are not his were not imperfect here, and begin only to be made up when Christ by his angels shall make a final separation between the sheep and the goats.'[13]

Indeed, since the elect were, in this life at least, subject to grievous temptations and sins, it was hardly surprising that the faith and obedience of even the best of churches should remain imperfect. As Cartwright remarked, 'the children of God have also their proud and presumptuous sins'.[14]

The church, argued Cartwright, could be compared to a disobedient wife: while her disobedience was a fault 'yet it followeth not that because she obeyeth not therefore she is no wife'. Hence, while the church could err, 'yet not having abandoned her husband by atheism nor by idolatry, she remaineth still the wife of Christ'. Indeed Cartwright went further. Though the church commit 'spiritual adultery' she retained her status as a true church of God 'until such time as the Lord taking away the ministry of the Word from her and the administration of the Sacraments hath as it were by bill of divorcement disabled her'.

In view of that, concluded Cartwright, it behoved the separatists to show a deal more tolerance towards their brethren in the English church. 'But who are you that judge your brother?' asked Cartwright, 'and why do you judge before the time? And herein not tarry until the day of the Lord shall open the hearts of all men? We profess that we do herein according to that we are persuaded out of the Word. If we be deceived, as you say we are yet is our sin in infirmity, that is to say in ignorance which in part cleaveth to the most perfect upon earth.'[15]

Hence, given the fact that all churches were necessarily imperfect, Cartwright went on to adduce from both the scripture and contemporary experience examples of churches which, although seriously in error over central issues of doctrine, were still to be accounted true churches of God. From the present he quoted the example of the Lutheran churches 'in high Germany' 'which are grossly deceived in the matter of the Supper', but which were still 'notwithstanding holden in the roll of the churches of god'.[16] Similarly, from scripture, Cartwright cited the example of Christ, who despite the fact that

there were corruptions crept into the holy things themselves, besides an open and professed enmity of the Jews against our Saviour Christ and his disciples. Howbeit our saviour by his calling not being able to remedy those evils he chose rather to join himself unto the company of most notorious wicked men than that he would separate himself from the holy things and in them from God, whose they are. And seeing that by being of the wicked unwillingly I take no harm and am greatly hurt by separation from the holy things of God, there is no cause why I should lose the fruit of one for the presence of the other.[17]

All of this, of course, was of direct relevance to the situation of the presbyterian divine. They too were not able 'by their callings' 'to remedy those evils' wherewith the church was affected. Furthermore, as Cartwright himself observed, the faults of the church of England, however grievous, could not be compared with those that afflicted the church of the Jews at the time of Christ. They had utterly 'renounced the son of God' and indeed crucified him. Yet notwithstanding, they were, in Acts, chapters 2, 3 and 4, 'dealt with by Peter and other apostles as brethren and fathers, as with those to whom the promises do apertain'.[18] The lesson was clear: the separatists should show at least as much humility and deference in their attitude to their fellow protestants as Christ had shown to the Jews.

Thus far Cartwright had managed to make his case without any positive claims on behalf of the present state of the church of England at all. To defend the church on these terms was to pay it, at best, a backhanded compliment. But since his whole argument rested on the distinction between what was essential for a true church and what was merely desirable, he could quite happily seek to justify his position within the English church almost without mentioning, and certainly without defending, any of the peculiar characteristics (and to Cartwright outright corruptions) of that church. Hence, he argued that 'whereas in the constitution of a man's body or of a whole man there are some parts required to the being of a man, as the head, the heart etc. So it is in the body of the Church there are some things required to the body of the Church...and there be some things [required] to the beauty and perfection of it.'[19] It was the essence of the separatist position, claimed Cartwright, to confuse the essential with the merely desirable: 'That if there be any thing wanting in the Church which the Lord hath required that instant you should conclude that therefore there is no church with us at all.'[20]

Judged on these criteria, maintained Cartwright, there could be no doubt that the church of England enjoyed everything that was essential for her continued existence as a church of God. Cartwright conceded that 'it is a piece of that discipline of our Saviour Christ that there should be certain which should be chosen out of the rest to preach the gospel, by preaching whereof the churches are gathered. Where, therefore, there is no ministry of the word there it is plain that there are no visible and apparent churches.'[21] The church of England, however, enjoyed just such a ministry of the word. Similarly, he continued,

it is another part of the discipline of our Lord that the rest of the body of the church should obey those that are set over them in the Lord. Wheresoever therefore there is no obedience of the people given to the ministers that in the Lord's name preach unto them, there also can be no church of Christ, but where these two be, although other points want, yea, although there be some defect in these, that neither the ministers do in all points preach as they ought, nor the assemblies in all points obey unto the wholesome doctrine of their teachers, yet do they for the reason above said retain the right of the churches of God.[22]

Hence, whatever the defects of individual ministers and congregations, the church of England enjoyed both a proper ministry of the word and, in the obedience of the people to that ministry, at least the rudiments of a proper ecclesiastical discipline.

But not only did the church of England enjoy the necessary prerequisites for a true church, the actual practice of large numbers of godly, learned ministers ensured that every opportunity to push the partially reformed framework of the church in a fully reformed direction was exploited to the full. Hence, over the vexed question of unpreaching ministers, Cartwright could argue that the efforts of the fully qualified ministers in the church could be taken to compensate for the shortcomings of their more

incompetent and ill-trained colleagues. Even in those congregations devoid of a preaching ministry, said Cartwright,

for as much as they both have and might have by some former
ministry or means which the Lord hath used towards them received
faith standing thereby in our saviour Christ as in the shaft of a
candlestick they cease not to be a branch in the Lord's candlestick
and being members of the same body they may well receive some
supply of their want from the light that shineth in the next branch
unto them.[23]

Hence, while the 'dumb ministry' was not something to be
passively accepted, the presence in the church of large numbers
of sufficient preaching ministers was enough to hold out the hope
of better things to come, and also, for the moment at least, to
safeguard the English church's status as a true church.[24]

Similarly, claimed Cartwright, even if one admitted that the
sacraments as administered by unpreaching ministers were invalid
(and Cartwright did not admit that) this still implied that the
sacraments as administered by the sufficient minister inside the
English church retained their validity as effectual seals on God's
covenant with the church of England and hence acted as guaran-
tees of that body's status as a true church.[25]

Cartwright dealt similarly with the issue of the power of the
keys, a function which the separatists sought to deny to the
minister in the present English church hierarchy. On the contrary,
argued Cartwright, the potential for a proper spiritual discipline
of the laity existed in England and, moreover, was vigorously
applied by many ministers: 'it is further untrue that the Church
of England useth no authority of Christ nor keys of the kingdom.
For first it bindeth by declaring the judgements against the un-
repentant and secondly it looseth in the preaching of the glad
tidings to those which do believe.'[26]

But Cartwright did not stop there. The English church enjoyed
other of the elements that made up a true and godly ecclesiastical
discipline:

namely that when a brother doth offend privately he is admonished
privately and not resting in the admonition there is proceeding by
2 or 3 and if the offence be either public or private without amend-
ment after such proceedings as hath been said then the minister
of the Church may put the offender from the Communion of the

Lord's Table unless he will humble himself in the congregation by an open confession of his sins and profession of his earnest sorrow for the same. And all this being (or at the least may be) by the laws of the Church of England exercised in every congregation of the land, it appeareth that it is a slander to say that there is no use of Christ's authority or of the keys of the kingdom with us.

Moreover the 'manifold troubles of godly ministers by them whom they have removed from the use of the sacraments or otherwise stung by the preaching of the word would not suffer you to be ignorant of their care and fidelity in such also'.[27] There could be no clearer example of Cartwright's use of the day-to-day practice and experience of the godly within the church of England to counterbalance, if not to justify or excuse, the corruptions inherent both in the institutional framework of the church and in the everyday practice of the unregenerate mass of ministers.

The same device can be seen in Cartwright's treatment of the separatist claim that it was essential for all true ministers of the word to be chosen by popular election. First he asserted that there were 'some ministers amongst us that had been chosen by the free voice of the people and therefore that it was no cause to deny that there was no church amongst us'. Second, and somewhat contrarily, he went on to claim that even when there had been no formal election

an after acceptance and liking of the minister whom they did at first so unwillingly admit is a manifest confirmation of their minister ...And of this kind of ministers of the Lord how many there be may in some part appear by those towns and parishes which have travailled for the holding of their ministers that have been threatened to be taken from them or for the recovery of them when they have been deprived of them.[28]

Hence Cartwright the presbyterian, confronted by the need to defend the English church, ignored the corrupt institutional framework of that church and emphasised instead the achievements of the godly acting within that framework yet all the time trying to transcend the partially reformed shell by infusing it with the values of a fully reformed church. In other words it was in practice the activity of the puritan movement, conceived in its widest sense as the zealous and godly ministers of England, that redeemed the church of England as a true church. The godly were 'the leaven that leavened the whole lump'. But while this view applied primarily to the puritan movement as a whole, it also provided the rationale for its narrower and more exclusive embodiment in the classis movement. For by attempting, as best it could, to implement the discipline within the existing structures and laws of the church (which was precisely how it characterised its own activities) the movement attempted to give formal shape to the activities of the godly ministers as they struggled to bring true religion to the mass of the people. In so doing it sustained and gave permanent institutional form to the concept of reformation as a process of militant struggle and spiritual regeneration rather than a mere act of state. Similarly, by propagating presbyterian principles the movement kept alive the hope that one day the church of England would enjoy a fully reformed polity. The classis movement can be seen as a bridge between the stark realities of the unreformed English church on the one hand and the dictates of scripture on the other. It was this function as a buttress for the moderate puritan world-view, rather than any reasoned estimate of its objective chances of success, that lay at the heart of the continued existence of the classis movement throughout the 1580s. On this view, rather than a 'political' organisation radically opposed to the status quo presbyterianism had become one of the means whereby puritan ministers accommodated themselves to a seemingly alien ecclesiastical regime. As the reformed *alter ego* of the English church, presbyterianism had established an almost symbiotic relationship with the corrupt church hierarchy – hence the separatist rejection of it as a vehicle for the pursuit of further reformation.

But if the classis movement played such an integral part in the maintenance of the moderate puritan world-view how did men like Chaderton or Cartwright negotiate the final collapse of the movement at the end of the 1580s with such apparent ease? How could they defend continued allegiance to a church now definitively deprived of its 'reformed shadow'? First, the sort of piecemeal accommodations and modifications set out by Cartwright did not rely on the classis movement for their continued validity. Such an institutional framework was useful but it was by no means essential. For it was intangibles such as the bonds of mutual admiration and respect between a pastor and his flock that enabled the godly to maintain a proper congregational dis-

cipline of morals even in the face of a hostile ecclesiastical
authority. Whilst externals provided a useful means to protect
and indeed advance the spiritual progress of the church of
England, that progress itself was not a result of mere human
institutions or traditions at all. It was the product of the autonomous action of the grace of God and, as such, in itself the
surest guarantee of God's continuing favour to the English
church. This very point had formed the foundation of Cartwright's letter to Harrison. For as he had claimed,

by believing that Christ is our righteousness we are made members
of his body and thereby as lively stones laid upon him as upon a
foundation we grow into one spiritual house with him, now that
they have the like precious faith with us, is convinced not only by
their own profession, but also by the testimony of the spirit of God,
who by manifold graces poured upon them, even unto an apparent
sanctification of numbers of them, do bear witness that they be
members of the body of Christ, who as the head hath partaked unto
them his holy spirit, they that have performed unto them the special
covenant which the Lord hath made with his churches of pouring
his spirits upon them and putting his words in their mouths are the
churches of God; but such are the assemblies in England...[29]

Indeed, so great was Cartwright's insistence on the testimony of
the spirit and the appeal to the inner certitude of the individual
believer that he enjoined the separatists to consider their own
experience of the workings of the Holy Spirit, the first stirrings
of which they had almost certainly felt while they were still
members of the English church. It was precisely that experience,
daily vouchsafed to countless ordinary members of the English
church, that provided the surest evidence for Cartwright that
the church of England still retained the favour of God. 'Before
you departed from us...you felt in yourself a desire of the
coming of the Lord Jesus, which you yielding unto me I concluded that thereof it followed that the true faith which you have,
you got in our church, it being the proper and peculiar voice of
the church, unfeignedly from the heart to desire the Lord
coming.'[30]
For Cartwright it was the progress of true religion based on
sound doctrine and furthered by the autonomous action of the
Holy Spirit in creating and sustaining the unity of the godly
inside the English church that validated the status of that church

as a true church. In the face of that the admitted institutional
faults of the church paled into insignificance.

> To say therefore it is none of the Church of God, because it hath
> not received this discipline, methinks is all one with this as if a
> man would say it is no city because it hath no wall or that it is no
> vineyard because it hath neither hedge nor dyke. It is not I grant
> so sightly a city or vineyard nor yet so safe against the invasion of
> their several enemies which lie in wait for them but they are truly
> both cities and vineyards.[31]

Such therefore were the opinions that made up Cartwright's
somewhat ambiguous attitude to the church of England. But
Cartwright did not limit himself to a purely defensive case. He
also moved onto the offensive and attacked certain central
elements in the separatist position. Here Cartwright's case revolved around the dominating figure of the godly, learned
minister. It was this exalted view of the ordinary minister that
stood at the very centre of presbyterianism and it was such men,
university-trained intellectuals, who both created and sustained
the presbyterian world-view and the classis movement that
embodied it. The almost complete absence of such men from the
ranks of the separatists constituted for Cartwright perhaps the
greatest weakness in their position. Hence, reported Anne Stubbe,
Cartwright had alleged that 'we are not the church because
none of us had the knowledge of the tongues wherein the scriptures were written and therefore they could not confute the
adversary'.[32] Indeed Cartwright went even further, claiming that
the separatists had amongst them no lawful ministers of the word
at all. If the church of England was no church of God because
it had no properly elected ministers (as the separatists claimed),

> how much more are you none of Christ's church, which have no
> ministers at all... Where I marvel it doth not cause you to tremble
> in this course you have entered into, for that our saviour Christ
> never saved you yet by any pastor which he, ascending into heaven
> hath ever given the church but that there is not so much as one
> among you that is fit for the function of the ministry, by those
> necessary gifts which are required in the minister of the word.
> Whereunto you answer that you believe that which Christ and his
> Apostles taught and which you teach one another. But how come
> you to know that you believe that when neither yourselves know
> the true exposition of the Scriptures (as having no gift to reach

unto it) nor have any to teach or to translate them unto you, but those alone which you reject as none of the Church?[33]

In all this the typical presbyterian insistence on a really high level of scholarship amongst ordinary ministers was, of course, crucial. In many ways it provides the key to the whole pheno- menon of presbyterianism seen as the expression of the profes- sional pride and self-esteem of a close-knit group of university- trained intellectuals.[34] On this view the whole classis movement can be characterised as a concerted attempt radically to trans- form the status and authority of the ordinary minister of the word and to accommodate the new recruits to the ministry who, for ideological reasons, were disillusioned with the antiquated career structure of the church at large but were totally un- prepared to accept the parlous social and financial standing of the ordinary minister in contemporary society. Hence, in reject- ing the separatists' populist revolt against any sort of ministerial elite Cartwright was defending the world-view and interests of those very university intellectuals whose aspirations were so clearly reflected in the classis movement and of whom Cartwright himself was so outstanding an example.

Confronted with Cartwright's insistence on the need for a properly trained ministry, Anne Stubbe resorted to the authority of the bare word of scripture and the workings of the Holy Spirit that attended the sincere and diligent study of it.

The Scriptures of God were not like men's words for no man knoweth the mind of a man but himself, but we see our own hearts in the word of God, and I think that so we of the Church of God have the knowledge of the interpretation of the tongues. But con- sider your own ministers: the word saith not some learned men among them but the minister, whosoever, now by this judge your own ministers. Truly my heart mourneth to see the general hard- ness of heart. And when we speak to any that standeth with you the word of God can take no place, you have so strengthened them in their sins, saying peace, peace, which you can do no way so much as to call them the Church of God, when you are without by the word of God.[35]

Cartwright had made virtually the same point in his vindication of vernacular translations against the papists.[36] But confronted in the person of his sister-in-law with the distorted mirror-image of his own principles he was forced to back down and emphasise once more the intercessionary role of the minister mediating between the actual text of scripture and the people of God. Here was the respectable face of puritanism. For while puritan divines did indeed emphasise the role of the spirit and the need for inner conviction, they also placed very severe restrictions and restraints on the workings of the individual conscience in its confrontation with the word of God. Indeed, the overwhelming puritan insistence on a learned ministry and the formidable array of linguistic, historical and theological skills which were held to be necessary for a proper understanding of the scripture can be taken as expressly designed to provide such a check. In practice, of course, this rendered the average layman totally dependent on the minister. Hence while the basic insights of true religion might be readily available to all through private study of the scriptures, questions of any difficulty had to be referred to those competent to decide them – the clerical intellectuals of the puritan movement.[37] Presbyterianism, of course, sought to give this de facto authority a solid institutional and legal basis. On this view presbyterianism can be seen as the product of a basically conservative impulse which led its adherents to place firm objective checks on the more radical tendencies inherent in many of the central doctrines of protestantism This of course closely parallels the presbyterian claim that the discipline represented the natural ally of the cause of social order, that it was society's readiest defence against the related threats of popery, atheism, popular immorality and social unrest.[38]

Throughout these letters, therefore, the radical tendencies inherent in Cartwright's position were subjected to the full checks and balances of the moderate position. For Cartwright was altogether unwilling to lose the substance of true religion for the sake of a few outward forms. In the church of England, he claimed, the basic tenets of the presbyterian platform (a godly, preaching ministry administering at least the rudiments of a proper spiritual discipline) were attainable and, indeed, in many parishes had already been attained. Of course, these were remarkable admissions for a committed presbyterian like Cartwright to make. And once the contents of his letter to Harrison became public knowledge[39] Bancroft, for one, fell upon them in triumph. As he wrote, the 'frenetical giddiness of the sectaries hath wrought a miracle in Mr Cartwright. For hear him, how for fear of falling into flat Donatism he was fain to plead against one (that had been his scholar) in the behalf of the church of England, so bitterly before by himself impugned.'[40]

Bancroft, of course, was hardly an impartial commentator. In his rush to extract the maximum party advantage from Cartwright's letter he rode roughshod over the delicate balance of the moderate position, so much of which relied on questions of tone, nuance and implicit qualification. What mattered in this case was not merely what was said, but to whom and in what form. Here it is instructive to compare Cartwright's dealings with the separatists with those of Robert Some. Certainly, Some reproduced many of Cartwright's arguments and even at one point obliquely cited his authority.[41] But where Cartwright's opinions had been contained in private letters, Some's were set out in printed polemics. Some's intentions were accordingly public and polemical. He wanted to isolate the puritan left – broadly speaking the separatists (like Barrow or Greenwood) and the semi-separatists (like Penry) but not the presbyterians – from the respectable protestant mainstream. Hence, despite the formal similarity of the arguments, the tone and intention of the two men could hardly have been more different. For Some, the professional administrator, had no sympathy with the separatists at all; his only aim in attacking them in the first place was the vindication of his own orthodoxy as a defender of the church of England. Unlike Cartwright he betrayed no sympathy with the separatist position, no recognition that though mistaken their intentions were of the best. For him they were merely subversives and sectaries to be denounced – his works were studied with appeals to the Magistrate to repress and control their activities.[42] Some had a personal stake in all this. He was, it seems, trying to make the transition from the patronage of the recently deceased Earl of Leicester to that of Hatton and Whitgift. Anti-separatist polemic appears to have been the means he employed to convince those two staunch anti-puritans of his reliability as a defender of the Elizabethan regime in church and state and thus lay the ghost of his own precisian past.[43]

Cartwright, of course, had no such axe to grind. Indeed for him to deal openly with the subject of separatism was an act of considerable courage. That he did so was a tribute to the strength of his pastoral concern for brethren who, though meanwhile in error, remained potential allies in the cause of true religion. It was perhaps indicative of the difference between presbyterian and non-presbyterian puritan opinion that when Cartwright wanted to win some sort of official approval he chose to write anti-papal polemic. When Some wanted to do the same he wrote anti-separatist polemic. As was suggested at the outset, one acid test of a man's position in the spectrum of religious opinion was his attitude to the relative significance of the opposite poles of popery and schism.

6

William Whitaker's position as refracted through his anti-papal polemic

In chapter 4 we examined the role of anti-papal polemic in the maintenance of the moderate puritan world-view. The theme of that chapter was the potency of such polemic as a gesture, a source of ideological leverage in the domestic disputes amongst English protestants. In the present chapter the content of some of those polemics will be examined in order to reveal the theological bases of William Whitaker's view of the world. Such a procedure involves an element of distortion. Whitaker's intention in his polemical writing was to refute the papists; our intention here is to gain some insight into his world-view as a whole. The end result will not, therefore, be a technical account or evaluation of Whitaker's performance against the papists, but a series of more general remarks about his style of divinity. As the title of this chapter suggests this position will be seen as, at best, refracted through his anti-papal works.

Such an approach is defensible on two grounds. The first is practical: Whitaker's anti-papal works provide the only source available for such an undertaking. His obsession with Rome ensured that this was the case. But the very extent of that obsession surely renders it legitimate to approach his thought through his works against Rome. Indeed, such an approach holds positive advantages since one of the themes of this account will be the way in which the overriding need to construct a case watertight against papist attack imposed constraints on elements in the protestant world-view which, unchecked, could lead to puritan conclusions. To underline that point comparative material from Thomas Cartwright's *A confutation* will be discussed in asides and notes.

In attempting to describe Whitaker's world-view let us start where all protestants started, with scripture.

The books of scripture are called canonical because they contain the standard and rule of our faith and morals. For the scripture is in the church what the law is in a state, which Aristotle in his Politics calls a canon or rule. As all citizens are bound to live and behave agreeably to the public laws, so Christians should square their faith and conduct by the rule and law of scripture.[1]

Hence, scripture provided the only basis upon which any church could be reformed. 'Pious princes and holy bishops always tried to reform and restore corrupt and deformed churches according to no other model save that contained in scripture and those churches were always the most effectively purged which accorded most closely to the word.'[2]

Whitaker was equally uncompromising in the matter of scriptural interpretation, particularly in the face of the popish emphasis on the mediating role of the church and human traditions.

We say that the Holy Spirit is the supreme interpreter of scripture because we must be illuminated by the Holy Spirit to be certainly persuaded of the true sense of scripture; otherwise although we use all means, we can never attain to that full assurance which resides in the mind of the faithful. But this is only an internal persuasion and concerns only ourselves. As to external persuasion we say that scripture itself is its own interpreter; and therefore that we should come to the external judgement of scripture itself, in order to persuade others.[3]

Only thus could the faithful attain to that certitude of spiritual knowledge, that assurance that was necessary for a true and lively justifying faith. Here Whitaker distinguished between 'understanding and knowledge of the scripture', 'one of the letter, the other of the spirit'. Thus Whitaker admitted the need for men skilled in the Greek and Hebrew tongues and other necessary exegetical techniques, but he reduced these merely human skills to a purely instrumental level in ascertaining the will of God. Only scripture itself allied to the workings of the Holy Spirit could bring that true assurance and spiritual knowledge that distinguished the true believer from the hypocrite. Hence Whitaker regarded any tendency to trust purely human faculties or authorities, or to leave them any remotely creative or free-ranging role in the interpretation of scripture, as directly inimical to this true knowledge. Thus, he claimed, 'the argument that is grounded only upon reason in matters of religion and faith we grant most unfeignedly to be no lawful weapon in the Lord's warfare...For reason must submit itself to faith, we know, faith must not be restrained or stretched according to reason.'[4] For Whitaker the subtleties and pretensions of human philosophy, which after all placed all its faith in unaided human reason, summed up the unreliability of man's natural faculties. It was this that explained the papists' fondness for subtleties and shifts of philosophy as compared to the plain and pious methods of divinity.

Campion, you see, hath a better mind to converse with philosophers than with divines; for being furnished with rhetoric and logic and having spent most of his time in often declaiming and inventing and answering sophistical captions he doubteth not of a famous victory, if philosophers were judges. But these matters are not to be disputed among philosophers, which are otherwhiles deceived with probability and appearance of truth, following that opinion which themselves judge most agreeable to reason. This question in hand must be discussed in the assembly of most grave and learned divines, whom no juggling of words, no subtlety in disputation, no wit, no cunning, no youthful insolent boldness in quarrelling, lying or foolish vaunting can once move, much less remove from the truth they are persuaded of. Here can you not have liberty to brag of your counterfeit devices; philosophy may not sit as judge in these controversies neither will those things wherein you chiefly trust be here of any authority; you must leave your own erroneous and endless walks and be drawn perforce, into the compass and limits of true scripture and divinity.[5]

These sentiments had, of course, a solid theological basis. Since the Fall all man's natural faculties had been, at least for spiritual purposes, completely corrupt. Although 'some relics of that most noble image [of God] do remain still, yet we hold that all that which may reconcile and make us acceptable unto God and be sufficient for us to salvation, is blotted out and extinguished'.[6] This being so, it was fatal to place any faith in, or attribute any value to, purely human powers or authorities. Accordingly, Whitaker roundly rejected the papists' excessive reverence for the fathers.

Councils, fathers, popes, are men; and scripture testifies that all men are deceitful. How then shall I acquiesce in their sentence? How can my conscience certainly determine so as to leave no room for my faith to waver that whatever they may pronounce is true? Surely, this is to leave no difference between God and man?[7]

Because they were but men, devoid of that special inspiration that had been the distinguishing mark of the Apostles, there could be no hope of consensus amongst the fathers. Since they disagreed even amongst themselves, Whitaker concluded, 'their authority will be but small'.[8] 'Learned and godly men we grant they were, but yet men having their infirmities and imperfections.' As such they were worthy of respect, but they could provide 'no stable and steady ground to build our faith upon'.[9] Hence, if protestants studied the fathers it was not as 'proofs of doctrine in themselves' but 'to stop your mouths that cry so loud in the ears of the simple that all the fathers are against us, it being most true that they are notably and generally (as I have said) for us'.[10]

As a further reminder of the frailty of human resources, and of man's reliance upon scripture as his only guide, there was the insidious influence of Antichrist. Whitaker, of course, fully subscribed to the contemporary orthodoxy that identified the papacy with Antichrist. He devoted an entire book to proving the point, defended it at least twice in the schools at Cambridge (once as his D.D. thesis), and referred to the doctrine constantly in all his polemical works.[11] All in all it formed a central plank in his confutation of the papist case. In this way Whitaker effectively wrote off fifteen hundred years of church history as a positive guide in determining God's will. For while Whitaker dated the final emergence of the fullyfledged Antichrist to the moment when the Emperor Phocas granted the title 'universus episcopus' to Pope Boniface,[12] he yet argued that the rise of Antichrist had been so gradual a process that it could hardly be dated at all: 'For the mystery of iniquity which in papistry is fully finished, began to work in the Apostles' age and so continued still forward in the fathers' days until it came to this height and perfection in the kingdom of popery.'[13] It was a gradual process of decline that Whitaker compared to the slow decay of a house.[14] Thus the fact that Antichrist had only fully emerged in the pontificate of Pope Boniface did not mean, he argued, that he allowed 'the

Church of Rome to have been pure, godly, Christian for six
hundred years after Christ'. On the contrary, no sooner had the
structure of true religion been established by the Apostles than
it had started to decay.

Thus far there is little to distinguish Whitaker's position from
the sort of theological presuppositions that underlay presbyterianism. It accorded no special role to any merely human authority,
claimed to base itself on the scriptures alone, and the writings of
the Apostles in particular, interpreted only by the light of the
Holy Spirit working through the collation and comparison of
various passages of scripture with one another. In its identification of the papacy with Antichrist it also subscribed to that view
of church history as a decline stretching from the golden age of
the Apostles to the very dawn of the reformation. This, of course,
was the view which, applied to church polity, lay behind the
presbyterian attack on episcopacy.

The affinities of Whitaker's thought with that of the precisians
did not end there. Just as in the definition of doctrine he had
denied a positive mediating role for human reason, so on the
individual level he denied any positive role to human free will
or reason in the process of justification. We have already quoted
his view on the effects of the Fall. Indeed, so complete was man's
corruption that mere concupiscence, even after baptism, was
sin.[15] Hence, to Whitaker, the popish position appeared simply
Pelagian. For this held 'that liberty of will remaineth in man's
corrupt nature, that it needed not to be given him from above
but only by the help of grace to be drawn out of certain difficulties in which the corruption of sin had left it'.[16]

On Whitaker's view, therefore, man's justification depended
entirely on God's grace. This, of course, raised the vexed
question of the relationship between faith and works. Here
Whitaker admitted the existence of two kinds of grace:

We make grace to be twofold...wherein we do not disallow the
philosophy of your schoolmen. For either grace declareth the free
good will and clemency of God toward us or else it signifieth those
gifts which flow out of that mercy of God to us. That, they commonly call 'grace making acceptable' and this 'grace freely given'.
Now, for that goodwill and favour whereby the Lord embraceth us
in Christ and forgiveth us our sins and receiveth us into favour, we
place it in God; but the effects of this grace are in us; which effects

are these, that we do, by the Holy Ghost, perceive that we are loved of God, that we believe in God and repose all hope of salvation in that mercy of God. We do not, therefore, take away all grace from man and place it only in God's favour; but that first grace, whereby he hath reconciled us to himself in Christ and wherein our salvation is contained, that alone we place in God; which being felt by us faith, hope and charity and other virtues do follow it, which are ours and resident in us. But we deny that position of yours, of infused grace, whereby you defend that the grace whereby we are justified is a certain habit situate in our minds within; and we acknowledge no other justifying grace but the great and free mercy of God, whereby he did elect and predestinate us in Christ before all eternity unto life everlasting and hath called us in time and justified us. For grace infused, wherein regeneration and sanctification consisteth and which the scriptures call the new man, is not strong enough to justify us, because it never satisfieth the law of God in this life and ought every day to be restored and aspire to greater perfection.[17]

Hence Whitaker sought to distinguish between what 'the divines call the first justice', which was nothing but 'the righteousness and innocency' of Christ 'imputed to us and apprehended by faith', and another different sort of righteousness, compounded of those infused virtues so beloved of the papists. This 'first justice' was of an entirely different order from that of these infused virtues. 'For with that remission of sins which dependeth on Christ's obedience, faith and hope and charity are joined which make us just also after a sort, but inchoatively not perfectly.'[18] This imperfection was inevitable and all important. Even the justified sinner could never aspire to complete obedience to God's will. There was no way to salvation through the law alone.

And if Christ by his death brought us grace to keep the law why not might the Galatians have kept the law and obtained righteousness by it? But the Apostle showeth them that Christ took the curse because he took both the sin and the punishment upon him and not that thereby he procured them grace to fulfil the law.[19]

For Whitaker, therefore, good works were necessary for salvation. As he remarked, 'Christians [by whom he meant the elect, since the reprobate were never freed from the demands and punishments of the law][20] are delivered from the curse of the law, but

not from the obedience of it.'[21] Hence, he concluded, a faith
devoid of works was no true faith. Good works 'do make show
and proof of faith'.[22] However, as he was quick to point out,
'the true and proper causes of salvation' lay elsewhere: firstly
in 'God's adoption in Christ...possessed by the right of inheri-
ance', and secondly in the 'eternal election of God when he
saith that it is a kingdom prepared for them from the foundations
of the world'.[23] It was to underline precisely that point that
Whitaker drew such a sharp distinction between justification
and that process of sanctification whereby the individual believer
was increasingly enabled (albeit imperfectly) to obey the will of
God. Certainly, as he admitted to Duraeus, 'justification and
sanctification are inseparable, yet must they be distinguished,
which, because you do not, you place justification in sanctification'.[24]

But even having made that distinction, Whitaker yet went out
of his way to emphasise that there was no element of human
merit even in this process of regeneration: 'That which the regenerate man hath of his own and proper to himself is vicious.'
It was only 'those things which he received from God' which
'are contrary to this corruption and contagion' that produced
the regenerate saint from within the shell of the old Adam.[25]

It was precisely because all was attributed to God and nothing
to man in the justification and sanctification of the individual
believer that God's elect could enjoy a comfortable assurance of
their salvation. Indeed to feel anything less, argued Whitaker, was
'to cut insunder the sinews of God's everlasting decree. For seeing
God's pedestination is everlasting and unchanging it doth cause
our calling, justifying and glorifying to be as certain as itself.
For is it in our power to dissolve and break insunder the golden
chain of the Apostles.'[26]

This, therefore, was the only certain foundation for the individual believer's faith.

This faith ought to depend most certainly and strongly upon the
promises of God, so as we may expel all doubting about the grace
of God, our adoption and salvation. For true faith cannot agree
with unbelief. It is the property of this to distrust God's promises
but the property of that is to overcome and drive away all doubting,
as much as may be. But if faith be full of doubting wherein doth it
go beyond unbelief?[27]

Closely linked with this view of assurance was the concomitant doctrine of perseverance – the idea that a true faith once experienced could never finally be lost. Whitaker ran the two concepts together in a remarkable piece of sustained logic-chopping that not only throws light on his particular views on the subject of perseverance and assurance but also on his whole method of argumentation and proof.

The Apostle termeth faith the ground of those things that are hoped for and the evidence of things which are not seen. Now how are those things extant which be hoped for or demonstrated which are not seen if faith be not perpetual? But they which are endued with this faith they do now after a sort enjoy those good things which are yet hoped for and they do contemplate those things which cannot be seen with men's eyes. So that faith admits us being alive here and as the Apostle saith walking by faith and not by sight into the very possession of heaven, so as because we are certain that we shall one day be there we seem now after a sort to live and converse in heaven. But all these things would be fading and light if faith could not persevere. Therefore Paul had a most certain persuasion that neither life nor death, nor things present nor things to come nor any other 'creature can separate us from the love of God which is in Christ Jesus'. (Rom. 8.38) But such as do not persevere they may be separated; but these cannot be separated therefore they persevere. And for this cause the pledge of our adoption even the Holy Ghost himself is given to us who assureth us most certainly that we are the sons of God so as now we do not doubt to call God Father. But how dare such a one call him Father who thinketh that he may be sometime not his son? For the saints may profess with the Apostle 'we know that we shall be like him'. (I John 3.2) Knowledge is certain and consisteth on assured principles; to doubt is the property of opinion not of knowledge.[28]

Here then is Whitaker's theological method. Taking certain key texts out of their immediate context in the scriptures, Whitaker used them as starting points for a process of rigorous syllogistic reasoning. Then, having set up his watertight either/or choices of logical compatibility or incompatibility he proceeded from point to point with an inexorable commitment to rational consistency. As he had need, Whitaker took up axioms from the realm of purely human learning. Almost punning on the word 'know' in his quotation from St John, he proceeded directly to a definition of 'knowledge' which virtually insisted on his own doctrine of assurance. How could Whitaker, who made such play with his sole reliance on the authority of scripture as against the papists' use of merely human authorities, justify such a procedure? Put simply, it would appear that, for Whitaker, while recourse, say, to the fathers, constituted a reliance on the mere opinion of particular men, his own reliance on a particular definition of the concept of knowledge constituted only an entirely objective and very necessary definition of terms.

The basic urge behind this style of reasoning seems to have been the reduction of all purely human authorities to a merely instrumental role in the definition of right doctrine. All human powers were to be effaced before the sovereignty of scripture. However, ironically, that process itself led to an overwhelming emphasis on the eminently human sciences of logic and dialectic. Now this 'rationalism' on Whitaker's part was almost certainly entirely unself-conscious. Dr Lisa Jardine has suggested that contemporaries regarded Ramist logic not as a largely artificial or arbitrary way of arranging or imparting a given body of knowledge or information but as a straightforward reflection of the workings of the human mind. In the Ramist method they felt themselves to be confronted with the basic structures of human rationality. In following that method an author was thus not engaged in a personal or subjective exercise, nor even simply following a body of impersonal rules, but rather proceeding in accordance with a sort of species rationality, the validity of which transcended all limitations of place and time and circumstance.[29] If that is so, then the application of such procedures to scriptural exegesis and theological argument by men like Whitaker and Chaderton represented an attempt to remove the human tendency to err from these activities. This was to be achieved by proceeding in accordance with a method of argument and exposition which, since it reflected the structure of all thought, could be assumed to be entirely impersonal and objective. Here was not the opinion of one man, or a group of men, but the product of a method so rooted in the basic structure of human reality as to escape any self-conscious epistemological analysis of the elusive human or subjective element in the definition of right doctrine.[30]

But to return to Whitaker's doctrine of assurance, this inward certitude of spiritual knowledge applied not only to the individual's apprehension of the truth of right doctrine,[31] but also to his conviction of his own ultimate salvation. Certainly, what was at stake here was not the possession of mere right opinion. Even hypocrites and the very devils in hell enjoyed that in so far as they were compelled to acknowledge the objective truth of right doctrine.[32]

The question is not whether things believed be so certain or no; for that the devils do certainly know; which is as much as you papists do believe by your own confession, and so you confess yourselves to be void of true faith. But the faith the Apostle speaketh of doth not only believe those things are true in themselves, but they are partakers of them.[33]

Here then was the subjective element that validated, indeed constituted, the very essence of a true justifying faith.

As we have seen, this concept of assurance was grounded on the will of God, expressed in his double decree of election and reprobation, laid down 'before all eternity'. But Whitaker did not always choose to emphasise this supralapsarian view of things. For instance, as we have seen in outlining 'the true and proper causes of salvation', Whitaker had ranked 'God's adoption in Christ' first before 'the eternal election of God'. And certainly Whitaker's view of predestination did not prevent him from emphasising the intercessionary role of Christ in displacing the old covenant of works and winning for mankind the new covenant of faith. Moreover it should be remembered that assurance was not only a doctrine but an experience, to be undergone by every true believer as he felt the testimony of the Holy Spirit. The emphasis Whitaker gave to the internal testimony of the Holy Spirit in vouchsafing the truths of scripture to us and in validating the faith of true believers should serve to warn us not to underestimate the importance of this experiential aspect of the doctrine of assurance. It has to be remembered that the doctrine of predestination formed but the objective basis of this subjective experience, and that the puritan style of divinity was just as concerned with the subjective as the objective side of the issue, as we shall see below. While we are here primarily concerned with Whitaker's works of theory and polemic, to forget entirely the practical, experiential side of puritan divinity would be seriously to distort his position as a whole.[34]

Nevertheless, this experiential side of Whitaker's thought did not lead him to ignore or shirk the logical implications of his own position. On the contrary, faced with Campion's taunt that 'the English Calvinists', following Beza, Calvin and Peter Martyr, made God the author of sin, Whitaker firmly grasped the nettle. He roundly denounced what he called

a certain inveterate opinion among men that whatsoever sin was committed by any, all that was done, God only permitting not willing it; now they did separate this permission utterly from all will of God, so as they affirmed that God did no way will those things which he had permitted...[But only permit that they may] be done, as if he did no whit intermeddle himself in those things nor had nothing to do therein.

On the contrary, Whitaker asserted that 'God doth by his special providence so govern all things as that nothing in the whole world happeneth against that that he hath willed and decreed; certainly it cannot be denied that God doth will after a sort those things which the wicked do and that this will of God is so effectual that in the wicked actions of men God doth execute his own decree.'

Having thus gazed into the abyss, Whitaker relented a little to make the distinction between 'the action itself and the corruption of the action'. This, he claimed, could be found in the works of both Augustine and Aquinas. For

the action so far forth as it is a thing and a work is good; for God effecteth it; but so far forth as this self same action is vicious, it proceedeth not from God but from the corrupt nature of man. Although therefore God who worketh all things in all and against whose will nothing can be done doth bring to pass a certain work of his in the evil actions of men; yet he doth those things that are just, nor ought he any way to be thought to be guilty of the sins of the men themselves; therefore that which a wicked man doth that as it is a sin and as it hath the proper nature of a sin the Lord neither willeth nor suggesteth nor biddeth nor effecteth; nay he detesteth and revengeth it and judgeth it worthy of everlasting punishment.[35]

These views are taken from Whitaker's attack on Campion of 1581, the earliest of his major statements against Rome, with some additions from his defence of that work against Duraeus of

1583. But he can be found defending precisely the same positions fifteen years later, at the very end of his life, in his two sermons against the Pelagians of 1595 and during the theological disputes of the same year.[36] It seems reasonable to conclude, therefore, that the uncompromising view of the liberty and sovereignty of God, contained in his view of predestination and also in his attitude to the authority of scripture, represents the central unifying thread running throughout his adult career as a university divine. Certainly it was this that provided the stable and unchanging basis for his massive output of anti-papal polemic. Indeed it was probably only the fact that he was expounding essentially the same case that enabled him to be quite so prolific. Certainly, I would argue, that it was this world-view that explains his long-standing links with the precisians analysed in the last chapter. But if these same theoretical assumptions and attitudes led others of the same generation and background as Whitaker to avowedly precisian and even presbyterian conclusions, why did they not have the same effects in Whitaker's case?

The answer to this question lies, I would argue, in the strength of Whitaker's obsessional concern with Rome. Certainly the need to construct a case easily defensible against the papists was a formative influence on Whitaker's view of the church. The papists placed great emphasis on church history and tradition, the visible succession of popes and bishops that linked their church with that of the Apostles. It was this that served to validate the equation of their visible, this-worldly church with the universal catholic church. Such claims were difficult to deny. Popery had indeed dominated whole centuries of church history. The protestant schema of world history that identified the pope with Antichrist took much of its potency as a polemical weapon from its capacity to explain that dominance while yet denying it any normative value. The fact remained, however, that the history of the visible church was of little or no polemical use to the protestant apologist. It was in response to this situation that Whitaker turned away from the visible church, as a this-worldly institution, to the invisible church, conceived as a spiritual body whose existence transcended the confines of everyday human society and history. This shift of emphasis allowed him to argue that this invisible, universal church could not, as the papists claimed, be identified with any one visible church or succession of churches. Hence Whitaker maintained 'that the true and catholic church of Christ consists only of those predestinated to eternal life'.[37] It was composed of the 'number of God's elect'[38] or again 'of the whole multitude of the faithful'.[39] The formula 'extra ecclesia non est salus' and Christ's promise that it should stand until the end of the world applied only to this church.[40] While the true invisible catholic church would indeed last for ever, all particular or individual churches were subject to the same vicissitudes of history that afflicted secular states. They could either fall into heresy and apostasy, as had happened to the church of Rome, or even cease to exist altogether as had happened to the churches of the ancient Near East.[41]

But Whitaker did not completely abandon the visible church to the papists.

Antichrist, that man of sin, could never prevail so far but a great multitude of the saints remained; and those whose names were written in the book of life did utterly abhor all those filthy and wicked superstitions of Antichrist. For in the church of Rome itself in the worst times of it, yet many were found who worshipped the God of their fathers and kept themselves unpolluted from that horrible idolatry.[42]

Moreover, defining a church with spartan simplicity as 'any number of those who retain the true faith',[43] Whitaker maintained that these small groups of true believers, meeting and worshipping in secret, constituted themselves a church. Here he cited the experience of English protestants under Mary and the predicament of the contemporary French churches. For in both instances the church had been driven underground, unable in the face of persecution to maintain a visible profession of faith or ministry of the word. Yet in neither instance could the church be said to have ceased to exist as – in England – the Marian burnings plainly testified.[44] In place of the papists' insistence on a visible succession of bishops Whitaker asserted an underground succession of true believers who, despite the corruption of the papist church, had kept alive the seeds of true religion.

But, in the absence of a public profession and a visible succession, how was their status as true believers to be vindicated? For Whitaker the quality of a church's doctrine was the touchstone of its status as a true church. 'Apostolica Ecclesia est quae in Apostolorum fundamento id est doctrina aedificatur ut omnes interpretentur.'[45] That, he claimed, was the 'rock' upon which the true church was founded, not 'externam sedem hominumque successionem'.[46]

By thus concentrating his attention on the invisible universal catholic church and keeping the requirements for an effective visible church in this world to a minimum, Whitaker certainly eased his position against the papists. But he also effectively placed his doctrine of predestination at the very centre of his view of the church. Indeed, his ecclesiology was dominated by precisely the same view of the liberty of God and its expression in the autonomous action of the Holy Spirit that we have already observed in his views on the authority of scripture and predestination. Starting with God's double decree as a direct emanation of that liberty, Whitaker saw all other issues from the perspective of that ineluctable process through which, throughout human history from the Fall to the Day of Judgement, God had gathered his elect to him. In view of the many centuries dominated by popery Whitaker was obliged to concentrate on the minimum conditions under which that process could continue. Hence, in response to the popish emphasis on the mediating role of the priest, the church and human ceremonies, Whitaker cleared away the paraphernalia of merely human institutions and customs to allow the will of God to work its way through history, gathering together the elect and rejecting the reprobate.

Having thus cleared the ground Whitaker was understandably reluctant to cloud the issue by taking a dogmatic stand on matters which he regarded as inherently indifferent. Hence, when he turned to the nature of the visible church unhindered by popish persecution, Whitaker remained determined to keep his position pared down to essentials. Discussing the marks of the church set out by the Apostle – namely Apostolic doctrine, mutual care and charity amongst the faithful, dutiful prayers to God, and proper administration and use of the sacraments – Whitaker came close to subsuming all four under the general heading of the first. It was the possession of true apostolic doctrine that distinguished the true church from all other human groups or societies. The second mark, the mutual care and charity amongst the faithful, could be construed as but an effect of possession of the word. Similarly, the saying of public prayers to God was but another facet of the ministry of the word. That left only the sacraments. These Whitaker conceded must be accepted as a mark of the true church in their own right. But even here he felt constrained to add that the sacraments should not be regarded as necessary in the same way as the word. For the sacraments were mere external signs of that good which was set before the believer in the word. As signs they added nothing essential to those spiritual goods implied by possession of the word. They could therefore be omitted without destroying or undermining the faith or profession of the group involved. After all, the believer was not dealing here with a fraudulent merchant but with God himself. His promises could hardly fail. There was no cause to doubt the veracity or efficacy of the promise of eternal life set out in the word merely because we lacked for a time the external signs which normally accompanied or sealed that promise. If, therefore, it was not possible for some reason to receive the sacraments, this did not automatically deprive a church of its status as a true church. Here Whitaker referred to the experience of the Israelites who during their forty years in the wilderness had omitted the sacrament of circumcision. Yet who would deny their claims to be considered a true church? Whitaker was not belittling the significance of the sacraments. They had a central role to play in any well-ordered Christian community. He was merely trying to avoid tying the power of the word (and the workings of the Spirit that accompanied it) to any external rite or ceremony. Certainly, he was very eager to point out that the sacraments in themselves contained no special properties or powers. Neglect of the sacraments was thus an offence not against any power or properties inherent in the sacraments, but against the will of God that had instituted them as central parts of his worship.[47]

Whitaker had thus reduced the marks of the church to two. In one of his rare references to the debates and disagreements amongst contemporary protestants he then expressly repudiated the view, which he attributed to Beza and Danaeus, that elevated an external, spiritual discipline into a third mark of the church:

If by discipline they understand a certain set form of church government by presbyters and the sanction of excommunication, I think they are in error. A church can stand without these. Certainly, the schismatics of our times are in no sense to be believed when they condemn as no true churches those which lack the discipline and church government current at the time of the Apostles. Certainly the administration of excommunication according to the canons of divine scripture is much to be valued and the form of government current at the time of the Apostles was most excellent. Who would deny that? But it does not directly follow that either characteristic is so necessary as to render any church which lacks either or both of them no true church of God. To hold that would be to condemn many excellent churches, like those at Zurich, Berne and many others...We will content ourselves, therefore, with these two marks of the church, the preaching of the pure word of God and the proper administration of the sacraments: If anyone should propose a third mark of discipline without imputing to it a degree of necessity equal to that to be attributed to the other two, we will not entirely repugn his opinion. For the society of the church cannot survive without those two attributes which involve its very life and being, but it can survive without those characteristics which affect only its safety, albeit it will then survive in a weakened and imperfect state.[48]

From Whitaker's views on the marks of the church let us turn to his attitudes to the polity and ministry of the church. Here again he was nothing if not circumspect. No one could accuse him of restricting the Queen's authority in causes ecclesiastical by making extravagant 'iure divino' claims. Hence he told his papist adversary that 'Christ ordained "Pastors and Doctors" to rule his church the scripture is plain so that you may not for shame deny it'.[49] For Whitaker the presence of these ordinary ministers was quite sufficient to guarantee any church's status as a true church. Such a position was necessary to sustain his claim of an invisible succession of true churches within the papist church:

Our church was never so straited that it might be found in all countries christened and our ministers had the chiefest rooms, till Antichrist by little and little had driven them out; and then afterwards the Lord continually raised up and provided for his church such pastors and doctors as were necessary for the gathering of the saints together. Further answer in this place is not needful.[50]

Elsewhere, however, we do find Whitaker being slightly more explicit in his attitude to episcopacy. For instance in his book against Campion he cited Jerome 'against your pope and other glorious bishops, when he writeth that a priest and a bishop by the law of God are all one'.[51] That avowal was made in 1581. But similar sentiments can be found in Whitaker's *Praelectiones* (published posthumously in 1599) which formed part of his unfinished *magnum opus* against Bellarmine. There he maintained 'nam quod Episcopi postea Presbyteris praelati sunt in ordo humanus fuit ad schismata tollenda, ut historiae testantur'.[52]

There is, however, a certain ambiguity about the way in which Whitaker used the word 'episcopus'. Whitaker himself frequently warned the reader that the word meant something very different in the primitive church from its contemporary meanings. 'Dictos esse vulge episcopos eo tempore singulos singularum ecclesiarum pastores et presbyteros ex more et consuetudine scripturarum'.[53] And quite often Whitaker himself seems to have used the term in precisely that sense. For instance, discussing the validity of the orders of leading reformers like Calvin and Luther, Whitaker asserted that 'Lutherum et reliquos illos nostros praeclaros ac nobiles heroas fuisse presbyteros etiam ex ordinatione Romanae ecclesiae ac proinde iure divino episcopos'.[54] For Whitaker, therefore, the term 'episcopus' could be taken as synonymous with 'presbyterus' in denoting an ordinary minister of the word. This emerges again when in answering Bellarmine's claim that 'ecclesia non potest esse sine episcopis' Whitaker argued that if by the word 'episcopus' Bellarmine meant simply a pastor, then he agreed with him: the church could not exist without pastors. If, on the other hand, Bellarmine meant papist bishops 'who usurp jurisdiction over others, and exercise a tyranny over the church and the people of God, who assume everything to themselves, unlike those who were true bishops', then Whitaker was far from yielding the point.[55] In discussing the same question elsewhere Whitaker likewise asserted that there were at the first in each church bishops ('episcopi'), that is to say pastors, not the sort now to be found in the church of Rome. He readily admitted that such 'episcopi' were indeed necessary, 'for by them the church was taught and instructed. Doctrine established the church, it provided the church's soul or life. It was necessary therefore that there should be those in the church who taught.' But that, of course, was not what Bellarmine had meant at all.[56]

For Whitaker, therefore, the term 'episcopus' seems to have had two meanings. Primarily, it was synonymous with the word 'presbyter' and meant an ordinary minister of the word. Amongst all such men there was a complete parity of spiritual function and authority. This was the sense in which 'episcopus' had been employed at the time of the Apostles and it was in this sense that Whitaker most often used it when comparing the corruptions of popish prelacy with the purity of 'episcopacy' in the primitive church. But Whitaker also acknowledged that the word could denote a purely human institution designed for the control of heresy ('ad schismata tollenda') whereby certain ministers were raised above their colleagues. In seeking to prove 'Pontifex Romanus non est verus episcopus' Whitaker compared the Antichristian papacy with the ancient bishops of Rome:

The Roman bishops ('episcopi') of today are not the same as the ancient and original bishops who occupied the place in the past; therefore they are not true bishops ('episcopi'). The bishops of old diligently taught their flock ('ecclesiam suam') and none were made bishops save those who faithfully fulfilled that function. Of old bishops regarded this to be their most important function, to teach and instruct the people entrusted to their care.[57]

Hence, for Whitaker, the principal function of a bishop ('praecipuum munus episcopi') remained the same as that of a minister – preaching.

As one might expect, Whitaker also strongly rejected any tendency for the bishops to develop into a ruling caste within the church. Rather he placed them very firmly under the authority of the prince. Hence, faced with Bellarmine's claim that only the pope could call a church council, Whitaker resorted to the power of the prince in causes ecclesiastical. Was it not the task of a prince, he asked, to provide for the peace and tranquillity of the church and was not that the express purpose for which church councils were called?[58] But once called, Bellarmine continued, only bishops should enjoy a fully active role in the council's deliberations and only they should sign the canons that emerged at the end. Whitaker, of course, would have none of that. It was the task of church councils, he maintained, to decide any questions concerning the nature and definition of right doctrine and to provide generally for the welfare of the church: 'But that could not only be done by bishops ("ab episcopis") but also by those who are learned, pious, skilled in the scriptures, who are possessed of knowledge, seriousness, faith and piety and all the other gifts which business of this weight and importance requires.[59] Citing Acts 20.17,18, Whitaker continued that if all those

charged with the care of the Lord's flock had a right to take part
in such councils then the ordinary presbyter enjoyed such a right
and it was for that reason in verse 18 that they were referred to
as 'episcopi'.[60]

But Whitaker went further than that. So far was he from
allowing the development of a clerical caste that he maintained
that laymen should be allowed a full and positive role in church
councils. In an interesting passage he took Bellarmine's claim that
only 'public ecclesiastical persons' should be allowed to take part
and turned it against him:

Are only bishops ('episcopi') ecclesiastical persons? What of presbyters, deacons, abbots, nuns and all other clerics? What of cardinals
who are not bishops? But the phrase 'ecclesiastical person' can be
taken in two senses. The first refers to all members of the church
and in this sense all Christians are ecclesiastical persons. The
second and more restricted sense refers only to those who hold some
office or ministry in the church. In neither sense can the phrase
'ecclesiastical person' be taken to refer exclusively to bishops.[61]

It was as 'ecclesiastical persons' in the first sense that laymen
were to attend. To back up this claim Whitaker took issue with
Bellarmine's reliance on the authority of Eusebius for his account
of early church councils. There were councils older than those
described by Eusebius; and with that Whitaker turned directly
to the practice of the Apostles as described in scripture. Taking
the account of a council held at Jerusalem, described in Acts,
Whitaker proved by a detailed analysis of the text in question
that apostles, presbyters and ordinary church members had
played a full and active part.[62]

As for general church councils, Whitaker denied that bishops
alone could somehow 'represent' their particular churches, just
as the pope, despite claiming a similar mystical authority, could
not be taken to represent the universal catholic church. What,
asked Whitaker, if some of the bishops in question should be
heretics; should they still be accepted as truly representative of
their churches?[63] Taking the example of lay gatherings and parliaments Whitaker asserted the right of each particular church to
choose its own representative, be he bishop or no:

Just as in civil gatherings magistrates are not always sent to represent their community, but sometimes some other person is chosen,

so bishops are not always to be chosen and sent to church councils but other pious, able and learned men who perhaps may be more apt to dispute and better able to delve into controversial questions than the bishops. Whoever is chosen by a church represents in his person that church.

To drive the point home Whitaker cited a whole series of examples of intense lay involvement in church councils culled mainly from the fathers: 'Princes, presbyters, senators, judges and other laymen were not merely present at sacred and ecclesiastical councils but also gave their opinion, voted and helped resolve the issues. Therefore, bishops do not possess the deciding voice in church councils.[64]

There were definite links here between Whitaker's theory, as set out in his polemical works, and his later practice as an administrator and ecclesiastical 'politician'. For instance, in 1595 he referred a theological dispute, already pending before the relevant ecclesiastical authority (in this case Whitgift himself), to Burghley, a mere layman.[65] Not only was this a cunning manoeuvre on Whitaker's part in defence of the privileges of the university; it can also be seen as an expression of his sincere belief, cited above, that laymen (particularly those as eminent as Burghley) constituted as legitimate a source of ecclesiastical authority as any bishop. In 1595 again, Whitaker almost certainly saw himself as one of those men, eminent for their learning and theological expertise, who, while not bishops themselves, were as able and eligible as any bishop to decide the future of the church. Significantly, it was the Heads' refusal sufficiently to defer to the authority of Whitgift as Archbishop that alienated his sympathies from their cause.[66]

It is not difficult to discern in Whitaker's views as summarised above the outline of the Elizabethan church. His vision of a reformed church, Calvinist in doctrine, presided over by a godly prince, governed by bishops whose authority was a direct emanation of the power of that prince over causes ecclesiastical, owing nothing to spurious claims of Apostolic succession and whose prime function, along with that of their fellow ministers, remained the preaching of the word, reflected very faithfully central elements in the Elizabethan church settlement. But Whitaker's position cannot be taken as a simple reflection of 'the realities of the Elizabethan church' if only because, for contemporaries, there was no such thing as 'the realities of the Elizabethan church'. On the contrary, the perceptions of contemporaries were inextricably mixed with a series of images of both what that church was and what it ought to be.[67] The religious controversies of the period consisted almost entirely of the manipulation for polemical purposes of such images. Sometimes (as in the Admonition controversy) the manipulation and polemical intention were completely overt. At other times they remained concealed. The latter was true in Whitaker's case. Aimed not at fellow protestants but at the papists, Whitaker's discussion of the contemporary English church was pitched at a very high level of abstraction. Moreover, it remained but one possible view of the Elizabethan church. As such it could not command the general assent of all English protestants – as Whitaker's clashes with Whitgift were to reveal, when he tried to put his principles into practice. In fact Whitaker's vision of the church summarised here can be seen as an idealised version of certain central elements in the church under Grindal synthesised into a seemingly abstract and theoretical picture of what a true reformed church should be.

If this was the case and Whitaker's career grew essentially from opinions formed by his early years in Grindal's church (and particularly by the circle around his uncle Dean Nowell), then it may be possible to say something about the evolution of Whitaker's views and in particular about Andrew Perne's allegation that Whitaker became more radical as he grew older and fell increasingly under the influence of his puritan in-laws. On this view Whitaker's 'puritan conversion' can be seen as a function not of any personal change of mind but of change in the ideological tone of the English church as the period of Grindalian compromise and consensus was succeeded by Whitgift's anti-puritan zeal. There is here more than a suggestion that the conformist campaign against puritanism, instead of dividing moderate puritans from their radical brethren (as it was designed to do and as, I think, Professor Collinson has implied it did), in fact drove Whitaker, at least, further into the puritan camp.

But where, then, did Whitaker stand in relation to the puritan position? His flight from the visible church to the universal invisible church and his insistence on doctrine as the only touchstone for a true church inevitably distanced him from the precisian/conformist debate, which after all was concerned primarily with the externals of church polity and ceremony. The point is nicely made by Whitaker's response to an attempt by William Rainolds to demonstrate a contradiction between the doctrine of many of the English Calvinists and the official position of the English church as set out in the Prayer Book and the Thirty-nine Articles. He dealt contemptuously with Rainolds' allegations regarding outward ceremonies:

From copes and such like ornaments, either approved or rejected, to gather an argument of our inconstancy in matters of faith is too childish and absurd. Our religion is not like yours, consisting in outward show of gestures, garments and behaviour; so that our external ornaments may be changed without any alteration or change of our doctrine.[68]

But when Rainolds made the same point in the doctrinal sphere Whitaker took him altogether more seriously. He met Rainolds' allegation of an incompatibility between the Calvinist view of predestination and the official doctrine of the English church on baptism with what amounted to a Calvinist gloss on the relevant passage in the liturgy:

Baptism is the sacrament of new birth, wherein our adoption by Christ is sealed unto us and we are made the sons of God, as many as believe both sacramentally and spiritually the unbelievers only sacramentally. Wherefore this is not to be understood as though whosoever is baptized shall therefore be sure to have eternal life.[69]

The assumption, encapsulated in that passage, of a complete congruence between Whitaker's own doctrinal position and the official position of the church of England was perhaps the central pillar around which Whitaker's whole position was arranged. Certainly, the strength of Whitaker's reaction when that assumption appeared to be challenged, first in the comparatively narrow circuit of St John's College and then in the wider context of the university, can in itself be taken as evidence of the depth of the initial assumption and its central importance for the maintenance of his view of the world.[70]

But while Whitaker in the main avoided the issues traditionally taken to have divided precisians from conformists, on at least one occasion, as we have seen, he had firmly dissented from perhaps the central principle in the presbyterian platform: the assertion of a proper discipline of morals as a third mark of the church, on a par with the word and the sacraments. But what was the significance of this denial? Did his reference to 'schismatici nostrorum temporum' in fact apply to respectable presbyterian divines like Cartwright and Chaderton? From what we know of Whitaker's contacts with both men that seems highly unlikely. Rather it was an attack on the separatists who did indeed attempt to 'unchurch' the English church over this very issue, and perhaps also on presbyterianism in its most coherent and aggressive form as set out in the early 1570s. But there was a considerable difference between Cartwright's position of the 1570s and that of the 1580s. True he was still a presbyterian, but his formulation of the presbyterian case was now modified by other considerations. For instance, his role as an anti-papal polemicist had subjected him to precisely the same pressures as Whitaker. He too had had to turn his attention from the visible to the invisible church, to reduce his criteria for the continuing existence of a true church to a minimum and to place the major emphasis in the validation of a true church on doctrine.[71] While such developments remained implicit in his work against Rome, in meeting the challenge of the separatists Cartwright was forced to make them explicit in a coherent defence of the church of England. In short, in common with other moderates, Cartwright had been forced by events to distinguish quite clearly between doctrine and discipline. As we have seen, the presbyterian case had been based on the denial of such a distinction, but now Cartwright was forced to admit that while deficient in the latter the English church was wholly orthodox in the former. Hence the difference between Whitaker's position and that of Cartwright can be seen to have amounted to little more than an academic quibble. Both men were agreed that a proper external discipline was a good, even a necessary thing, for a reformed church. All that remained in question was the precise degree of necessity that should be attributed to it. That, beside their almost complete agreement on every doctrinal issue of importance discussed in this chapter, is not a very significant disagreement.

7

Theory into practice: puritan practical divinity in the 1580s and 1590s

Thus far this study has been largely concerned with formal theology. Certainly, the theological kernel of the moderate puritan position has been sought in essentially polemical situations where the proponents of the protestant case were concerned to assert, and defend from attack, their doctrinal position. In part this is unavoidable since it was precisely in such situations that doctrinal issues were formulated most clearly. However this is to ignore the way in which the formal principles of Cambridge Calvinism were translated into a style of practical divinity. This is a serious omission since the internal spiritual dynamic of puritan religion can hardly be understood if the formal doctrinal underpinning of that position is discussed in isolation. That formal basis has to be balanced by an analysis of the puritan style of preaching and of the ways in which the truths of right doctrine were actually presented to lay audiences. The sources for such an analysis are somewhat sparse. There are some, however, which allow such a study to be attempted. Firstly, we have a series of lecture notes taken from a course of lectures given by Laurence Chaderton in 1590/1.[1] These are remarkably full and appear at times to amount to a verbatim account of what was said. To these can be added the contents of a commonplace book which from internal evidence appears to have belonged to a member of St John's College during the 1590s. It contains notes from sermons by a whole series of men, many of them prominent in Cambridge puritan circles. In what follows most frequent use has been made of the material from Chaderton's sermons.[2] This material can be augmented by Chaderton's one printed exercise in practical divinity, his St Paul's Cross sermon of 1578.[3]

The other major source on which the following analysis is based is the commonplace book of Abdias Ashton.[4] Ashton was at St John's throughout the 1580s and became a fellow in 1590. The admiring biographer of William Whitaker, he was also one of those irate puritans who testified against Peter Baro and petitioned against William Barrett in 1595/6. In 1589 he had petitioned in favour of the puritan and future separatist Francis Johnson and in 1595, following Whitaker's death, he was one of the fellows of St John's who petitioned Burghley in support of Henry Alvey's candidacy for the mastership. In addition he was one of a group of young puritan divines – Samuel Ward, Thomas Gataker, William Bedell and others – who toured the villages around Cambridge supplementing the meagre diet of sermons preached by the local incumbents. There can, therefore, be little doubt of the centrality of Ashton's position within Cambridge puritanism.[5] Moreover, it is clear that the commonplace book in question dates from his days in the university since, according to a date on the title-page, it was apparently begun in 1584. And as the work is a large one, it is reasonable to suppose that Ashton kept adding to it throughout the 1580s and 1590s.

The book comprises about two hundred and eighty pages, each with a separate heading. These cover a vast range of subjects; to take a random sample under 'a' we find 'ancient way vid. truth, adultery, angels, arts manual, apparel, authors of evil, air, actions upon particular motions, anger, adverbs their use, godly acknowledge unworthy God's benefit'. Or again under 'd' we find 'devil, doctrine, God's decree, the last day, death, dearth, dancing'. Under each such heading is arranged a list of scriptural references and quotations together with similar references to the fathers, contemporary reformed theologians and classical authors, all designed to buttress the assertion contained in the heading.

Lest this sound too much like a mere student's notebook, it should be remembered that the book's contents evidently held a real personal significance for Ashton. On the first page he had given the book a title: 'Sacra scientia est quae veram et aeternam hominis faelicitatem docet fide et cognitione Christi.' This was followed by two short remembrancers in English:

When contrary to thy first vow and against the resolution of thy heart sinning day after day thou art ashamed to ask so oft pardon for the same crime call to mind the sweet comforts ministered to the prophet...I am God not man.

The second was more in the form of a prayer:

Merciful father vouchsafe to sanctify me by thy spirit that I may read thy word with all reverence and by thy gracious blessing thereby profit in knowledge, judgement and holiness of affection through Jesus Christ.

Here, then, was no mere mine of theological argument. In this context it is worth noting that popery was hardly mentioned in the book. Ashton's intentions were not polemical, rather the book was an exercise in personal piety. As the passage cited above might suggest, Ashton's aim was to attain to the 'veram et aeternam hominis faelicitatem' through his faith in the immutable mercy of God's nature, mediated by the figure of Christ.

Hence, Ashton's theme was the existential significance of right doctrine – 'sacra scientia' – but it seems reasonable to assume that his purposes in compiling the book were more than personal. The book formed a directory of quotations and references organised around certain central themes. Its purpose, I would suggest (apart from providing a source of spiritual solace and guidance for Ashton), was to provide a source of material for the writing of sermons. This is rendered inherently more likely by the fact that the headings under which it was organised did not come from the lecture room or the disputation. Rather it was set out under a series of themes and topics of the sort to which a preacher would need to address himself. If this view of the book can be accepted then we have here a virtual compendium, an epitome of Ashton's sermons throughout the 1580s and 1590s. Here, it can be argued, is the distilled essence of the puritan style of preaching. If this is so, then in identifying the central organising concerns of the work and in analysing the correspondences and differences between these and the formal structure of Calvinist orthodoxy we have some claim to have identified the central nexus of concerns at the heart of Cambridge puritan divinity at the end of the sixteenth century.

Perhaps we should start with a few remarks about the view of the authority of scripture and scriptural exegesis inherent in the format of Ashton's book. The very diversity of the topics under which the book was ordered can be taken as a sign of the assumed omnicompetence of scripture as a guide to all aspects of human life. The concatenation of disparate scriptural references, unified by the single assertion that they were being amassed to support, betrays a very similar attitude to the authority of scripture to that exemplified by Chaderton and Whitaker. Moreover Ashton revealed himself as enamoured of the bifurcated diagrams so typical of puritan rationalism in its application of the insights of scripture.

Chaderton's procedure in his lectures on St John was somewhat different. Rather than seeking to arrange a whole series of references under one heading, he was trying to give a detailed reading of one particular course of scripture. In the notes in question Chaderton can be seen teasing the meaning from particular passages, drawing moral and doctrinal lessons, leaping from the particular to the general and back again. Chaderton's discourse also provides us with sustained passages of rhetoric and argument not found in Ashton's rather terse and compressed commonplace book. The juxtaposition of the two sources thus allows a more rounded picture to emerge than would otherwise be the case. Moreover, given the very different forms and functions of the two sources, the fact that they reveal precisely similar attitudes and deal with precisely the same issues and concerns is a powerful indication that those same concerns were central to the puritan world-view as a whole.

As we have already seen in the case of William Whitaker, protestant scripturalism of the sort outlined above was but a product of the Calvinist view of the all-surpassing power and sufficiency of God's will and sovereignty. 'Nothing done without God's providence', ran one of Ashton's headings. 'Who is he then that sayeth and it cometh to pass and the Lord commandeth it not...wicked worldlings advance fortune.'[6] Similarly, Chaderton remarked that the very frequency with which the phrase 'it cometh to pass' occurred in the scriptures was a sign to man that all events proceeded from the great providence of God.[7]

The entire creation had to be viewed as a vast monument to God's providence:

The disposing of the heavens, the equal course of the stars in variety and the heavenly lights, the constant and marvellous description of times, the diverse fruitfulness of the earth, the plain fences of the fields, heaps of hills. The greenness and plentifulness of woods, the wholesome springs of fountains, the commodious overflowing of rivers, the rich and abundant running in and through the earth of the sea. The diverse and profitable blowing of the winds. In these shineth out the marvellous disposition of our most provident God.

Yet more impressive and significant than the regularities and harmonies of nature were the irregular but awesome eruptions of God's will into the natural world interventions which entirely cut across the normal laws of nature.[8]

Indeed, there was a sense in which man had been created in order to provide an appreciative audience for the exercise by God of his over-ruling providence. Under the heading 'wherefore God made man' Ashton quoted Isaiah 45.7:

Everyone shall be called by my name for I created him for my glory and formed him and made him. This people have I formed for myself and they shall show forth my praise. Lesser creatures the earth at God's commandment brought forth but man as a special creature to set forth his glory he made by his wisdom (Gen. I.26). He made him to behold with his eyes and wonder in his mind and speak forth with his mouth God's providence in disposing his reason in creating and power in finishing his works.

It was man's role as this uniquely appreciative audience that underwrote his lordship over the rest of creation:

He is endued with authority over all creatures (Gen. I.26,28, and 2.19) wherein his excellency doth consist not so much in speed and reason which in some sort are imparted to others as in religion.

In that sense man's lordship over nature was a function of his own subjection to God. 'He should resign himself to God (Exod. 3.5). See what God requires at man's hands (Deut. 10.12,13).'

The world was made for man, man to know the maker of the world. Our knowledge is to worship him. Worship to receive immortality as a (free) gift promised to our labour. Therefore we obtain the reward that we may be like to the angels and serve our sovereign lord and father forever.[9]

But if man provided the audience in a theatre presided over by God's providence, he was, unaided, an obtuse judge of the performance. 'The Lord both in his judgments and mercies disposeth all for his own glory but man is an evil judge thereof.'[10] He was an evil judge because of the sin and corruption inherent in his fallen nature. As Ashton observed, 'all are in darkness till God give the light of his spirit'.

Certainly, as Ashton admitted, 'God hath not taken away every spark of light from natural man and wicked.'[11] As the passage cited above shows it was possible to gather something about the power of God from the mere contemplation of nature. It was possible to 'see there is but one God whose power hath made and will govern hereafter all things' and 'yet from this such slip as grant one God yet being entangled with philosophy or some other captious reasons do conceive otherwise of his majesty than the truth may seem to require'.[12] 'Even the godly consulting with reasons do sometimes stagger.'[13] Chaderton similarly denounced as 'atheists' those who 'acknowledge one God, the creator of heaven and earth and doth this by the light of nature and therefore when he cometh to worship God, he conceiveth amiss of him'.[14] Popery was a direct product of such a trust in mere natural reason:

And therefore knowing everyman to be by the instinct of nature given to acknowledge God and with some kind of watchfulness to serve him, they have out of the folly and vanity of their own brains drawn out of a kind of service which standeth only in outward ceremonies and bodily exercises wherein they have been and are very watchful...All which inventions of men are directly contrary to that worship which our saviour Christ witnesseth to consist in spirit and truth and therefore justly condemned.[15]

Hence the believer was forced back to the scriptures.

Who [asked Chaderton] could have ever searched out what was the cause why the earth being barren and dry should bring forth fruit except it had been revealed unto us by his word. And this is the great mercy of the Lord which will make us acquainted with his eternal decree. Certain it is that the philosophers did search deeply into nature yet none of them all could ever search forth this which the holy ghost here teacheth unto us.[16]

Elsewhere, speaking of the variety of God's creation, Chaderton observed that some 'that meaneth to apply themselves to study may here receive a warrant from God to study philosophy'. But this only applied 'to such knowledge as may enable them to understand the scriptures'.[17]

Hence God could not be conceived as immanent in the cosmos. He could not be approached merely through the contemplation of external reality. God himself was no object of contemplation, nor the world a static structure both hiding and showing forth the divine essence. On the contrary, this God was a God of the will and all that was possible for man was the apprehension of what this God of the will chose to reveal of himself when and where he chose to reveal it. Some idea of the implications of this attitude can be gleaned from Ashton's answer to the question 'what did this God before he made this world?' In response he wrote:

Wilt thou call God to give thee an account of his life and deeds; he made a bottomless hell to torment such inquisitive and curious hearers as thou art being not content with knowledge of things pertaining to thy salvation. But yet hear further, he was not idle but was occupied in his works...he was marvellously delighted at the contemplation of himself. He enjoyed his own unspeakable glory and was busied in his large and incomprehensible light of his essence.[18]

It was typical of the tension in puritan divinity between a codifying rationalism and an equally strong emphasis on the existential significance of right doctrine that, having denied the validity of the question, Ashton should attempt to answer it. But it was no less typical that he should make the attempt by a mere reassertion of the liberty of God couched in pseudo-philosophical terms.

On this view the gulf separating God from man was so vast that nothing could be known of God's intentions save what he himself chose to reveal. But precisely because that gap was so great the process of revelation could only take place within the limits of the human world. In other words, God could only be known in terms of his relations with man. The result was an intensely man-centred view of the world which tended to see in any and every event – indeed in the very structure of the world – an expression of God's concern for man. The distinction between night and day – the seasons themselves – had been arranged, like the markings on some cosmic clock, to help man gauge the passing of time.[19] It was also a view that saw the entire course of human history, from the most personal and private griefs to the most general national and international crises, as direct emanations of the divine will. For as Chaderton observed, 'all afflictions come from the eternal providence of the Lord'. In the public sphere, he claimed, 'we must know that when any people doth abide in any land and remove into any other it cometh to pass by the providence of God'.[20] By thus removing mere contingency from existence, by picturing the social and natural worlds as part of some divine plan, the world was in some sense explained and appropriated as a field of human action. Certainly this was true for the godly since it was their eventual salvation which lay at the centre of the divine plan. It was this assumption which enabled puritan ministers to interpret events in the natural and social worlds as rebukes from God intended to return his people to the straight and narrow path of godliness. In 1579 Chaderton saw an outbreak of the plague in London as just such a rebuke. He was to repeat this direct link between 'the judgements of God' and the sins of the English nation having 'had this word this thirty-seven years' during the 1590s. George Estye was to take a precisely parallel view of the widespread famine during that same decade.[21]

For nothing was so certain as the care of God for his people. It was this that prompted the eruption of his will into the human world. Ashton maintained that 'the salvation of the righteous is joined with the honour of God'.[22] Whatever the appearance to the contrary, 'in the very midst of all his threatenings against the wicked he remembreth his (Jer. 33.6 and 44.28)'. 'He will sift the wicked but none of his shall fall through (Amos 9.9).'[23] As Ashton remarked, 'God will always have a remnant'. It was this that underwrote the continuance of a true church through all afflictions and persecutions.[24]

But not only did this infrangible bond between God and his people provide an objective guarantee for the continuance of the church, it also provided a major element in the subjective experience of the godly. Hence Ashton could assert that 'we must stay ourselves in patience upon God's providence'. 'God's providence is a safe and sure ground for God's children to build on (1 Sam. 3.17)...It is a sure castle against all temptations (Gen. 22.8, Gen. 24.7). This only is safety enough that God all sufficient is their defence (Gen. 35.11, 39.10, Exod. 14.13).'[25] In many ways that attitude to the providence of God, as the underlying principle of their lives, was the defining characteristic of the godly.

The difference between their position and that of the ungodly can be seen most plainly in their divergent attitudes to the experience of suffering. It was axiomatic to both Chaderton and Ashton that all affliction came from God. As Chaderton wrote, 'all are guilty of [sin] by the fall of Adam' and therefore 'all are subject to infinite calamities'.

All afflictions come from the eternal providence of God and therefore according to the greatness or the smallness of the same he
afflicteth his punishment upon men. Where he showeth that there
is no evil connected to man which the Lord hath not done and for
the better proof of this John saith the Lord hath made the light and
created darkness, he hath formed good and created evil, as if he
should have said if that I have made all prosperity and adversity
then am I a true God for by creating these things he proveth himself
to be God.[26]

God would use any and every means to afflict mankind. He was
quite capable of using the ungodly as instruments against the
godly. 'God useth the wicked to execute his judgements which
have not that intent but do it for some other proper end of their
own.'[27] Yet always such actions were directed toward the eventual
destruction of the wicked and the salvation of the righteous.
Chaderton noted 'the proceeding of God in persecution who
although he suffer his children to be persecuted of the ministers
of the devil thereof he openeth the way to his own glory and to
the profit of his own children'.[28] Ashton went into greater detail
concerning God's intentions in afflicting his people: 'They are
humbled thereby (Lam. 3.20, 29). To try them (Jonah 4.8). It
is not for their overthrow (Zech. I.15)...Thereby God as a
father nurtureth them (Deut. 8.5) and humbleth them (Deut.
8.16).'[29] Hence, Ashton concluded, 'paenae non sunt piorum
afflictiones sed castigationes paternae'. The case could hardly
have been more different with the ungodly: 'The godly chastised
in mercy, the wicked plagued in God's fury and justice' ran
one of Ashton's headings.[30] Chaderton made basically the same
distinction when he divided the afflictions of God under two
headings, the 'judiciary' and the 'castigatory'. The judiciary was
when the Lord 'in judgement doth punish the wicked for their
sins'; as such it was a 'forewarning of their everlasting damnation'. The castigatory was that 'whereby we are chastised which
our saviour Christ calleth the cross...As the other belongeth to
the reprobate so this belongeth to the godly. If we hope to be
partakers of the glory of Christ then we must also be partakers of
his afflictions.'[31]

This difference in God's intentions in chastising the righteous
and the wicked was paralleled by the very different subjective
response of those two groups to the experience of affliction. By

their sufferings the godly were genuinely brought to God. Their sense of their own sin and impotence before the all-sufficiency of God was genuinely enhanced. The wicked, on the other hand, if they were brought to God at all, were drawn only by fear for their immediate safety. No heightened awareness of their spiritual condition was awakened within them. They remained trapped in a carnal security:

The wicked tremble under God's judgements (Dan. 5.6) and are astonished (Amos. 6.10, Zech. 1.6) and when they are out of sight the wicked wax straight presumptuous and rebellious (Num. 16.34).[32]

The wicked are more ignorant of God's judgement then is the stork of his appointed season (Jer. 8.7 and Jer. 44). Though he be beaten to pieces by God's judgements yet he will not leave his foolishness.[33]

Hence, 'the Lord's lenity maketh the wicked presumptuous'. They were incapable of realising that 'his hand is heavier the longer it is in falling (2 Chr. 36.15,16,17)'.[34] Indeed, even when 'they perceive them [the judgements of God] coming yet will they not yield but use policy and force to withstand them'.[35]

Accordingly, while 'the wicked in trouble shall seek for help by man'

the righteous always in extremity flee unto God for succour (Mic. 7.7). For he will hear them (Gen. 25.22 and 32.9-11) and it is not in vain (Gen. 33.4 and 35.1). For he is the shield of their help, the sword of their glory and rideth upon the clouds for thine help (Deut. 33.29) and find comforts (I Sam. 30.6, 2 Sam. 17,18,19).[36]

In this congruence between the intention of God 'to win us to repentance' or to make 'us to desist from some sin',[37] and the subjective response to affliction on the part of the godly, we can see summed up the reciprocal relationship between the Calvinist God and his followers. Ostensibly these relations were entirely dominated by the all-surpassing power of God. But the very extent of the gulf between God and man ensured that God's interventions in the world could only be understood in terms of his chosen human agents, the subjects of his guidance and protection here on earth. Moreover, it was only members of this group who could be expected to perceive and understand these divine interventions. Hence, on one view, it was the group consciousness and self-image of God's people that kept alive God's presence in the world. They were the only mirror in which the majesty of God could be seen accurately reflected. God's people, confronted by the seemingly impenetrable palimpsest of events had to preserve an interpretation of these events, and in particular of their own fate within them, that centred on the providence of God and kept alive their special relationship with that providence. But they had to do this in the face of rival interpretations put forward by the ungodly. External reality was not theirs by right, rather they had to appropriate it. It is in this sense that the warning, cited above, against too great a trust in mere human reason, or the worldlings' trust in fortune, should be taken. The godly were fighting for their view of the world and for their own place in it.

The paradigm for this integral relationship between God and his people was provided by that which pertained between God and the Jews before the coming of Christ. Then the link between Jewish social space and true religion existed for all to see. The situation under the gospel was less clear cut. Nevertheless Ashton, by his frequent citation of Old Testament examples, tended to transfer the Old Testament relationship between God and his people to the new dispensation of the gospel. In the process he was forced to stress the division between the godly and the ungodly, in many ways a far more nebulous division than that between Jew and gentile. The identification of the defining characteristics of the ungodly thus became a central element in the raising of godly consciousness. For the godly validated their status as the special objects of God's concern almost as much in terms of their separation from the ungodly as in their union with God. As Ashton observed, 'true felicity is to rest upon God. An high degree therein is to have no dealing with the wicked.'[38]

The objective basis for that subjective apprehension of God's purposes and power that marked off the godly from the ungodly was provided by scripture. To an extent what was involved here was simple information, the brute facts concerning God's providence and the liberty of his will. Certainly such knowledge was a *sine qua non* of true belief. 'Knowledge', Ashton wrote, 'required both of priest and people (Hos. 4.6). My people are destroyed for want of knowledge. Because thou hast refused knowledge I will also refuse thee that thou shalt be no priest to me.'[39] But there was more involved here than a mere formal knowledge of the text. Even the wicked could attain to that and use it to justify their own iniquities. 'When it serveth their humour the wicked shall use it as a most certain oracle (2 Kgs. 9.11).'[40] As Chaderton observed, 'it is not the bare naked knowledge of great mysteries that are available to salvation'.[41] On the contrary, he defined faith 'as a sure and certain persuasion of the heart grounded upon the promises of God and wrought in me by the holy ghost whereby I am persuaded that whatsoever Christ hath done for man's salvation he hath done it not only for others but also for me'.[42] Since 'faith is a persuasion ignorance must be avoided and since it is a certain persuasion here is all doubting confuted'.[43]

Such a faith, added Chaderton, 'cometh by hearing'. As Ashton observed under the heading 'the power of the word':

it quencheth the devil's darts (Matt. 4.4,7). It is like a fire, like a hammer that breaketh the stone. It hath power to slay the wicked (Hos. 6.5, Prov. I.2–5). It giveth knowledge and information to all, sharpness to the simple, increase in learning to the wise.[44]

The holy spirit useth outward preaching as a conduit pipe whereby he pierceth to the inward parts of the mind (Heb. 4.12, Jas. I.18, I Pet. 1.20) and maketh the understanding capable of the under-standing of the mysteries of salvation. It beateth down the holds of the imagination and whatsoever is exalted against the knowledge of God and captivateth the thoughts to the obedience of Christ (2 Cor. 10.4,5).[45]

Chaderton himself provided the perfect example of the preacher in the role of a 'conduit pipe' for the Holy Spirit, linking the realm of objective doctrinal truth to the subjective response of the godly. At St Paul's Cross his whole intention had been to lead his audience from the empty formal profession of true religion typical of 'hypocritical and faithless worshippers' to the 'sincere and faithful profession' of true believers.[46] To take a specific example, Chaderton started with the general proposition that events in the external world – war, famine, pestilence, translation of monarchies and kingdoms – represented the punish-ment of God on the sins of his people. Yet the English, living 'in this peaceable land flowing with milk and honey and in the light of the gospel shining unto us for the space of twenty golden years', had repeatedly ignored such warnings:

But who hath shed forth as yet the Christian tears of repentance? Not four years ago the Lord did as it were with his own hand set a star in the heavens, whereof the wisest astronomer that liveth can give no reason. Since then we have been admonished by a great and strange comet in the air, by earthquakes, inundations of waters, all which signs and forerunners of God's wrath are returned to him again as being unable to mollify our stoney hearts that we might turn unto the Lord.

If such hardness of heart were to continue Chaderton much feared that the gospel will 'within short time' 'depart from us and by the commandment of God go unto a people which shall receive it not as the word of men but as it is indeed the word of God'.[47] Thus were the impersonal truths of right doctrine, and even that most impersonal of all doctrines concerning the ultimate sovereignty of God, given immediacy and force by the word preached.

Hence, while Ashton noted 'none are exempted from hearing the word of the Lord', he felt compelled to add that 'to this hearing is annexed doing that the action may be acceptable before God. Hear we the words of the convenant and do them and learning to fear the Lord (Deut. 31.13).[48]

But as that passage reveals, the word preached did more than awake the believer to the need to obey. It was also a principal means to enable him to obey. Here the objective realm of scriptural truth and the subjective realm of true belief were fused and the concept of knowledge, at least in the case of the godly, combined with a whole series of spiritual graces without which a mere formal knowledge of the scriptures was useless. Hence Chaderton insisted on the need to so 'use this outward ministry of man that then all our affections may be changed that we may become new creatures',[49] 'for hereby he confereth the power of the spirit whereby all the faculties of his mind are moved'.[50] What was involved here was a basic reorientation of the personality as the truths of right doctrine were fully internalised by the individual believer. The results could be nothing but disturbing: 'Some will say', observed Chaderton, 'that I would go to sermons but I am so troubled that I cannot be at peace with myself many days after and yet I can go to such and such sermons and never feel such effects; but these are the true effects of the word.'[51] Indeed, the lack of such effects was enough to cast doubt on the authenticity of the individual's profession of true religion. It was perhaps the defining characteristic of puritanism that it did not shirk, indeed welcomed, the disruptive, discomforting effects of protestant doctrine on the lives of individuals and on the life of the whole social organism. For neither the individual nor society itself could hope for true peace and order except on the basis of true religion (that, of course, had been the theme of Chaderton's presbyterian sermon of 1584). Yet given man's fallen state such a solid foundation could not be established without a struggle. It was this struggle between the old Adam and the new that produced that feeling of unease identified by Chaderton as among the proper effects of the word preached.

Such disorder was, moreover, inevitable since 'we are in these dangerous times, the last age of the world where Satan doth work mightily in the hearts of the wicked that he carrieth away with him a very great company'.[52] Even at the time of Christ 'we see that there was dissension come then. But yet his doctrine and life was most perfect.' 'If any church could have been free it was most likely that that church should be free wherein he taught.' 'What use', asked Chaderton,

have we to make of this to teach not to mistake the doctrine of Christ for the dissensions of our times. Surely this is very necessary for us present for do we not see in all places diversity of opinions. Shall we call therefore into question the foundation of religion? God forbid for he hath taught us that there must needs be errors that the good may be tried. Notwithstanding diversity of opinions search the scriptures.[53]

But, Chaderton warned, it was easy to misunderstand the word. Since the disciples had contrived to misunderstand Christ when they were in his presence 'how are we subject to error which have the scripture but written'.

Seeing therefore the great evil of false interpretation how are we to take heed, therefore we must read the thing diligently and we must compare the end of the writing with the words; and make a comparison with other places of scripture and use hearty prayer unto God that he would reveal the light hereof to us.[54]

Given this situation, with the godly constantly subject to error, tempted by Satan and led astray by his minister Antichrist, it was essential, Chaderton maintained, that 'the true sheep of

Christ' be able 'to discern his doctrine from the voice of Antichrist here therefore is commanded to every man and woman that they be not so ignorant but may discern the voice of Christ from Antichrist'.[55] This was to place a heavy burden on the individual believer, both in his own study of the scriptures and in his hearing of the word preached.

But if anything it placed a greater responsibility on the minister of the word. Given their emphasis on the word preached neither Chaderton nor Ashton could avoid an exalted view of the ministry. For Chaderton preachers were 'the light of the world'.[56]

They shall hear his [Christ's] voice by his ministers...Therefore he will send his ministers to gather and call his sheep and that we reverence as the voice of Christ. By this means we shall be brought to Christ.[57]

For Ashton they were 'dei dispensatores'.[58] Under the heading 'their authority' he cited Jer. I. 10, 'behold this day have I set thee over the nations and over the kingdoms to pluck up and to root out and to destroy and throw down, to build and to plant'.[59]

The good pastor and prophet discovereth to the people their iniquity; the false not (Lam. 2.14). He is sent as a means to purge the uncleanness of the people...All their graces they acknowledge to be God's for his glory...Their duty to bring man to God (Hos. 9.8).[60]

'As the Lord's emissary', wrote Ashton, 'the minister must speak all the words of God.' 'He must speak none but the words of God (Jonah 3.2)...and for this cause I suppose they are called virgins or maidens (Prov. 9.3) as not infected with men's wisdom or doctrines of men.'[61]

Of the ministers' functions Ashton wrote:

they should have knowledge to teach others...On the priests' breasts was Urrim and Thurrim; light and perfection, knowledge and holiness (Exod. 28.30). The discharge of their duty consisteth in these I. by pure preaching of God's word to instruct their flock in pure doctrine and godly, 2. to administer the sacraments according to Christ's institution, 3. to admonish, reprove, comfort and to wipe away the uncleanness of...and offences by the spiritual discipline of the church.[62]

It was, therefore, 'a great honour to be called to the office of pastor'. 'The contempt of their preachings shall be punished (Mic. 1.2,3). For they are fathers whose instruction is to be regarded (Prov. 1.8, Deut. 18.19). The scorning of their persons shall be punished...They that believe them shall prosper (2 Chr. 20.20, 2 Chr. 24.22,23).'[63]

There was in such a view of the ministry an implicit division between the true minister and the false, the puritan and the conformist. For what of those ministers too ignorant or corrupt to denounce the sins of the people effectively, whose sermons were 'infected with the doctrines of men' and who did not seek to exercise an effective spiritual discipline over their charges? It was a division Chaderton had made explicit in 1579:

Where [he asked] are the lips of those ministers which do preserve knowledge or those messengers of God at whose mouths his poor people should seek his law? Nay rather where be not whole swarms of idle, ignorant and ungodly curates and readers who neither can nor will go before the dear flock of Christ in soundness of doctrine and integrity of life? The cause of which enormity resting principally in the persons themselves and then in those which sent them and now suffer them in the church; I charge in the Lord, the one, that they seriously weighing the worthiness of the Lord's embassage for the which they are most unworthy would voluntarily forego that calling wherein they cannot do the fathers will and betake them to some other which they may in a good conscience without offence and in some godly and profitable measure discharge. The other I council and beseech as a brother in the Lord that they would more diligently look unto their ministry committed to them, lest not only this grievous offence but also all other their sins against God and their brethren be laid upon their charge.[64]

But Chaderton did not restrict his censures to unlearned ministers and the bishops who ordained them, he also condemned those who, although they preached, preached in the wrong way. Preaching in England, he maintained, was 'clean contrary' to the example of St Paul, 'for it giveth no life to those which are dead in sin, it hath no power to strike insunder or to unloose the hold of sin'.

Our words are of our own making not such as the spirit of God teacheth; our matter for the most part is the devices of men; the disposition of our hearts prophane, worldly carnal; our intent and purpose is to get honour and worldly preferments.[65]

Wherefore many do stuff their sermons with new devised words and affected speeches, of vanities, not being content with the words that the Holy Ghost teacheth. Many with unnecessary sentences, proverbs similitudes and stories collected out of the writings of prophane men; many with curious, affected figures, with latin, greek and hebrew sentences without any just occasion offered by their text, with multitudes of human authorities and divers opinions of men in whom there can be found neither certain rule or truth neither constancy in judgement.[66]

Later, in 1590, Chaderton implicitly acknowledged the polemical – indeed bitterly divisive – nature of this position and tried to pre-empt conformist counter-strokes. It was, he claimed, 'the inquity of our time' to resist 'every mean which the Lord useth'.[67] 'If that the Lord being thus hated by men for preaching was slandered nowadays therefore his ministers be slandered and hence cometh these slanderous names of puritan and precisian.'[68] Hence the polemical use of such labels was dismissed as a sign of disaffection with the cause of true religion and those against whom such insults were levelled established as the guardians of orthodoxy and zeal.

However, while both Ashton and Chaderton can be seen to have had a high opinion of the ministry, it would be a mistake to suppose that they regarded the ministers as forming some sort of caste or elite within the community of the godly. On the contrary, for Chaderton the assent of the godly was to provide the touchstone of the minister's legitimacy. 'It is the property of the true sheep to follow the Lord and confess his doctrine only.' If there 'be any that the sheep of Christ do not follow he is not a true pastor'.[69] Similarly, the laity were urged to compare the preaching of various ministers as a check on the orthodoxy of their doctrine.[70] For their part the ministers were to avoid all arrogance and harshness in their dealings with their flock. By his own example Christ had taught them not to reject 'them that come unto them although they be simple'.[71] Christ's readiness to teach his disciples and any others 'that be desirous to learn' 'is to teach the minister to instruct his auditory and when any of them shall move any question then to be ready to answer'.[72] But perhaps the clinching example of the interpenetration and mutual reliance of clerical and lay members of the community came in Chaderton's discussion of 'conferences of the children of God'. 'Therefore let us', wrote Chaderton, 'if we doubt of anything ask questions of them which be able to dissolve them.' For it was the practice of Christ and his disciples 'to use conference in points of divinity by the way when they walked from place to place'.[73] Chaderton did not differentiate between the clerical and lay elements in such conferences. Evidently skill in interpreting the scriptures and spiritual insight in applying them was no clerical monopoly.

We have here a picture of a godly community brought together by a common experience of, and response to, the doctrine and reality of the providence of God, called to that common experience by the word of God as preached by his ministers, and united against the profane, the sinful and even those who, while they might outwardly profess the same beliefs, did not inwardly share the same experiences and attitudes based on those beliefs.

And so we are back with that basic division between the righteous and the wicked, the true believer and the hypocrite. There can be no doubt that both Chaderton and Ashton conceived of the community of the godly as a living organism with an objective existence in the social world. Hence Ashton held it to be one of 'the virtues of preaching' that 'it serveth to winnow and fan the good from the bad (Matt. 3.12)'.[74] 'The godly have great danger by fellowship and living with the wicked.' 'The Israelites being present at the sacrifice of Moabites to their God's committed whoredom and idolatry (Num. 25,1,2)'; 'The godly being harmless are often deceived by the wicked sometime to the loss of their lives'; 'If the godly will not leave them being admonished they shall taste of their plagues (Rev. 18.4, Gen. 19.15).'[75] As Ashton remarked, 'the world' was 'no dwelling place for the godly' for 'here they are hated'. However 'it is profitable (Gen. 46.34) to them. For they being separated from wicked men may more freely serve God.'[76] One result of this separation from the ungodly was the mutual reliance and recognition of the godly. Hence Chaderton could maintain that:

it behoveth us to be moved when we hear any such report of any of our brethren for he is no lively member of the mystical body of Jesus Christ which hearing that his fellow member is cut off will not have compassion of him.[77]

But he could also assert that:

the man of an upright life he despiseth the vile man and he will not keep company with them and he must not show him a merry countenance...The society of concord must be with all men, but the society of amity must only be amongst those which are of the church of God...we must learn that there is no countenance to be showed to the works of darkness and therefore if you will lend your ears to the preachers [of] the word of God you must stop your ears to vain plays.[78]

There was, therefore, a separation in practice between the godly and the ungodly. But how precisely was one group to be distinguished from the other? To an extent external conduct could provide a rough guide. As Ashton noted, 'the wicked by continuance in sin are shameless'.[79] However even this was not foolproof. After all, Christianity was a religion based on repentance. As Chaderton observed, 'he came not to call the right but the sinners'.[80] Men could be called to God even at the end of their lives – at the eleventh hour as the parable had it.[81] 'It is not enough', wrote Chaderton, 'to say that this man is a sinner. If, therefore the whole church doth avouch any man to be a sinner we may not believe it except God hath revealed it.'[82] But that raised rather more questions than it answered.

Moreover, as we have seen, much of the difference between the godly and the ungodly proceeded not from their external actions but from the inward spirit that informed them. As Ashton admitted in his section headed 'how to discern true professors from dissemblers', 'the hypocrite will serve God outwardly but not inwardly from the heart as he hath commanded (Zech. 7.9, Prov. 20.11). For outward testimonies there is small difference betwixt the good and bad (1 Kgs. 22.11).[83] Elsewhere he remarked that 'God regardeth not the sacrifice but the sacrificer's faith and mercy.' 'These outward things be but lying words and not to be trusted to.'[84] Throughout the book Ashton contrasted the spirit in which the godly undertook the profession of true religion with that which informed the profession of the ungodly. But he was forced to admit that even the godly were subject to the same faults as the ungodly. Hence, having compared their reliance 'wholly upon God' with the wickeds' trust in purely human and worldly powers, he conceded that 'the godly consulting with reason do sometimes stagger'.[85] Elsewhere, commenting on the carnal security in the face of God's judgements so typical

of the wicked, Ashton added that 'sometimes the godly are over-
taken with this security – Jonah asleep when his ship was like
to be broken'.[86] Conversely, the ungodly might give every appearance of enjoying the same positive attributes as the godly. Hence
Ashton remarked that 'the people of God shall agree...The
false prophets agreed well. For whatsoever one said another
avouched to be true (Ezek. 13.11). One built up the wall and
another tempered it with untempered mortar. Their agreement is
called conspiracy.'[87]

Thus, while there was obviously a link between godly status
and external conduct, in the final analysis that status sprang not
from any external act or attribute but from God's attitude toward
the individual. Hence in one section Ashton listed a whole set
of examples of 'infirmity in God's children' before pointing out
that 'God turneth the faults of his children to their benefit.
Peter's weakness to increase his strength (Matt. 26.74, 75). Paul's
persecution caused him to be more fervent for the truth.'[88] Before
all else came the individual's status as a child of God, but that
hardly rendered the task of distinguishing between the godly and
ungodly any easier.

While one cannot deny the centrality to the puritan world-
view of this division between the godly and the ungodly, there
was a real tension, almost a contradiction, inherent in their position concerning the precise nature and extent of that division.
Hence at one point Ashton could observe, under the heading
'reprobates not to be prayed for' that 'the Lord's determinate will
towards the wicked shall stand and therefore but vain to pray for
them'.[89] Yet elsewhere he could cite Beza's opinion that 'the
law of charity biddeth us to reckon for faithful so many as give
out a true confession of faith until their hypocrisy be detected'.[90]
Hence what on one view could appear to be a very exclusive
and integrated definition of the godly community could also
appear as a rather loose and open-ended category, notionally
including 'so many as give out a true confession of faith'. In
part this was a reflection of the position of the puritan member
of the national church, but more importantly this tension had
deep roots in the spiritual predicament of the true believer.

For instance there was, apart from the ambiguity over the
exact nature and extent of the division between the godly and
the ungodly, a similar lack of clarity concerning the nature of

the eventual triumph of the one group over the other. Such a triumph was certainly inevitable, but how precisely was it to be interpreted? There was a sense in which Ashton wanted to say – and indeed implied – that the godly would prevail in this world. Hence he could assert that 'blessings upon the wicked last but a while'. 'The earth is for the righteous (Ezek. 33.25,26, Prov. 2.21,22) and the wicked shall attend upon them (Prov. 14.19).'[91] Ashton went so far as to claim that not only were 'creatures at the first ordained to serve his [man's] use' but that 'they serve specially for the use of the godly'.[92] Under the heading 'the godly are safe under God's protection' Ashton first listed 'the instruments Satan useth in assaulting God's children' only to conclude that 'those that vex God's children shall be rewarded'.[93]

However Ashton was well aware that mere outward prosperity 'was no proper token of God's child'[94] and that 'wicked men are not always plagued but sometimes have prosperity'. This, he admitted, 'is a great temptation to the godly to see them flourish and the righteous in adversity'.[95] In part he resolved this tension by asserting that 'the wicked shall not fly from God's punishment'. 'He delayeth to punish but it is for their greater plague.' And here he cited a whole list of tyrants who had suffered sudden death, including Caligula, Claudius, Nero and Domitian.[96] The wicked, he claimed, lived under the constant threat of punishment: 'The wicked shall be cut off (Eccles. 8.13). God threateneth to cut off princes in the mid-way if they with reverence adore not his son (Ps. 2.12).'[97]

This was in direct contrast to the position of the godly. As we have seen, their afflictions were always designed for their own good. For them great affliction was simply a token of greater joy to come.[98] 'As the Lord delivereth into captivity so he doth bring back again.'[99] Statements such as these were subject to a literal interpretation. God had indeed delivered the Jews into captivity and then restored them to their homeland. There is no reason to doubt that Ashton used such instances to keep alive the expectations of God's people of a deliverance from their enemies in this world.

However, the same passages were equally susceptible to an entirely other-worldly interpretation: whatever their station or fate in this life the godly would triumph in the next. There was a real tension here in Ashton's rhetoric. Hence, under the heading 'the joy of God's children', Ashton cited several passages of scripture that were deeply ambiguous on precisely this point. He quoted Isaiah 65.13: 'therefore thus saith the Lord God behold my servants shall eat and ye shall be hungry'. Or 'they which are delivered shall rejoice in the company of the faithful. Then shall the virgin rejoice in the Lord's holy name.'

The destruction of God's enemies is a cause of rejoicing (Ps. 21.13). Then the heaven and the earth (not only God's children) and all that is therein shall rejoice for Babel; for the destroyers etc. And they are destroyed when as God's people turn to the Lord.[100]

Such passages could well refer, albeit through terrestrial imagery, to the final triumph of the godly over the ungodly on the last day. They could also refer to this worldly victories of the godly over the ungodly, prompted, as that last passage suggests, by a collective turning to God on the part of his people.

But did this distinction between the godly and the ungodly, however ambiguous, give rise to a distinctive puritan social theory? Did either Chaderton or Ashton recommend to their audiences distinctively puritan social forms to mark their behaviour off from that of the ungodly? It is very difficult to judge the level of social visibility inherent in the view of godliness put forward by Ashton and Chaderton. Even on so central and seemingly clear-cut an issue as conformity it is extremely difficult to pin Chaderton down. Ashton was similarly guarded. He certainly produced what appeared to be resounding statements of puritan principle: 'Whatsoever we do ought to have his warrant out of the scripture', he claimed.[101] This had a particular application to

the worship of God after his own commandment...otherwise he accepteth it not (Hos. 8.13, Mal. 1.7,8) and for this cause he prescribeth particulars in his worship and service even the matter of the altar and manner of making the same (Exod. 20.24,25, I Sam. 13.9,13).

Accordingly Ashton asserted 'our own inventions must not be meddled with God's commandments in his worship (Mal. 1.8)'. These sentiments were given further point by Ashton's claim that 'the commandment of the Prince is good religion to the wicked'.[102] Add to this his caveat that simple obedience is not always to be given to his [the magistrate's] commandments seeing that if we do evil we may not thereby be excused before God (Mic. 6.16, Exod. 1.17). Disobedience commended, a wise heart knoweth time when to obey and when not (Eccles. 8.5, I Sam. 22.17).

and Ashton's position appears to offer a perfect rationale for precisian non-conformity.[103] However elsewhere Ashton can be found categorising ceremonies under three heads:

1. legal, which are abolished concerning the letter but remain as concerning the spirit for their truth abideth as the word of God. 2. evangelical as sacraments. 3. indifferent, not forbidden by the word for which we should not condemn another.

Moreover he added that 'legal ceremonies give place where love of thy neighbour hath to deal' and that 'ceremonial and lighter matters have their time when to be done'.[104] In other words such matters were subject to the law of expedience and edification, considerations which, as Chaderton's experience will prove, left the divine ample room for manoeuvre.

Nor is it any easier to pin down the puritan position on more general issues. On these their attitudes were conventional in the extreme. Chaderton and Ashton were, predictably perhaps, proponents of a rigidly hierarchical and static view of the social order. Social peace, Ashton claimed, was a gift of God to those that served him. Civil dissension, on the other hand, was 'the great plague with which God will bring down the enemies of his church'.[105] 'Humana est ordo a deo institutus de rebus administrandis ad humanae vitae sanctitatis felicitatis adiumentum (Gen. 2.15, Col. 2.5).'[106] From this Ashton deduced the duty to obey those set over us by God:

He sendeth none to honour and authority in the commonweal but such as have his gifts to discharge the same (Gen. 41.38)... Resistance to them is no less than against God.[107]

Rebellion to Princes – such shall be punished (Prov. 17.11). Beware of withdrawing thyself from obedience and thy oath (Eccles. 10.20). Grouching and obloquy punished in Miriam with leprosy (Num. 12.20).

Even idolatrous monarchs enjoyed the same standing. 'Zedekiah was punished for rebelling against Nebuchadnezzar (2 Kgs.

28.6,7).'[108] Chaderton too, after his diatribe about avoiding the company of the ungodly, had added a significant caveat – 'none may despise the wicked magistrate, he may despise the sin yet not his person'.[109]

To underwrite this vision both Ashton and Chaderton espoused a severe version of the doctrine of callings:

We must not be ashamed of our calling or condition of life, how base soever it be (Gen. 46.34) but stay therein, lowly without all pride (Prov. 11.2) and not seek to intrude themselves into another.[110]

'Whosoever despise to do the works of their calling in the appointed time they are the greatest sinners condemning themselves.'[111] Ashton posited a society based on condescension from above and deference from below, stressing the tutorial role of the dominant groups:

Husbands and masters ought to take heed they permit no evil for fear of further inconveniences...It is their part and duty to instruct their wives, children and family.[112]

Elsewhere Ashton outlined the reciprocal duties of masters and servants: on the servants' part obedience and loyalty, on the masters' lenience and the reward of faithful service. (In the process he pointed out that 'the godly servant is most profitable to his master'.)[113]

Similarly Ashton could recommend the correction of children by their parents as a model for social relations in general. 'Correction' was 'profitable for others either at their parents' hands or by the voice of the minister'.[114] At the head of this essentially patriarchal hierarchy of instruction and correction stood, of course, the magistrate. His duty was to preserve social peace through the impartial application of the law, the repression of crime and the defeat of external threats. But over and above these secular tasks he had a duty 'to observe the laws of God'[115] for which he was given the authority 'to deal in ecclesiastical causes'.[116] More generally he was 'to resist evil...and to punish the wicked'. He was in harder cases to follow 'the direction of the priest (Deut. 17.9,10,11); for this the priests meditate in God's law that he may judge wisely (Josh. 1.8)'.[117]

In the face of this model of an integrated society Ashton deprecated those sins and failings that were most likely to undermine this careful equilibrium. Covetousness came in for particular comment:

Covetousness nought in all especially governors for in them covetousness leadeth to oppression, oppression to outrageous dealing...It perverteth judgement (I Sam. 8.3) it causeth lying and procureth plagues (2 Kgs. 5.22,25,27).[118]

Similarly Ashton identified ambition and a desire for honour as a 'provoker to injustice'. 'Ahimelech for this usurped without right (Judg. 9.2,6)...Saul cared as much for honour amongst the people as for the favour of God (1 Sam. 15.30).' He went on to show 'how wicked men seek preferment':

by accusing them of negligence and injustice that be in place, by making fair promises of themselves if they were...outward courtesy and gentleness by bribing, false accusations of others whose state they seek.[119]

In the same vein Ashton explicitly condemned wicked and flattering councillors. 'Good and godly council' on the other hand was 'not to be condemned'. 'Good and aged councillors are to be harkened unto and not dismissed as did Rehoboam (1 Kgs. 12.8).'[120]

In 1579 Chaderton had echoed these sentiments. 'Where be those parents and masters', he asked,

which do teach in their families unto their children and servants the law and fear of God, walking themselves in the midst of their houses in uprightness of heart. And where be those governors to defend the fatherless and widow that receive no bribe to corrupt justice, that prolong not the sentence for lucre sake, that respect no persons in judgement and that are ready also without regard of fear or favour of men to cut off the workers of iniquity from the city of the Lord and to establish the seat of the faithful.[121]

Similarly, when in 1579 Chaderton had been discoursing on the judgements of God visited upon the sins of England, he had come at last to the plague at that time raging in London. He thereupon called both the mayor and the bishop to co-operate in 'a general and public fast according to the commandment of God and the necessity of this present time'.[122] Here, then, was the puritan view of the social order. True religion was to be brought to the people, the social order sanctified, through the conversion of the leaders of society from the level of the individual household to local and national magistrates. Both spiritual and secular leaders were to co-operate in the task of leading the community to repentance and godliness. In the particular instance of the plague in London in 1579, it was only after the failure of the bishop and the mayor to respond to this signal judgement of God that Chaderton turned to the spiritual self-help of the godly. He admonished 'everyone privately both to use this [fastings] and all other good means to turn from us and this city all those punishments which our sins have most righteously deserved.'[123]

This is typical of the puritan impulse. The social norms embedded in puritan thought were entirely conventional. They might be pressed with a peculiarly intense moral force, but that aside the only impact that Ashton or Chaderton's puritanism had on their social thought was that limitation (in itself highly ambiguous) on the duty to obey the higher powers, cited above. This should not surprise us. Certainly it need not call into question the status of the puritan outlook as a free-standing view of the world. For what was important about puritanism was not the external forms, the social categories that the puritans used, but the religious experience that structured their priorities and shaped their attitudes while they themselves yet remained wedded to those conventional forms and categories.

Here a central role was played by the linked concepts of Satan, the world and the flesh. According to Ashton it was against these that 'the battle which the godly fight' was waged. But what did Ashton mean precisely by these last two terms? 'The weakness of man's nature is called flesh. Cursed is he that trusts in men and maketh flesh his arm.'[124] The wicked were pictured as almost entirely enslaved to the flesh:

Wicked men make no spare of anything to satisfy their lust... Carnal pleasure the Lord as it were forbade in challenging from me the fat (Lev. 3.17). The lusts of the flesh fight against the soul (I Pet. 2.11).

Lust is blind and without all judgement...crafty, impudent and untrue.[125]

Hence the consequences of lust were 'to be deceived, to be weakened, to fall into the enemies' hand'.[126]

As for the 'world', by this Ashton appeared to mean in certain contexts simply terrestrial existence itself, with all the limitations and corruptions implied by that:

All worldly things are passing from one stay to another and God only is immutable. The sun goeth daily to his setting, the wind driveth away and the rivers fall into the sea.[127]

More specifically Ashton used the term to refer to the insertion of the godly into the hierarchies and structures of human social life. Hence 'the love of the world' was

an hinderer in the proceedings of religion. Nicodemus is thy example who durst not for fear of losing his place defend the innocency of Christ (John. 7.50,51).[128]

Nicodemus' failure of nerve was a product of fear – fear of 'the loss of his credit and favour amongst the pharisees' and 'the loss of his place and dignity'.[129] Elsewhere Ashton discoursed on the spiritual dangers of prosperity:

Prosperity breedeth pride (Deut. 8.14) and pride forgetfulness (Deut. 31.20). Assurance of our estate breedeth contempt of God (2 Chr. 7.12) and prosperity disobedience (Neh. 9.25,26,28).[130]

Chaderton similarly discoursed on the reasons why 'a rich man shall not enter into the kingdom of God'. The reason was not simply the fact of his wealth but

in the disposition of the person that is rich, for a natural man having riches cannot but abuse them by resting in them and by the carnal disposition of his soul. No marvel though it be hard for them to enter because the kingdom of heaven is not of this world but they are of this world. And it is a kingdom of humiliation, and a kingdom of suffering affliction in which a rich man cannot enter. The kingdom of God is a kingdom of righteousness but the rich man he is given over to unrighteousness. The kingdom of God is a kingdom of peace with God but the rich man he doth not seek peace with God and it is a kingdom of peace with men but these rich men are full of malice. The kingdom of God is altogether a spiritual kingdom. Now the natural rich man that hath never tasted of the spirit can not have any affinity with it. The rich man is further off of the kingdom of God in respect of his riches than is the poor man in respect of his poverty. For he speaketh this in comparison. The mariners in Jonas' ship void of the fear of God yet they crave of the

Lord's mercy so that the state of adversity is more near unto God. Nebuchadnezzar that proud monarch of the world did never confess the Lord til his time of adversity.[131]

But 'the world' was more than a mere distraction, an insidious net of preoccupations and attachments, waiting to ensnare the unwary. There was a natural opposition between the people of God and the people of this world. The godly could expect nothing from this world but hatred and persecution. Hence Christ had told his disciples

that the world should not persecute them for their vices or for their ill behaviour or for any unjust cause but for a most just cause namely for Christ his own name sake, for his goodness, for his truth and for his justifying and redeeming all mankind.[132]

The forces of the world and the flesh thus opposed to the godly were summed up in the person of Satan. He was 'the prince of this world'. All those who sin 'are the instruments of Satan seeing that all injuries done to the children of God do proceed from Satan'. Hence, when Satan had come against Christ he had come not himself but in the 'persons of those in whose souls he reigned, Judas, Pilate and the high priests'.

Now the government of the prince of this world consisteth not only in governing but also in binding and ensnaring men. By world is to be understood all manner of men [except] such men as God hath taken from the kingdom of Satan. The reason is because all men by nature are the children of Satan not saints of God...As Christ is the saviour of mankind so is Satan the destroyer of all mankind and therefore he is called the prince of the world.[133]

Now Chaderton went to considerable lengths to prove the objective existence of Satan. Many imagined, he claimed, that the devil was a mere 'foul cogitation of the mind'. But that was quite wrong. For in scripture the

holy ghost doth attribute to the devil these actions going, coming, moving from place to place, persuading men to injure Job and to kill his children, so that thereby it appeareth that we must not imagine (as many do) that the devil is only a foul cogitation of the mind because no cogitation can be said to go from place to place.

In addition to the testimony of scripture the existence of the devil could be proved from everyday experience:

First, if a man shall examine his own heart he shall find that he is continually tempted of Satan to do those things which his own conscience telleth him are unlawful. Secondly, if we consider the manifold hatred which is between man and man, yea man and wife, brother and brother, father and child we shall find that all these proceed from the regiment of Satan which he hath over mankind. True it is that mankind's nature is weak and prone to sin yet for a man to commit sins against his own nature it must needs proceed from Satan.

Thirdly, 'seeing it is certain that there is a unity of the deity', the multiplicity of god's worshipped throughout the world could only be attributed to the malice of Satan, deliberately leading man to destruction. 'Besides this the horrible superstition which is in the world could not possibly be invented by the wit of man without the help of the devil.'[134] In short, Satan was behind all the myriad assaults made upon the godly in this world.

The result of all this was an almost Manichaean view of the world. As Christ was our redeemer, so Satan was bent on man's destruction. So close was the parallel between these two opposite poles, implied Chaderton, that to deny the existence of Satan was but the first step on the road to atheism. For not to be totally and unequivocally against Satan was to be for him.

For if the spirit of God doth command us to hate the evil which is in us much more doth the spirit of God command us to hate the devil which doth always oppose himself both against God and men and whosoever doth not hate the devil it is evident that he doth consort with the devil and that he is of the devil and that the devil is his father.[135]

The individual was confronted by a cosmic struggle between Christ and Satan, good and evil, darkness and light; a struggle in which he had to choose sides.

By the kingdom of light is meant that power which the son of God hath over all the saints of God, the which power Satan always goeth about to pull down.

This stark choice was invoked by puritan preachers to stir up the godly to a renewed zeal in the cause of true religion. The threat of hell fire, especially prepared for Satan and his devils, lent a certain urgency to these exhortations.

If Satan be nothing but a kingdom of darkness it behoveth everyone to hate and abhor these works of darkness. Satan's kingdom is a kingdom of lying, stealing, murdering, whoring and such like and therefore it standeth everyone in hand which will avoid the kingdom of darkness to shun all these and such like sins; we must therefore try and examine ourselves if we have not the works of darkness it is well and yet it is not well enough for we must go further and have the works of light.[136]

But the precise nature of this zeal was ambiguous. For instance Chaderton's contention that in negotiating the toils of this world wealth was a positive disadvantage has already been cited. The result, however, was hardly a radical repudiation of material prosperity. Ashton took up the same point:

The benefits of adversity bridleth a poor man from doing evil (Prov. 10.15) but extreme poverty sometimes causeth stealing and taking of the name of God in vain (Prov. 30.9) 'ergo mediocritas est optima'.[137]

This last remark was typical of a central strain in the puritan world-view. For the godly were not to respond to the obvious tension between their commitment to true religion and their social environment – and indeed their own instincts – by a campaign of simple repression and rejection waged against the world and the flesh. On the contrary, in such matters puritan stress was placed on the need for moderation. Hence Ashton remarked that 'a godly mind is contented with sufficiency of all things necessary'.[138] In mourning the dead Ashton remarked that 'it is lawful for the godly to mourn in measure therein', adding however that 'the heathen were more excessive in this than the godly'.[139] In more mundane matters Ashton commanded 'sobriety in meat and drink':

It is a good means to help in the service and religion of God (Dan. 1.8) for Daniel calleth excessive fare to defile himself and Nebuchadnezzar offered the same unto them as a way to draw them from their religion. After excessive drinking Lot fell into horrible incest (Gen. 19.33,35).

It was, Ashton concluded, dangerous 'not to refrain the appetite'. However, as he swiftly added, 'all meats are lawful modo moderate'.[140] Ashton, then, could scarcely be accused of an excessive asceticism. Having commended fasting as a means of humbling 'thyself before God' he went on to explain that in itself 'fasting deserveth nothing toward God'. As if to underline the extent of man's spiritual freedom in these matters, Ashton went on to expound the lawfulness of feasts in the celebration of marriages, or more generally to mark the defeat of God's enemies. He even listed the 'feasts appointed by God to be solemnly observed among the Israelites'.[141]

Typically the prime concern was not with the external action, what was eaten or when it was eaten, but with the spiritual state that informed the action. Hence Ashton remarked, 'lusting for that which God hath not exhibited unto us always evil having other sufficient'.[142] It was this that prompted his later remark that 'daintiness' was 'a great fault and severely punished' and that 'sober diet and simple fare with God's blessing is as able to feed as the most dainty dishes'.[143]

A similar moderation was to be exercised in responding to the claims of the world. Here Chaderton cited the example of the woman who asked Christ to appoint her two sons to positions of pre-eminence in his kingdom. Certainly she showed a touching faith in the imminence and the reality of that kingdom but, argued Chaderton, her request

betrayeth her great worldliness which is a great infirmity and common to all parents. She loved her children more in the flesh than in the spirit. She betrayeth her ignorance of the kingdom of Christ, errors both in the state of her sons and the kingdom of Christ when she would have them change the state of their callings...Let us therefore see that our petitions be suitable to the calling in the which the Lord hath placed us. Here they betray an infirmity that they being placed in the spiritual kingdom look for a worldly kingdom. So let us learneth by these to content ourselves in that calling in which the Lord hath placed us, for as the hand is not to meddle with seeing or the eye with handling so we must not go further than our calling will permit us.[144]

Indeed, since the cause of the fall of Satan (and to an extent that of Adam) had been a product of the drive to transcend the spiritual position or estate in which God had placed them, Chaderton argued that the godly should beware of any dissatisfaction with the calling or gifts which God had bestowed on them:

Seeing the devil misliking his estate came to ruin we ought to learn to take heed that the devil do not draw us to mislike our estate which God hath put upon us for if we be drawn to this it is to be feared that we fall from God as the devil did.

The need for vigilance was acute since man was a naturally restless and envious creature, and the devil was constantly at work, playing on these impulses.[145]

Professor Collinson has noted this puritan stress on moderation (albeit in a slightly different context). He attributes it to the wholesale importation into the reformed tradition of the Aristotelian concept of the golden mean. He then goes on to contrast this stress on moderation with what he takes to be the conventional view of puritan zeal.[146] However if we examine Ashton's position this stress on moderation can be found subsisting next to an equally strong insistence on the need for zeal:

They which be zealous of God's glory hearing that their brethren have gone after strange Gods must seek them and enquire after the truth and slay them (Deut. 13.13)...Nine tribes and a half prepare them to battle against the two who had built an altar as they thought to worship on which would be a mean to bring in idolatry to the dishonour of God's name (Josh. 22.12).

Admittedly, Ashton added that

the true zeal of God's glory is with advice and prudent discretion. The nine tribes and a half afore they took revenge of their building the altar which seemeth to bring another worship than was in Shiloh sent ambassadors to expostulate with them and to learn the truth of the matter for what end they set it up (Josh. 22.13).

There can, however, be no doubting the intensity of Ashton's concept of zeal. Under the heading 'defects in zeal' he cited Asa 'for deposing only and not putting his grandmother to death (2 Chr. 15.13,16)'.[147]

It could be argued that all the objects against whom such zeal was to be directed were idolators. Ashton's examples were nearly all taken from the Old Testament and involved a clear-cut apostacy from the true God of the Jews to some other deity. Since this was the plainest and most heinous offence imaginable against the majesty of God, a certain extremity of response was perhaps understandable. However the position was hardly as clear-cut as that. The puritan concept of idolatry was not a well-defined analytical tool. As Ashton himself observed, 'under

idolatry and vain confidence in men all other sins are contained'.[148] Indeed, the concept came to imply the preference of
any secular or worldly aim before the worship of God. Hence it
is by no means clear whether the sort of militant zeal described
and endorsed here by Ashton should be limited to the repression
of apostates and idolators (most obviously of papists), or whether
it should be extended to include that much vaguer category, the
ungodly.[149]

And so we are back to that central ambiguity concerning the
precise nature of the divide between the godly and the wicked.
It was this ambiguity that provided the key to the puritan position. Certainly it enables us to integrate that stress on moderation
discussed here into an enlarged and deepened concept of zeal.
For despite the intensity of their insistence on a division between
the godly and the ungodly both Chaderton and Ashton agreed
that such a division could never, in this life, be final. For in this
life the righteous were inextricably mixed with the wicked, indeed
such contact formed a central part of God's design for his people.
'The wicked are to keep them in continual exercise (Gen.
12.1,21,22). They are to prove our faith.' Similarly, Chaderton
remarked that

in the militant and visible church, the field floor and net of the Lord
there are not only sincere and faithful but also hypocritical and
faithless worshippers of God, not only upright and constant doers
of the word, but also vain and idle talkers of the same; finally not
only such as with good consciences, pure hearts and faith unfeigned
do serve the Lord and his church but such also as be reprobate to
every good work whose end is to be cast eternally from the presence
of God and to be burned as chaff in the fearful furnace of God's
wrath and everlasting indignation.[150]

Likewise, neither Satan nor his acolyte Antichrist could be
finally destroyed until the last day. There always had been and
always would be devils, hypocrites and false believers to tempt
and destroy the godly until God consigned them once and for all
to destruction in eternal hell fire.[151] Hence the godly had to live
in constant tension with Satan, the world and the flesh. They
could never, in this life, finally escape from them since these
temptations were locked into the basic structures of human social
life. The doctrine of callings outlined above made a virtue of
this necessity. But if withdrawal from temptation was not a

possibility and the godly had to live in this world, they were not to live of it. They had to fulfil their secular duties with a will, but they were not to view their lives in primarily secular terms.

The insistence on moderation was a product of this position. On this view, rather than the exercise of some 'classical' virtue tacked onto the reformed tradition, puritan moderation was the product of a real battle between extremes and the only means by which the tension between complete submergence in the world and complete withdrawal from it could be controlled. For the calm, distanced moderation envisaged here should be seen as the product of a longstanding, indeed, endless process of self-discipline and sublimation through which the true believer handled and circumvented the temptations strewn before him by Satan. It was, in short, the demonstration of the believer's spiritual freedom in the face of the world. But such a demonstration was not an end in itself. On the contrary, it was at best a holding operation, a preliminary designed to make room in the individual's life for that union with God, through Christ, that had to dominate the thoughts and actions of every believer.

However, enough has been said here to demonstrate that the puritan emphasis on moderation in ethical and social matters can be integrated into a wider definition of zeal against the flesh and the world, albeit a zeal tempered by the knowledge that in this life those two threats could never be definitively defeated but merely controlled and resisted. Such a tension was, of course, typical of the ambiguities and contradictions inherent in the position of the godly, trapped in the world and inextricably mixed with the ungodly.

What are at stake here are not logical contradictions, but divergent tendencies and a certain resulting ambiguity and tension. For logically all the positions outlined in the previous sections were compatible when viewed within the context of the wider Calvinist position. It was quite possible for the godly, in this life, to gather together against the forces of Satan, the world and the flesh and to achieve a certain measure of separation from the wicked. It was just that in this life such a separation could never be definitive. Similarly, the godly could sometimes hope for, and sometimes achieve, piecemeal victories over their idolatrous enemies. But again those victories could never be complete in this life. The final separation from the ungodly, the final victory over Antichrist, could only come in the next world.[152] Certainly it was this final victory and separation that provided the aim of the puritan quest. But the other-worldliness of that final aim did not prevent its providing a model or paradigm for earlier victories, deliverances and separations here on earth. And often, as we have seen, puritan rhetoric tended rather to blurr that distinction. Hence the basically spiritual, other-worldly vision inherent in puritan religion should not blind us to the sharply critical attitude adopted by puritanism in its confrontation with contemporary social reality. Neither should it allow us to see puritanism, only, or primarily, as an attempt to transform contemporary society. Even to conceive of the problem in those terms is to perpetuate a false dichotomy. Rather on this issue there was an unresolved tension within the puritan world-view, a tension that is almost *the* defining characteristic of that world-view.

The theological resolution of these tensions, crudely summarised above, was based on the Calvinist doctrine of predestination. Now this doctrine of predestination provides the essential frame of reference without which much of the position expounded by both Ashton and Chaderton cannot be understood. The discussion of its role in underpinning their discourse has been delayed until now precisely because it did not play a central, organising role in either of the two works under discussion. This is not to say that either Chaderton or Ashton was ashamed of his predestinarian theology. Neither tried to hide it: it is clear from the works under discussion that both men held the orthodox, supralapsarian position, outlined by Whitaker.[153] It is just that neither organised his discourse around the doctrine of predestination.

Nevertheless, the doctrine remains central to an understanding of many of the issues raised in the present study. It was, of course, the division between the elect and the reprobate, grounded on God's double decree made before the foundation of the world, that underwrote the distinction between the godly and the ungodly that was so central to the puritan position. It provided the objective basis for Ashton's assurance that 'God will always have a remnant'; his absolute conviction that, whatever the appearances to the contrary, God was in fact caring for his people. We have already examined the way in which, Ashton maintained, God always used the failings of the godly (often failings they shared with the wicked) to their eventual spiritual advantage. The logical concomitant of that was that their status as godly people came not from their own behaviour or qualities but from some prior relation with God, and that that relation proceeded from their status as members of his elect.[154] Similarly, Ashton could maintain that the 'optima impiorum opera' were 'abominable even those which are done with the best mind'.[155] Again, their status as ungodly persons had logically to proceed from some cause prior to their own behaviour, and in their case that prior cause was provided by the decree of reprobation. To take another instance, Ashton's contention that, while the godly and the ungodly might both fall prey to a carnal security, the godly would always emerge unscathed, was but a particular application of the doctrine (defended by the Cambridge Calvinists in 1595/6) that members of the elect could fall from grace neither finally nor totally.[156]

However, if the doctrine of predestination provided objective roots for the divide between the godly and the wicked, it also ensured that puritan attitudes to that divide could be nothing if not ambiguous. For it was not permissible simply to transfer the division between the elect and the reprobate to contemporary social reality. Only God knew the identity of his elect and to anticipate the final revelation of his will would have been a heinous offence against his sovereign liberty. It was this that produced the intense ambiguity in the puritan attitude to the community of the godly that we have outlined above.

It was an ambiguity compounded by both Ashton's and Chaderton's language. They both seldom referred to the elect and hardly ever to the reprobate. Far more commonly they referred to the godly and the ungodly, the wicked and the righteous. For both, it would seem, were wedded to the language of voluntarism. Hence, Ashton spoke of 'the fruit and benefit of our obedience' and quoted Isaiah 48.18,19: 'O that thou hadst harkened to my commandments then had thy prosperity been as the flood and thy righteousness as the waves of the sea.'[157] 'The threatenings of God are ever with a condition...If the condition be not taken they are most certain and inevitable and without all doubting.'[158] God, it appeared, made demands on men and then responded according to the extent of their obedience. Even the presence or absence of faith Ashton appeared to attribute to the individuals involved:

For that Moses and Aaron did not believe the Lord saying he would bring water out of the rock and in this dishonouring him before the rebellious people, they were debarred from entering into the land of Canaan.[159]

The implication was clear: Moses and Aaron could have acted differently and had they done so God's response would have altered accordingly. Similarly, in condemning the deliberate refusal of the pharisees to acknowledge Christ, Chaderton denounced the sins of pride and self-love, which led them thus to harden their hearts, in a way which implied that they had some choice in the matter and in an exhortatory context designed to persuade his audience to avoid such sins themselves.[160]

But both Chaderton and Ashton were orthodox Calvinists and there were certain contradictions between the assumptions apparently underlying the statements cited above and basic elements in the Calvinist position. Speaking of 'the fruit and benefit of our obedience', Ashton remarked that 'obedience to God [is] voluntary'.[161] Yet later he admitted that 'God's calling is effectual to make obedience thereto'.[162] Similarly, under the heading 'an exhortation to come to Christ', Ashton cited scriptural texts like Isaiah 55.1, 'everyone that thirsteth cometh ye to the waters and ye that hath no silver come buy and eat'.[163] Chaderton dangled a similar prospect before his audience:

Never any were frustrate of their expectation which follow Christ, for he is now ready to give them life. Although they had no justifying faith yet because they had a liking of him he would not make them frustrate.[164]

Yet later in the same passage Ashton asserted that 'none come without drawing'.[165] 'God prepareth the heart to desire and then harkeneth thereto.'[166] Yet this did not prevent Ashton from appearing to exhort the true believer to 'give God thy heart'.[167] Even the stress on 'how greatly the Lord detesteth sin' and the concomitant notion of God responding to human frailty had to be modified. For

God's punishments are not always alike to offenders in the same things. The Jews sinned more than Sodom (Ezek. 16.48) and yet were not so strangely consumed. The reason of this inequality of punishment set down in the v.30 I took them away as pleased me.[168]

There seemed, therefore, to be a basic contradiction between the voluntarist rhetoric employed by both Ashton and Chaderton and the theological presuppositions that underlay it. Now to an extent these contradictions have to be accepted. Indeed, it may well be argued that their presence in Ashton's and Chaderton's work merely reflects their fidelity to the insights and tensions contained in scripture. Certainly it is no part of my present purpose to iron out their position into a consistent whole. For the fundamental question at stake here was that concerning the relation between man's free will and God's providence. How, in a universe so dominated and determined by God, could sin be explained by man without at least appearing to hold God responsible for it? The problem arose at its starkest in Chaderton's discussion of Satan's fall and subsequent role in the divine plan. Thus, in order to avoid a lapse into pure Manichaeism and to redeem the liberty and omnipotence of God, he needed to argue that Satan and his devils acted only when and as God permitted; that in all their doings they acted simply as instruments of God's will. Hence, when Satan came 'of purpose to take Christ yet God had determined and ordained it before'. Similarly, in the case of Job, Satan only took away his goods, 'he could not destroy Job's body having not power of God to do it'.[169] Yet at the same time Chaderton wanted to argue that

the wickedness that is in Satan proceedeth only from himself that is from the freedom of his own will. We must not then think that the wickedness in Satan proceedeth from his creator which was God who is goodness itself. For God did make the devil the goodliest in wisdom, power and knowledge of all his creatures and therefore it is great blasphemy to think that the wickedness of Satan proceeded from his creator especially seeing the scripture also teacheth us that it proceedeth only from the abuse of his own will.[170]

Of course these two positions were extraordinarily difficult to reconcile. On the one hand Chaderton argued that while Satan's fall (or Adam's or indeed Christ's death and Judas' role in it) were all part of the divine plan, laid down before the foundation of the world, yet, on the other hand, Satan acted out his part in that plan for reasons of his own (broadly speaking because of his initial desire to rival or surpass the honour of God and, after his fall, because of his malice and hatred toward mankind). That presumption and malice stemmed directly from the evil of his own nature, an evil created by the exercise of his own free will. On this view 'there is no cause that God permitting Satan to sin is to be blamed for that God's permitting him did not corrupt Satan'.[171] Summing up his attitude on this point (in the more congenial context of Christ's willing obedience to his father) Chaderton concluded 'the providence of God doth not frustrate the will of man nor the will of man take away the providence of God'.[172]

It was, however, undeniable that God could have prevented Satan from falling if he had chosen to do so. Did that not render him culpable? Here Chaderton had recourse to the liberty and sovereignty of God's will, defined in terms of his complete freedom from any of the laws, divine or natural, that bound men in similar situations:

True it is if a man do not hinder his neighbours from sinning if it be in his power he is greatly to blame because man by the law of nature is bound to do the same yet is not God therefore to be blamed because he did not hinder the fall of Satan when he could because there is no such law to bind God to do the like in that he is creator of all.[173]

As Chaderton remarked elsewhere:

there are two kinds of sufferers one which is above all law absolutely free and this is God himself. God suffering one to commit sin sinneth not because he is not bound to permit. The other sufferer is man. He is bound to the law and therefore mans permission is evil.[174]

But Chaderton did not leave it there. 'God', he continued,

did permit Satan to sin because God is of that infinite power and wisdom that he is no less able to glorify his majesty by the sins of the world either in Satan or in men then by the obedience of the righteous. Lastly, God suffered Satan to fall because he had so decreed and determined in his everlasting decree from eternity so to put the keeping or losing of salvation in the hands of the devil that if he would himself he might either keep that estate or lose it.[175]

Ashton's treatment of these issues echoed that of Chaderton. 'Freedom', he wrote,

is a thing properly pertaining to will whereby voluntary appetite without foreign coaction it may will either good or evil but to will good cometh of grace, which maketh to will and to do. Freedom is an activity of reason and will whereby good is chosen by the assistance of grace and evil if grace be absent.

Free will, therefore, was to be found 'in God chiefly',

whose will is of itself simply and absolutely most free from all bondage of sinning and infection of sin not because any force restraineth him but because of his own nature he cannot so will; so that God is both holy of necessity and yet this necessity doth not seclude free will from God...[176]

Passages such as these amounted to little more than restatements, rather than resolutions, of the issues involved. However such theoretical treatments of these issues were relatively few and far between in the main texts under discussion. Their presence is enough to show that puritan divines were neither afraid nor embarrassed to confront the implications of their exalted view of the providence and will of God. But their relative scarcity also shows that such discussions, unsurprisingly, did not play a central part in their practical divinity.

However these issues and tensions, while they might resist effective theoretical resolution, could still be used by puritan ministers to provide the central spiritual dynamic for their style of practical divinity. Protestant religion had two sides to it: firstly the objective realm of doctrinal truth, and secondly the subjective religious experience undergone by the godly in their internalisation of those truths. The doctrines of predestination and the providence of God belonged unequivocally to that first category; and they provided the objective basis for the existence of a true church and a godly community in the world. But while it was clear that such a group existed, it was by no means as clear precisely who belonged to it. In this life the answer to that question could never be definitive and hence could not belong to that same realm of objective doctrinal truth. Scripture, after all, did not comprise a roll call of the elect. Scripture did provide, however, a basic corpus of right doctrine and any number of examples of godly behaviour based on those doctrines. It was the task of the preacher to provide the link between the objective and subjective levels in protestant religion by presenting those doctrines and examples in the most persuasive way possible.

Puritan practical divinity centred around the exploitation of the gap, the anxiety-filled rift, that separated those two levels. This was done by a subtle shift of perspective from the objective basis provided by the doctrine of predestination to the situation of the individual believer confronted by the knowledge that some men were elect and others reprobate and yet denied an answer to the key question of his own status relative to those two groups. The preacher thereupon confronted the believer with a description of the objective characteristics of a godly or elect person. But in the final analysis the individual's position depended on his own view of himself, on his own choice of whether fully to internalise and appropriate those qualities or not. Hence we have already seen Chaderton informing his audience of the difference between a 'judiciary' and a 'castigatory' visitation or affliction from God. The one belonged to the reprobate, the other to the elect. The difference between those two types of affliction and the two groups towards whom they were directed belonged to the realm of objective doctrinal truth. But, from the perspective of the individual believer, whether an affliction was judiciary or castigatory depended entirely on how he allowed it to affect his attitudes and behaviour. He could choose to view it as a warning or punishment from God and amend his life accordingly. If he did so choose it was presumably castigatory and there was a presumption that he was elect; if he did not there was an equal presumption that it was judiciary and he was reprobate. When directed to other people such judgements were obviously provisional (although they clearly formed the basis for that practical distinction between the godly and the ungodly that both Chaderton and Ashton habitually made); but seen existentially (once the initial decision had been taken to perceive his life in these terms and so long as he contrived to sustain that vision in the face of rival interpretations and despite whatever sufferings he might undergo), such considerations allowed the individual believer to regard himself as saved; his elect status was vindicated.

To take another example, Chaderton expounded at length on the text 'many are called but few are chosen'. Here Chaderton distinguished between two different sorts of calling:

1. the calling of the minister of God. 2. of God himself... The second calling is the voice and calling of God himself which is

applied to the inward ear of the inward man. This kind of calling is the proper and peculiar office of God himself and of his spirit...

Since many are called not only the good but the bad we must not content ourselves with this outward calling concluding thereby that we are in a good case but to seek further till we obtain to that gift that shall never forsake thee.[177]

Again, that second calling, the calling of God himself, can be taken as the prerogative of his elect, and the believer who felt he had attained to that, as long as he took no credit for that attainment himself, had achieved a powerful validation of his status as an elect vessel of God.

Moreover, since all true faith and knowledge was seen as a direct gift of God even the smallest impulse toward true belief could be interpreted as a sign of elect status and hence be elevated at once from the level of subjective impulse to objective proof. The psychological mechanism at work here was fairly clear-cut. 'Some may say', said Chaderton,

if the Lord will not hear their prayers why should not they surcease to pray until such time as they have faith. No for how knoweth thou when the Lord will hear them and grant them faith therefore thou must continually pray even in the day of thine anguish and those that do thus they shall not find their prayers to be in vain, even from their infancy.[178]

In this way the very impulse toward God became a sign of God's presence and the capacity to pray a comfort in itself. Not that the first impulse toward God could be equated with a proper justifying faith. On the contrary, Chaderton implied there were several stages through which a believer might pass before achieving or rather receiving such a faith. Even before a full justifying faith was achieved a consciousness of, and a penitence for, sin, expressed in a turning to God in prayer, would win a merciful response from the Lord.[179] Similarly a simple historical faith – for instance the mere acknowledgement of Christ's divinity, devoid of any application of such doctrine to the self – could be regarded as a step on the road to a proper justifying faith.

This historical faith is a preparation to receive the justifying faith ...For whatsoever we may know concerning the will of God, that may grow by the consideration of his works.[180]

But Chaderton went further. 'Of justifying faith there are two sorts', he wrote:

The first is a weak faith...which is an unfeigned desire of reconciliation with God, with a loathing of sin which is the cause that he which hath this faith desireth reconciliation.

Such a weak faith was subject to many failings; for instance

1. where knowledge faileth. 2. where the apprehension of God's promises faileth as in the Apostles when Christ asked them who he was which wanted knowledge of his resurrection and ascension. Also it is called weak faith which faileth in apprehension of God's promises for many good Christians cannot say with good consciences 'my sin is pardoned'. But yet he is not to be said to want faith. A man may be saved by this faith, for this faith will apprehend Christ as truly as a stronger faith though not so strongly...This faith is but for a time and will be stronger afterwards. The second is a strong faith when a man hath great knowledge and also strong apprehension of Christ. This faith cometh not at the first but is only in corrupt man in part. For this good apprehension ariseth out of the observation and experience of God's favour and love, yet this faith is imperfect. Neither can a man have perfect faith because he can never have perfect knowledge, therefore a man shall always have some doubt of salvation and they have no faith which never doubted of their salvation.[181]

Chaderton had thus set up a progression through various stages of spiritual development, each of which, if the individual were in possession of a true faith, would inevitably lead on to the next. And so the zealous searcher after a true justifying faith was led through a series of self-fulfilling prophecies.

However, always in the back of his mind there was that nagging doubt as to his own spiritual status. 'They have no faith which never doubted of salvation' Chaderton had said, and since faith could never be perfect there was always room for that seed of doubt which incessantly threatened to stand between the subjective experience of the believer and the objective reality of the decree of election. Moreover, much of the spiritual dynamic enjoyed by the puritan style of divinity stemmed from the exploitation of that doubt by puritan preachers. For while on one view the merest impulse toward God could be seen as a sign of true belief, a genuine gift of the spirit working within the individual soul, on another, as Chaderton had observed, 'many are called but few are chosen'. The line between true belief and hypocrisy was a thin one. Chaderton rubbed the point home:

The wicked may willingly hear, understand, joyfully receive and profess the word, yea endure for a season and falsely persuade themselves to believe...Again they may abstain from evil and do the outward works of charity whereby they seem very righteous unto men as did the scribes and pharisees;...They may be lightened with the knowledge of the truth taste of the heavenly gift and the good word of God and the powers of the world to come and be made partakers of the holy ghost and yet fall from the grace received; finally they may suffer banishment and persecution for the outward profession of the truth, yea they may do all the outward works in serving God and helping their neighbour, which the godly do, but when the question shall be demanded of Christ who indeed and in truth is his brother, sister and mother he will answer – 'whosoever shall do my father's will which is in heaven'.[182]

How in such circumstances could the individual be sure of his spiritual status? It was the need to reach that certainly that provided the internal spiritual dynamic of puritan religion. For in such a situation no true believer could rest content with those initial stirrings of faith. He was compelled to push on up the path of spiritual development outlined by Chaderton. Indeed, the very fact that his faith must in this life remain imperfect provided a further incentive as the individual strove to distinguish his profession from that of the wicked and the hypocritical believer.

As George Estye claimed in some lectures delivered during the 1590s, such a growth in grace was a distinguishing mark of a true faith. True faith was an active faith:

As it is impossible that if there be the sun there should not be light and where there is fire there should not be heat so impossible is it that where true faith is there should not be a lively operation of the same comforting the hearts of them in whom it is, for faith is such a thing as cannot suffer a man to be idle. Here we may learn whether the examination which a man hath of himself is true examination. If the man do not labour to go forward to increase his faith it is an evident token though he seem to himself to have faith and to examine himself rightly yet he doth it not as he should do. Shall his faith save him, as if he should say shall such a faith which maketh him idle save him, surely it is so far from saving him that it is the readiest way to bring him to condemnation. The chiefest thing to be learned is that we always seek and labour for such a faith which may not make us idle but which may bring forth sweet and plentiful fruits.

Those 'sweet and plentiful fruits' Estye described as 'good works and actions done according to the will of God'.[183] Good works had a central role to play in this process of differentiation between a true and a false or hypocritical profession. True belief to qualify as true belief had to find an external expression in good works. That had been the basic theme of Chaderton's St Paul's Cross sermon. Ashton summarised 'the use of good works' thus:

1. to assure thee of thy election 2. to testify thy faith to the world and thy obedience to the commandments of God 3. to provoke others to glorify God.[184]

In 1579 Chaderton had concluded that

works are necessarily required not only for doing of the father's will but also for the declaration of our faith, for the confirmation of our hope, for the separating of us from infidels and hypocrites, for the example of those which are without and within the church, for the relieving and succouring of all, especially of those which are of the household of faith, for to justify our religion to be pure and undefiled before God the father.[185]

Works, then, were the means by which true religion entered the social world; they provided the only way in which the subjective experience of true belief could be given external expression and validation, both in the individual's own eyes and those of his fellows.

However, the actions or works were in themselves worthless. Their only value came from their status as the expression of internal spiritual realities. Chaderton had put the point with great force in 1579:

to do the father's will is in faith, hope, love and fear, with all manner of careful watching and perseverance to work those things which he commanded in the law and the word that God thereby may be glorified; for to do the thing commanded and fail in the manner of doing is an half and maimed yea rather no service of God at all; to fail in both is atheism, to fail in the work and yet to boast of the affection of the mind and to be persuaded to have the right manner of doing is carnal liberty and licentious presumption. Contrarily to have and delight in both is sound godliness and pure and undefiled religion, even before God the father.[186]

All of which throws us back to faith:

For it is that gift of the holy ghost which makes God's children careful and studious not only to do the father's will (for that may be after some sort in the reprobate and castaways) but to do it with that assurance of faith, with that steadfastness of hope, with that zeal of his glory, that love of our brethren that reverent fear of his majesty which is commanded to us in the word also which is most convenient and proportionable to such spiritual graces of know-ledge as we have received; of which things carnal professors have little or no care at all. And therefore although they may do the works which God hath decreed to be done for good and necessary purposes yet being void of this right manner of doing they can never do the will of the father as he hath commanded.[187]

It was, however, only too easy, once his spiritual intentions had been externalised in good works, for that externalisation to become fossilised, taken over by other consciousnesses and hence to become valued, as an external observance, in and for itself. To avoid this it was essential for the believer to place no faith in his own works; that way lay perdition. 'What', asked Chaderton,

is the cause that few are chosen? To omit the cause known to himself in us the first cause is that the sins of man are so great that if he should not call us at all yet was he right. But why are not all chosen that are called? Some that are called are of this judgement that they think by their own righteousness to inherit the kingdom of heaven and so are rightly deprived of election. Some although they rely not so much on their works as others yet they rely more upon works than on faith and such was the reason why Paul speaketh against this sort that giveth a second point to merits against whom Paul contendeth that we are justified by faith without the works of the law.[188]

It was this that explains an apparent contradiction in puritan rhetoric. At one moment Ashton could stress the need to obey God's commands and promise that 'righteousness...receiveth a sure reward'.[189] Yet at the next, under the heading 'all men are sinners', he could assert that 'all our righteousness is as filthy clothes'.[190] The point here was not that all men were so tainted with sin that no amount of effort on their part could affect the

degree of their sinfulness. Chaderton distinguished between
original sin and personal sin. Original sin was common to all,
it was 'the mother sin of the world' and none could escape its
effects. The same was not true of personal sins, as Chaderton
maintained:

contrary to the false opinion of some that think that none can live
so but as they must needs commit some personal sins for the word
of God is clean other ways. It is in the power of man to eschew
these actual sins for God will send us his spiritual grace to keep us
from them.[191]

The efforts of the godly in resisting and repressing sin were not
in vain, in a relative sense. It was just that human nature was so
vitiated by sin that before the justice of God it was not possible
to merit salvation. For even after conversion 'there was never
found any man ever so perfectly endued with grace but he
sinned deadly'. Men could be made free from the imputation
of sin, but not from sin itself.[192] 'We must therefore confess our
sins (Dan. 19.20) and be ashamed of them as the church is and
so shall Christ call us to him and show forth his mercy.'[193] This
was not to say that good works did not receive a reward, merely
that such a reward could never be deserved or merited. 'It is not
in vain to serve our God', wrote Chaderton, 'no it is not in vain
to come into the church, there are rewards.' It was just that 'when
we look for a reward we must not look by the eye of our works but
faith, from the last to the first'.[194]

The godly were thus placed in a paradoxical position of having
to produce good works without setting any absolute value on
them. Indeed, the believers realisation of the worthlessness of
works before the justice of God and his confession of his own
corruption were central elements in his profession of true religion.
There was, therefore, a cycle set up whereby the believer sought to
express and validate a necessarily imperfect faith in a series of
good works. These works, however, were themselves similarly
imperfect and, moreover, carried with them the spiritual danger
of presumption and security. This prompted a return to that
reliance upon God, to that faith which had originally produced the
works themselves. Hence Chaderton cited amongst the spiritual
graces necessary for the production of truly acceptable works a
'reverent fear of God'. Such a fear was necessary to break through

that pride, that trust in purely human works that would otherwise impede the believer's progress to a true faith:

Such is the pride of our nature, the dullness of our hearts, and the lack of wisdom that we should behave ourselves presumptuously, securely and rashly before the presence of our heavenly father, were it not for this reverent fear and trembling we have received at his hand.

This fear was not to

proceed from any diffidence or distrust in the accomplishments of God's merciful promises towards us; but rather from a most vehement sorrow and inward feeling bred in our hearts by the earnest consideration of the heavy burden of all our sins and the deep serious weighing of the everlasting wrath of God most justly deserved.[195]

Hence, such a fear should serve to force the believer back on to a total reliance on 'the promises of God concerning eternal life in Christ' to which his faith should be totally directed.[196] But then it was precisely that faith which the believer had sought to express in the production of good works and which still demanded such an expression and validation in the world at large. What was involved here was not an unchanging oscillation between a delusory faith in his own works and a true faith in God, but an upward spiral whereby the true believer without ever, in this life, freeing himself from sin, fought a gradually winning battle against the corruption inherent in his own nature.

The motive force that drove the believer up this spiral of sanctification was provided by the concept of repentance. Hence Ashton outlined 'the fruit of repentance'. This included

humility and mourning, remission of sins (Zech. 13.1), mercy (Col. 3.16). It is itself a sign of sins forgiven (Prov. 16.6, Deut. 30.2,3,4, 5,6,9). The melting of the heart and humbling before God (2 Kgs. 22.19). The confession of the sin and yielding to punishment (I Chr. 21.17, 2 Chr. 32.26).

Hence 'the use of repentance' was to reconcile us again to God, 'to stay his wrath (2 Chr. 12.7, 34.26, 27,28). To move the Lord to mercy.'

But what, asked Ashton, were the causes of repentance? These he divided under the headings 'inward' and 'outward'. The outward causes comprised 'the thundering of God's judgements...

affliction his [God's] lenity and mercifulness....'. The inward causes consisted of the proper internalisation of these outward causes by the individual through 'meditation upon his mercies and curses' and 'remembrance of the forewarnings from God'. Finally Ashton outlined the 'ordo paenitendi'; first came 'believing the prophets', then 'acknowledging of sin, hearty sorrow returning to God tota corde, tota anima, loathing of the former manner of life, hoping and believing in the remission of them, putting away the evil and serving the Lord'.[197]

Here, therefore, described in voluntarist terms, was the individual's journey toward God and a true justifying faith already outlined by Chaderton above. But this mechanism was not a once and for all experience; it was to be repeated at each and every lapse from godly behaviour. It was in this sense that God always employed the faults of his children to their ultimate spiritual advantage since each lapse provided the occasion for a fresh turning to God through a recapitulation of the processes of repentance outlined above.

These processes provide a perfect example of the links between the objective realm of doctrinal truth and the subjective realm of religious belief resulting from the application by the godly of the truths of right doctrine to their own experience. But while such a process of repentance might have been existentially necessary in order for the individual believer to come to a true belief and knowledge of his own elect status, seen from the perspective of Calvinist theory that necessity melted away. For if repentance were elevated into an essential requirement for salvation then the will of God would be seen to be dependent on the will of man. Yet it was a central principle of the Calvinist case, as Chaderton observed, that 'the Lord in his election he only respecteth his own will. For if he should respect our works then it may be thought to be mutable.'[198] Hence, during the Cambridge theological disputes of the 1590s, John Overall can be found arguing that a full repentance was a *sine qua non* for salvation, even in the elect, while his Calvinist opponents were adamant that a member of the elect who died without the least sign of repentance would nevertheless be saved.[199] This is not to argue that the Calvinists held such an eventuality to be usual. As we have seen, puritan divinity assumed that repentance was a central sign of elect status and for the individual believer an existentially necessary step on the road to a true faith. Yet it was necessary to assert that such a situation was logically possible if the sovereign liberty of God's will were to be vindicated from the reliance on man that Overall's position entailed. The difference here was that which separated the rationalist defence of a basic corpus of right doctrine from the delicate balance normally maintained by practical puritan divinity. The puritan position can only be properly understood when these two spheres are taken into full account.

The central link in the chain between God and man that an undue concentration on the formal theology of the Cambridge puritans might lead us to overlook, but which nevertheless stood at the very centre of practical puritan divinity, was provided by the figure of Christ. For Christ was the sole mediator between God and man. 'So that our Saviour Christ is the sole raiser of Lazarus from the grave, so he is the sole raiser of the soul from sin.'[200] He was the only true object for our faith. 'Objectum exaequatum fidei est promissio vitae aeternae in Christo benedictionis per hoc semen.'[201] 'All salvation is only begun, continued and perfected in him.'[202] 'This is the height and depth of the mercy of God. He upon his mere mercy should lose his life for the sheep which was come astray.'[203] It was Christ alone that made up for the failings of our faith. 'Christ will cherish any small measure of faith (Matt. 12.20). If thou canst touch Christ by faith his virtue shall heal thy sore.'[204] 'Fides vincit omnia in Christi sanguine (Rev. 12.11).'[205]

Hence, that search for the true interior calling of God, cited from Chaderton's lectures above, came to be characterised as a search for Christ.[206] Not only was Christ responsible, through his sacrifice on the cross, for our freedom from the imputation of sin, he was also the moving force in our gradual liberation from our own sins, in the process of sanctification. 'Jesus Christ by faith dwelling within us after a spiritual manner and by virtue exerciseth his power within us which is called by the terms of regeneration and sanctification because that by them we become altogether new men.'[207]

In short, Christ personified the merciful, loving impulses of God toward man (or rather toward his elect). As such he provided the positive side of that oscillation between anxiety and assurance that has been described above. The negative side was provided by the law. The complete impossibility of achieving salvation through the law alone was the hammer which drove home the fact of man's corruption to the believer and hence forced him to Christ.

Let us therefore be taught that we never content ourselves with a bare knowledge of the laws without Christ...And this must admonish us to know that which is worthy of knowledge, that is the knowledge of Christ and then we shall find peace of our conscience betwixt God and us.[208]

Chaderton used the enormity of the threat posed by Satan and his superhuman powers of knowledge and persuasion to drive the believer to Christ. Since men 'were overmatched of our enemy in knowledge' 'we are taught to go unto Christ to reconcile ourselves to him and in all our adversities flee unto him that as he hath so we may overcome the devil, for there is no other name under heaven whereby we can be saved'.[209] 'The more infirmities we find in ourselves the rather must we be encouraged to come unto him and then we shall have him ready to offer our petitions with his own hands.'[210] For

all his petitions are meritorious so that God in justice cannot deny them, therefore seeing all his petitions are for us we must have our faith fixed in him, so through him we shall obtain what we desire, so that if Satan tempt thee that thy petitions are doubtful and therefore God will not grant them thou must say that if he weigh them by his law they are worthy to be rejected, but my petitions are Christ's petitions and therefore he heareth them and receiveth them at my hands, through his merits.[211]

Hence Christ provided the ground for the individual believer's assurance of his own salvation.

Nothing shall be able to pluck us out of Christ his hand. This is the promise, for nothing neither the devil, nor the flesh, nor the world shall pluck us out of his hand.

Since therefore that the father of Christ is greater then all then it is impossible that all the creatures should pluck one of his sheep out of his hand. Hereof, therefore, is taught the assurance of our salvation except we should speak this blasphemy that there is one in hell more able to condemn than God is to save. This therefore doth minister great consolation to those that are engrafted into the body of Christ that none is able to disinherit them of the kingdom of God.[212]

This doctrine of assurance provided a central element in the protestant critique of popish doubtfulness – 'the doctrine of the church of Rome that teacheth us to mistrust of our salvation in this life'. Its basis was the doctrine of election. 'Everyone is to labour that there is a certain knowledge to be had of our election in the Lord.' But there was an 'order we are to observe in making it sure, that we must begin at our calling and so ascend to our election. For if we shall begin at our election then we shall never have assurance.'[213] In other words, viewed from the perspective of objective doctrinal truth, or at least abstract doctrinal proof, the root of this assurance was God's decree. But seen existentially the individual believer had to start with the workings of the Spirit within his own breast and ascend via Christ, the only mediator.

There was, of course, no logical contradiction between such an emphasis on Christ and the Calvinist view of predestination. Christ simply provided the ground for the salvation of the elect. Hence Ashton cited God's words, 'behold my servant I will stay upon him mine elect in whom my soul delighteth'.[214] Christ was the 'fundamentum electionis'. 'Christus qui ab aeterno vocatus est a patre ad officium mediatoris (Heb. 5.5, Isaiah 49.1).' 'Electio aeterna and aeternam salutem ad fidem in Christum ad praeceptorum ipsius obedientiam et ad perseverantiam in fide Christi.'[215] According to Chaderton there were 'four causes of our salvation; the efficient cause is the love of God, the material cause is Christ Jesus, the instrumental cause is faith, the final cause is life everlasting'. But while it was true that 'God so loved the world' that 'he gave his only begotten son' for its salvation, Chaderton maintained 'by world are meant the elect of God, not the whole world'.[216]

It has been suggested of the Calvinist divines of the late sixteenth and early seventeenth centuries that their heavy emphasis on the doctrine of predestination seriously disturbed the balance of the earlier Calvinist tradition as it had been handed down from Calvin to Beza.[217] These strictures might well apply to the moderate puritan divines of Cambridge University if their position were to be judged on their formal theological and polemical output alone. But when this is juxtaposed with their style of practical divinity a somewhat different picture emerges.

For while predestination played a central role in their worldview and provided the objective doctrinal basis for many of the major themes and motifs in their thought, they never concentrated on this objective, doctrinal sphere to the exclusion of the subjective realm of individual belief. Puritan religion always retained a very strong experiential bias. Rather than offer to the believer the decree of election as the object towards which his faith should be directed, both Chaderton and Ashton presented instead the figure of Christ. For Christ was to mediate not merely between God and man, but between the objective realm of right doctrine and the subjective realm of true belief.

8

William Whitaker at St John's:
the puritan scholar as administrator

The purpose of this chapter is to examine the career of William Whitaker as Master of St John's College, Cambridge. The controversies and disputes that dogged his regime can be seen, it will be argued, as the result of his reputation as a puritan and his subsequent attempts to impose a distinctively puritan discipline on the college. Under Whitaker St John's was to become a godly seminary similar to the new foundation, Emmanuel, whose master, Laurence Chaderton, was Whitaker's brother-in-law. But Emmanuel was a puritan institution; ideological consensus was the foundation on which it was built. Whitaker's attempt to achieve a similar consensus through the imposition of puritan discipline on an established institution with its own history of factional and ideological squabbles, was to provoke considerable opposition. In Whitaker's career at St John's we can see 'puritanism' not as some oppositionist movement, operating in contention with the predominant ideology of hierarchy and degree, but as the informing principle behind the regime of the eminently respectable Dr Whitaker. Whitaker's opponents in the college hence found themselves having to denounce Whitaker as a puritan. Yet Whitaker was neither a non-conformist nor a presbyterian. He was also, as Master of St John's, their immediate superior. The normal conformist, anti-precisian rhetoric was hence placed under considerable strain as the dissident fellows struggled to place the evasive Dr Whitaker within their recognised framework of dispute. Their attempts to resolve this dilemma provide an essential background both for the theological disputes of the 1590s and for the wider shifts within conformist thought as the old rhetoric of anti-puritanism merged into a wider critique of puritan divinity and Calvinist theology. For the school of conformist opinion at St John's not only gives us a glimpse of an intellectual milieu very different from the style of Calvinism then predominant in the university but also provides us with some idea of the sort of person who would have welcomed and supported the stance taken by William Barrett and Peter Baro in 1595/6. The existence of such potential support thus helps to explain the vehemence of the Calvinist response. On this view, the disputes of 1595/6 represented less a bolt from the blue than the culmination of longstanding tensions within the university, tensions engendered by the dominance of moderate puritans like Whitaker and Chaderton and the emergence of an increasingly vocal and coherent conformist opposition to that dominance. The disputes at St John's provide perhaps the most clear-cut example of this process.

From the first Whitaker's regime at St John's was fraught with difficulty. The trouble began even before he was formally installed as Master. In 1585 Howland, the then Master of the college, was appointed Bishop of Peterborough at Whitgift's behest. Almost immediately Whitaker's name was linked to the post. The mere prospect of his appointment was enough to rouse opposition. This was the occasion of Andrew Perne's subtly derogatory letter to Burghley and Whitaker's pained defence of his own suitability for 'that post' cited above.

However, judging from the apologetic tone of Perne's letter, it would appear that Whitaker already enjoyed Burghley's support. For Burghley St John's was 'my best parent that gave me nurture to know God truly and to detest popery'. Who better, then, to guide the college's fortunes than the staunchly anti-papist Dr Whitaker. Thus in June 1586 a slightly harassed Howland was acting, at Burghley's instigation, as a sort of campaign manager for Whitaker. Howland clearly did not relish the job. He found opinion in the college equally divided between rival candidates. Whitaker, however, was not amongst them. No doubt Whitaker could be 'chosen by voices' but only if Burghley were to insist. Should he do so and impose Whitaker on an unwilling college, the resulting tensions and resentments would 'greatly hinder his government and alter the quiet state of the college'. Should, however, Burghley continue to press for Whitaker's election, Howland professed himself willing to 'vouchsafe your letters unto the fellows in the favour of Mr Whitaker upon my relinquishing the place, I do not doubt but to draw them if not to a general consent yet not to repugn the same at the least'.[1]

Even that, however, appears to have been too optimistic a forecast. Howland himself remained as Master until February 1587. The delay in appointing his successor was almost certainly the result of a stalemate between Burghley's determination to have Whitaker elected and the equally firm resolution of the fellows that this 'puritan' outsider should not be imposed on the college.

Not everyone in St John's was opposed to Whitaker's cause. In 1586 a group of fellows wrote a long Latin letter to Burghley praising Whitaker's virtues profusely and imploring him to see that Whitaker was elected. The letter was signed by Downes, Munsay, Harrison, Furnes, Woolaston, Bodes, Hill, Alvey, Johnson and Higgins.[2]

St John's, then, was deeply divided. After Howland's eventual resignation the Ecclesiastical Commisioners (Burghley and Whitgift amongst them) had to apply considerable pressure to secure Whitaker's election.[3] Their pious hopes that the fellows would now unite behind their preferred candidate, Whitaker, proved ill-founded. Indeed it appears that the fellows actually tried to elect someone else. Andrew Downes, the new Regius Professor of Greek and a fellow since 1571, and John Palmer, a fellow since 1573, were rumoured to be the leading candidates (though Howland for his part had thought that Laurence Stanton was the leading contender).[4] As Whitaker was to observe during a later dispute, 'those that were most against my coming in were either seniors or immediately to succeed in place of seniors'.[5] It seems likely that the opposition to Whitaker within the college was led by fellows of long standing who resented having been passed over in favour of Whitaker.

Whitaker's first actions as Master can only be explained as a response to this potentially explosive situation. Rather than smooth the ruffled feathers produced by his election Whitaker seems to have decided to smash all such opposition by making an example of one of his most vocal critics – Everard Digby. Digby had been a fellow since 1573 and a senior since 1585. In 1587 he became an object for the hostile attentions of the new master. A list of eighteen complaints against Digby drawn up by Whitaker gives a comprehensive picture of the characteristics which, in Whitaker's eyes at least, marked Digby down as an undesirable:

1. Publica infamia et suspitio Papismi which is...maiora crimina.
2. He hath preached in commendation of voluntary poverty and in the said sermon complained that copes and vestments were turned into cushions.
3. He hath inveighed against Calvinians as schismatic and enemies of the church.
4. When one in the hall said that the papists had raised a report that my Lord of Leicester was forsaken of his soldiers, he immediately affirmed it openly to be true.
5. In the time of communion in the college at the beginning of the term he hath fished with a net in the river before the college in the sight of many...
6. He useth not to come to chapel in our college.
7. He is notoriously non-resident from his benefice, never almost coming at it and yet being within a day's journey.
8. He never preacheth any sermons more than of necessity he must neither at Cambridge nor else where for anything we know.
9. He chooseth his text out of Apocryphal books as are not read in our church...
10. He hath lately in a commonplace given great suspicion that he is corrupt in religion, delivering nothing almost but magical, suspicious and popish conceits of angels.
11. He hath often put off his punishments, set on his head by the officers.
12. He being a senior and warned to come to our meetings absenteth himself of purpose for the most part.
13. He hath threatened to set the president in the stocks being chief in the master's absence and has otherwise openly abused him foully.
14. He hath openly encouraged the younger sort to break a decree made by the master and the seniors.
15. Being told by some of one which was expelled for his ill demeanour he hath said openly 'Come let us take him and set him at the bachelors table and see who dare stir him.'
16. He being deprived hath notwithstanding sat as President in the hall before anything was done for his restitution.
17. Being warned by the master not to give a question for fear of contention and stirr notwithstanding would needs give the same and none other, and set up bills upon diverse places of the town provoking all to come and dispute if they durst at St John's college...
18. He being sent for twice by the master to come before the company that he might be charged with his faults refused to come,

whereupon he was judged by the greater part of the seniors to have incurred contempt.[6]

The charges can be subsumed under two headings: those concerning doctrine – his alleged popery – and those concerning his attitude toward the college authorities. Both were a direct product of what amounted to his deliberate campaign to outrage the puritan sensibilities of Whitaker and his sympathisers. A more accurate sense of the tone and polemical thrust of Digby's attitudes can be gained from his answers to the charges cited above.[7] He dismissed the charge of popery with contempt: 'I have been and am ready to take the oath of supremacy, to subscribe unto the articles of religion; to the book of common prayer; therefore there is no such suspicion made by any honest man, but only by some schismatical precisians my professed adversaries.' He had already accounted for his preaching on voluntary poverty before William Fulke, the then Vice-Chancellor, thus: 'to this effect if we give all to the poor and follow Christ Jesus it is acceptable in the sight of God'. 'Concerning copes', he continued, 'the use of them is very solemn and religious as may appear by the service used in her majesty's chapel and cathedral churches.' On this point Digby confronted the authority of Calvin cited by some against the surplice or the sign of the cross. But Calvin, observed Digby, 'had his errors' and just to rub salt in the wound he cited the authority of Whitaker's uncle, Dean Nowell, to prove it.

So much then for doctrine, but what of Digby's attitude to the college authorities? Digby stood on his rights. He had gone fishing during communion, but what of it? 'The company which did not receive being come out of the chapel walked abroad some...as usually they do going to tennis some walking, some fishing, so did I and so I might do lawfully.' As for his failure to attend chapel, Digby compared his own record favourably with that of Whitaker: 'Though the master be often absent, lying all night with his wife in the town, yet am I either at our service at home or at King's college chapel thrice for any of their once.' To his admitted absence from the meeting of the senior fellows, Digby replied that he had absented himself ever since the master had overridden six of the eight seniors who had wanted to punish 'a precisian who preached openly in the chapel that non-residency is a great sin and that they that chose them to any office in the college were in the gall of bitterness'.

The antagonism and bitterness of feeling between the conformist and puritan members of the college come out very strongly
in all this. Digby was clearly trying to provoke the puritans at
every turn. For their part they were attempting to impose their
own rigorous standards of conduct on the college. The issue of
non-residence illustrates the point perfectly. While all might agree
that in principle it was reprehensible, the extent of its reprehensi-
bility – whether it was an abuse entirely to be eschewed or, given
the present state of the church, a necessary evil which provided
the only means to maintain a properly learned clergy – was an
open question. Moreover, in an enclosed community like St
John's, general pronouncements of principle could not but have
highly personal implications. By explicitly linking the issue to the
appointment to college offices the anonymous preacher had made
a thinly veiled personal attack on those members of the college
who, like Digby, possessed a benefice outside the college. While
under Howland such an attack would probably not have escaped
censure, Whitaker's arrival had seriously altered the balance of
power in the college. He was clearly not disposed to punish people
for the expression of opinions with which he was himself in sympathy. This closed to Digby the normal means of redress within
the college. But Digby was not a man to take such a slight lying
down. He took steps to protect himself:

The precisians having preached that non-residence is a grievous
sin I gave this question 'non residentia est licita' to be defended
against any of them in public schools or elsewhere and when they
durst. I did defend it and am ready to defend the same at this day.

In the same vein Digby admitted encouraging the 'younger sort'
to disobey one of Whitaker's decrees. It was

a precise decree against statute made by deputy seniors most of
that sect and forbidding us to play at cards in Christmas at such
time as we are permitted by our statute. I did play and did signify
that it was lawful for the whole company to play at convenient
time notwithstanding this new fangled decree of theirs concerning
their Christide.

In his campaign to ridicule and defy the new precise order in
the college Digby's principal weapons appear to have been a
painstaking adherence to the letter of statute and his own singularly abrasive manner. He indulged in a satirical 'work to rule'.

From his own account of his conduct during the dispute over the payment of commons, which finally led to his dismissal from the college, it seems that he abided very closely to the precise letter of the college statutes. But from Whitaker's account of the same events it would appear that the very strictness of that observance was designed to ridicule the college authorities.[8] The dispute revolved around the question of who should come to whom. Digby claimed that the custom of the college enjoined that the steward should come to the senior fellow and ask for payment. Whitaker insisted that this custom had been rendered obsolete by the new statutes of 1580 and was in any case no longer 'convenient' since debts were now collected not by the seneschal, a mere college servant, but by the steward who was a fellow and often a senior.

But Whitaker's case against Digby did not consist entirely of alleged minor breaches of statute. For Whitaker Digby was more than a mere troublemaker – he was a papist. 'Sir Birch a known papist persuaded one Mr Heyward, a gentleman's son in our house whom he would have induced to popery with this reason amongst other that Mr Digby and some others of account in our house were so.' Digby, it was alleged, 'liveth familiarly with some known papist in our town and giveth countenance unto all that are suspected'. Whitaker concluded that 'the common opinion of him abroad doth for the most part condemn him [to be] a man of corrupt religion'. It was this popery that prompted Digby to 'speak dangerously and undutifully and that openly of the matters in the Low Countries and of Sir Francis Drake'.[9]

This was hardly conclusive evidence. Indeed, it might appear that Whitaker's invocation of popery was a mere shift in order to justify his own high-handed and oppressive dealings. That there was more to Whitaker's position than this, however, can be established from a fuller study of Digby's underlying views as expressed in his published works. Of these the first was his *Theoria analytica* of 1579. This was followed in 1580 by two more: *Admonitioni F. Mildapetti responsio* and *De duplici methodo*. Both were designed to defend his own peculiar brand of platonised Aristotelianism from the Ramist assaults of William Temple. Then in 1582 came a Latin treatise on swimming, and finally in 1590 his most overtly polemical work, *Dissuasive from taking away the livings and goods of the church.*

Digby's thought amounts to a considerable subject in itself.

For the moment suffice it to say that Digby was not a papist. But he was also certainly not a protestant of the Whitaker school. In his *Theoria analytica* Digby had erected a highly personal, neo-platonic view of the world in which insights and references taken from the Cabbala, Paracelsus, Pythagorean number mysticism, the Italian neo-platonists Ficino and Mirandola, Plotinus and Plato himself were integrated into a carefully articulated whole. Digby's vision of the ascent of the individual soul through the various levels of reality (the sensible and the intelligible) to the final state of pure contemplation and knowledge in the 'mundus suprasupremus' was very much at odds with the view of human nature and its dealings with the divine contained in Whitaker's works. His view of a corpus of ancient knowledge independent of the scriptures and the revealed will of God contained therein was also sharply divergent from the rigorous scripturalism of Calvinists like Whitaker. Hence, as well as providing the epistemological basis for his critique of Ramism, Digby's neo-platonism also provided the basis for a critique of Whitaker's entire world-view.

Unfortunately Digby never undertook such an explicit exposition of his theological views. However, in his *Dissuasive* he produced a work which not only denounced the puritans as enemies of the church, bent on despoiling her of her remaining wealth, but one which also contained a view of church history very different from that put forward by Whitaker. Digby's work contained not one reference to the popish Antichrist and appeared to put forward a far more positive evaluation of the mediaeval heritage of the church than any Whitaker could formulate. Similarly, Digby appeared to regard human ethical choice as playing a central role in the justification and salvation of the believer.

It is clear from all this why Whitaker should not have taken kindly to Digby's presence in St John's. For Whitaker saw the world stretched between the opposite poles of true religion and popery, Christ and Antichrist. Whatever did not further the cause of the gospel or accord with his view of right doctrine must of necessity savour of popery. Hence, however Digby might equivocate about his readiness to subscribe to the Thirty-nine Articles, to Whitaker he was a papist. By thus assimilating Digby to popery Whitaker was able to justify his own harsh proceedings and to present the dispute not as some trivial disagreement over college statutes but as a test case in which the religious status and spiritual condition of the entire university was at stake. Hence, he could tell Burghley that

the state of the whole university is such at this present time that Mr Digby's cause being heard if he be relieved and restored by superior authority it will not be an easy matter to restrain the insolency of a number with whom I have to deal in this college ... It is a pity and unspeakable grief that the state of this most excellent university should be such. Many were good but never so many bad. Papistry doth secretly increase and namely in this college as hath appeared of late since my coming into the college and among others Mr Digby a man most notoriously suspected and one that by confession of some hath given encouragement to papists in their opinions in this house. Besides a man continually scandalous, as it shall be declared to your honour. For which respects I was the more willing to have the very extremity of the statute to pass against him.

Nor was Digby without his favourers in high places. Not every one was as vigilant against popery as he ought to be. Here Whitaker referred to 'Mr Dr Legge':

Once I was deposed in a matter against him for papistry and he enjoined by your honour to make a kind of public satisfaction before the Heads of the university. It may be perhaps he will not be altogether indifferent in hearing and reporting the whole cause for me and against Mr Digby as were requisite.

Indeed, Whitaker complained, 'such commissioner had been appointed as Mr Digby most desired which in the opinion of many here somewhat already prejudiced our case'.[10]

Whitaker, then, was well aware that there were those in authority who did not share his perception of the popish threat and who might baulk at his assimilation of Digby's position to popery. This explains why Whitaker did not simply charge Digby with popery and have done with it. While Whitaker, Chaderton or Fulke (who had denounced Digby's view on voluntary poverty as 'popish')[11] would have accepted the doctrinal case against Digby without hesitation, men like Legge, Perne or Whitgift would not. Hence, rather than stake everything on doctrine, Whitaker based his case on statute and on his own position as Master, with the doctrinal charges used simply as a background to justify the severity of his proceedings. For Digby's offence was trivial. Whitaker admitted as much. What mattered, however, was his 'contempt of authority in taking his commons not having paid, being warned to the contrary by the magistrate. . . it was parva res but magna culpa'.[12]

Whitaker had been right to proceed carefully. But even these tactics did not succeed. When Digby appealed to Whitgift against his expulsion, Whitgift upheld the appeal. Baulked by Whitgift, Whitaker turned to Burghley and bombarded him with a series of letters justifying his treatment of Digby and freely invoking the spectre of popery. But it was all to no avail. In April 1588 Whitgift and Burghley wrote jointly to Whitaker. The case against Digby, so carefully composed in terms of college statute and respect for authority, they found totally unconvincing. If Digby had been provocative, Whitaker had been high-handed. As for the sinister doubts raised about Dibgy's 'popery', these were to be carefully investigated and if proved true Digby denounced as 'unfit to remain either in that or any other society'. In the meantime, however, Digby was to be restored to his fellowship immediately.[13]

Whitaker was thus left in something of a quandary. The leading figures in the English church, upon whose support his career had hitherto been based, had found against him. Nothing daunted Whitaker looked elsewhere for backing and turned to the Earl of Leicester, Warwick and Essex, all three of whom now took a hand in the affair. Leicester first wrote to Whitgift on 30 April 1588 asking him to proceed no further until he had had a chance to put Whitaker's case to the Archbishop in person.[14]

Leicester, however, got short shrift from the Archbishop. The college visitors had examined Whitaker's proceedings and found them sadly wanting. They were such 'as if they might be tolerated would bring too violent a government into that college and breed many inconveniences'. Whitgift showed himself well aware of the issues at stake:

If there be so great matters to charge Digby withal (as is now pretended) then they are much to blame in suffering the same to be so long unpunished or not complained of and in expelling him for so small a trifle when as they might have done it for so great and weighty causes.

He was shocked that Whitaker

whom I have always so greatly tendered and did not lack my help for extraordinary favour to obtain that mastership should in a case of his own (wherein he is thought to seek his private revenge) use this uncharitable and indirect course, I think I might say contrary to his oath and statutes of the college.[15]

Whitgift was having his arm twisted and he resented it. He gave vent to his feelings in a letter to Burghley. Whitaker had acted contrary not only to statute and the law of charity but even to plain honesty. He had

privately laboured to the Earls of Leicester, Warwick and Essex and informed their lordships of diverse matters against Digby that he is a papist, a seducer of the youth in the college, a depraver of some doings beyond seas and such like whereof they neither have complained to us nor punished the same at home as they ought to have done, if it be true...I do not think that Mr Whitaker who hath received so many and good turns from your lordship especially would have so used himself. It is far from divinity to seek to overrule justice by letters and it is most contrary to the rule of charity to backbite a man and to condemn him in corners especially to such noble personages, before he be judicially heard and convicted. I am sorry Mr Whitaker doth so far forget himself but without doubt it is the violence of preciseness which desireth a rule and government absolute without controllment be it never so vehement and unjust. It were convenient that Mr Whitaker should understand his evil dealing herein for so much as in him lieth he goeth about to breed some hard conceit in these noblemen towards me especially who have least deserved any such thing at his hands.[16]

Whitgift would seem to have been genuinely shocked and saddened by the behaviour of his erstwhile protégé. There could hardly be a clearer illustration of the ambiguity of his relationship with Whitaker and with Whitaker's puritan leanings. Whitaker had worked his way to respectability and preferment through his efforts against Rome and it was in that role that Whitgift valued and respected him. Yet Whitaker's cast of mind had far more in common with puritans and presbyterians like Chaderton and Cartwright than with the aggressively conformist Whitgift. Whitgift and Whitaker differed not on the content of right doctrine but over its implications. While they might both agree on the Antichristian nature of popery, their applications of that doctrine to the person of Everard Digby diverged sharply. For Whitaker any divergence from his own school of Calvinist divinity and anti-papal zeal amounted to popery. Whitgift, on the other hand, required conclusive doctrinal proof before he would allow any such accusations to stand and regarded Whitaker's ready recourse to the spectre of popery with grave suspicion. However these differences remained implicit, hidden by Whitaker's studied moderation on the issues normally taken to divide puritan from conformist and by the solid orthodoxy of his anti-papal works. Certainly the Digby affair does not seem to have caused a permanent rift between the two men. As early as 1590 Whitaker was confident enough of Whitgift's good opinion to cite the Archbishop's longstanding support of his career against his conformist opponents in the college.[17] The very real differences between his position and that of Whitgift, however, remained a constant source of potential misunderstanding and conflict as the theological disputes of 1595 were to prove.[18]

To return to the fate of the unfortunate Digby, Leicester's involvement in the affair was to prove crucial. He wrote again to Whitgift on 6 May. He had received, he insisted, 'very strong and credible informations that this Digby is a very unsound and factious fellow'. However he understood that having committed himself thus far the Archbishop could not back down without considerable loss of face. He therefore suggested a compromise. Digby should be reinstated but only for a 'short time of stay in that college so that he be gone within a quarter of a year. Whereby neither this Your Grace's action shall be undone and the college shall be disburdened of a lewd fellow which disturbeth the government and hath empoisoned the youth.' Failing that, Leicester suggested, Digby should lose his status as a senior.[19]

It says much for Leicester's influence and Whitaker's determination that Leicester's first proposal was adopted. The college accounts verify Digby's restoration to his fellowship. For the year December 1587 to December 1588 Digby's name does not appear on the list of fellows for the first quarter. Then following his restitution in May his name has been interlined by the steward and he is credited with two quarters' allowance, presumably in compensation for his suspension during the first quarter. For the third quarter he received his due allowance.[20] After that his name disappears from the college records. Whitaker (with Leicester's help) had carried the day.

Having dealt with Digby and thus (he hoped) broken the opposition in the college, Whitaker turned to the positive side of his programme. This was contained in a series of projected changes in the college statutes put forward by Whitaker in 1588.[21] These leave no doubt concerning his plans for the college. The primacy of religion in the life of the college was to be established beyond challenge. Hence his fifth suggestion was that divines be favoured before others in the appointment of senior fellows:

The senior's duties must needs especially concern matters of religion because the house is founded for divines. And such as now direct their studies to other professions because they see the way open rather for them than divines to the best places among us will by this means something be persuaded to change their course.

As things stood, the prevalence of physicians was so great that there was a danger that they would come 'to occupy all the places of the eight seniors. The want of this hath of late been apparent when physicians were chosen for deans and likewise a lawyer which are necessarily bound to moderate the divinity problems.'[22]

There was to be a general tightening of discipline amongst the fellows. Whitaker proposed

that all acts be performed of every fellow, fellow commoners (except noblemen's sons) also of all scholars and other students in the house whosoever, in their own persons, unless there be some just cause to the contrary approved by the master, president and senior dean and likewise that the duties of all officers, lecturers and sublecturers and examiners be done in their own persons.

The benefits of this were self-evident: 'It is best for increase of learning, for the greater good of the youth, for the state and benefit of the college, for the keeping of everyone within his bounds.' Many had been consistently avoiding the performance of their duties: 'many have been in the house long time and scarce done acts in their own persons in seven years and so both their learning and religion not so well known'. In addition,

lecturers laying their duties upon others, grow themselves to be idle and given to play and pleasure, become factious and busy in by-matters; exercises and acts by that means either wholly omitted or foully neglected in the hearers and in the officers, are posted over to deputies some seek them that are not fit for them, propounding nothing else but ease and continuance, benefit and gain and so pass over their year they pass not how, whilst in the mean time the college goods are committed to the bare credit of men and all things administered by deputies unsworn.[23]

In future things were to be ordered to favour the diligent and penalise the lazy. Thus the dividends from corn money were to be distributed once a week rather than in a lump sum once a year. This, Whitaker claimed, 'will be a good means to keep men at home and so be a great furtherance to learning. Such as stay at home take pains and care for the house and therefore the rather to be considered; and those that are abroad be either of pleasure or for their greater good and commodity.'[24]

Similarly, greater attention was to be given to religious duties. Whitaker demanded that all students

in our house from the highest to the lowest that be of years and knowledge be bound to receive the communion together in the college, if they be at home at Christmas, Easter, Whitsuntide and beginning of terms unless their reason to the contrary be approved by the master before.

For besides

the particular good of every man to breed and maintain unity and love in the society it will take away both all suspicion of corruption in religion and also that offence which is justly taken by the absence of many of all sorts being notwithstanding at home when communion is administered.[25]

Strict measures were also to be taken to ensure that only sound doctrine was taught. 'The questions to be disputed of in problems of divinity upon Friday be allowed by the master and senior dean. On Wednesday by the master and junior dean.' At present, Whitaker claimed, 'factious and seditious questions are sometimes propounded...which move altercation and strife'. Not only that but 'the same questions are handled diverse times and questions nothing profitable not any controversies nor points of learning but rather witty and affected conceits'.[26]

In the same spirit of reform the distribution of college livings was to be taken in hand. No one was to be allowed to hold such a living and a fellowship concurrently for more than a year.[27] Pluralism and non-residence were hence to be controlled. 'Such as be preachers of our house having obtained a benefice abroad and with it a pension, annuity, feofment, inheritance etc. may lose his place within one year of the enjoying of both', for 'men that are so well provided for will not take pains in lectures and with the youth as tutors should do'.[28]

Morals too were to be subject to more stringent control. Whitaker was particularly concerned about gambling and card playing at Christmas and upon the sabbath. 'Upon the receiving of the Lord's supper and upon the sabbath day as it hath been a custom continued scholars fall to their game.' Yet 'there be better exercise and more seeming scholars which would be practised of us if the other were not permitted'.[29] Playing cards at Christmas had been one of the points in contention between Whitaker and Digby. William Ames, in a parallel example from Christ's College was to be expelled following a particularly vehement sermon against playing cards at Christmas. The Master of Christ's then was Valentine Cary, at one time a fellow of St John's under Whitaker. It was over such apparently trivial issues that the tensions between puritans and conformists tended to reveal themselves.[30]

All in all Whitaker's proposed changes in the college statutes represented a comprehensive programme of reform. St John's was to be converted into a seminary of proper godliness on the lines of Emmanuel. Religion and the training of divines and preachers was to dominate the life of the college. All the changes proposed by Whitaker were designed to increase the college's efficiency as a teaching institution, to reform morals and manners within the college and ensure that the ministers trained there were forced to take their place in the church at large, in the forefront of the struggle against popery and irreligion.

But Emmanuel had been built as a godly seminary from the first. Whitaker, on the other hand, was trying to impose his puritan regime on an established institution. Inevitably his proposed reforms aroused resistance. Why should any fellow support changes designed to make him work harder, to reduce his income and opportunities for advancement and to restrict and control his private pastimes and pleasures? Only those personally committed to the puritan purposes behind Whitaker's reforms were likely to welcome changes such as these. With these proposals following hard on the imposition of the outsider, Whitaker, on an unwilling college, and Whitaker's own expulsion of Digby, a senior fellow of long standing, Whitaker was well on the way to creating a unified opposition to his regime. Moreover, such an opposition had a ready-made set of polemical weapons to hand in the sort of conformist anti-puritan rhetoric employed by Digby. Nor was Digby the only fellow with strong anti-puritan views. In 1590 Eleazor Knox engaged in a sharp exchange of views with one Hugh Gray over an anti-puritan sermon in which he had denounced both Whitaker and a certain Mr Woodcock (almost certainly Ranulph Woodcock, scholar and fellow at St John's from 1592).[31]

Digby too had undoubtedly had his friends in the college. Three fellows contributed laudatory poems to the preface of his *Theoria analytica* in 1579 (Robert Booth, Samuel Hodgson and Samuel Perkins) and Booth, John Bois, Ottwell Hill and Samuel Gooder contributed more poems to his *De arte natandi.* Given Digby's outspoken and abrasive nature it is unlikely that any of these men were unaware of or opposed to his views. Moreover, both Bois and Hill remained in the college throughout Whitaker's period as master and signed a series of conformist petitions to Burghley drawn up immediately after Whitaker's death in 1595. There is evidence, then, for an anti-puritan or conformist tradition in the college which both predated and survived Whitaker's regime. But if the college contained conformists it also contained puritans and always had done.[32] Given the alignment of forces in the college under Whitaker, with an assertive puritanism once more in the ascendant it was inevitable that opposition to Whitaker's policies should be expressed in the language of conformist polemic and that moderate members of the college would be driven toward the conformist camp.

Certainly the opposition to Whitaker's regime was both persistent and vocal. In response to the projected changes advocated by Whitaker his (unfortunately unnamed) opponents drew up a list of forty-three 'flat breaches of statute' perpetrated by him during his short time as master.[33] Whitaker was accused of consistently passing over the claims of the senior fellows to preferment to leading college offices and of favouring men entirely unsuited to, and unqualified for, the posts in question.[34]

Some idea of the methods Whitaker used to thus override can be gained from an anonymous account of an election to the post of lecturer in physic.[35] First Whitaker had waited until only two of the eight seniors were in residence. Then he had called a sudden meeting, with five of the seven fellows present being merely deputy seniors, on the grounds that the appointment could be deferred no longer and that he was constrained by statute to hold the election immediately. Despite his clear determination to proceed four of the deputy seniors argued that since the election was already late, and the statute therefore already broken, it would be better to wait a few more days until more seniors could be present. This suggestion did not please Whitaker and despite the fact that he was supported only by Henry Alvey he refused to give way. The meeting broke up in disarray only to be reconvened after lunch when the candidature of Whitaker's protégé was canvassed. Here doubts were raised as to his medical expertise. He had, it was claimed, only a cursory acquaintance with the works of Galen and had been heard publicly to express his intention to enter the ministry. Whitaker, however, simply asked him if either of these allegations were true and accepted his assurance that they were not. With that the man was elected to the post. Perhaps it was not necessary to be a rabid conformist to object to behaviour of this sort.

In another example Whitaker had bestowed a vacant college living not on any of the suitably qualified senior fellows, or indeed on any member of the college, but on 'one who was a stranger and none of the house'.[36] Whitaker had already expressed his disapproval of the fellows' holding benefices away from the college and he was hardly likely to encourage the practice while simultaneously petitioning for a change in the college statutes to forbid it. Nevertheless such an attitude hardly accorded with the material interests of the fellows. Once again the clash between Whitaker's essentially ideological drive toward puritan reform and an opposition composed of an amalgam of personal interest and conformist principle can be clearly discerned.

For Whitaker's opponents were not merely accusing him of playing favourites. Their complaint was not simply that he favoured some more than others but that he consistently favoured puritans and non-conformists.[37] Hence in 1590 an unknown critic asked 'whether a senior of honest life and against whom no lawful exception can be taken be not to be preferred before his in being suspected vehemently and probably to be a favourer of precisianism, the senior by the maior part of the seniors being chosen?' Again the same critic posed the question whether

the negative voice granted by the university statute were not to strengthen the master his authority in keeping out papists and precisians and such other heretics and schismatics and notorious malefactors and not to be used against honest men against whom they can take no lawful exception much less to bring in or advance precisians and such like.[38]

The college, therefore, was in the grip of a puritan clique and, with Whitaker as Master using all the power and influence inherent in his position in support of the puritans, there was little the dissident fellows could do about it. While they might seek to stick to the letter of statute, their cause transcended such legalistic equivocation. They were upset by Whitaker's whole demeanour as master. 'Though we can find no statute to the contrary yet is it against the custom of the house and all good order for the master to take such absolute authority to himself as he doth.'[39] Given Whitaker's connections and reputation the seniors had little chance of having him removed from the college. They confined themselves therefore to petitioning for changes in the statutes that would shift the balance of power in the college from the master to the senior fellows and would hence render it impossible for Whitaker to govern the college without the consent of a majority of the seniors. Their main proposals were: firstly that no decree whatsoever be valid without consent of the master and at least four seniors; secondly that no one should be deprived of his place in the college before his case had been heard by the master and at least four seniors (not deputies); and thirdly that the master was to lose his negative voice which, as things stood, allowed him to appoint whom he chose to college offices unless he were opposed by seven of the eight seniors. Elections to all fellowships and offices should be decided by a simple majority verdict in an election held amongst the seniors.[40]

Whitaker's objections to these proposals and the seniors' replies provide us with a vivid picture of the state of the college. It is a picture of a college divided against itself. For their part the seniors feared that the fate of Everard Digby might befall any of them. 'By taking advantage of the time in the senior's absence' Whitaker might 'injure and grieve both the seniors themselves and the rest of the fellows'.[41] The dissident fellows had, they claimed, good reason to fear

hard measure by reason of a speech which Mr Alvey (who is the master his right hand and whose advice and council he followeth together) uttered not secretly in a corner but openly and boldly before all the seniors. For whereas some complained that is was no indifferent dealing but an unjust practise to watch times to determine of criminal causes when as the seniors themselves either are sent abroad upon college affairs or are forced by reason of their business to go abroad, Mr Alvey boldly affirmed that he saw no reason why the master should not watch his times and take all advantages, protesting that if he were in his place he would do it and praetermit no opportunity whereby we may justly fear that if it be not already determined yet it will be put in practice for the master is wholly led and directed by him. As also it is an opinion not only nourished privately but openly maintained at the fellows' table by some of those that favour the master his proceedings that he may lawfully watch opportunity to expel any how honest, learned or sufficient soever that in all opinions, elections and so forth do not consent and join with him, which they call by this term 'which cross his government'. As also it is a speech given out and heard in every place that it is necessary that some in St John's his college should be expelled for the reformation of that house.

They added that if the statutes had been as they now desired the whole unfortunate Digby affair would never have happened.[42]

The seniors thus raised the spectre of an arbitrary personal rule by the master and his clique. On his side Whitaker conjured up the equally unpalatable prospect of a self-perpetuating oligarchy of seniors, opposed to true religion, dominating the college. If the present proposals were accepted, he warned, five seniors acting in unison could effectively govern the college. 'They might be of any religion safely, they might together with their fellowships enjoy as many promotions as they could get, have leases at the college land and keep their places still and finally they might live in the college as they list.' Hence,

if the five seniors or some of them were corrupt in religion and yet could keep in with others (as is easy in colleges) they might bring into the college in time a number of ill-affected in religion, which is principally to be foreseen.

But the real cause of these complaints, Whitaker claimed, was personal and factional animosity. The master's powers, devised by the college visitors to meet 'the troubles and disquietness of St John's', were even more necessary now when 'those that were most against my coming in are either seniors or immediately to succeed in place of seniors'. Should the seniors' proposals be accepted, 'the master shall be but a shadow and in disgrace and contempt withall, as having no authority either to reward any that do well or to punish any that doth amiss, all being in the power of the seniors'.[43]

The seniors, of course, denied these accusations of faction and personal malice:

Some misliked his coming in, fearing all that which now they find and the rest being indifferent to all parties were rather against the manner than the man and that we all are very willing (he using the place of master as he ought) to behave ourselves in all duty as becometh fellows.

It was merely that

we think it not reasonable that the master or any one man his conscience (which often is in truth but a conceit) should without good proof be any man his hindrance or without publishing be other men's direction who are by the same oath and duty to do for the best as well as he and to admit of this were to hinder the preferment of any man how worthy soever who shall not be squared altogether according to the master his own only conscience.

The seniors, they continued, 'are always home bred whereas the master is most commonly a stranger and our desire is that he may not dissent from the seniors but upon the most weighty considerations'. False religion was more greatly to be feared in the master who, with the help of one or two toadies, could more easily do as he pleased than could a group of five seniors. As for Whitaker's dark hints about popery, they dismissed them with contempt:

As for this present time we are assured that there is no doubt of popery, whatsoever they for the advantage of their faction do suspect and wish that precism had not so many favourers then should we have less cause to be so careful to obtain this petition and be sure of better agreement among ourselves.[44]

Hence by 1588 the alignment of the forces in St John's was

complete. What had started as a slanging match between Digby and Whitaker had developed into a full-scale confrontation between the new master and his adherents and the old-established fellows. Moreover, it was a confrontation conducted in terms of the wider debate between puritan and conformist – only in this instance it was the puritans who were in authority and the conformists who were forced into the position of dissidents.

The disputes of 1588 over the proposed changes in the statutes ended in stalemate. There were no alterations in the college statutes. But after this attempt to give formal expression to his view of St John's had failed Whitaker certainly did not slacken his grip on college affairs. In December 1590 Whitaker forced through the election of Henry Alvey as president in the face of the opposition of a majority of seniors. At that the five seniors walked out of the chapel threatening to complain to the Queen. In a letter explaining his action to Burghley it is notable that while Whitaker described Alvey as a 'man singularly well deserving of the college' he nevertheless based his defence purely on his own powers as Master. He was quite within his rights as defined by statute and that, he argued, was justification enough. He had, he explained, encountered this sort of obstructionism from the seniors before. Then he had hesitated. Now, fortified by the advice of Dr Byng (a lawyer and Master of Clare), he had simply gone ahead with the election. Evidently Whitaker was learning to live with opposition, if only by ignoring it.[45]

Certainly the incident illustrates perfectly Whitaker's continuing determination to appoint his own men to key college posts. Moreover, coming from Whitaker's own pen, the account cannot be said to exaggerate the situation for polemical purposes. On the contrary, Whitaker's own account echoes closely the complaints of the conformists. Whitaker, it seems, continued to pursue such policies throughout his period as master. The complaints levelled at the puritan party in a series of petitions written after his death in 1595 reproduced almost word for word the earlier conformist complaints outlined above.[46] The only difference was that by 1595 the situation was even worse. Things had progressed from the question of undue puritan influence at the elections to college offices to the whole issue of the admissions policy:

They preach in their private sermons that we ought to choose fellows and scholars 'religious' and 'godly' men (as they term them) that be unlearned rather than our greatest scholars; and following this principle they have pestered our house with unlearned puritans picked out of the whole university and schoolmasters out of the country and drive away all the best and most towardly scholars that be of our own college.[47]

But were the puritans really guilty of drawing such a crude dichotomy between scholarship and godliness? Even a cursory examination of the career of a Chaderton or a Whitaker would reveal the unfairness of such an allegation. Scholarship played a central role in puritan godliness as it was espoused by these men. But there was a difference of approach involved here. Writing of one Mr Benson (probably George Benson, a fellow of St John's in the 1590s) Samuel Ward recorded that this Benson had been persuaded by the devil 'that he was reprobate...for that he had sinned against the holy ghost'. Apparently Benson had risen in the night and amongst other things renounced 'his overmuch delight in the Greek as also of Mr Downs, Bois, Cook and how he neglected other more profitable studies and ever when he came to divinity cried "O sweetness" with iteration'.[48]

Here, therefore, was the difference between the puritan and conformist attitudes to the university. For the puritans the main aim of the college should be the training of a godly learned ministry. In that process mere learning was not enough; scholarship without godliness was as useless for spiritual purposes as reason without grace. For the puritan the right ideological commitments were as important as mere scholarly aptitude, although the one did not preclude the other as the conformists seemed to imply. And certainly godliness was a good deal more important than any considerations of college privilege. Similarly ministers, once trained, should take their place in the church at large. For the conformists, however, the college was a place for scholars, a haven where career academics could devote their lives to study, safe in their enjoyment of college offices and livings. While theirs was a commitment to a 'humanist' ideal of learning for its own sake, the puritans instead sought to integrate their view of scholarship into a wider ideological commitment to further reformation and the pursuit of godliness.

The period of domination by Whitaker's puritan clique undoubtedly left its mark on the college. By 1595 the conformists were claiming that the puritans 'so have altered the state of this college since the Lord Bishop of Peterborough went from us as is incredible to be told'. There was a good deal of truth in these allegations. In 1586/7 the majority of fellows had opposed Whitaker's election and only ten had actively supported him. But in 1595, following his death, thirty-four fellows supported the puritan candidate to succeed him – Henry Alvey – while only fifteen opposed him. Even the conformists conceded that they were in a minority in 1595. In other words, during Whitaker's period as Master the ideological tone of the whole college had been decisively altered. Of the thirty-four Alvey supporters only nine had been fellows before Whitaker's appointment. Whitaker had indeed packed the college with his own adherents. On the other hand, of the fifteen conformists in 1595 only five had been fellows before Whitaker arrived and, of the remaining ten, five had been elected since 1590. It was still possible, therefore, for a conformist to get into the college even at the height of puritan influence. In fact the conformist faction retained its identity throughout Whitaker's period as Master. It retained a hard core of men from the Digby era – men like Ottwell Hill who had been a fellow since 1577, John Bois since 1580, Christopher Powell since 1583 – all of whom were still fellows in 1595. In addition there were others like Robert Booth, a contemporary of Digby, who retained his fellowship until 1592, or Eleazor Knox who kept his from 1579 until his death in 1590. Moreover the two most senior conformists in the college in 1595 – Bois and Hill – had both become seniors in 1593. Hill was junior bursar in 1589 and senior bursar in 1592. Bois was junior dean in 1591 and senior dean in 1590 and again in 1593. He was also founder's chaplain between 1590 and 1596 and Greek lecturer in 1588, 1590, 1593 and 1595. The road to office was evidently not completely closed to conformists.[49]

Whitaker's partiality cost him dear. He started as the master of one college and ended as the master of two for by the early 1590s St John's was divided into mutually exclusive and antagonistic groups. When John Bois was senior dean, in 1591 and 1593, his biographer records that his junior colleague, who was a puritan, refused to attend Bois' commonplaces but went off to hold meetings of his own.[50] Similarly, on the other side, Whitaker wrote to Burghley in 1590 complaining that there were some in the college who almost never attended college communion.[51] If puritans would not go to conformist commonplaces neither, evidently, would conformists attend puritan communions.

Since the puritan faction continued to enjoy the support of Whitaker as Master there was no way, within the college, that these tensions and antagonisms could find expression or redress. Instead they gradually built up until in 1590 they spilled over into yet another unseemly public row. This centred on the alleged presence in the college of a presbytery in 1589. It is probable that the modern historian, in possession of the Star Chamber depositions taken from various presbyterians in 1590 and the fruits of Professor Collinson's researches, may be in a better position to evaluate these charges than were many contemporaries. This, briefly, is what happened. In 1589 the last national synod of the classis movement met in St John's. It was attended by all the leading presbyterian divines of the day. Once assembled they discussed such central issues as the final form of the book of discipline, the exact status of unpreaching ministers and the validity of the bishops' courts. According to one deponent all this took place in Whitaker's chambers, although all the witnesses were agreed that Whitaker was not present at the meeting but away in Lancashire visiting his family.[52]

By October the first rumours of a presbytery started to circulate. The source was John Palmer, a fellow of the college. These culminated in a list of complaints against Whitaker's government (now lost, although we have Whitaker's point by point refutation of them) and a letter from Eleazor Knox to Burghley denouncing 'the master and his favourers'.[53]

Whitaker's response to these rumours was immediate. It was a mere three years since the Digby affair, two since the disputes over the statutes, and only the year before he had felt the need to reassure Burghley that he had not forbidden the traditional Queen's oration.[54] Now there was this fresh report of a presbytery coming at the height of Whitgift's final drive against the classis movement. Whitaker was in a tight corner. He went quickly to London and wrote to Burghley from his uncle Dean Nowell's house protesting his innocence.[55]

Meanwhile in Cambridge a group of fellows in St John's had joined together to deny all knowledge of a presbytery in the college. Surprisingly the petition was not signed only by active members of the puritan faction: Ottwell Hill, John Bois, Christopher Powell, William Billingsey, William Mottersham and Owen Gwynn – all of whom were later to come out against Henry Alvey – were also amongst the signatories. However, the names of Palmer, Knox, Booth, Robson, Morrell, Higgins and Clayton were conspicuous by their absence.[56] Whitaker, it seems, had taken steps personally to orchestrate this 'spontaneous' protestation of innocence. As he later told Burghley,

I thought it good and necessary to bring the testimony of the fellows with me, especially such as are most suspected that way. I persuaded no man to subscribe but showing them the matter briefly set down left it unto themselves, whether they would set to their hands and names to it or not. I sent for them all at one time by messenger but some came sooner than other as it fell out.[57]

Whitaker, it seems, had had to work hard for his petition and even then he had not managed to drum up a unanimous response.

Similarly on 20 October the Vice-Chancellor and certain Heads also wrote to Burghley. Again their letter had been written only after close consultations with Whitaker. Asked about the presbytery Whitaker had denied all knowledge of it and offered to have all the fellows interrogated about it under oath. The Heads, however, had decided to proceed no further until they had been briefed by Burghley. In the meantime they took this opportunity to assure him 'that none of us ever did hear any fame or speech in the university of any such presbytery or any such like disorderly meeting there before this present and we are persuaded there is no such matter'.[58] Hence, before any move for an official enquiry could get under way, Whitaker had contrived to get his version of events accepted by the university authorities and was well on the way to achieving the same with Burghley.

It is worth noting which of the Heads signed this letter. Preston as Vice-Chancellor, John Still, Roger Goad, Edmund Barwell, John Duport, John Jegon and Laurence Chaderton all supported Whitaker. However, names like Lancelot Andrewes, Humphry Tyndall, Thomas Legge, Thomas Byng, Thomas Neville and John Copcot were all conspicuously absent. In short, the moderate puritan (or evangelical protestant) establishment in the university was closing ranks to protect Whitaker and his regime at St John's and, more generally, to stave off the threat of a new visitation of the college, or, indeed, of the whole university.[59]

By thus exploiting his links at court with Burghley and in Cambridge with his fellow Heads, and by leaning on moderates in St John's like Bois, Whitaker had succeeded in largely isolating his enemies. They reacted in rather different ways. Eleazor Knox frantically tried to persuade Burghley to undertake an official enquiry.[60] John Palmer, the supposed source of the rumour, was more submissive. He did not deny the truth of the story – if anything he implied it was true – but he did deny his own complicity in any plot to discredit Whitaker. There was apparently a move afoot to force him, as the alleged cause of all the trouble, out of the college. Palmer was scared.[61]

Eleazor Knox thought that Whitaker was involved in a cover-up. 'He justly feareth the strict examination of the High Commission as such, as he knoweth to be fully acquainted with the deceitful and deceiving nature and conditions of these and which know their starting holes.'[62] But how much did Whitaker know about the synod of 1589? Chaderton certainly knew about it. He had been present as the Cambridge representative and Whitaker, of course, had close connections with Chaderton. Indeed there is clear evidence that they were in close consultation over the matter. Apparently Whitaker had been charged with planning a cover-up with Chaderton, the noted precisian, the very night before his departure for London. Whitaker vehemently defended his association with Chaderton:

I lodged that night in St John's college in mine own chamber. I perceive I am narrowly searched into when such things are marked. If I had lodged in his house that night for some convenience of taking my journey in the morning this had been no great fault I trust. My brother Chaderton is able to answer for himself; and I trust I may without offence use his company still being a man godly and learned and studious of peace for any thing that I have seen in him.[63]

Similarly Henry Alvey had been at the synod and he too was very close to Whitaker (his 'right hand' if the conformists were to be believed). It seems almost impossible, therefore, that Whitaker should not have known of the synod. On this view his absence from the college at the time can be seen as a carefully contrived coincidence which allowed his precisian friends the use of the college whilst leaving Whitaker free, if necessary, to deny all knowledge of their proceedings.

The whole episode neatly illustrates the balanced ambiguity of Whitaker's relations with 'puritanism'. Eleazor Knox tells a story that further underlines the point. Apparently Daniel Munsey had preached an openly presbyterian sermon before the whole college, including Whitaker, at the height of the furore over the presbytery. Essentially he had made five points:

1. That we wanted that holy discipline which is grounded and commended in the scripture.
2. That that discipline was the very sinews of doctrine which strengthened it and which set an edge upon the word to make it effectual.
3. That it was so necessary as that all the profit and good which in so long time hath been or is done in this realm; for the want hereof was and is altogether extraordinary.
4. That if we had this discipline we should have a paradise upon earth.
5. That it was our sins which hindered so great and necessary a blessing from us.[64]

Despite such an open and scandalous display of subversive and unlawful opinions Whitaker had taken no action against Munsay. Whitaker's explanation is of considerable interest:

Concerning Mr Munsay his sermon preached in the chapel I was as much grieved therewith as any of them; yet where they say he made this petition in his prayer that God would establish amongst us a presbytery in this church is untrue. He named no presbytery neither in his prayer nor in his sermon. Indeed, he prayed that God would establish discipline in this church, which may be indifferently construed and in some sense is not an evil prayer, there being such want of good order and discipline everywhere. The next day I sharply reproved him for it before all the seniors and more (I think) I could not do; it being a public sermon and therefore if any thing were spoken therein amiss the punishment belongeth to the vice-chancellor. If Mr Munsay had offended never so much must I bear the blame? Must this be a complaint against me?[65]

Whitaker, then, had begun by denying that Munsay had done anything particularly terrible, then admitted rebuking him and ended by disclaiming all responsibility, no matter what Munsay had said. Not himself a precisian or presbyterian, Whitaker was nevertheless prepared to countenance the expression of such opinions by others. Indeed, in so far as they could be taken to assert the need for a more effective godly discipline, Whitaker was ready to regard such sentiments as a sign of zeal rather than sedition.

But if Whitaker knew about the synod, how could he in conscience deny its existence? Here it has to be remembered that what was being denied by both Whitaker and the Heads was not a national presbyterian synod held in the college but merely the existence amongst the puritan faction of St John's of a 'presbytery'. This provided almost infinite scope for hair-splitting and academic quibbling. Knox complained that the puritans refused to address the substance of the charges but persisted in 'resting themselves upon the word and definition, upon genus and differentia of a presbytery'.[66] Whitaker certainly confined himself to the issue of a presbytery within the college and made great play with the somewhat imprecise nature of the charges. 'Who are the officers? Where hath been their meetings? When have they met? What have they done?' he asked. 'What that part of discipline is and what be those classes and synods I know not nor cannot imagine; neither this informer himself. And therefore he sayeth as it is reported.' On another occasion it had been alleged that 'we have something analogon to the presbytery although we have not the thing itself in perfection'. But that, argued Whitaker, was 'a mere shift to relieve and succour a manifest untruth that is now in danger to be deprehended'.[67]

The allegations of a presbytery are best seen as a confused amalgam composed of vague rumours about the synod of 1589 and more definite reports concerning the private meetings and commonplaces held by the puritan faction in the college. There was almost certainly nothing particularly sinister or even expressly presbyterian about these 'exercises' but the very fact that the conformists were excluded from them was enough to ensure that they fell under suspicion. This, combined with the atmosphere of uncertainty and suspicion that accompanied Whitgift's final drive against the classis movement, was sufficient to account for the conformists' charges. By means of the rigid distinction between involvement in the classis movement and a 'presbytery' in the college both Chaderton and Whitaker were able to reconcile their precise but very subtle consciences to the strenuous denial of rumours to which there was more than just a grain of truth.

Nothing came of all this. Even at the height of the anti-puritan reaction of 1590 the conformists in the college had failed to break Whitaker's stranglehold over St John's. His position strengthened by yet another victory, Whitaker went on as before, riding roughshod over opposition (viz. his appointment of Alvey as president in 1591) and muttering darkly about popery.

After the furore over Alvey's appointment as president the college seems to have quietened down. This was probably due more to the stoical acceptance of their fate by the conformists than to any spirit of reconciliation or consensus. Certainly, on Whitaker's death in December 1595, the rift between conformists and precisians revealed itself to be as wide as ever. No sooner had the last breath left Whitaker's body than both sides were petitioning Burghley to further the election of their preferred candidates. The puritans supported Henry Alvey and wanted a free election. The conformists pointed out that the puritans were now 'the greater number of the society so if the new master be chosen by them we must needs greatly fear what they will do'. They wanted Burghley to appoint the new master himself.[68]

They were, therefore, very anxious to blacken Alvey's name. It was Alvey, they claimed, who had been behind the puritan policies pursued in the college during the past decade. Whitaker, they admitted, had been 'a man renowned for his learning throughout all Christendom and a great pillar of our church'. But he had given himself wholly over to 'his study and being by nature quiet and tractable and putting in trust some others who contrary to his mind suffered conventicles in our college of Cartwright and his associates'.[69] He had, in short, lost control of the college. Alvey was cast in the role of a sinister 'éminence grise' who had consistently duped and misled the naive and ingenuous Whitaker: 'for the space of seven or eight years last past [Alvey] hath in all elections and bringing young students to the house ambitiously continued a plot for the mastership as may clearly appear from his proceedings from time to time'. Alvey's part in the agitation in support of Francis Johnson was dragged up again and he was made to appear responsible for all the precisian irregularities that had afflicted the college during Whitaker's period as Master. Whitaker, apparently, had spent his time in

St John's in a state of blissful ignorance; only at the very end had he realised what was happening. 'Our master inclined in his latter time to do good to our company in many things and as he professed oftentimes he was drawn by Mr Alvey to do things against his mind.' The puritans themselves had noticed the change in Whitaker. Both Munsay and Alvey had preached sermons warning Whitaker to stick to the straight and narrow path of godliness and 'not to be joined in friendship with those that hate the Lord'.[70] The conformists assured Burghley that 'if our master had lived he would as he often professed since he made an end of writing against Stapleton have reformed all things'.[71]

Whitaker of course was in no position to challenge these assertions (he was after all dead) and we should beware of taking them at face value. For the conformists had a vested interest in painting this picture of Whitaker as the retiring and gullible scholar: they needed to be able to denounce the events of the past few years without denouncing Whitaker. For they wanted Burghley to intervene in college affairs on their side. But Burghley had been Whitaker's greatest patron and was unlikely therefore to be won over by a denunciation of his dead protégé's mismanagement of college affairs. The conformists admitted as much when they told Burghley that they had not mentioned these abuses and grievances before because of the 'reverence and kind affection' they had felt for 'that learned and grave man our master'.[72] Yet if their accusations of puritanism and faction levelled at Alvey and his supporters were to stick they had to explain away Whitaker's consistent backing of the puritan party during his period as Master. This the picture of Whitaker as the vague and unworldly scholar allowed them to do.

But does it represent a credible version of the events described above? Whitaker's career as Master of St John's revealed him as anything but a quiet and impractical scholar. On the contrary, his considerable political and polemical skill, used consistently on the puritan side, had been the sole cause of the conformists' dilemma. Whether playing Leicester off against Whitgift and Burghley in 1588 or orchestrating the suppression of the presbyterian rumours of 1590, Whitaker had always stayed one step ahead of his opponents. The very consistency of conformist complaints from 1588 to 1595 is in itself a tribute to Whitaker's determination to turn St John's into a puritan seminary and to prefer only those who would support him in that intention. Alvey's advancement was not in spite of his puritanism but because of it.

As for the claim that his polemical activities against Rome had prevented him from giving college affairs the attention they deserved, Whitaker himself had used entirely the opposite argument in a letter to Burghley. Burghley had asked him to 'set forth in print more of my readings against the adversaries', but if the conformists ('the parties that are grieved'), wrote Whitaker, did not leave him alone, he would have no time left for study.[73] Similarly, the alleged split between Whitaker and Alvey and Munsay cannot be accepted at face value. It is quite likely that Whitaker felt called upon to restrain the zeal of his younger colleagues. During the anti-puritan purges of the early 1590s the position of the moderate puritan administrator was subject to considerable strain.[74] Whitaker was very keen to keep the prying eyes of conformist authority away from his college and from the university as a whole. It would have been quite natural for him to seek to moderate and stifle outbursts of some of the fellows alienated by the sudden hostile turn of official policy. In turn it was equally likely that firebrands like Alvey and Munsay would construe such moderation in the face of the drive toward conformity as backsliding and cowardice. But this represents the difference between radical and moderate members of the same party rather than any deep divide of principle. As Whitaker went to great lengths to prove, St John's was his college and such flimsy rumours as these provide no basis upon which to characterise him as the victim of some puritan plot.

But such a view of Whitaker has proved surprisingly influential. It can be found first repeated in the early seventeenth century in a letter from Richard Neile (a St John's man and a future Arminian Archbishop of York) of 1612 in which he referred to 'Alvey's government in Dr Whitaker's time' and claimed that 'the college had not recovered of that prejudice that Alvey's government had brought upon it'. Neile, of course, was committed to an extreme view of the puritan threat to the English church and that view would have been called into serious question if a man as respectable and respected as Whitaker were acknowledged to have pursued 'puritan' policies. Neile was engaged here in the same sort of covertly polemical exercise as that undertaken by Bancroft when he denied the mediating role of men like Fulke, Whitaker and Chaderton between 'puritanism' and the mainstream of protestant opinion. Once established, however, this view of Whitaker passed swiftly into the literature and Neile's opinion can be seen cited and endorsed in Thomas Baker's history of St John's and adopted wholesale by Dr Porter in his account of these disputes.[75] The effect of all this has been to foreshorten or compress the spectrum of Elizabethan religious opinion so that the 'puritan middle ground' of Elizabethan protestantism, so clearly personified by Whitaker himself, has been squeezed out of its rightful place by the great confrontation between puritanism and conformity. However, as this chapter has attempted to demonstrate, a moderate scholar like Whitaker could prove himself both ruthless and determined in the pursuit of ends which, while neither formally presbyterian nor avowedly non-conformist, can nevertheless meaningfully be described as puritan.

9

The theological disputes of the 1590s

THE OPENING SHOTS

On 29 April 1595 William Barrett, a fellow of Caius College, preached a sermon to the university from the pulpit of Great St Mary's.[1] His sermon concerned the nature and extent of Christian assurance. He denied, in short, that such assurance was either possible or desirable for the ordinary believer. No one, in this uncertain world, he argued, could aspire to believe in the certainty of his own salvation, at least not with the certainty of faith, unless he had been vouchsafed a personal revelation from God concerning his own spiritual state. As for Christ's prayer that man's faith should not fail, which was often cited in support of the extreme view of assurance, Barrett restricted its application to the Apostle Peter alone. He concluded that to be thus certain and secure concerning one's own perseverance (something by its very nature dependant on contingent circumstances and events) was to be guilty of very great pride and impiety. While the remission of sins was to be accepted as an article of faith, that did not extend to its application to individuals. Men neither could nor should believe with complete faith or certainty that their own sins were forgiven and remitted. For Barrett faith was unitary. There was no distinction to be drawn between different types of faith, merely between different types of believer. Applying such ideas to the doctrine of predestination he asserted that 'sin was the proper and first cause of reprobation'. Moreover, all these positions had been maintained with a series of side-swipes at Calvin, Martyr, Beza, Zanchius and Junius and 'other men of similar opinions, the very lights and ornaments of our church', all of whom Barrett had branded with the name 'Calvinist'.[2]

Such a performance was calculated to cause the maximum

offence amongst the Calvinists in the university. For by seeking to impugn the doctrine of assurance Barrett had attacked the whole Calvinist view of predestination at its weakest point – the supposedly antinomian consequences of any view of reprobation that located its cause not in sin but in the mere will of God. The sermon, in short, constituted a frontal assault on the uncompromising style of Calvinist theology, then predominant in the university, which can be found embodied in the polemical works of William Whitaker and underlying the world-view of Abdias Ashton.

Barrett's sermon provides the natural starting point for any discussion of the theological disputes that dominated Cambridge divinity for the remainder of 1595 and much of 1596. Certainly it marks a major escalation in the running fight between Calvinist and anti-Calvinist that can be traced throughout the 1580s and 1590s. Hitherto the initiative in those disputes has been assumed to lie with the anti-Calvinists with this sermon representing the opening shot in their campaign. The Calvinist reaction has been seen as just that – a reaction or defence. For Dr Porter the disputes constituted a 'Calvinist rearguard'; a belated last-ditch stand against a growing groundswell of anti-Calvinist opinion that could no longer be simply ignored.[3] Certainly, as the careers of Peter Baro or indeed of Everard Digby prove, such ideas had a long history in the university. But given that very fact, why did Barrett choose that precise moment to bring the issues into the open and challenge the Calvinist supremacy when, as he must have known, the anti-Calvinists were heavily outnumbered and outgunned? For, as subsequent events were to prove, all the leading members of the university, with the notable exception of John Overall, ranged themselves on the Calvinist side. Moreover the anti-Calvinists had no one to match the theological reputation and political connections of William Whitaker. Why, therefore, did Barrett put both his own career and the future prospects of the anti-Calvinist cause at risk in so disadvantageous a situation?

The answer is that he had little choice. Far from being an unprovoked attack on an unsuspecting Calvinist majority, Barrett's sermon was but a response to a longstanding Calvinist campaign. Certainly Barrett was not responsible for the opening of hostilities. Two months before, in February, William Whitaker had preached a highly polemical sermon on the extent of the atonement.[4] Posing the question of how an omnipotent God could want all men to be saved when many were in fact damned, Whitaker denounced the Pelagian equivocations that this thorny issue had elicited from many divines. He would have no truck with those who sought to resolve the problem by distinguishing between different aspects of God's will and who claimed to be able to identify two different wills, an antecedent and a consequent. On this view, by his antecedent will, God wishes all men to be saved, but since many men abused God's goodness and turned away from the proffered salvation, he commanded the damnation of those wilful sinners by his consequent will.[5] This, claimed Whitaker, was nothing more than a slander against the divine will. It rendered God's will dependent on that of man, left the fact of man's salvation hanging by a mere thread and called the whole concept of predestination into serious question. Most seriously it implied that God's will was mutable, that God could, in short, contradict himself. For Whitaker that was sheer nonsense, an open contradiction of the divine nature. It was, he argued, a popish, jesuitical opinion, totally at variance with scripture and the works of all sound theologians.[6] Here Whitaker cited the authority of Augustine and the papists' own Thomas Aquinas. However, this sermon was not merely another exercise in antipapal polemic for Whitaker. He went to considerable pains to establish the errors in question as not merely popish but also Pelagian.[7] Indeed so great was the appeal of Pelagianism to the corrupt reason of natural man that it was a heresy which was almost endemic in the Christian tradition. It could, therefore, spring up at any time and in any church.

In conclusion Whitaker drew up a list of six points or principles to be defended as bastions against the spread of Pelagian heresy:

1. The number of the predestinate is fixed; it can be neither augmented nor diminished.
2. It is not possible to identify any cause of predestination other than the simple will and good pleasure of God.
3. God can, without injustice, decide whatever pleases him regarding all men and their membership of either the elect or the reprobate.
4. No one can aspire to salvation unless the will and faculty has been given to him by divine providence.

5. God does not give his grace to everyone; he does not call all men, he does not inspire all with the will to come to him; not everyone recognises Christ as the only way to eternal life.

6. Those, therefore, whom God wishes to save he inclines their minds with his grace to yield to the divine voices and allows them to make an impression on the hardness and wickedness of their hearts; we are all born slaves of wrath and destruction. We cannot be liberated from this misery unless God lifts us out by his grace which he does not impart to all since he does not choose so to do.[8]

Whitaker had, therefore, some three months before Barrett's sermon, set out the basis of the Calvinist position on precisely those central issues of predestination, assurance and free will that were to provide the key elements in the coming disputes with Barrett, Baro and Overall. He had done it, moreover, in an aggressive and uncompromising polemic aimed not merely at papists but also at Pelagians. While Whitaker avoided naming any contemporary proponents of this Pelagian position, he did inform his audience that it was a heresy particularly in need of refutation at that time. The implication was clear: there were those in the English church who held such opinions and Whitaker's sermon served notice that he intended to weed them out. It was, in short, a thinly veiled attack on the anti-Calvinist elements in the university. Moreover it was delivered before a highly influential audience, which contained the Earls of Essex, Shrewsbury and Rutland, and hence can be taken as an attempt by Whitaker to enlist powerful lay backing for his campaign against the 'Pelagian' party. As such it should be set beside a letter of 1593 from Whitaker, Some and Goad to Burghley in which they had asked the latter for special extended powers to deal with secret papists; those men that while 'they come to church' 'had by their malicious and bold speeches and otherwise betrayed themselves' and who 'lurking in the colleges amongst us' presented such a serious threat to the well-being of the church and university 'through the corrupting of youth'.[9] As we shall see, the charge of popery was to bulk large in the Heads' case against Barrett and Baro, just as it had in Whitaker's denunciation of Digby. I would contend, therefore, that both the letter and Whitaker's sermon of February 1595 constituted part of a concerted attempt by the Cambridge Calvinists, notably

William Whitaker, to discredit their anti-Calvinist opponents in the university. This campaign must itself be set against the background of Whitaker's clash with Digby and his continued running fight with the conformist and anti-Calvinist elements in his own college, which can perhaps be taken as having alerted him in the first place to the threat to true religion presented by the spread of such pernicious opinions.[10] As for the campaign itself, it was notable for its complete lack of personal abuse or public polemic. Whitaker had, after all, had his fingers badly burned by the unexpectedly hostile reaction of Burghley and Whitgift to his expulsion of Digby. This time he was proceeding by stealth (as he had done finally over Digby) in the hope of gaining his ends by private influence rather than by public suit and dispute with their inevitable concomitant accusations of personal malice and interminable appeals to higher authority.

Heavily outnumbered in the upper echelons of the university as they were, the anti-Calvinists, had they allowed things to go much further, would have found themselves confronted by a *fait accompli*, their case defeated without a hearing, lost by default, as it were. But if this were to happen it was essential that the machinations of the Calvinists remain covert. In that way the anti-Calvinists could be picked off one by one, as Digby had been in 1588 or as Baro was to be in 1596, without the general doctrinal issues ever getting an airing or the Calvinists' activities ever being subjected to the sceptical gaze of Whitgift or Burghley. But Barrett's sermon and the inevitable reaction it produced ended all chance of such an outcome. At a stroke the doctrinal issues were thrust into the open and the Calvinists forced to act under the general scrutiny of superior authority. After all, it was easier to appeal against a formal conviction in the Consistory Court than against the nebulous but all-pervasive influence of Whitaker's lay supporters.

Certainly, if Barrett was trying to provoke a reaction, he succeeded. He was roundly dealt with by the Heads in three sessions of the Consistory Court and forced to recant publicly.[11] But Calvinist opinion in the university remained unappeased and a petition, signed by fifty-six dons, was raised demanding further action against Barrett.[12] However, had things stopped there, the affair would probably have died a natural death. Interestingly enough, though, it was Barrett who once more took the offensive.

This time he appealed to Whitgift. The terms of the appeal are themselves instructive. Barrett singled out Some as the main source of his troubles. Some claimed to have acted with the full consent of his colleagues in the university. But in fact Some himself had been the prime mover in the affair, seeking to mobilise puritan opinion in the university against Barrett. Most of his support was drawn from such men ('amicos suos quosdam puritanicos') and consisted of the most puritan ('puritanissimorum') elements in the university.

Many of Some's supporters, Barrett continued, were young men, with little or no theological training, not merely led but dragged into the argument by Some and other leading men in the university who shared his opinions. The Heads, Barrett claimed, had seriously misrepresented the contents of his sermon and, moreover, were being considerably less than impartial in their application of the law. Here Barrett cited a book written by one Perkins ('hominuncio quidam, nomine Perkins'). This had contradicted openly an article of faith professed as true by the English church. And yet far from censuring Perkins or suppressing the book the university authorities had approved it and allowed its publication. Even now it was available for purchase in London. But how different had the Heads' attitude been to Barrett. He had said nothing against the articles of faith professed by the English church, he had spoken in Latin while Perkins had published in English, yet Perkins' conduct had been approved and his condemned. Where was the justice in that? Similarly, a libellous version of Barrett's initial sermon had been printed and distributed in London by Daniel Munsay of St John's. Barrett had complained to Some, as Vice-Chancellor, 'of this kind of inveighing and of others also using the like liberty against me in St Mary's pulpit', only to be told by Some 'that he had countenanced and would countenance all those that would appear against me to the uttermost of his power'.[18]

The implication behind all this was clear: Barrett was presenting himself as the victim of a puritan plot, a plot that comprised senior members of the university like Some as well as firebrands like Munsay. By singling out Some for particular complaint Barrett avoided the charge of disloyalty to his superiors in general and allowed himself to pose as the victim of an extremist plot without denouncing the majority of the Heads as puritans. In short Barrett was exploiting Whitgift's great dislike of what he had called, in connection with Whitaker's attack on Digby, 'the violence of preciseness'. Excesses like the pamphlet attack by Munsay and the known puritan sympathies of the likes of Whitaker, Goad and Some, not to mention Chaderton, gave Barrett's accusations and innuendoes more than enough basis in fact to arouse Whitgift's interest and concern.

To pre-empt Barrett's attempt to enlist Whitgift's support the Heads themselves wrote to the Archbishop. They took the doctrinal issue as having already been decided:

For our part the sermon being so offensive to the church, so injurious to the worthy learned men of our time, so strongly savouring of the leaven of popery and contrary to the doctrine of the nature and quality and condition of faith set forth in the articles of religion and homilies and appointed to be read in the church and that hath been taught ever since her Majesty's reign in sermons and defended in the public schools upon commencement, without contradiction in the universities we thought it meet to repress these novelties of doctrine by such means as our statutes do appoint and hath been used in like case when your lordship was in the university.

Barrett's popish proclivities were clearly shown, the Heads claimed, by his

impudent challenging of Calvin, Beza, Peter Martyr, Zanchius and others of error in the doctrine of faith in most bitter terms...and taking upon him to answer those places which are alleged of protestants for certainty of faith and alleging most places and speeches which are used in the Tridentine Council and popish writers to prove popish doubtfulness and that we cannot assure ourselves of our salvation. These things gave us occasion (besides his words and answers especially at his first convention and his familiarity and conversation with recusants and papists) justly to charge him with corrupt doctrine.

Thus, taking their stand on the undoubted popery of Barrett's doctrine and on the powers granted to them by statute to deal with heretical statements, the Heads further justified the severity of their response by reference to the present state of the university. As ever popery was on the increase. If such opinions as those expressed by Barrett were allowed to pass uncensured and Barrett let off scot-free, 'it will not only be a great discouragement to the

godly professors of the religion established but also an embolden-
ing to such as are unquiet and evil disposed to proceed both in
these points already begun and in other not yet mentioned'. For
'corruption in religion' had already spread to such an extent that

in those times instead of godly and sound writers, and among our
stationers the new writers are rarely bought; there are not books
more ordinarily bought and sold than popish writers; Jesuits, friars,
postill writers, Stapleton, and such like...upon the search that was
made by your Grace's appointment many divines' studies being
searched there were found in diverse studies many friars', schoolmen's, Jesuits' writings and of protestants either few or none.[14]

In this letter, therefore, all the major elements that have been
identified as central to the moderate puritan attitude were present.
Religious matters were characterised as a straight choice between
popery and reformed purity, Christ and Antichrist, with orthodoxy presented as a rigid adherence to a closely defined body of
doctrine, the smallest divergence from which constituted *per se* a
tendency toward popery. And popery, of course, was seen as an
ever-present threat, its proponents always on the alert to exploit
any lapse of concentration or vigilance on the part of the godly.
It is also worth noting that there was no real idea of the English
church as an autonomous institution with its own traditions and
prerogatives separate from those of any other reformed church.
On the contrary, she was seen as merely the English extension of
an international, or rather supranational, protestant position.
Admittedly the Articles of Religion were mentioned but only to
be immediately identified with the doctrine of foreign divines and
churches, criticism of whom was taken, seemingly, as an offence
in itself.

Hitherto these had remained the unstated assumptions behind
Whitaker's anti-papal polemic and indeed the entire attitude to
the English church. Now they had been set out in black and
white; set out moreover in a letter to none other than Whitgift,
Whitaker's patron of twenty years' standing, and Whitgift did
not take kindly to them. The Heads, he claimed, had ignored the
proper procedures. He condemned their

hasty and rash proceeding against him not giving unto him liberty
to confer with others nor time to consider those points wherewith
he was charged; a peremptoriness not used by the papists nor in

any well governed church of protestants and indeed a rash and intolerable and consistorian-like kind of proceeding.

But, more importantly, they had ignored Whitgift's own authority in such matters:

In that they knowing my care to have these new occasions of contention appeased and to that end writing my advice therein to the Vice-Chancellor to be imparted to the rest of the Heads; knowing also...that in matters of religion it hath pleased her Majesty to commit the especial care to me, that university also being within my peculiar charge in respect of the vacancy of the Bishopric of Ely, yet they would not vouchsafe to make me acquainted therewith as in duty they ought to have done, which I cannot take in good part neither yet suffer. Thirdly for that they have proceeded in matters wherein they have no authority no not by the statute by them alleged, these points not being within the letter or meaning thereof, although they have suffered and daily do suffer both in their colleges and in other places in the town men to offend against the very letter of that statute without reproof.

Evidently Barrett's accusations of puritanism had struck a chord with Whitgift since it was precisely the Heads' precisian disregard for his authority, together with the stark contrast between the harshness of their treatment of Barrett and their indulgence toward puritan non-conformity, that had so angered the Archbishop. This formed the kernel of Whitgift's indictment of the Heads' actions. Admittedly he did discuss the purely doctrinal aspects of the case in the same letter but only in order to back up his assertion that the Heads had exceeded their authority in forcing Barrett to recant since, claimed Whitgift, Barrett had not contravened the Thirty-nine Articles.

Indeed Whitgift went even further than that. The Heads, he asserted, had actually forced Barrett to approve views

contrary to the doctrine holden and professed by many sound and learned divines in the Church of England; and in other churches... and the which for my own part I think to be false and contrary to the Scriptures, for the Scriptures are plain that God by his absolute will doth not hate and reject any man without an eye to his sin. There may be impiety in believing the one, there can be none in believing the other, neither is it contrary to any Article of Religion, ...but rather agreeable thereunto.

To underline the point Whitgift ran through the four major contentions of Barrett's sermon. The first – 'neminem debere esse securum de salute' – Whitgift denied to be contrary to any of the articles of religion 'seeing security is never taken in good part neither doth the scripture so use it. And what impiety is it to affirm that a man ought to be certus de salute but not securus?' The second point, that faith may be lost 'totaliter' but not 'finaliter', he again denied to be against the articles of religion. It was, he said, 'a matter disputable' 'wherein learned men do and may dissent without impiety'. However Whitgift admitted that Barrett's claim that there was no distinction to be made in the nature of faith but only 'in credentibus' was an error. But it was 'yet without the compass of their authority having no article directly against it'. It was, he concluded, 'an error worthy of reprehension not recantation for anything I can yet understand'. As for the fourth point – that the remission of sins while it remained an article of faith was not so in its application to particular men – Whitgift conceded that that was 'likewise untrue and if he did in that manner and sort affirm it he showed therein his ignorance, wherein he should have been better instructed and in a more Christian manner'.[15]

On this basis alone it cannot be justifiably inferred that a genuine difference of doctrinal opinion existed between Whitgift and the Heads. Whitgift's main concern at this stage was the high-handed attitude of the Heads in seeking to settle the matter on their own initiative; in other words, their precisian disregard for his authority as Archbishop of Canterbury. His handling of the doctrinal issues was shaped by that concern. Indeed, far from prejudging the theological aspects of the affair, he was reprimanding the Heads themselves for having done so. Hence, whatever Whitgift may have said in the heat of the moment must be treated as, at best, a preliminary judgement conceived when the desire uppermost in Whitgift's mind was to put the Heads in their places.

Well aware of the assumptions that underlay the Heads' attitude to Barrett, Whitgift's overriding concern was to refute their implicit assimilation of the doctrinal position of the English church to the opinions of foreign divines. He was determined to vindicate the authority of the Thirty-nine Articles as the only yardstick of doctrinal orthodoxy in the church of England. To that end he made his attitude on the question of foreign divines quite clear:

> To traduce Calvin and other learned men in pulpits I can by no means like, neither do I allow the same towards Augustine, Jerome and other learned fathers who nevertheless have often and many times been abused in that university without controlment. And yet if a man should have occasion to control Calvin for his bad and unchristian censure of King Henry VIII or him and others in their peremptory and false reproofs of this Church of England in diverse points and likewise in some other singularities, I know no Article of Religion against it much less do I know any cause why men should be so violently dealt withal for it or termed ungodly popish impudent for the doctrine of the Church of England doth in no respect depend upon them.[16]

There could be no clearer demonstration than that of the role played by Whitgift's very strong anti-puritan instincts in determining his initial highly critical reaction to the Heads' action. Both their high-handed attitude in proceeding on their own initiative and their seemingly excessive reverence for the authority of Calvin raised the spectre of puritanism and that was enough to ensure Whitgift's hostility. Barrett's tactics had worked perfectly.

Whitgift likewise dismissed out of hand the Heads' typically 'puritan' use of the popish threat as a justification for their own protestant extremism. When they had first made a search for popish books they had found no cause for alarm. Why, then, had they suddenly changed their minds? Besides, even supposing their fears were justified, the university authorities already possessed ample powers to deal with any such glut of popish books without seeking to wreck young Barrett's career in the process.[17]

Whitgift, then, was opposing his own view of an autonomous and broadly based national church to the narrower, more constricted view of the Heads. Central to Whitgift's position was his concept of 'things disputable'. This was the equivalent in doctrinal matters of his concept of adiaphora, which had played such an important part in his rejection of the presbyterian case. In both cases, of course, he was dealing with a rigid scripturalism, and in both cases he opposed it with a more limited view of scriptural authority whereby the general rules laid down by scripture were to be interpreted and applied by the relevant human authorities, which in this particular instance meant the Archbishop of Canterbury. Consequently, while the Heads implicitly claimed that true unity was only to be soundly based on the full acceptance of a detailed and closely defined body of doctrinal orthodoxy (which hence, in effect, limited membership of the English church to those who were in full agreement with their style of Calvinism), Whitgift, recognising the 'precisian' impulse behind this view, was concerned to define membership of the national church in terms of a limited number of essential doctrines (enshrined in the thirty-nine articles), thus leaving a fairly wide area of inessentials open to scholarly debate. It was an attitude in sharp contrast to his rigid application of conformity in externals.

Faced with a hostile and incensed Whitgift, the Heads turned to Burghley who, after an interview with the persuasive Dr Some, emerged convinced that Barrett's appeal to the Archbishop over the heads of the university authorities was a breach of the privileges of the university. Accordingly Burghley authorised further proceedings against Barrett.[18] Thus fortified the Heads decided to stand their ground and, basing their case on the powers over such matters ceded to them by their statutes, they waited for Whitgift to come round.[19] They seemed fairly confident that he would do just that. In a letter of 7 July they even went so far as to attribute Whitgift's initial highly unfavourable reaction 'rather to the sinister report of Mr Barrett and his favourers than to your Lordship's own disposition'.[20] The Heads, of course, had good reason to be so confident. Close links of patronage and friendship bound both Robert Some and William Whitaker to the Archbishop. Whitaker, of course, enjoyed equally close links with Burghley. Such personal ties must have bulked large in the Heads' calculations. Certainly Whitaker used his influence for all it was worth to win the Archbishop over. In June, in the course of a routine letter to Whitgift recommending one Mr Powell, a fellow of St John's for preferment, Whitaker took the opportunity, in a quite off-hand manner, to assure the Archbishop of the propriety of the Heads' actions. 'I was present and heard with mine ears, to my great grief. I humbly beseech your Grace and for the love of God's truth which I know is planted in your heart to repress by your authority those ungodly proceedings.'[21] When that, together with the collective efforts of the other

Heads, failed to work the desired changes in Whitgift's attitude, Whitaker wrote again. This time it was a formal letter which went into a detailed discussion of the theological points at issue and in which Whitaker defended the action of the Heads in terms of the need to preserve order and respect for authority in the university:

How necessary a thing it is to have the government of the Vice-Chancellor and his assistants maintained and what a perilous example this will be to have one man of that condition thus to oppose himself against the same; and in his opposition to find such encouragement from superior authority, I leave it to your Grace's wisdom to consider.

Whitaker made great play with Barrett's lowly status in the university hierarchy: if a man like that could defy his superiors and get away with it, where would it all end?[22] As an attitude it makes an interesting contrast to Whitaker's lenience towards the precisian excesses of the equally junior Francis Johnson.[23] Whitaker's judgements were based on an implicit but nonetheless rigid distinction between the 'godly' and the 'ungodly'. Whereas Johnson, however irresponsible he may have been, belonged unequivocally to the former group, Barrett belonged to the latter. Whitaker could cite 'the grief that the godly conceived and the encouragement of the evil disposed' as an argument for a hard line toward Barrett; the same sensitivity to the dictates of 'godly' opinion led him to precisely the opposite conclusions with regard to Johnson. Whitgift, it seems, was well aware of this inherent bias in Whitaker's judgement.

Not that Whitaker's role as a go-between or political broker for the Heads was limited to his dealings with Whitgift. While it was Some, as Vice-Chancellor, who first involved Burghley in the affair, Whitaker repeatedly tried to invoke the influence of the Chancellor on the Calvinist side. For instance, having defied Whitgift's ban on further public discussion of the doctrinal issues pending an enquiry, Whitaker wrote to Burghley in November assuring the Lord Treasurer of the righteousness of the Heads' cause and expressing his fears 'of greater offence and trouble' 'if good order be not taken and provided to the contrary on time'.[24] As ever, baulked in one direction, Whitaker immediately took steps to enlist fresh support on his side. As he had invoked the influence of Leicester against that of Burghley and Whitgift over the Everard Digby affair, so here he was seeking to play Burghley off against the Archbishop.[25] Similarly, it was Whitaker who was to insist on involving Burghley in the promulgation of the Lambeth Articles. An adept at political manoeuvre, Whitaker evidently did not believe in leaving any loose ends for his enemies to exploit.

But there was more at stake here than personal ties of friendship and patronage. For many years both Whitgift and Burghley had taken a close personal interest in the career of William Whitaker. With good reason Whitaker had understood this interest as a sign that the doctrines enshrined in his works of anti-papal polemic represented the official doctrinal position of the English church, if not as set out in the Thirty-nine Articles then at least, as he told Whitgift as 'the religion of our Church publicly received and always held in Her Majesty's reign and maintained in all sermons, disputations and lectures'.[26] Now that the orthodoxy of that doctrine was being publicly challenged for the first time, Whitaker had every reason to expect the help and support of both his illustrious patrons in defending it. Indeed, the key to the Heads' attitude throughout the summer and autumn of 1595 was their conviction that, despite all appearances to the contrary, Whitgift was doctrinally on their side. In the event that was how it proved, with Whitaker playing a leading role in bringing the two sides together and drawing up the theological concordat that expressed their basic agreement. Of course, for the Heads, it was the doctrinal issue that was all important. That was not Whitgift's view and if the Heads thought that it was the Archbishop swiftly disillusioned them.

Further incensed by two indiscreet sermons by Some (the first denouncing Barrett and the second directly critical of the Archbishop) Whitgift wrote a long letter to the Heads which can have left them in no doubt as to his real feelings.[27] Whitgift expressly denied either siding or sympathising with Barrett:

> I am not so light of credit as to believe Mr Barrett in his own cause and you do me wrong so to charge me. Your own proceeding and doing have drawn me into this dislike wherein I am not as yet by your letters satisfied.

How could the Heads thus brazenly deny the Archbishop's jurisdiction in the university when Whitgift himself with others have sat as Commissioners sundry times in Great St Mary's as it is notoriously known and by that authority censured in matters of religion as well scholars as others. And who well advised can or dare doubt whether her Majesty by the laws of this realm or by her prerogative royal may grant such a Commission or not? None but an undutiful subject. It is a most vain conceit to think that you have authority in matters of controversy to judge what is agreeable to the doctrine of the Church of England and what not. The law expressly laying it upon her Majesty and upon such as she shall by her commission appoint for that purpose. And how far my authority under her Highness reacheth therein I hope you will not give me occasion to try.[28]

In the face of an open threat the Heads had to back down. In a long letter to Whitgift they elaborately excused themselves and their past behaviour. The question of the university statutes had not yet been decided, they claimed, all the Heads being not yet present in Cambridge. They, of course, had no intention of impugning the authority of either the Queen or her appointed agents in causes ecclesiastical. Neither had they intended to arrogate to themselves the power to define the doctrinal position of the national church,

but only to signify our care to testify our own opinions for the defence and preservation of that truth of doctrine in some substantial points which hath been always in our memories both here and elsewhere taught, professed, continued and never openly impugned amongst us but by some persons of late.[29]

The Heads painted a picture of godly peace and unity rudely shattered by the novel opinions of Barrett and his supporters. To recover that former peace and concord, they argued,

it is necessary that the one sort be enjoined silence... If the doctrine that hath always since reformation been received and allowed begin now in these points not only to be brought into question but by authority either charged as untrue or suppressed as dangerous or unprofitable what may the papists think of the whole substance of our religion? What a grievous offence will this be not only to malicious enemies but also to weak professors.

Hence the Heads argued that it was the innovators who should be compelled to silence and they used the threat of popery and the need to protect the weak in faith to buttress their case.

The strong similarity between their arguments and those put forward to justify precisian non-conformity in ceremonial matters would not have been lost on Whitgift. But however strongly the Heads might argue their case, they at least put it to Whitgift as if he had some choice in the matter rather than merely presenting him with a *fait accompli* as they had done in the past.[30]

His authority thus vindicated by this admission from the Heads that the dispute fell within his sphere of competence as Archbishop, Whitgift could now turn his attention to the doctrinal issues. In September he drew up a list of questions to be put to Barrett.[31] The Heads sent Barrett's answers to Lambeth and in turn Whitgift supplied his comments.[32] He now admitted to the Heads that he was 'partly of your mind'.[33] Only on one point did Whitgift side with Barrett against the Heads, agreeing that Christ's prayer in Luke 22 could 'not be drawn to all the elect'. Even here, however, he added that it was a point disputable whether Christ was praying for the apostles in general or only for Peter, and that elsewhere in scripture (John 17) Christ was recorded as praying explicitly for the elect as a whole.[34] He agreed with the Heads that Barrett's distinction between 'fides formata' and 'informata' was popish and he also condemned Barrett's attitude to penitential acts.[35] Also, he 'misliked utterly' Barrett's intemperate attacks on foreign divines, although here he added the typical caveat that 'we must take heed that their bare names and authorities carry not men so far as to believe their errors or to yield unto them that honour and forbearance of reproof which is not yielded to any of the ancient fathers'.[36]

Whitgift's greatest doubts concerned assurance. Where Barrett asserted that 'electi' or 'fideles' can only be 'certe de salute', 'I do not take it', said Whitgift, 'that he denyeth that fideles may be assured of their salvation by the certainty of faith; but he denyeth that they are assured "ea certitudine fidei qua tenent omnipotentiam, unitatem et sacrosanctitam personarum trinitat".' Whitgift asked for further information on Barrett's attitude to these particular questions. He wanted to know precisely what Barrett meant by 'certitudinem fidei'.[37]

Whitgift, then, was demonstrating his doctrinal independence (and by implication that of the whole English church) by taking each point in isolation, judging it on its merits and sticking to his category of things disputable. By prolonging matters thus, he was making it perfectly clear to the Heads that he was the ultimate authority in such cases. He was also making it quite clear that while he would defend orthodoxy (summed up in his interpretation of the Thirty-nine Articles) he was not prepared to sanction a precisian witch-hunt. However inadequate Barrett's theological position, Whitgift claimed,

the conclusion of all wherein he offereth to submit himself to the judgement of those who have chiefest authority to decide these controversies and to reform that which they shall think to be erroneous ought in conscience and charity to satisfy you, if you seek his reformation and not his overthrow and destruction. The fierceness and peremptoriness of some in these causes doth more harm than good.[38]

Having made his point, Whitgift at last took steps to bring the affair to a close. He arranged that Barrett and two representatives from the Heads should come to Lambeth to thrash the matter out finally. The end product of this meeting was almost complete doctrinal agreement between Whitgift and the Heads. In Whitgift's own words:

I found that Barrett had erred in diverse points. I delivered mine opinion of the propositions brought unto me by Dr Whitaker; wherein some few being added I agreed fully with them and they with me. And I know them to be sound doctrine and uniformly professed in the church of England and agreeable to the Articles of Religion established by authority.

He added, 'if this agreement be not maintained further contentions will grow to the animating of the common adversary the papist, by whose practice Barrett and others are set on, some of his opinions being indeed popish'. In view of which, the Archbishop concluded, 'I thought it meet that Barrett should in more humble sort confess his ignorance and errors and that none should be suffered to teach any contrary doctrine to the foresaid propositions agreed upon'.[39]

Having established his independence of the Heads Whitgift had dropped his earlier qualifications and settled for a general condemnation of Barrett's doctrine. Hence in Barrett's second retraction, which was drawn up with Whitgift's full approval, while no mention was made of the text Luke 22 (on which point Whitgift had found himself in agreement with Barrett), the doctrines which Barrett had used that text to substantiate were denounced explicitly. Barrett had to deny that 'Petri solius idem deficere non potuisse' and that 'Christum pro Petri solius fide precatum esse ne ea deficerit'. He was also to deny that 'remissionem peccatorum esse articulum fidei sed non specialem huius aut illius', that 'Davidem necisse se non posse excidere', that 'perseverantiae donum esse futurum contingens'. He had to admit that there was a distinction between different kinds of grace (efficacious and sufficient). As for assurance, while Whitgift had not fully accepted the rigid views of the Heads, Barrett had still to deny that 'nemini datum esse certo cognoscere certitudine fidei se esse electum' and that 'neminem posse in hoc fragili mundo certum de salute sua certitudine fidei'. Barrett was to conclude, 'me paenitet de sumis illis viris Martyre, Calvino, Beza, Zanchio quos fateor optime meritos esse de ecclesia Christi tam contumeliose loquutum esse'.[40]

Whitgift, therefore, had sided with the Heads at the end of it all. Elaborately impartial to the last, he had vindicated his own authority and the doctrinal autonomy of the church of England, he had refuted the 'precisian' assumptions and pretensions of the Heads, but he had finally agreed with them. That agreement was enshrined in the Lambeth Articles, and it is to those that we must now turn.

THE LAMBETH ARTICLES: JOHN WHITGIFT AND CALVINISM

The standard account of the Lambeth Articles is given by Dr H. C. Porter in his book *Reformation and reaction in Tudor Cambridge*.[41] He presents the Articles as occupying an intermediate position between that of the Heads and that of Barrett. But in the light of the background we have outlined in the previous chapter it is possible to modify that view.

The word 'Calvinism' and the appellation 'Calvinist' are often used as though they retained a stable and consistent meaning throughout the period. But as a number of scholars have pointed out, there was a considerable shift of emphasis within the mainstream of Calvinist orthodoxy during the second half of the sixteenth century.[42] Briefly, Calvin's thought was subjected to a process of systematisation by a group of 'second generation'

Calvinist scholars who, faced with a resurgent Rome, were concerned to weld the protestant case into a coherent and self-consistent whole. This process, although generally taken to have started with Calvin's colleague and successor Theodore Beza, was not restricted to Geneva. Scholars like Zanchius in Heidelburg or William Perkins in England played an equally important role in the modification of Calvin's thought to meet the needs of the later sixteenth century. Common to them all was a view of predestination even more uncompromising than that held by Calvin. In many ways the difference was one of presentation. Where Calvin had been silent where scripture had been silent, content to accept the apparent contradictions inherent in the text, his followers felt compelled to dot every 'i' and cross every 't'. Hence, finally to undercut any possibility that human effort had anything to do with salvation or damnation, Beza placed God's sovereign decree not under the doctrine of salvation (as Calvin had done) but under the doctrine of God and providence. The doctrine of predestination was in this way included in a logically necessary progression which, from the nature of God and his omnipotence, led inexorably through his double decree to salvation for the elect and damnation for the reprobate. This involved the change in attitude to scripture summed up by Professor Breward in his comparison of Perkins' *Armilla aurea* with Calvin's *Institutes*: 'whereas the *Institutes* had patterns of biblical thought interwoven into the fabric of the argument *Armilla aurea* used texts to buttress positions deduced dogmatically from scripture'.[43]

In England this tendency to reduce the role of scripture to that of a buttress for a logically consistent and 'necessary' system was not confined to the issue of predestination. 'Iure divino' presbyterianism was based on the same attitude to the authority of scripture. Here a full-scale platform of church government was dogmatically deduced from a relatively small number of key texts and then applied directly to contemporary conditions as the embodiment of the will of God. The close connection between presbyterianism, anti-papal polemic and a rigid attitude to predestination and related issues – a connection which has already been noted in the thought of William Whitaker, Thomas Cartwright, Laurence Chaderton, William Fulke and Walter Travers – had, as a result of a common attitude to scriptural authority and theological argument, a strong underlying theoretical basis.

Whitgift's relationship with this nexus of concerns was complex and contradictory. During the Admonition Controversy he had written page after page outlining the dangers of just such an over-rigid attitude to scriptural authority in matters of church polity. Similarly, Beza's support for 'iure divino' presbyterianism, as well as his outspoken attacks on the English church, had done little to endear him to Whitgift. As he remarked in a letter to the Heads, referring to foreign divines in general, 'we have been little beholding to some of them who rashly, and uncharitably, have believed reports of this government and taken upon them to censure us in books printed, which I am persuaded they would not now do if it were to do again'.[44]

Whitgift was also quite aware that a considerable gap separated the position of Calvin from that of many of his supposed supporters. Hence, in his anti-presbyterian works, Whitgift invoked 'the opinion of Mr Calvin of things indifferent' and went on for several pages to prove that in the context of the precisian/conformist debate Calvin was on the conformist side:

If Mr Calvin were alive and understood the state of our church and controversy I verily believe that he would utterly condemn your doings; and I am the rather induced to think so because I understand him to have allowed many things in the English church being at Geneva which you altogether mislike...and therefore he would not think his words racked one whit to establish anything that he would have had overthrown. The rest of my collections are most agreeable to Mr Calvin's words, most necessary for this present time and most apt for my purpose; and your passing over them so slightly doth argue your lack of ability to answer them. Indeed, they flatly determine this controversy and in effect overthrow your whole book.[45]

Here, then, are two rival claims for the Calvinist heritage. Whitgift was, in effect, claiming to be a better Calvinist than his puritan adversaries who made so much of the Genevan example. It was an attitude in marked contrast to the derogatory use of the label 'Calvinist' employed by men like Barrett and Everard Digby.

That the puritan platform rested on an over-credulous – even slavish – admiration for foreign churches and the opinions of foreign divines remained a basic plank of Whitgift's anti-puritan position. It was a criticism that could be applied just as easily in the doctrinal sphere. Whitgift, therefore, was hardly likely to be caught expressing too high an opinion of Calvin, who had occasionally criticised the English church, albeit not as severely as his successor Beza had done. Whitgift, of course, was well aware of all these nuances. As we have seen, he had spent a great deal of time during the Barrett affair in asserting both his own and the church of England's doctrinal independence.

Nevertheless he was also quite capable of using the considerable authority attached to Calvin's name to rebuke the precisians. Hence, in so far as he retained considerable respect for Calvin as a divine and accepted the basic insights of his thought, we are justified in referring to him as a Calvinist. But that does not mean to say that he was a Calvinist of the same sort as Chaderton, Whitaker or Cartwright. On the contrary, he had explicitly rejected the developments inside the Calvinist tradition that had made it the basis for the presbyterian platform.

Whitgift's conduct during the Barrett affair fits this view perfectly. His main concern in opposing the Heads had been to contest their narrow 'precisian' view of the nature (not the content) of doctrinal orthodoxy in favour of his own vision of a broadly based national church, independent in its doctrine from the interpretation of any private individual or foreign church, particularly where inessential or doubtful points were concerned. In theological terms, to put it rather crudely, Whitgift remained true to Calvin's awe before the mysteries of God's will. This was in direct contrast to the Heads' 'Bezan' search for complete logical rigour or consistency. His attitude to assurance typified the difference. Without departing from a view that could be meaningfully called Calvinist Whitgift had pulled the Heads up short. He had let them know in no uncertain terms that if all Barrett had done was to deny that we can be as sure of our own salvation as we can of the doctrine of the Trinity then he had done nothing contrary to the Articles of Religion. But once the Heads' assumptions and pretensions had been defeated and the affair referred to him, Whitgift's basic allegiance to the central insights of Calvin's thought reasserted itself and he found decisively for the Heads and against Barrett.

Some corroboration for this view can be found in Whitgift's relations with Matthew Hutton, the Archbishop of York. Hutton

was a contemporary of Whitgift's and his early career in the
university had closely paralleled that of Whitgift. But while
Whitgift had taken the shorter route to preferment, through his
direct and polemical espousal of the conformist case, Hutton
had taken a more roundabout route to the top, remaining loyal
to his old patron Grindal and the ideal of an evangelical protestant consensus in the church.[46] Hutton's progress up the career
ladder of the established church was accordingly far slower than
that of his more dynamic contemporary. But whatever their
previous differences, Whitgift undoubtedly regarded his northern
colleague as a fellow survivor from a past golden age of protestant
orthodoxy and moderation.[47] It was very likely that it was in
that role that Whitgift had consulted Hutton concerning the
Cambridge disputes. Hutton was aware of them as early as
August 1595 and kept in constant touch with the latest developments until the conclusion of the affair the following spring.[48]
In his letters to Whitgift Hutton took a consistently Calvinist
line. Asked for his opinion of the Lambeth Articles he fully
endorsed them as an accurate statement of the doctrinal position
of the church of England. He was similarly unequivocal in his
rejection of the individual doctrines put forward by the anti-
Calvinists. Baro's distinction between an antecedent and a
consequent will of God was dismissed as simply popish. It was
an error to be found in the works of Pelagius, Damascenus, Biel
and Scotus and one which had been amply refuted by Augustine.
Baro's contention, that merely because man had been created in
God's image in the first instance, all men were therefore framed
for salvation, was likewise rejected as heretical. It ignored,
claimed Hutton, the severity of Adam's fall which had all but
destroyed the image of God in the natural man. As for Baro's
comparison of God with an earthly governor who adapts his
laws to the capacities of his subjects and to the farmer who plants
a tree so that he can see it grow, not merely so that he could
have the pleasure of rooting it up again, they too were popish.
As for Peter Baro, Hutton wished that he were in his own
country and not sitting in Cambridge disturbing the peace of
the English church. 'Let one be in his place', Hutton advised,
'who is learned, godly and mild of nature, Cambridge affordeth
store of such.'[49]

Hutton enclosed with his letter a short treatise of his own on predestination. This he wanted Whitgift personally to see through the press as a public demonstration of the Calvinist solidarity of the episcopate. 'I am sorry to hear', he wrote, 'that the court should boil at the doctrine of predestination. It may be that when they see that your Grace and I do agree in all points (which will be if your Grace do publish my treatise) they will take better liking of it.' Certainly Hutton himself was in no doubt that his doctrinal position was in complete agreement with that of Whitgift. 'I do not think that we dissent anything at all from St Augustine' whom 'God hath used as a special instrument to set forth that comfortable doctrine'.[50]

By thus harking on the authority of Augustine Hutton avoided that slavish adherence to the opinions of Calvin and Beza that Whitgift had discerned in the attitudes of the Heads. Rather than resort to such foreign authorities, Hutton was invoking the broad doctrinal consensus of the English church which both he and Whitgift had experienced in the years before the spectre of presbyterianism had arisen to shatter the unity of protestant opinion. Hutton sought to do this in two ways: firstly by recalling their days as academic colleagues and theological allies in the Cambridge of the 1560s, and secondly by trying constantly to assimilate the position of Baro and his ilk to that of the papists. Hence at one point he remarked that Baro's doctrine reminded him of nothing so much as the opinions that he had heard expressed at a disputation in Cambridge during Mary's reign.[51]

On this view, Hutton and the protestant tradition that he personified can be seen playing a central role in reconciling Whitgift to the Heads on the basis of a strongly Calvinist doctrinal concordat. But that was not the limit of Hutton's involvement in the affair. In the Chaderton Mss at Lambeth there is part of a manuscript copy of his treatise on predestination, dated 1595.[52] This is the same treatise as that Hutton sent to Whitgift. It seems possible, therefore, that in addition to his official contact with Whitgift, Hutton had also sent a copy of his treatise to Chaderton. In effect, then, Hutton had privately encouraged the Heads to withstand the irate Whitgift until the latter's basically Calvinist outlook had had time to reassert itself, suitably encouraged by Hutton. Such co-operation is rendered inherently more likely when it is remembered that when Hutton's little book was finally published in 1613 it appeared in a volume containing works by Chaderton, Some, Andrew Willett and George Estye, all dealing with issues raised during the disputes of 1595/6 and all taking a strongly Calvinist line.[53] There could, of course, be no better illustration of the continuing validity of the protestant consensus of the English church than the mediating role of Hutton in bringing Whitgift and the Heads together. Here, surely, in the person of the venerable Hutton, was a Calvinist tradition that pre-dated the more recent 'Bezan' developments in English divinity, and it was on the basis of this style of Calvinism that Whitgift found for the Heads.

Certainly, if he disagreed with the Heads, Whitgift had a funny way of showing it. Referring to the first draft of the Lambeth Articles given to him by Whitaker Whitgift wrote, 'wherein some few being added I agreed fully with them and they with me'.[54] Dr Porter makes great play with those 'some few being added'. By comparing the initial draft drawn up by Whitaker with the final version approved by the Archbishop Dr Porter has identified the changes introduced at Whitgift's behest and attempted to show that they constitute a distinct move away from 'Calvinism' on Whitgift's part.

But what were these changes?[55] In Article 2 the phrase 'efficient cause' was changed to 'moving and efficient cause'; 'predestination' was altered to 'predestination to life' which in effect meant that election alone was grounded purely and simply on the will of God. Reprobation was not mentioned. This allowed the implication to be drawn that reprobation was in some sense caused by, or grounded on, man's sin. But it was only an implication and it could just as easily be drawn the other way. While such reticence was not typical of the Calvinism of the 'Whitaker school', it was quite compatible with an earlier style of Calvinism, a style typified by what Basil Hall has called Calvin's 'refusal to be too systematic, too precise, too logical about God's purposes'.[56] Lastly, the phrase 'absolute and simple will of God' was modified to 'the will and good pleasure of God' ('voluntas beneplacitas dei'), a phrase almost directly scriptural (Ephesians 1.5).

In Article 5 Whitaker had maintained that true faith cannot 'fail in those who have once partaken of it'. In the final version this was changed to 'in the elect', which implied, or at least allowed the implication to be drawn, that people other than the elect could, for a time at least, enjoy a true faith.

In Article 6 the phrase 'certus est certitudine fidei' became 'certus est plerophia fidei'. This Dr Porter calls 'perhaps the most significant change'.[57] Certainly, as we have seen, it was over assurance that Whitgift's opinion diverged most clearly from that of the Heads. But even this change was merely a modification, a toning down of the rigidity of the Heads' wording to emphasise the scriptural elements in it. Certainly it did not alter the basic thrust of the article. As a formula it seems to have served the Heads perfectly well in their continuing campaign against Barrett and, later, Baro. In Chaderton's account of an interview with Barrett held after the formulation of the Articles in their final form we find the former using precisely the same phrase without Barrett gaining any material advantage from it.[58] I would contend that all the changes made by Whitgift in the original draft were of this nature. The basic orientation of the Articles remained the same, and in the context of the Cambridge disputes this was entirely in favour of the Heads and against Barrett. Moreover, the Lambeth Articles remained a watch word for unrelenting Calvinist orthodoxy well into the seventeenth century. For instance, at Hampton Court, it was one of the puritan demands that the Lambeth Articles should be given confessional status, a proposal opposed by both Bancroft and Overall.[59] Similarly, in 1615, that high Calvinist, Archbishop Ussher, was to include the Lambeth Articles as an adjunct to the Articles of Religion in the Articles of the Irish church.[60] Hence, if Whitgift had intended to produce a via media between Calvinism and anti-Calvinism, it would appear that he did not make a very good job of it.

But if Whitgift was intent on putting a basically Calvinist gloss on the Thirty-nine Articles, why did he change Whitaker's version at all? Firstly, I would contend that he felt the need to avoid the appearance of complete agreement with the Heads, for the sake of his personal prestige. As we have seen, the whole point of his initial intervention in the entire affair had been to vindicate his authority in doctrinal matters. Having entered the arena with a flurry of criticisms directed at the Heads, to have ended in complete and unqualified agreement with them would not only have looked like an admission of defeat: it would have left the Archbishop looking very silly indeed. Moreover, as we have seen, Whitgift had 'missed' the developments inside the

Calvinist mainstream that had occurred during the Admonition controversy, and consequently he had been left with a style of Calvinism rather different from that of the Heads. Hence he had sought, in Dr Porter's phrase, to render the Articles 'less uncompromising and more scriptural'.[61]

But it was not merely theological considerations that motivated Whitgift. We have already noted the parallel between his concept of 'things disputable' in doctrinal matters and 'things indifferent' in externals. Almost certainly Whitgift felt himself to be confronted with the same overrigorous preciseness in the Heads' doctrine as he had already encountered in the classis movement. The only difference was that in matters of doctrine the Archbishop was in substantial agreement with his precisian opponents. But Calvinist though he was, it is worth remembering that Lancelot Andrewes and Hadrian Saravia were both Whitgift's chaplains at this date. While this does not justify the assimilation of Whitgift's theological position to that of Andrewes and Saravia (any more than his role as Whitaker's patron justifies the assimilation of his opinions to those of Whitaker), it can be taken as evidence that Whitgift was considerably more charitable in his application of doctrinal orthodoxy than the Heads. Hence, in altering the Articles, it does seem likely that he was prompted by a desire to render them acceptable within a wider spectrum of doctrinal opinion than that readily accepted by the Heads as orthodox. Certainly it can have formed no part of his intention in drawing up the Articles to make membership of the church of England more difficult for a man like Andrewes. Whitgift wanted to regulate the terms within which theological debate was to be conducted, but he was not going to sanction a precisian witch-hunt.

Given these circumstances, Whitgift's production of a document as avowedly Calvinist as the Lambeth Articles was a tribute to the strength of his assumption that the broad Calvinist consensus of the 1560s and 1570s was still intact. The Lambeth Articles, therefore, stand as a monument to Whitgift's rather ingenuous, not to say old-fashioned, conviction that the opinions of every English divine of significance could be accommodated, without undue strain, within a framework of thought that was recognisably Calvinist.

THE CASE OF PETER BARO

The Lambeth Articles were received in Cambridge with a sigh of relief. The Heads evidently interpreted them as a belated but nonetheless very welcome sign of official approval for their doctrinal stand. In that sense they provided an ample reward for, not to say vindication of, their initial recalcitrance in the face of Whitgift's disapproval. In a letter to the Archbishop (dated 13 December 1595) they thanked him for the 'good issue' of the affair and pledged themselves 'everyone on our places for the preserving of that peace to employ our special care and endeavour and to continue the course of doctrine in those points amongst us according to the directions and cautions your Grace hath thought meetest'.[62] What those pious and seemingly innocuous sentiments entailed for the anti-Calvinist elements in the university soon became clear. Goad, the new Vice-Chancellor, wrote around to the other Heads and, as he told Whitgift, gave special warning 'unto some particular persons of whom I doubted, as namely Dr Baro the Frenchman...by causing him to see and read over the propositions as also that clause of the said letters that nothing should be publicly taught to the contrary'.[63] The Heads had already stated their view that the controversies could be brought to an end only by the silencing of one of the two parties. Evidently they considered the Lambeth Articles to give them *carte blanche* to do just that – to silence their enemies.

For the Articles had far greater implications than Whitgift appeared to realise. Carried away by the basic agreement of his own doctrinal position with that of the Heads and by the personal influence of his old friend Whitaker, Whitgift had committed himself to the definition, in numbered theses of something that had previously belonged to the intangible realms of tacit assumption and implicit agreement – namely, the 'Calvinist consensus' of the English church. Ironically, in so doing, Whitgift was himself committing precisely the offence of which he had earlier accused the Heads: he was arrogating to himself the power to define the doctrine of the church of England. That Whitgift could risk so much without realising the full implications of his own actions was in itself a telling tribute to the depth of his assumption of an abiding doctrinal consensus in the church. But if, as seems likely, Whitgift believed that he was merely committing to paper the theological commonplaces of the age, he was to be swiftly disillusioned.

On 5 December 1595 Robert Cecil wrote to the Archbishop telling him that the Queen 'mislikes much that any allowance hath been given by your Grace and the rest of any point to be disputed of predestination being a matter tender and dangerous to weak ignorant minds and thereupon requireth your Grace to suspend them'.[64] It is instructive to enquire how precisely the Queen came to hear of the Articles. Shortly after the meeting at Lambeth that had produced the final form of the Articles, Whitaker had decided to inform Burghley of what had taken place. As we have seen, Burghley was Whitaker's special patron and Whitaker was afraid 'lest if he should understand of it after it might be taken in evil part'. Whitaker told Humphrey Tyndall of his intention and although the latter did not altogether agree that it was a good idea he consented to accompany Whitaker on his mission. They showed Burghley a copy of the Articles. He read them over and also acknowledged receiving the text of an earlier sermon by Whitaker on the points in dispute.[65] With becoming modesty Burghley admitted that the

matters were too high mysteries for his understanding and seemed to dislike of the propositions concerning predestination and did reason somewhat against Dr Whitaker's in them, drawing by a similitude a reason from an earthly prince inferring thereby they charged God of cruelty and might cause men to be desparate in their wickedness. Mr Dr Whitaker seeing then his Lordship's weakness did in wisdom forebear to answer my Lord but only said that nothing was in that behalf set down but was delivered in the articles set out by public authority.[66]

And with that assertion of the complete congruence of the Lambeth Articles and the Articles of Religion they took their leave of a perplexed Burghley.[67] The latter's robust common sense had, it seems, revolted against the extremes of Whitaker's Calvinism. After years of consistent support, during which he had given Whitaker every reason to believe that he regarded his doctrine as the acme of protestant orthodoxy, this sudden defection on the part of Burghley must have been a nasty shock. Neither could it have come at a worse time. It is highly likely, therefore, that it was Burghley who told the Queen about the Lambeth Articles. Certainly, judging from his later consistent support for Baro against the prosecution of the Heads, Burghley continued to sympathise both with Baro's personal plight and with his doctrinal position. For once Whitaker's attempts to hedge his bets by involving lay authorities in ecclesiastical disputes had backfired badly.

The personal intervention of the Queen put Whitgift in a very embarrassing and exposed position. Her unstinting support had been the rock upon which Whitgift's career had been founded. Now, having committed himself further than he knew, that support had been suddenly removed, leaving the unfortunate Archbishop high and dry. The extent of his embarrassment can be gauged from a story told by Thomas Fuller, wherein the Queen is reported to have told Whitgift jokingly that by having thus called a council without her consent as Supreme Head he had forfeited all his goods to her.[68] Of course, all might yet have been well. Had the affair come to a peaceful conclusion with the promulgation of the Articles and Goad's circular to the Heads, the Calvinist case would have prevailed by default and the very tenuous claims of the Articles to confessional status would have gone unchallenged. However, it was precisely at this most crucial of moments that Peter Baro chose to reopen the whole affair by commenting publicly on the Articles and subjecting them to a thorough reinterpretation from the anti-Calvinist point of view.

Whitgift's discomfort at this is shown plainly in a letter to Dr Nevile, the Master of Trinity, written on 8 December 1595. In it Whitgift tried vainly to salvage something from the wreck of the Articles. The Queen, he claimed, 'is persuaded of the truth of the propositions, but doth think it to be utterly unfit that the same should any ways be publicly dealt with either in sermon or disputation'. Certainly Whitgift himself had intended no such thing. 'For indeed', he claimed, 'my meaning...was only that in these points I do concur with you in judgement and will to the end, and mean not to suffer any man to impugn them openly or otherwise'. At this stage Whitgift was still determined to stand by his doctrinal concordat with the Heads, and hoped to see the Articles installed as guidelines for theological debate both in the university and in the church at large. But Whitgift had been embarrassed in front of the Queen and he was looking for someone to blame. It seems he still harboured a grudge against the Heads, 'you that refuse advertisement and think yourselves to have no need of advice'. Had they acted otherwise 'these things had never grown to this extremity'. But if he blamed the Heads, he blamed Baro more. 'You may also signify to Dr Baro', he told Nevile, 'that Her Majesty is greatly offended with him for that he being a stranger and so well used dare presume to stir up or maintain any controversies in that place of what nature soever. And therefore advise him from me utterly to forbear to deal therein hereafter.'[69]

Obviously Whitgift and the Calvinists needed more than anything else a period of quiet to allow the memory of the Archbishop's indiscretion to fade. Faced with such an awesome display of Archiepiscopal ire Baro looked for a moment as though he might provide just such a respite. He wrote a long letter in Latin to Whitgift which purported to summarise his doctrinal position. He had asserted only that God was not the author of sin; that God condemned men only for their sins, which alone formed the object of his hatred; that the faithful or the elect should not rest secure ('securos') concerning their own salvation. According to his own interpretation and that of others, the Lambeth Articles hardly touched on such points.[70] Called to Lambeth to justify himself further Baro continued in the same vein. According to Whitgift he made 'some frivolous and childish objections against some one or two of them only; yet did he confess that they were all true and that they did not impugn any of his assertions'.[71] After Baro had thus gone through the bare motions of compliance, Whitgift was only too glad to let the whole matter drop.

But Baro was not to let the Archbishop off so lightly. Once more he dealt publicly with the Articles, in a *concio ad clerum* on 12 January 1596. According to Goad's account, the *clerum* was unusually vehement for the mild-mannered Baro. It was delivered, wrote the Vice-Chancellor, 'with more earnestness and vehemency than is remembered that ever he showed before; to the great offence and grief of all the soundly affected to the truth and to the encouragement and stirring again of the minds of his disciples and adherents'. As far as Goad was concerned, no sooner had the moderation of the Calvinist party created an atmosphere of godly peace and concord than this outrageous intervention on the part of Baro arose to shatter it.

In public divinity exercises either in the schools or in Great St Mary's where I have been continually personally present I have not heard the least contradiction on the other side so far off from personal provoking as there hath been seldom or never maintaining or mentioning the truth set down in any of these points, their texts of scripture not occasioning thereunto. So, as it was like within short time the former troublesome controversies would have worn out of men's minds and been forgotten.

But now, thanks to Baro, all such hopes were dead, shattered by this 'unhappy and unlooked-for reviving which I did hear yesterday at the *clerum* sermon'.[72]

Of course Goad's analysis was far from impartial. It was entirely in the interests of the Heads to let the controversies subside. If the validity of the Articles was allowed to pass uncontested then the Calvinist case prevailed by default. For however elaborately impartial Whitgift had been in 1595 by agreeing to the Articles, he appeared (whatever his intentions) to have sided definitively with the Calvinists. Whitgift's signature at the bottom of the Lambeth Articles put Baro in a situation where he had to fight for his theological life. He summed up his situation in a letter to the Danish Lutheran divine Niels Hemingsen, written in 1596. 'In this country', complained Baro, 'we have hitherto been permitted to hold the same sentiments as yours on grace, but we are now scarcely allowed to teach our own opinions on that subject much less to publish them.'[73] Calvinist repression was forcing Baro out into the open. The *clerum* of 12 January was probably the first overtly polemical act in a career otherwise notable for its utterly unpolemical nature. Baro had been in the university for over twenty years and, with the exception of his earlier skirmish with Chaderton, had never been involved in a similar dispute before which, given the nature of his doctrinal position, was in itself an achievement. Ironically, this was precisely the sort of polarisation of opinion that Whitgift had wanted to avoid but which, unwittingly, his approval of the Articles had helped to bring about.

Baro's persistent attempts to reopen the controversies in December and January were almost certainly part of a calculated campaign to overturn the assumption that with the drawing up of the Lambeth Articles the whole affair had been decided in the favour of the Calvinists. Of course the hostile attitude adopted by both Burghley and the Queen to the Articles presented Baro with the perfect opportunity to do just that. Moreover the position he took up to justify his defiance of the Calvinist authorities was perfectly calculated to take full advantage of that opportunity. The Articles, he claimed, did not impugn his positions. Indeed, he was not commenting on the Articles at all but merely attacking the errors of Piscator and those who tried to assimilate the Articles to those same errors. In this he claimed to be saying no more than was contained in a letter of Bishop Hooper's which he had always been taught to regard as a perfectly orthodox exposition of the doctrine of the English church.[74] Baro was thus seeking to align himself with a tradition of 'liberal' English theology which, he implied, stretched from the reign of Edward VI, through the Book of Common Prayer, the Book of Homilies and the Thirty-nine Articles, to the 1590s. In effect, by taking this line Baro was presenting Whitgift with a choice: either he must repudiate that tradition as heretical or else he must leave the likes of Baro alone. But to denounce such views, claimed Baro, was to equate the doctrine of the English church with the errors of Piscator and to effectively replace the Thirty-nine Articles, established by the authority of Parliament, with the completely unofficial Lambeth Articles. That, certainly, was what many of the Heads, who angrily invoked the Articles against Baro's doctrines, were doing. Of course, Baro assured the Archbishop, he did not for one moment include him in his strictures against the Calvinists. Nothing, he was sure, could have been further from the Archbishop's mind when he framed the Articles. For, as he was sure Whitgift appreciated, rightly understood, there was nothing in the Lambeth Articles that impinged on the Articles of Religion. Subtly, therefore, but very skilfully, Baro was exploiting the weakness of Whitgift's position.

It is interesting to note that in a letter from Whitgift to the Heads concerning Baro's second outburst Whitgift had remarked that:

I doubt indeed that he hath received some kind of encouragement here from some that seem to make some account of his judgement in these points and take their pleasures thereof both publicly and privately. It may be also that he hath heard of some misliking of the said propositions by some in authority. But therein peradventure in the end he may deceive himself.[75]

Baro, then, had been put up to it by someone in authority, in the hope that by exploiting the Queen's dislike of the Lambeth Articles the anti-Calvinist cause might be advanced to new heights of respectability. But at the end of the passage quoted above Whitgift seemed to imply that he hoped to overcome his enemies at court and vindicate the Calvinist cause with the Queen. But until that were done, Whitgift advised the Heads to proceed against Baro with caution. Goad, as Vice-Chancellor, should call Baro before him and ask for a full copy, or at least an accurate précis of his sermon. But, warned Whitgift,

> forasmuch as there is some thing ado here about the same propositions I would not have you proceed to any determination against him till you have advertised me of his answer and the particular point of his sermon and received back again from me what I think fittest to be done by you in this matter.[76]

With Whitgift impotent until the situation at court had resolved itself, the Heads struggled on alone as best they could. They called Baro before them but nothing came of it because of Baro's 'uncertain and insufficient answers'.[77] Depositions were then taken from nine witnesses and Baro was examined yet again; again nothing happened.[78] Throughout these proceedings Baro stuck to his basic claim that since he had not contravened or in any way maligned the Thirty-nine Articles or the Lambeth Articles, 'certe et orthodoxe intellectus', he had committed no offence.[79]

In an attempt to break the deadlock, Goad turned in desperation to Burghley. The Chancellor, however, had not changed his attitude since his interview the previous December with Whitaker. 'The matters', he said, 'I cannot conceive as others take them.' The Heads had treated Baro 'as he were a thief,' particularly as 'the witnesses do not agree'. As for the Heads' doctrinal claims, 'as good and as ancient are of another judgement'. The irate Burghley concluded, 'You may punish him if you will but ye shall do it for well doing in holding the truth in mine opinion.'[80] The Heads were baulked on all sides. Whitgift's hands were tied by the disapproval of the Queen, Burghley was openly hostile and Baro remained obstinate. All they could do, therefore, was to exploit their numerical preponderance in the university and keep up the pressure on Baro in the hope that he would crack under the strain.

In defending his doctrinal position it was inevitable that Baro should have offended Whitgift. But isolated as he was in the university, he could not afford to treat the Archbishop in too cavalier a fashion. Hence, having made his doctrinal point, he set about appeasing the Archbishop. First he wrote to Lancelot Andrewes, who was one of Whitgift's chaplains and in whom Baro recognised another proponent of the anti-Calvinist cause, and asked him to intercede on his behalf with the Archbishop.[81] Then on 27 January he appealed directly to Whitgift. All the doctrinal points of his first letters were rehearsed, but this time in considerably more suppliant tones. But now Baro's purpose was not so much to vindicate his doctrinal position as to win his way back into the Archbishop's favour. Like Barrett, he denounced the Heads as themselves in error. The Calvinists, he implied, were the true instigators of those disputes. Only recently Mr Perkins had preached 'in templo Mr Chadertoni' against the doctrine (asserted both by Baro and by Overall) that Christ had died for all men. This was a point, claimed Baro, that was quite fundamental to the Christian faith; a point, moreover, that had never been a subject of debate between true Christians before. Yet, complained Baro, while the Heads allowed every sort of excess to pass unpunished on the Calvinist side, they denounced him for preaching the true doctrine of the apostles. Baro begged Whitgift not to leave him at the mercy of such men; men whom everyone knew to have been ill-affected towards him for years and who were themselves at odds with the present discipline of the church.[82] Like Barrett before him, Baro was trying to exploit Whitgift's anti-precisian instincts by presenting himself as the innocent victim of the Heads' misplaced puritan zeal.

When Whitgift gave no sign that this attitude had softened, Baro wrote again in despairing and importunate tones. He repeated his accusations of malice, singling out both Chaderton and Goad as two men who had been attacking him for years, simply, he added, because he was well-affected to the present state of the church. Moreover, Chaderton had a special reason to dislike him since he still harboured a grudge from their earlier clash of 1583. At present, Baro complained, there were no constraints placed on the Heads' powers. They could indulge their personal prejudices as they pleased. Hence, when Goad had warned Baro not to deal publicly with any of the questions covered by the Articles, he had refused to go into details. This meant that the Heads might seize on any statement of Baro's and construe it as a breach of the Articles. Baro was alone and at the mercy of his enemies. He threw himself, instead, on Whitgift's mercy.[83]

Baro's letters to the Archbishop had become more desperate and imploring as time passed, and the reason is not difficult to see. At first he had been concerned not with Whitgift's personal favour or protection but with doctrinal issues; only later had he come to see that he needed Whitgift's support. As he himself confessed, he was isolated in Cambridge. Admittedly, in a test case of national significance, Baro, with friends at court, might defy the Heads successfully. But in the long term weight of numbers would surely tell. As things stood, Baro could be assailed by his enemies in the course of some purely personal dispute and no one would come to his aid. His overtures to Whitgift in January and February 1596 were hence an attempt to protect himself from the inevitable wrath of the Calvinists.

Given this series of letters to the Archbishop, it was natural for Baro to attribute the conclusion of the Heads' campaign against him to the intervention of Whitgift: 'quod tua reverentia factum esse non dubito'.[84] But this was only an assumption and, I would contend, merely wishful thinking on Baro's part. Certainly there is no reason to 'legitimately infer' (in Dr Porter's phrase)[85] that Whitgift had intervened postively on Baro's behalf. It is surely more likely that the Heads' campaign dragged on until March when, denied 'official' support from either Whitgift or Burghley, it died a natural death, and that once it was clear that the cause of the Lambeth Articles was utterly lost at court, Whigift took no further part in the affair, merely allowing events to take their course.

Certainly, later in the year, Whitgift displayed no great enthusiasm for Baro's continued presence in the university. On 26 November Whitgift wrote to Jegon, the Vice-Chancellor, concerning the forthcoming elections to the Lady Margaret Chair of Divinity. 'I am loathe to commend any man unto you for the Lady Margaret's Lecture', he wrote, 'partly because I would give no impediment to Dr Baro's re-election, if any of his friends be disposed to help thereunto, but especially because I know your wisdoms and discretions to be such as that you will make choice of the best and fittest for that office. Notwithstanding if there be no intent again to elect Dr Baro, then I would pray you to be favourable to Mr Dr Playfere.'[86] The letter was not a little disingenuous. By thus leaving the decision to the university authorities, Whitgift had made it virtually certain that Baro would not be re-elected. As we have seen, the university was dominated by

Calvinists (Baro's only real supporter during the disputes had been John Overall) and after his experiences of the previous year Whitgift must have realised how high feelings were running. Hence Baro's only chance of re-election was through the intervention of some authority outside the university. By denying Baro precisely that sort of support, Whitgift had effectively sealed his fate. In the event Baro did not even stand in the election which turned out to be a straight fight between one Mr Dr Gray and Playfere. Needless to say, Whitgift's choice won by a margin of twenty votes to twelve and, interestingly enough, proved during his period in office to be a staunch champion of Calvinist orthodoxy.[87]

Whitgift, then, had ended on a Calvinist note, and the Calvinist elements in the university had won a piecemeal, but notable, victory. But however many battles the Calvinists might win, they had already lost the war. With the collapse of the Lambeth Articles, the Calvinist claim to represent the sole fount of orthodoxy in the church of England was definitively discredited. This is not to say that the claim was not made, merely that it could never become the basis for an effective purge of the university or church after 1596 in the way that the Heads had hoped. The failure of the Articles, then, to achieve confessional status ensured that.

Moreover, there were elements left in the university whose presence gave that failure a more than academic significance. Here the crucial figure was John Overall. His election to the Regius chair in succession to Whitaker was in itself a blow to the Calvinist cause. While there is no evidence to link Whitgift to that appointment, it is extremely unlikely that he disapproved of it and entirely possible that Overall's preferment represented a typically Whitgiftian ploy to deflate the pretensions of the Heads even as he was concluding the theological dispute largely in their favour and presiding over the removal or departure of the two trouble-makers, Barrett and Baro, from the university. Certainly, shortly after the conclusion of the theological disputes, Whitgift can be found protecting Overall from what looks like the hostile attention of the Calvinist Heads. The occasion of Whitgift's intervention was a disputed election to the mastership of St Catharine's College in March 1598.[88] The college had only six fellows. Of these the three seniors wanted Overall as master, the other three wanted Dr Simon Robson of St John's. The two factions found it impossible to agree, and at the end of the time appointed for an election the seniors declared their candidate, Overall, elected, they being 'senior et sanior pars and so to be deemed the maior pars'. At this the three junior fellows 'expecting...the last moment of the time appointed assembled themselves in the chapel...to make another scrutiny for election of the master and admonished the rest of the fellows to be present at the last scrutiny'. However, the three seniors, 'presuming they had made a sufficient election before...refused to come into the chapel to that scrutiny'. Thereupon the juniors proceeded alone and declared Robson elected. St Catherine's now had two masters and the task of choosing between them fell on Jegon the Vice-Chancellor. Acting on legal advice and in association with Tyndall, Nevile, Barwell, Duport, Clayton, Byng, Legge, Chaderton and Montague, Jegon found for Robson, who took possession of his new post.[89] At this point a letter from Bancroft arrived instructing Jegon 'not to meddle in that matter (unless it be to justify the election for Mr Dr Overall)' for the Queen was 'made acquainted with that controversy' and intended 'to take order therein'.[90] Overall, it appears, had powerful favourers at court. Certainly he had been Whitgift's preferred candidate – the senior fellows had cited his instructions to elect Overall in their case against Robson and Jegon felt constrained to write a fulsomely apologetic letter explaining his role in the affair to the Archbishop and denying charges of bias against Overall.[91] Overall's backers were certainly determined to get their own way for despite the support of the Heads and a week of 'quiet possession'[92] Robson was removed and Overall installed.

There was no mention in any of this of any doctrinal issues. However, the Heads who chose to justify their proceedings to Burghley were none other than Jegon, Tyndall, Chaderton, Barwell and Montague (Master of the new 'puritan' foundation Sidney Sussex).[93] It may well be that the Calvinist elements in the university were closing in on Overall in an attempt to prevent his further rise up the ladder of preferment. In the manner of Whitaker in his campaign against Digby, they based their case on the minutiae of college statute, unwilling, after the debacle of 1596, to risk any reopening of the doctrinal issue. Whitgift and Bancroft's crushing intervention on Overall's side might then be seen as a response to precisely those tactics and hence as a part of the continuing struggle to control 'the violence of preciseness'.[94]

In any case, the incident reveals the strength of Overall's backing and when in the later 1590s he again aroused the ire of the Calvinists by continuing to spread the anti-Calvinist gospel the Heads found themselves unable to act. They investigated, they drew up a list of supposed errors from Overall's lectures, and they confronted him with a list of their findings at a meeting of the Consistory Court. But when the point was reached at which definitive action should have been taken, Jegon, the Vice-Chancellor,

> put forth a question which appeared to put them into a great muse; whether they thought it not meet before they proceeded any further herein to acquaint my Lord of Canterbury his Grace herewithal? Whereunto was said diversely that it was needless; it would be a trouble to his Grace; his Grace would not like it; that his Grace's judgement was utterly against those points; that it would diminish the authority of the university.[95]

In other words, the Heads were in the same dilemma in 1599 as they had been in 1595/6. Given their experience during the Barrett affair, they were bound to consult Whitgift. Yet after the fiasco of the Lambeth Articles they could hardly hope for a favourable response from that quarter. Accordingly, the charges against Overall stayed in Cambridge. There was much denunciation of Overall from the pulpits, but no action.[96] When the latter finally appeared before a meeting of the Consistory Court (headed by Some as Vice-Chancellor) in June 1600, he was once more in a minority of one. At length 'the Vice-Chancellor earnestly desired Dr Overall to join with him and the rest in the acknowledgement of the same truth whereof all present would be most glad. To which he answered he was not so persuaded in his conscience and therefore could not.' The Vice-Chancellor tried to salvage something from the mess. Citing a precedent

> in like case occasioned by a letter from the Lord Grace of Canterbury there read [Some enjoined Overall]...to forbear impugning the said points of doctrine in any of his public exercises considering that thereby not only themselves there present but many others in the university could not but be greatly offended and excited to a needless and dangerous contention.[97]

Weight of numbers counted for something, therefore, but only in a limited, piecemeal way. Overall's activities could only be hindered, they could not be definitively stopped. As Some said in 1600, 'the university is a precious fountain; if that be corrupted it must needs be wide with the rivers and give a grievous blow to truth and peace'.[98] It was a fountain that from the Calvinist point of view was irretrievably polluted after the debacle of 1595/6.

Of course the heyday of English Calvinism, which was produced by the alliance between godly bishop and moderate puritan in the defence of right doctrine (termed by Dr Tyacke the 'Calvinist consensus' of the early Jacobean church), was yet to come.[99] But that should not blind us to the significance of the events of the 1590s. For in 1595/6 the foundations of high Elizabethan protestantism started to crumble. For the essence of that protestantism had been a basic doctrinal agreement or consensus within which differences about the extent and nature of divine sovereignty and the authority of scripture had centred almost exclusively on the debate about church polity. After that debate came to a close with the final collapse of the classis movement in the early 1590s, while mutual suspicion might persist (as it certainly did between Whitgift and the Heads), there was no great theoretical divide. Admittedly there was, from the dispute about church polity, a 'carry over' into the doctrinal sphere which can be seen, for instance, in Whitgift's concept of 'things disputable' and in the relative lack of rigidity in his formulation of Calvinist orthodoxy. But here, as we have seen, the difference between Whitgift and the Heads was one of nuance and degree and not one of kind.

That basic agreement was enshrined in the Lambeth Articles, which were in essence an attempt to set out in numbered theses the hitherto undefined doctrinal consensus of the English church in order to use the resulting formulae to regulate future theological debate. That attempt failed as it inevitably had to. Such shared assumptions are at their most effective when they operate at a level at one remove from conscious formulation. Once they cease to operate automatically but have to be formally defined and enforced, their days are numbered.

Moreover, such a process of systematisation, by giving potential opponents something to react against, often ends up by increasing the solidarity and self-consciousness of the very people it is designed to discourage and intimidate. Certainly this was true of the Lambeth Articles. There the attempt to codify the basic canons of Calvinist orthodoxy merely served to provoke further opposition. The threat of virtual outlawry forced both Barrett and, more particularly, Baro out into the open. In the process opinions that had been current in the university for decades were suddenly forced into coherent polemical shape and Baro's ideas transformed from the disparate thoughts of a foreign professor of divinity into a rival claimant for the heritage of English protestant orthodoxy.

Isolated as he was, Baro was forced to cast around for allies. Mention has already been made of his letter to Lancelot Andrewes, which was intended to stir the latter into further efforts in the anti-Calvinist cause. The dividing line between theological parties was becoming more and more acutely defined. In that letter Baro had conveyed very sharply his own appreciation of that division, with himself and Andrewes ranged on the one side and Perkins and his allies on the other. Similarly, in a letter to Hemmingius in Denmark, Baro enjoined the Danish Lutheran finally to commit himself in the confrontation between Calvinists and anti-Calvinists. The whole tenor of the letter is indicative of Baro's attitudes in the face of the Calvinist assault. In the present climate of opinion, wrote Baro,

We must not on any account desist from the defence of the truth which we have undertaken. But the eyes of all men are turned towards you, a man of the greatest celebrity on account of your age, your piety and your erudition; the matter itself also requires this at your hands – to continue drawing out of the storehouse of your riches whatever your prudence may have considered to belong to the elucidation of a question of such vast importance.

The particular issue that concerned Baro was a recent edition of a short work by Hemmingius published in Geneva, with a preface by Beza.

In that preface although he appears wishful of giving a favourable and just interpretation of your sentiments yet he draws it over to his own meaning in such a way as to make it difficult to perceive what are your real opinions. By this means he has excited doubts in the minds of many people which you can remove if you please and no longer allow your opinion to be thus unfairly wrested.[100]

It would be difficult to conceive of a more explicit call to arms than that. For Baro a period of theological detente was over; it had been succeeded by a period of confrontation in which modesty or ambiguity were luxuries which no prudent divine could afford.

Certainly, this realisation of the increasingly polarised situation in the church was reflected in the stark contrast between Baro's attitude during his earlier dispute with Chaderton in the early 1580s and his attitude in 1595/6. Then Baro had seemed somewhat bemused by the hostile response his views had provoked; he had tried to reason with his detractors, whom, despite the vehemence and unfairness of their attacks, he had still regarded as fellow protestants and potential friends and allies. By 1595 he had come to regard the same men as enemies, puritans to be denounced to the authorities, implacable opponents to be defeated not so much by reason and scripture as by political and polemical manoeuvre and party solidarity.

The ambiguous legacy of these events found expression in a minor incident in the early months of 1597. In January, one John Rudd, a graduate of Christ's College and now parson of Shephall in Hertfordshire, preached in Great St Mary's. Amongst other things he maintained:

1. That the use of humanity and human arts and profane authors in sermons was and is altogether unprofitable and unlawful.
2. That not the tenth part of the ministers of this our Church of England are able ministers or teachers but dumb dogs.
3. That a curate not being a preacher is no minister nor doth edify any more than a boy of eight years old may do.
4. That papists and Lutherans in Cambridge are lately reconciled and dismissed for which the university doth here well abroad.[101]

In the present context points one and four are of particular interest. But Rudd's conjunction of them with traditional precisian complaints against the established church was scarcely less significant. Evidently, the whole performance can be taken as an indicator of the attitude of the puritan rank and file to the outcome of the disputes and their view of them as yet another instance of the corruption of the English church and the inability of even the more godly elements in the university establishment to safeguard the cause of true religion. As such it was surely indicative of that pressure from below, exerted by puritan opinion in the university and its environs, that must have been a constant factor in the Calvinist Heads' calculations throughout the disputes. Certainly, the sermon registered their discontent at the outcome of the disputes, which they apparently viewed as an unworthy compromise forced on the university from outside (as, of course, it was).

It seems that Rudd was doing more than merely voice his own opinions. No longer a resident member of the university, he may well have been acting as the spokesman for others more directly vulnerable to the wrath of the university authorities. Certainly, those authorities experienced enough trouble in bringing Rudd to book. He promised to retract the offending statements, but, like Barrett before him, his retraction proved merely to compound his offence. Indeed, his remarkable stubbornness may have represented an attempt to reopen the whole dispute. However, the university authorities, rather than allow that to happen, referred the matter to the High Commission. The letter explaining the affair to Whitgift was signed by John Jegon, as Vice-Chancellor, Richard Clayton, John Overall and Simon Robson.[102] Evidently the fatal conjunction of anti-Lutheran sentiments with precisian polemic against the established church had served to hand the initiative back to the anti-Calvinists. Now it was they who could pose before Whitgift as the guardians of order.

Certainly Bancroft and the other High Commissioners seem to have impressed Rudd with the gravity of his offence and extracted an apology and assurances of future good behaviour from him. The letter from the Heads accepting this reprimand as punishment enough and restoring to Rudd his preaching licence and degrees was signed by an entirely different set of people from those who had complained against him in the first place. Jegon (again as Vice-Chancellor), Tyndall, Barwell, Some, Cowell, Chaderton and Montague signed this second letter.[103]

There could be no clearer example of the divisions in Cambridge opinion opened by the disputes nor of the ambiguous and uncomfortable position occupied by the moderate puritan Heads. Despite their numerical superiority in the university, they were unable to embody their own principles in effective punitive action against their opponents. This in turn did little to bolster their standing with their erstwhile supporters amongst the godly, whose explicitly precisian pressure from below could only confirm Whitgift's worst suspicions and undermine the moderate Heads' own position. As ever the lot of the committed reformer, enmeshed in the contemporary establishment, was not a happy one.[104]

IO

Conformity: Chaderton's response to the Hampton Court Conference

After the collapse of the classis movement in 1590 the puritan cause, taken in its most polemically developed form as a series of propositions concerning the liturgy and polity of the church, was faced with a crisis. For that cause was now deprived of its most coherent and polemically effective weapon – the presbyterian platform. If nothing else the debacle of 1589/90 had served finally to remove presbyterianism from any realistic agenda of incipient change or reform within the English church. But the accession of James I rekindled puritan hopes for further reformation. Those hopes came to centre on the conference at Hampton Court called by James to settle the religious position of his new realm once and for all.

Professor Collinson has demonstrated the considerable overlap of personnel and approach which linked puritan organisation and agitation prior to Hampton Court with the classis movement.[1] However, not all the puritan aspirations centred on Hampton Court were presbyterian in form. In this chapter I want to examine the theoretical position adopted by Laurence Chaderton toward the issue of subscription, raised in its most acute form by the failure of the puritans to win a definitive victory at the conference and by Bancroft's subsequent drive for conformity. Chaderton's position here can be seen as a continuation of that developed by Cartwright and others in the late 1570s and 1580s. However, by 1604/5 it was no longer accompanied, in Chaderton's case, by any overt expression of presbyterian principle. The aim here is to examine the ways in which Chaderton sought to accommodate himself to the new conditions produced by the relative failure of Hampton Court (in which he, as a puritan delegate, was implicated) and Bancroft's drive toward conformity without fatally compromising his puritan principles. Some idea of the success with which Chaderton was able to sustain this delicate balancing act can be gleaned from the nature and tone of his contacts with two men, both more radical than he in their attitudes to conformity and both threatened with suspension and even deprivation as a result of their refusal to subscribe. For the moment, however, let us turn to Chaderton's developed position on the issue of subscription.

Whereas in the 1580s it was necessary to tease out the moderate position on the issue of subscription from a series of relatively ambiguous documents, by the end of the century Chaderton had obligingly set out his own attitudes on the subject in the notes for a full sermon 'de licitis'.[2] He took as his text 1 Corinthians 6.12: 'All things are lawful but all are not profitable; all things are lawful but I will not be brought under the power of anything.'[3] His theme, predictably, was the nature and extent of Christian liberty in externals. In his best Ramist fashion, Chaderton divided 'lawfuls' under two headings – those that were directly commanded and those that were left to 'man's liberty and choice'.[4] Of the former, pertinently enough, he cited the example of the minister's duty to preach the word.

But it was the second half of the distinction – things licensed – with which he was primarily concerned. It was to these that the 'liberty of doing or not doing'[5] of the Apostle referred. But it was 'liberty not licentiousness' that was at stake here.[6] This freedom 'though it be purchased by a great price and given by Christ left in man's choice yet it must not be used licentiously, but with due observation of the circumstances of expediency, to wit of order, decency, edification and inoffensiveness, the careful keeping whereof maketh the licensed expedient as the undue regard of these maketh it inexpedient'.[7] In order for this law of expediency to be observed it was necessary for some positive benefit to accrue from the action in question. Mere lawfulness was in itself a neutral quality and hence was insufficient on its own as a warrant for positive action.[8] For something in itself lawful 'may be used both with a repugnant and with a doubting conscience and so not profit but hurt the user; also with offence and scandal to the weak in faith and therefore hurt others'.[9] Such considerations obviously depended on a whole series of variable circumstances, and Christian liberty consisted in the determination to modify one's use of externals in accordance with the exigencies of the immediate situation; hence the Apostle's refusal to bind himself in perpetuity 'using it ever or using it never; but as a Lord over it I will use it when I see cause and when I see no cause I will not use it, so making it serve to me and not myself to serve it'.[10]

Chaderton proceeded to apply these principles to 'our ceremonies of kneeling at the communion and the surplice'.[11] To do so he had first to prove that as ceremonies they were indeed indifferent. Certainly, he maintained, they were not forbidden in scripture. Some had tried to invoke the second commandment against them, but Chaderton rejected that. He asked

How can this be seeing nothing is there forbidden but as it is a serving of God by him not commanded and prescribed? Now we know [and this was precisely what the radicals denied] that the church professeth that these ceremonies are neither propounded nor to be used to serve God with all or to be any parcels of his worship. (For if they were they should be detestable abominations), and therefore they are not, neither can be, forbidden in the second commandment.[12]

Yet, as things indifferent, they were still subject to abuse. 'For what is more lawful than to eat and to drink or more unlawful than to be drunken...?'[13] While such abuses were indeed forbidden by God, they did not and could not alter the inherent lawfulness of the thing itself or its licensed uses. In short, 'abusum non tollit usum'. All of which, of course, applied to the abuse of the ceremonies in question by the papists. Of themselves, therefore, such things could not contaminate a man or an institution.[14] It was 'the lust of man's heart coveting to use them otherwise than the Lord hath commanded that is with breach of the eternal law of love and of the rules of expediency. And these are the ill thoughts that defile a man and not the ceremonies themselves.'[15] To think differently was a sin against the will of God. Chaderton catalogued the errors of such men. 'They make that sin which God hath made none, that unlawful which he hath made lawful, they make themselves servants whereas Christ hath made them Lords.' In short, 'having begun in the liberty of the spirit they end in the servitude of the flesh'.[16] The ceremonies should neither be urged nor used 'of necessity' but 'voluntarily as indifferent things judged fit for the present time and the common state of this church'.[17] To do otherwise was to 'do wrong to our church and the governors thereof as if they required these to be observed as parcels of God's worship, which they do not'.[18] Such sentiments had implications for both precisians and conformists. For precisians evidently were not to prefer the 'servitude of the flesh' to 'the liberty of the spirit', but were to conform to the present state of the church for the sake of their God-given ministry. But if precisians could 'do wrong to our church and the governors thereof' by taking a hard line on the issue of subscription, so too could conformists by seeking to give the ceremonies in question a necessity they did not possess through enforcing conformity too severely. For since the ceremonies in question were indifferent, all men should be 'ready and willing with like duty to admit the change hereof made by like authority'.[19] Moreover, such ceremonies could only be observed (and hence conformity enforced) according to the law of expedience. 'We must beware that we use them not with a repugning or doubting conscience but with a mind fully persuaded of the lawfulness and indifferency thereof for else we sin being condemned of our own conscience.'[20] Similarly, 'we must use them without giving offence to any present that shall signify his weakness in faith unto us or which otherwise shall be made known unto us'.[21] To enforce the ceremonies in such circumstances would be to 'break the law of love' and to 'offend those whom God's word commandeth to be edified and brought up to a perfect building in Christ'.[22] Chaderton, then, fully accepted what were perhaps the two most common reasons put forward by ministers to avoid or at least to modify the demand for subscription: the integrity of their own conscience and the weaknesses or scruples of their congregation.

But Chaderton was far from giving way entirely to precisian scruples. The demands of conscience were not absolute; they could be exercised only within fairly constricted limits. Hence, Chaderton claimed, we should 'avoid singularity of practice' and 'conform ourselves to the accustomed manner of the church to show that we neither are nor will be refractory for matter of indifferency'.[23] But this duty to use the ceremonies to 'testify peace and obedience not to weaken unity but to strengthen it as the bond of peace' applied with equal force to the conformists. They were placed under an obligation not to enforce conformity in such a way as to threaten that unity. But this raised the crucial question of 'who shall be judge in case of controversy whether the lawful be profitable or not?' Chaderton's answer was immediate. The matter should be left to

every superior in his own calling and limited charge; the husband amongst his wife and children; the householder in his house; the magistrate in his precinct; the king in his kingdom; the pastor in his flock; the council in the church and to be short every superior to whom God hath given the spirit of discerning things that differ.[24]

In its complete omission of any mention of the authority of the bishop in his diocese, its implicit division between the temporal and the spiritual spheres (the king in his kingdom and the council in the church), its location of authority in the spiritual sphere in church councils rather than the Supreme Head and its implicit assertion of ministerial parity, that passage was reminiscent of nothing so much as the presbyterian platform. But perhaps more interesting still is the very strong resemblance between Chaderton's description of the English church and its actual practice. Chaderton, in fact, was putting forward a defence of the de facto workings of Elizabethan church government. Rather than a centralised, rigidly hierarchical system whereby the bishops mechanically applied an 'official' policy, inflexibly laid down at Canterbury, Chaderton was arguing for a decentralised system whereby general principles (drawn initially from scripture but no doubt confirmed by authority) were to be applied to particular cases by a whole series of autonomous or semi-autonomous magistrates – 'every superior in his own calling and limited charge'. It is not difficult to see here the godly laity, the well-affected local, and indeed national, magistrates and councillors, and the sympathetic bishops, all of whom in practice made 'space' for the puritan party within a seemingly uncongenial, even hostile, ecclesiastical regime. Finally, remembering the general principles laid down by Chaderton concerning the need for a fully resolved conscience and the avoidance of offence of the weak in faith, we can see quite clearly the process whereby the tender consciences of many puritan ministers were reconciled to a still unreformed church.

It was, of course, perfectly possible to argue for further reformation on the basis of the demands of expediency and edification set out here. Chaderton's presence as a puritan delegate at the Hampton Court Conference must be taken as evidence that he himself favoured such change. Indeed, the puritan case at the conference was conducted by Chaderton and his colleagues in precisely such terms. The puritan delegates studiously ignored and avoided those more radical formulations of the puritan position which sought to characterise the situation facing the church as a simple choice between lawful and unlawful liturgical forms and ceremonies. Instead, the issues at stake were considered at the conference in isolation and purely in terms of their relative offensiveness and inoffensiveness. The result in polemical and propaganda terms was perhaps unfortunate. The puritan case was made to appear trivial, a series of piecemeal objections to the liturgy, quite capable of resolution without further change in the structure or nature of the English church. This is not to argue that the puritans came away empty-handed or that all the concessions granted them were trivial. Some – like the decision to embark upon a new translation of the Bible or James' public commitment to the 'puritan' doctrine of predestination (in direct opposition to the anti-Calvinism of John Overall) – patently were not trivial. It is, however, to observe that such piecemeal concessions did not amount to that definitive change in the ideological tone of the English church for which the puritans had hoped and which a consistently favourable royal response to their demands would surely have represented. If, as is likely, the studied moderation of the puritan delegates at the conference was a ploy designed to elicit such a response from the King, those tactics backfired.[25]

For a moderate like Chaderton, however, the conference was far from a disaster. At worst it was a tie: but most importantly it was a tie from which the puritans had emerged to fight another day. For by the very moderation of their conduct during the conference the puritan delegates had avoided a head on clash between the precisian conscience and the demands of authority. Once more conformist attempts to paint puritanism as an underground conspiracy inimical to all order in both church and state had been turned aside. But in that larger struggle the conference itself had represented a mere preliminary skirmish. The real battle would only commence after the conference when Bancroft, with his renewed demand for subscription, would once more attempt to squeeze the mass of puritan ministers between the demands of puritan principle on the one hand and their commitment to the national church and their role as preachers within it on the other.[26] It was precisely during such periods of official repression that the middle ground was most difficult to hold. Yet it was also precisely at such times that moderate councils were needed to hold puritan opinion together and stave off the threat of mass deprivations or, worse still, of open schism and separation. In short, moderate puritans had to turn aside the 'either/or' choice posed by the authorities between a meek conformity and deprivation, and yet convince their more radical brethren that such a course of action represented more than mere careerist hypocrisy.

Chaderton's position as a renowned moderate ensured that in the face of the renewed demand for subscription men would turn to him for advice. And so we find Chaderton applying the general principles outlined above to particular cases. One such minister who turned to him for help was Walter Jones of Benenden in Kent, who wrote to Chaderton in 1605. The last time he had been in London, wrote Jones, the city, 'because of these troubles, did abound with ministers and many did talk of you [Chaderton]'. 'I was sorry to see', he continued, 'what variety of opinions I found among those that stand in those controversies and, as far as I could see grounded upon final judgement.'

Jones himself was in trouble. He had appeared four times before the authorities (three times before Bancroft himself) and had hitherto refused to conform. In his hour of extremity he had turned to the godly learned scholars of his old university. Bancroft, however, had 'misliked' the idea of his coming to Cambridge in person, fearing that 'we would there meet to no good', so Jones had to consult Chaderton by letter.[27] Notwithstanding the fact that Jones' livelihood and vocation were at stake, their discussion concerned itself almost entirely with details of scriptural exegesis. Jones' main contention was that the church did not have authority 'to appoint signs of spiritual things'.[28] Only if such an authority were demonstrated out of the scripture would he conform.[29] Chaderton responded by citing Joshua 22.34, a favourite proof text of his. This concerned a dispute amongst the tribes of Israel over the building of an altar. One side accused the other of apostasy in building an altar for religious purposes, whereupon the other side replied that the altar was not built for a religious purpose at all, but as a witness 'between us and you and between our generations after us' to the effect that both sides worshipped the same God. The altar was, therefore, but a 'similitude or pattern of the altar of the Lord', and as such its construction could not constitute apostasy. That, claimed Chaderton, offered conclusive proof that the church had the power to signify spiritual things.[30]

Jones, however, challenged this interpretation of the text. Reverting to the Hebrew, he questioned Chaderton's translation of certain key words. Rather than 'signis', the altar in question should have been termed 'testis' or witness. It was intended to 'bear witness between man and man', and to do that, claimed Jones, 'is a thing civil'.[31] But a witness is not a function of the thing to which it bears witness. A witness of adultery 'is not therefore to be a sign of adultery'. As a witness between man and man, even though it was intended to signify a spiritual thing (viz. that Jehovah was God), the altar was civil. But, if the church could not 'signify spirituals' as Jones claimed, then the ceremonies in question could not be merely indifferent. That 'only God ordains signs of spiritual things' was not only to be 'observed throughout the course of the whole scriptures', but the second commandment expressly forbad 'all images, signs, similitudes for religious uses'. Yet what was the sign of the cross but 'a sign of spiritual things as of our signifying Christ crucified which is a holy and religious use'.[32] Moreover, if the church's power in such matters were once to be admitted, Jones could see no end to it. This was surely to open the way to all sorts of popish abuses like 'the blood of a lamb or bullock shed to signify Christ's blood shed for us... or candles to signify that we are passing from darkness to light'. Chaderton, he felt, 'seemed somewhat to approve' all this when he quoted from Tertullian 'examples of that time for this purpose... as that in the supper [they] did mix water with wine'. But Jones answered one patristic source with another. 'But I answer out of Eusebius', he said, 'that the church of God was a pure virgin 110 years after Christ;... but after as he saith the generation of Apostles being worn out then the church began to be defiled and so fall more and more from that time to the full setting up of Antichrist'. Now with these ruins 'men are foiled which maintain the sincerity of the gospel and the estate of churches as they were planted by the Apostles'.[33]

There in outline was the radical case. The need for direct

scriptural warrant for all things contained in the worship of God and the drive to destroy all the works and remnants of Antichrist. Chaderton, however, confined himself to Jones' particular arguments. First he addressed himself to Jones' distinction between the civil and the spiritual. Was every bearing witness civil? asked Chaderton. What of baptism, was that not a bearing witness between the party baptised and other men? Was that merely civil? Jones needed to 'better define what is a civil thing'. If functions and duties ordained by God could be signified in civil matters why not in the ecclesiastical and spiritual sphere itself? asked Chaderton. Chaderton knew of no passage in scripture where God had allowed the one but forbidden the other and therefore suspected that Jones' distinction 'is not from heaven but from man'. 'Consider and judge I pray you according to the judgement of the spirit and not according to man's judgement.' Likewise, Jones' distinction between 'signis' and 'testis' was dismissed by Chaderton as specious. He challenged Jones to say 'what difference there is between these two. This altar is a witness testifying that Jehovah is God and this altar is a sign signifying (by his likeness) that Jehovah is God.'[34]

As for things indifferent, Chaderton admitted that sacramental signs could be instituted by God alone. But he denied that the signs and ceremonies involved here were sacramental in nature. They were commemorative or admonitory and as such they had been left to human authority. Hence, while the second commandment forbade 'images to resemble God' it did not forbid images of any other thing or creature for uses other than divine worship – hence it did not forbid the ceremonies in question.[35]

Finally, Chaderton dealt with Jones' citation of Eusebius. The passage in question had provided a consistent source of support for the presbyterian platform and its citation by Jones in the present context might be thought likely to have caused Chaderton, as a former stalwart of the presbyterian position, a little discomfort. But if it did he betrayed no sign of it. The passage, Chaderton claimed, did not mean that there 'was no stain in the church at the time of the apostles' but merely that she was 'pure and incorrupted from the stains wherewith she was stained in his [Eusebius'] time'.[36]

But here Chaderton's concentration on his minimum position

– the mere insistence that these ceremonies were not, in themselves, unlawful – gave way. Chaderton was no simple conformist and he let slip a personal preference into his otherwise 'objective' analysis of Jones' case in order to 'sugar the pill' of conformity:

I would never advise any church to bring into the church any such signs or ceremonies, nor being brought in to retain them long nor to urge the observation of them by necessity or so as the observation of God's commandment ought to be urged. For being indifferent things they should be permitted to be used indifferently...So likewise should the omission of such indifferents though ordained, be censured with proportionable censure.[37]

That 'should' was of great significance. It provided eloquent testimony to the strength of Chaderton's distaste for strict conformity as Bancroft was enforcing it. As we have seen, Chaderton's view of the law of expedience had as many implications for the authorities who administered conformity as for the ministers who accepted or rejected it. The fact that Chaderton was unable to influence the former while he could influence the latter put him in a somewhat invidious position. But he refused merely to tailor godly opinion to suit the dictates of a peremptory authority. On this view of the situation subscription did not entail the tacit acceptance of Bancroft's view of the church. It was in order to underline that point that he explained his own preferences to Jones, implying in the process that the mere act of subscription need not preclude a continuing commitment to the removal of the offending ceremonies at some unspecified time in the future.

But Jones was not the only man to consult Chaderton on the issue of subscription. Thomas Brightman wrote in the same year (1605) trying to convince Chaderton of the unlawfulness of the ceremonies in dispute. But this letter differed from that of Jones in that whereas Jones had wanted Chaderton's help in resolving his own doubts, Brightman had no such doubts to resolve. He did not want advice from Chaderton. On the contrary, he was attempting to persuade Chaderton, as a leading moderate, to come over into the radical camp and declare the ceremonies to be simply unlawful. That Brightman thought such an attempt worthwhile is in itself eloquent testimony to the fact that Chaderton still retained the respect of even the more radical spirits in the puritan movement. Moreover, at the outset Brightman admitted that there was no question of time-serving on

Chaderton's part. It was, he wrote, 'no change of mind in you to admit a toleration of these things at some time and place and in some sort, but the same you have long heretofore both held and taught esteeming them as things indifferent, and therefore such as when and where expediency doth suffer maybe lawful'.[38]

The particular bone of contention between them was the way in which conformity was being 'enforced' inside Emmanuel College. Brightman referred to a paper wherein was 'required by the fellows of your college...assent to this effect' that the use of the surplice and hood 'after the manner of the university in your college' need offend no one.[39] However, such equivocation cut little ice with Brightman. His arguments, he admitted, applied mainly to 'that use which is enjoined us in the country' and not to that current in colleges. 'There seemeth to be some difference', Brightman concluded, but 'the similitude of an evil thing' is 'a poison not to be touched'.[40] For Brightman the ceremonies were simply unlawful. Scriptural commandments 'abolishing all idolatrous monuments' certainly applied to contemporary usages such as the 'religious use of a surplice'.[41] In all 'things unnecessary' we should never 'be conformable' to idolatry.[42] It was unlawful to accede even for one hour to the demands of 'false brethren' over things indifferent. In the present situation there could be no doubting 'what is the desire of many false brethren' or 'what advantage they hope from this conformity'.[43] Having thus divided the church of England into true and false brethren, Brightman proceeded to invoke the spectre of Antichrist. Did we not have the warrant of scripture 'to go out of Rome under the name of Babylon (Rev. 18.4)'? And that warrant, according to Brightman, applied to any 'unclean thing'. 'The things of Rome are the inventions of Rome or that which is appropriated to the Romish superstition. These and such like places make me think the religious use of a surplice is not indifferent.'[44]

For Brightman, therefore, Chaderton was equivocating; worse, he was temporising with the remnants of Antichrist. Now, the difference here between Chaderton and Brightman was one of degree, not of kind. Certainly Chaderton shared Brightman's belief in the great divide that separated Christ from Antichrist. For him too the church was divided between true and false brethren. What was at issue between them was not, therefore, the existence of that division, but whether it could be based on the issue of subscription and the acceptance or rejection of ceremonies that Chaderton held to be inherently indifferent. In matters essential to salvation (broadly matters of doctrine) Chaderton's attitude was an uncompromising as that of Brightman. The severity of his reaction to the doctrine of Baro and Barrett proved that. But in this case he accused Brightman of 'a lack of charity' in calling those who either used or urged the use of the ceremonies in question 'false brethren'.

> To speak my conscience I think that they who hold and teach that the ceremonies now urged are impious and therefore of necessity never to be used for any cause in God's service come liker to the false brethren meant by St Paul than they that urge and use them.[45]

Thus to restrict the membership of the godly only to those who refused subscription, which was what Brightman, for all his respectful deference toward Chaderton, was in effect doing, was tantamount to separation. Certainly, it drastically reduced the potential support for any broad protestant consensus to be constructed on the basis of the admittedly orthodox doctrine of the English church. Chaderton was, in effect, defending that commitment to a genuinely national church which had always characterised mainstream puritanism and which had been one of the underlying assumptions of the presbyterian movement. In a sense, therefore, Chaderton was still playing the orthodox presbyterian, here defending the concept of the national church from a new style of pseudo-separatism.[46]

But while such issues were implicit in the whole argument they were never explicitly stated. Instead the debate was carried on on the level of detailed scriptural exegesis. Brightman tried to stretch general injunctions against idolatry and Antichrist to apply to the immediate situation of 1605, while Chaderton denied that the texts in question could be applied directly to the ceremonies in dispute and tried instead to restrict them to more immediate contexts.[47] The exchange is notable for its unpolemical and gentlemanly tone. The two men were genuinely concerned to persuade one another. There was no attempt by Chaderton to tar Brightman with the brush of separatism, nor any attempt by Brightman to denounce Chaderton as a time-server. Both ac-

cepted the other's implicit claim to belong within the magic circle
of ideological respectability – the way in which the exchange
was contained within the limits of detailed scriptural exegesis
proves that.[48]

But, given the fact that the discussion took place within the
assumption of a basic protestant consensus, the almost purely
scriptural nature of the exchange should not surprise us. Such
exegetical rigour was the only reply that moderates like Chaderton
could make to conformist claims that the puritan appeal to
conscience, regulated only by scripture, was a mere shift to
justify personal prejudice and singularity. But if it was necessary
for Chaderton to be seen to follow the dictates of a scrupulous
scholarship to refute the conformists, it was also necessary to
control the excesses of the precisian left. For Chaderton well
knew that undisciplined subjectivism could easily prompt a so-
called principled opposition to authority. At one point Chaderton
set himself to answer the argument that no ceremony 'whereof
we have just cause to doubt whether we shall please God in the
use thereof' should be used in the church. Certainly conscience
counted for a lot. But there could be many causes for doubt.
'Men may have just cause to doubt by reason of their ignorance
or error though there be no just cause indeed on God's behalf or
of men of understanding.' In the case of the ceremonies, Chaderton continued, 'this just cause of doubting ariseth from
ignorance or error and not from God's word which maketh all
these lawful'. Hence subjective error could not detract from the
objective truth as set out in scripture, and in this instance the
inherent lawfulness of the ceremonies, since it proceeded directly
from the word, could not be affected by purely human considerations.[49] It was, therefore, the duty of every man to ensure
that all his doubts and scruples were soundly and solidly grounded
upon scripture. 'Is it anything else but either ignorance of God's
word or error or hardness of heart to believe that which is plainly
taught out of God's word?' Doubt on its own was simply not
enough. One must ask 'what leaveth the mind doubtful?'[50]
Chaderton, therefore, could take a hard line with his radical
brethren. But on other occasions he could sound extremely in-
dulgent toward the vagaries of the precisian conscience.

In these we are commanded every one to be persuaded in his own
mind of that he doth or leaveth undone but if any doubt whether

of just or unjust cause let him abstain till his conscience be persuaded.[51]

While these two statements were not logically incompatible, they did pull very strongly in opposite directions. The tension between them encapsulated the tension inherent in the moderate position as a whole. Committed both to the national church and to godly principle and unwilling to denounce as sectaries those who pushed their protestant principles to more radical conclusions, Chaderton could not be said to have resolved the moderate puritan dilemma: rather he was merely expressing it in theoretical terms.

But even supposing the ceremonies to be in themselves in-different, as Chaderton argued, it was still possible to refuse subscription on the grounds that, indifferent or not, given the present state of the English church, their use was so inexpedient as to be unlawful. Walter Jones had put just such an argument. 'In those places where men are not offended' ministers should leave their ministry rather than subscribe because 'they that hear of it afar off may be offended'.[52] To this Chaderton replied that questions of expediency were entirely dependent on 'variable circumstances of time, place, person, manner of doing'. The proper use of an indifferent thing was inherently lawful, yet this proper use may notwithstanding 'in regard of mutable circumstances be both expedient and inexpedient'.[53] Generalisations about questions of expediency or inexpediency were hence ipso facto inadmissable since according to Chaderton it was our duty 'to please all men in doing all lawful things'.

Now in pleasing all being of such different opinions and affections as men are we must necessarily respect those persons with whom we are present and they with us and not such as are absent. For if we should regard the absent also it is impossible to please all with the same useage of indifferents.[54]

Hence,

if in any congregation the minister infallibly know that there are infirm in fide that will be offended with the use of these it is certain that he ought first to seek by good instruction to heal those weak ones before he use the ceremonies. But for a minister having no weak ones in his own flock I never could see any scripture to warrant him to deny the use of these only because he will not offend the weak elsewhere abroad.[55]

This, of course, severely restricted the argument from offence as a justification for refusing to subscribe. For Chaderton held that having once by his preaching removed all cause for offence amongst his flock, the minister should give the authorities their due and conform. For since such matters were still the subject of sharp debate, he argued, 'ought we not to rest in the judgement of the church pacis ergo?' For 'though the imposer keep not the rules yet the user may especially if by former teaching he have removed all scandal from those in the congregation that are weak in faith'.[56] By so doing the minister declared 'a uniform conformity to superior powers', testified to the 'agreement of ministers touching the indifferency of these ceremonies' and served 'the liberty of preaching the gospel and to keep ministers in their livings and ministerial functions'.[57]

Here, then, was Chaderton's final resolution of the conflicting claims of edification and obedience. However, in order to function, it required the sympathetic enforcement of conformity by a bishop prepared to give sufficient time for a minister to resolve his own doubts and those of his congregation. Where this was not forthcoming even a man espousing principles as moderate as those of Chaderton could find himself deprived.[58] It was this reliance on a sympathetic hearing (which under Bancroft did not materialise, at least at a national level) that constituted the major weakness of the moderate position. Chaderton, of course, had his own views on how this impasse could best be avoided. They did not figure at all prominently in the letters and lectures cited above. But then the main thrust of those papers had been toward the reconciliation of the radicals to the idea of conformity. It was hardly likely that in such a context Chaderton would expatiate on the faults in the present state of the church, or on his own proposals for reform. Such subjects he reserved for discussion with his friends and fellow moderates. Happily we have a letter to one such friend – Ezekiel Culverwell – in which Chaderton handled precisely these points in the course of answering a series of formal questions, presumably put initially by Culverwell.

The first of these raised the central issue – 'who shall judge whether these ceremonies be expedient?'[59] Chaderton's reply gave a rather radical tinge to his earlier statements in his sermon 'de licitis' where he had maintained that such matters should be determined by 'every superior to whom God hath given the spirit of discerning things that differ'.[60] For now Chaderton concluded that 'every minister in our church to whom God hath given in any measure a spirit of wisdom or spirituality to discern the differences between things expedient and inexpedient is (iure divino) a judge declaratory meet to give his judgement according to his measure whether these ceremonies be expedient or not'.[61] Now a 'spirit of true spirituality' obviously had little to do with one's rank in the church. Chaderton had here produced a modified version of the presbyterian doctrine of the parity of ministers. It was the godly learned clergy of the type produced by Emmanuel College who were to judge.

As the content of this doctrine was reminiscent of presbyterianism, so was the method of arriving at it. For to back up his earlier statement Chaderton cited the practice of the Apostles. As the 'Apostles admitted the judgement not only of presbyters but the brethren also even the whole church; much more the judgement of the presbyters of our church be admitted in the question of expediency'.

Again if all in the church of Corinth, having the gift of prophecy, might prophesy why may not all ministers in our church, having the gift of discerning expediency and inexpediency, be admitted as meet judges of the same, it being more easy to judge herein than to prophesy and the determination no less concerning them than any other man.

Seeing the Lord Jesus Christ hath given to them a spiritual ministry of remitting and retaining sin who can justly deny them a ministerial and declaratory judgement of expediency considering the spiritual man judgeth all things.[62]

'Is it better', asked Chaderton, 'to use the judgement of the convocation only (whereof few or none nor all jointly together know perfectly the true and particular state of every parish)' rather than 'all sufficient men according to the permitted custom to view and make a particular search of parishes of the land?' The question was rhetorical and the answer immediate:

Nay considering the manner of making canons in the convocation (as the speeches of divers that have been of that synod report) it may be thought very probable that if liberty were given to every one freely to speak his mind and that they were charged to utter their conscience as before God without all respect of persons, these ceremonies at least the cross would have been judged inexpedient to have been longer pressed upon men under pain of losing their liberty of preaching and livings. And for my part I am verily so persuaded, the rather because the church (in my opinion) judging in this matter of expediency can hardly err for mere want of spiritual gifts.

For the matter in question was 'whether these ceremonies do yield a spiritual fruit of edification in this or that church, in some only or in all churches, being a matter of fact why may it not be known as well as all other facts'. Hence if errors were committed they 'were only committed for lack of due search and right proceeding in such assemblies'. It was a fault to which synods and church councils had always been subject. It was always easier to 'rest contented with a general information... and to be drawn into an erroneous judgement'.[63]

Turning from the convocation to the issue of the ceremonies themselves, Chaderton addressed himself to the second proposition put to him – 'that ministers in conforming to the orders of our church cannot give offence to any'. Here Chaderton demonstrated once and for all that his view of the law of expediency applied with equal force to both precisian non-conformists and to conformist administrators. For since questions of expediency or inexpediency were entirely dependent on circumstances, in some situations the ceremonies could be 'no occasions of spiritual edification or profit but rather of destruction of the weak in faith'.[64] Hence, conformists were no more able than precisians to draw generalisations with which to bolster their case from the formulas of the law of expediency.

What a weak means were this seeing the bare judgement of the church without evidence of the spirit is so far from grace and power to resolve a doubting conscience, that St Paul maketh little reckoning of it where he saith, as for me I pass very little to be judged of man, or of man's judgement; accounting that to be man's which is not the Lord's, who alone is he that properly judgeth him and us all.

To be effective in such cases the authority of the church 'must be spiritual and ministerial not worldly nor coactive ex ordinatione dei'. Only if the 'judgement of the church be an evident manifestation of the spirit as St Paul's ministry was' could it deal effectively with doubting consciences. And in Chaderton's opinion the deliberations of the convocation were hardly to be regarded as manifestations of the spirit.[65]

Having thus graphically described the defects of the present system Chaderton went on to suggest the means by which many of these faults could be corrected. Such constructive criticism, he claimed, could by no means be construed as disloyal. As if further to underline his respect for authority Chaderton invoked in support of his schemes not the practice of some foreign churches or even the practice of the Apostles, but the traditions of the English reformed church:

> to let pass all censure we may without all offence call to mind those golden rules and necessary cautions which our English church under their hands ordained in K. Henry the 8 days to be necessarily observed in making church laws and ceremonies. The first whereof is that such ordinances to be made as shall tend to the peoples profit and increase in Christian religion to the honour of God and the good tranquillity of them. The 2 that they be made with the consent of the people which profess the name of Christ. The 3 that they be made without intent to punish the breakers thereof by corporal violence. The 4 that being duly and rightfully made by the ministers and received by common consent of the people and authorised by the laws of Christian Princes there be no other obedience required to them but that men may lawfully omit and do otherwise than is prescribed if they do it not in contempt or despite of the power or jurisdiction but have some good and reasonable cause so to do; and offend not nor slander their neighbours in so doing.

In other words, they should not be made 'ordinances of necessity or perpetuity for such in time cannot but become superstitious'. They should also, as a matter of course, carry a proviso excusing 'all of the weak in faith'.[66]

Here, then, were the sort of attitudes that prompted Chaderton's presence at Hampton Court on the puritan side and which formed the basis of his opposition to the style of conformity in externals propounded by Bancroft. It is sentiments like these that answer the question of what happened to the presbyterian impulse after the demise of the classis movement. The insistence on the normative status of the practice of the Apostles that had characterised 'iure divino' presbyterianism had been transmuted, in

Chaderton's case, into a more flexible attitude to the authority of the Apostolic church. Chaderton had, of course, retained, in a slightly modified form, the presbyterian tenets of ministerial parity and the collective or 'pluralist' view of authority in the church. And as his letter to Culverwell showed, he could still cite the practice of the Apostles as a guide to contemporary conduct. But his insistence that the ceremonies in question were basically indifferent allowed him to play down the 'iure divino' nature of his claims. As things indifferent they were subject to the law of expediency and matters of expediency varied with circumstances and hence could only be resolved as a result of empirical investigation. Hence, if things went wrong the convocation could at worst be convicted of slackness and inaccuracy. While these were serious faults, they did not constitute outright sins against the liberty of God. Consequently, while they were worthy of censure they were not, should the church fail by some chance to reform itself, of sufficient moment to justify outright schism. They could, in short, be accepted for the sake of order without provoking a head-on clash between the will of God and the will of man. Hence, as ever, Chaderton's use of the doctrine of Christian liberty provided a basis for both the control of precisian excess and a critique of the ecclesiastical establishment.

William Bradshaw: moderation in extremity

At first sight Bradshaw's opinions might appear to be so radical as to deny him a place in any study of supposedly moderate puritan opinion. However Bradshaw is important for the present study for three reasons. Firstly, having examined the moderate response to Hampton Court, it might prove instructive to compare that with the response of more radical spirits and Bradshaw provides just such an example. Secondly, given his status as one of Chaderton's protégés, he also provides a striking example of Chaderton's continuing links with men whose opinions were considerably more radical than his own. Thirdly, moreover, his views, on closer examination, appear to have been subject to precisely the same sorts of constraint as had earlier checked the radical overtones of Chaderton's presbyterianism. Hence Bradshaw's career and opinions provide an interesting case-study of the logic of the moderate puritan situation in a period when presbyterianism and the movement that sustained it were no longer a living force.

We last encountered Bradshaw having been deprived of his living in Kent.[1] Thence he returned to his native Leicestershire, where by the good offices of Arthur Hildersham he gained a post in the household of 'a religious gentleman' by the name of Alexander Redich. Bishop Overton of Coventry and Lichfield was, to quote Gataker, 'a moderate man', and he gave Bradshaw a licence to preach twice every Sunday in a chapel of 'some capacity' on the Redich estate. But so popular did these lectures become that, 'when the resort from other parts more remote grew so great that the place could not well contain them', Bradshaw transferred his preaching activities to the local parish church where, according to Gataker, 'a reading Vicar only was'.[2]

After his brief sojourn in the Redich household Bradshaw was hence back in the mainstream of the national church. He owed that position to the networks of godly influence, comprising laymen like the Hastings brothers or Mr Redich, and ministers such as Hildersham, Chaderton himself, and even well-affected bishops like Overton, all of whom had, in effect, conspired to find a place for Bradshaw inside a church that, in theory at least, had no room for a man of Bradshaw's radical opinions. Moreover, instead of driving him into the moderate fold, Bradshaw's experiences at the hands of the conformists had served only to sharpen the radicalism of his views. Before, as we have seen, he had been content to squeeze puritan forms in and through the anomalies and inconsistencies of the official administration of conformity. Now, it seemed, he felt the need to stand out against conformity and in the years after 1604 he defended the radical position on subscription in a whole series of books and pamphlets.

He began by asserting the all-sufficiency of scripture. 'It is a sin', he wrote, 'to force any Christian to do any act of religion or divine service that cannot evidently be warranted by the same.'[3] Divine service he defined uncompromisingly as 'any action or service that is immediately or directly performed unto God himself'.[4] Hence, 'all special things therefore done in the service and worship is worship' and must on that account bring a special honour unto God. But the only means to render him such honour was by complete and absolute obedience to his direct commands. 'All ceremonies therefore of religion that are an honour unto God must be commanded by God himself and to bring in such ceremonies into his worship as are no honour to him is to mock God.'[5] Bradshaw thus cut out the middle ground of adiaphora, so central to the moderate position, and left the minister with a straight choice between direct scriptural warrant on the one hand and outright profanity on the other.

There could be, he maintained, nothing entirely indifferent. For indifferent meant equidistant between a created good and a created evil, but since nothing in the world was created absolutely good or absolutely evil, nothing in turn could be taken as absolutely and inherently indifferent. Hence, while he admitted that 'herein such actions of man's will are most frequent that are neither commanded nor forbidden in the word of God', he still maintained that 'there is no action of man's will so indifferent but the doing thereof (by some circumstance) may be repugnant to the love of God and by consequent be hurtful to the soul of man'.[6]

Chaderton, of course, had admitted that. All things 'licensed' were still subject to the law of expediency. But Chaderton's position seemed to Bradshaw to contain a contradiction. Chaderton, probably in a reference to Bradshaw, actually addressed himself to just such an objection, made by one M.B., in his paper asserting the lawfulness of the surplice. According to M.B., since all things were subject to the law of expediency, which came directly from God, the category of adiaphora, while possible in theory, could never exist in practice. To maintain that it did was to imply that it was lawful to do something which, according to the law of expediency, was better left undone or to omit something which, again by the law of expediency, ought to be done. That was to oppose the supposed inherent indifference of a mere object to the dictates of God's law of expediency.[7]

Chaderton replied with a renewed insistence on the role of mutable circumstances in rendering an action expedient or inexpedient:

As lawfulness and unlawfulness are adjoined to things by the law of God alone: so expediency and inexpediency are adjoined to things clean of themselves and lawful by circumstances of time, place, person and manner of doing which though they are not of the nature of the lawful; yet standing about it as being adjoined to it they may distribute it into expedient and inexpedient as the apostle hath done.[8]

Hence, in the case of ceremonies, circumstances could be changed by the preaching of right doctrine and once all cause for offence had been removed the ceremonies could be used quite lawfully and safely. Since circumstances were mutable, and varied so much from place to place, generalisations were impossible, and in practice the clash between theoretical indifference and practical inexpedience, posited by Bradshaw, need never occur.

For Bradshaw, however, in the present situation, such offence was virtually impossible to avoid:

How dare a Christian having knowledge kneel in the presence of any, who, for want of knowledge, receive superstitiously. Of which sort seeing there be so many even until this hour and ever likely to be that we know not when and where to communicate without some such, whether old or young; it followeth that as sitting at table in the idols' temple could not be without sin in the Apostles' time so kneeling cannot be without sin these days when the number of faithful teachers is much decreased but of papists much increased and by our kneeling much confirmed in their bread worship.[9]

Elsewhere Bradshaw listed the evil effects of the continued use of the ceremonies:

They have been and are the special means and occasion of the schism of many hundred Brownists. Of much superstition in many thousand ignorant protestants and of confirmation of many infinits of wilful papists in their idolatry...Also (if it be a sin to dislike our Lords Spiritual), there is no one greater cause that moveth those that the profane call puritans to do it then these ceremonies which if they might be freed from as all other reformed churches are, there is no other civil obedience or subjection due unto them that they would refuse to perform in as low a degree as any other whatsoever.[10]

Besides, these ceremonies were popish in origin and could no more be indifferent than the popish doctrine with which they were integrally linked:

As there are diversities of religion and churches so there are diversities of rites and ceremonies by which they are distinguished and ceremonies are the partition walls whereby (for the most part) one church is divided from another. The more one church differeth from another in rites and ceremonies the more it useth to differ in substance of doctrine.

It followed from this that 'he that hates the religion itself hates all the shadows and shows of the religion; and he that loves the shadows and rites of a religion, he loves the religion itself...he loves a mass priest with all his heart that is mad upon his massing attire or any part thereof'. Inevitably, therefore, 'some in the Church of England that do strive to come to Rome in ceremonies come so much the nearer to her in doctrine, as might appear by divers instances if the matter were not too apparent'.[11] In a later work Bradshaw was more explicit. Writing of the conformists he claimed that 'sithens their late strong patronising and urging of these things',

they have fallen from that that heretofore hath been constantly and generally held by our church now teaching these things which have been accounted and are in truth popish or lutheran errors; viz: touching general grace and the death of Christ for every particular person; against particular election and reprobation; for images in Churches...that the pope is not Antichrist which is the next step to say that he is Christ's vicar and whereby they hinder (what they may) the zeal of Christian Princes from executing that against him in general and against his members in particular which the word partly foretelleth and partly commandeth to be done; concerning also the necessity of baptism; also touching auricular confession for ignorance (according to the popish saying 'that ignorance is the mother of devotion') that it is not necessary for the people to have much knowledge and that therefore not much preaching.[12]

Since the sovereignty and authority of God and his word were one and the same, any offence against that authority in one sphere could not fail to have repercussions in others. Certainly, the popish nature of much of the conformists' doctrine was to supply a prominent strand in one of Bradshaw's later works.[13]

Bradshaw was, of course, taking arguments central to the moderate position in its opposition to popery and applying them to the remnants of popery in the established church. Certainly there is, in Bradshaw's *A plaine and pithy exposition of the second epistle to the Thessalonians* (published posthumously by Gataker in 1620) a classic exposition of the threat posed by Antichrist (in the shape of the pope and the Roman church) to all true believers. 'How have the people of God need to take heed of such a monster?' he asked;

What blocks and sots are they that cannot discover him and know him? Let us therefore, beloved, that live in God's church take heed to ourselves; look to our religion and worship, and all the parts thereof; that we do not serve Antichrist rather than Christ and that we mingle not both together. It will be hard to live in God's church in his times and to keep wholly free from him who if he cannot wholly draw men from Christ will be attempting yet to do it in part.[14]

Such sentiments had, of course, a direct application to the debate about conformity and the ceremonies. Hence, in one of his most directly polemical works, Bradshaw could ask 'what communion hath the light of the word with the darkness of man's inventions? What concord hath Christ our Saviour with

Belial the Antichrist of Rome?. . . Wherefore come out of Babylon (that is the confusion or confused worship and government of Rome) and touch no unclean thing.'[15] Certainly his view of the 'mystery of iniquity' contained in the Roman Antichrist allowed Bradshaw to deny any of the ceremonies a proper use in the primitive church before the rise of popery. For 'though at this time popery was not hatched yet the mystery of iniquity was then a working and the beginning, as it were, of the whorish fornications was found even in the fathers' time'. Hence 'ceremonies ratified by the popish canons and constitutions may well be taken for popish and Antichristian, even in the fathers' times, seeing they then made a way for the beast and since have received further impiety and authority from him'.[16] Similarly Bradshaw was able to discount the authority of individual church fathers cited in support of the right use of the ceremonies. 'For there being no one father that wrote since the Apostles' times but have erred in some matters of doctrine why may they not as well err in matters of ceremony.'[17] This diminution of merely human authorities was but the obverse of Bradshaw's scripturalism and as such can be taken as a hall-mark of his radical world-view. By thus pushing elements within the puritan mainstream to radical conclusions Bradshaw was, of course, cutting away the middle ground occupied by moderates like Chaderton. As we have seen in the case of Chaderton, Bradshaw was not above exposing what he took to be the inconsistencies in the moderate position. On a different occasion he cited the arguments advanced by another leading moderate scholar, John Rainolds, against the use of the sign of the cross during communion. But, asked Bradshaw, if it was idolatrous to use the sign of the cross then, as Rainolds alleged, was it not equally iniquitous to countenance its use during baptism?[18]

But the differences between moderates and radicals transcended the realm of mere theory. The issue of subscription threatened to tear the godly party asunder by dividing both the ministerial elite and their lay followers and by alienating precisian congregations from conformist, or at least conforming, ministers. In an attempt to ensure 'that sincere teachers of the same truth may either be conformable together or seek reformation together'[19] Bradshaw actually addressed his conforming brethren in print. He denounced 'this lie or politique subscription' which, he claimed, 'draweth a curse not a blessing upon the ministry of subscribers against their own conscience'.[20] Certainly he rejected the argument that 'by obedience to these ceremonies many souls by means of preaching are saved, which shall want the means in the refusal'. For, he claimed, 'we must not destroy the souls of some that we may save the souls of others. We must do that which is just, though the whole world go to wrack for it.' 'He that preacheth cannot assure himself of the salvation of one soul by the same, for that is wrought by the work of the Spirit of God. And he hath little cause to hope for a blessing upon that preaching which he purchaseth with the price of blood, yea the blood of souls.'[21] Moreover, Bradshaw claimed, 'this enforced or temporizing subscription' did inestimable damage to the cause of further reformation:

For if an hundred godly ministers were suspended for not subscribing to all the Archbishop's Articles I doubt not but that their silencing would preach reformation very effectually. Whereas your temporizing subscription doth hurt many ways...Is not then your politique subscribing the cause why those few be so hardly dealt with that no mediation can prevail in their behalf? To say nothing of professors who seeing you (who have stood in the gap) to subscribe at the last do think those few that now stand more precise than wise and become therefore less comfortable to them than they have been...your temporizing subscription hath been and daily will be an occasion to many weak ones if not of falling yet of stumbling...So that few be now so zealous for reformation as they have been which must needs be a great offence and that given by you, if (in your judgement) there be need of reformation.[22]

But Bradshaw did not restrict himself to the reiteration and development of the radical line on ceremonies. In 1605, in his book *English puritanisme containinge the maine opinions of the rigidest sort of those that are called puritanes in the realme of England*, Bradshaw finally grasped the nettle and outlined his own views on the polity of the church of England. As such the book can be seen as Bradshaw's attempt to recapture the coherence and polemical edge that puritanism had lost with the collapse of the presbyterian movement. Coming up to Emmanuel in 1589 Bradshaw had learned his puritanism after presbyterianism, both as a movement and as an ideology, had ceased to offer a viable alternative to the established church. The comparative failure of Hampton Court compounded this loss of coherence so that radical puritans like Bradshaw found themselves facing a veritable crisis of identity. For some more eirenic spirits like Thomas Sparke it was a crisis that could only be resolved by the virtual repudiation of their precisian past and a consequent drift into straightforward conformity. For Bradshaw, on the other hand, this situation had the opposite effect: rather than repudiate his precisian opinions he gloried in them. The very title of his book, by taking the term 'puritan', normally regarded as an insult, and seeking to invest it with a positive content, announced his intentions clearly enough. In effect it served to assert the longstanding existence, within the national church, of a puritan, non-conformist tradition, and to defend its status as the true guardian of the English protestant heritage. It was this that prompted his claim to speak for 'the rigidest sort' and his quotation on the title page, from Acts 24.14, 'but this I confess unto thee that after the way (which they call heresy) so worship I the God of my Fathers believing all things which are written in the Law and Prophets'.

But if Bradshaw's position was based on a longstanding puritan tradition it did not comprise a mere recapitulation of the Elizabethan position. Gone was the comprehensive hierarchy of presbyterian synods and classes. It was replaced by an insistence on the complete self-sufficiency and autonomy of the individual congregation as the basic and irreducible unit of church structure. Bradshaw retained the kernel of the presbyterian platform, with its provision of both a pastor or preacher and a teacher or doctor in each parish, backed up by a properly elected eldership to administer a decent spiritual discipline. But by relinquishing the national focus of ecclesiastical power, summed up in the synodical hierarchy, he tried to avoid that clash with the Royal Supremacy which had formed the basis of the conformist rejection of presbyterianism.[23] It was the essence of Bradshaw's position that it infinitely strengthened the power of the king: ecclesiastical discipline was to be purely spiritual and there could be no spiritual authority greater than that lodged in the individual congregation.[24] Hence all the functions and jurisdictions which, under the presbyterian dispensation, would have been exercised by provincial or national synods and which at present were exercised by the bishops and their officials, would revert to the king.[25] In fact, for Bradshaw, there were no intermediate ecclesiastical authorities standing between the individual congregation and the universal catholic church. This last comprised 'all protestants, pastors, ministers and governors living this day in Europe and all the painful resident pastors in our own country', for, maintained Bradshaw, 'the pastors and governors of churches...are reputed the church-representative'. It was to this 'catholic church' that Bradshaw appealed, against the prelates and their hangers on, over the issues of church polity and ceremonies.[26] Since, for Bradshaw, it was only individual churches or congregations that existed as jurisdictional bodies, and not the national church, he could not be accused of submitting the power of the prince to the authority of the church. Under Bradshaw's scheme the king could only be subject to the purely spiritual powers of that particular congregation which he had honoured with his presence.[27]

It was Bradshaw's basic contention that it was not the principle of ministerial parity, but rather the principle of inequality or hierarchy, that limited the royal prerogative:

> The equality in ecclesiastical jurisdiction and authority of churches and church ministers is no more derogatory and repugnant to the state and glory of a monarch than the parity or equality of schoolmasters of several schools, captains of several camps, shepherds of several flocks of sheep or masters of several families Yea they [the puritans] hold the clean contrary that inequality of churches and church officers and ecclesiastical jurisdiction and authority was that principally that advanced Antichrist unto his throne and brought the kings and princes of the earth unto such vassalage under him and that the civil authority and glory of secular princes and states hath ever decayed and withered, the more that the ecclesiastical officers of the church have been advanced and lifted up in authority beyond the limits and confines that Christ in his word hath prescribed unto them.[28]

Primarily, of course, these strictures applied to the papists, but they also had a certain application to conformists who

> holdeth that the king may not without sin remove these offices out of the church and dispose of their temporalities and maintenance according to his own pleasure or that these offices are iure divino and not only or merely iure humano; that all such deny a principal part of the king's supremacy.[29]

In part Bradshaw's 'congregationalism' was a device to circumvent the stock charges of subversion that had so often been levelled
against the puritan position.[30] As such it allowed him to turn
the tables on the conformist proportions of a 'iure divino' theory
of episcopacy. As Chaderton had before him, Bradshaw was
quite ready to claim that the puritan position was infinitely more
compatible with the hierarchies of lay society than the present
episcopal structure of the church.[31] In thus lighting upon the
individual congregation as his basic unit rather than the national
church, Bradshaw sought to avoid the impasse that the presbyterians' 'iure divino' claims had produced without relinquishing the ideal of a scriptural model for the basic organisation of
the church. In so doing Bradshaw was taking up the insistence
on the universal catholic church, as opposed to the particular
arrangements of individual visible churches, developed in their
anti-papal polemics by the likes of Whitaker. But instead of using
that perspective as an argument for a passive acceptance of things
as they were, he added to it a fierce commitment to the precisian
critique of the established church. The result was the presbyterian view of the arrangements within each parish, with the
unity of the national – indeed international – protestant church
preserved on the spiritual level by a basic uniformity of doctrine
and, in the final analysis, by God's decree of election, but bereft
of any institutional structure or hierarchy of ecclesiastical
power.[32]

This concentration on the individual parish allowed Bradshaw
to claim that the basis for this view of church polity had already
been laid amongst the godly in the English church. On this
view the church of England already possessed 'the rudera and
(as it were) the stumps' of the discipline 'yet remaining in our
parishional church-wardens and sidesmen, though instituted with
other names and wanting that ordination and authority which
with the pastors within their own parishes elders ought to have'.
Also the practice of many godly parishes, or groups within
parishes, corresponded very closely with Bradshaw's theoretical
opinions. His own experience at Chatham was ample evidence
of that. Hence, by denying the need for the synodical hierarchy,
Bradshaw was able to claim even more plausibly than the presbyterians that the godly represented the 'leaven that leavened
the whole lump'. Indeed, in his view, virtually all that was

needed to bring the English church into line with the scriptural ideal was the removal of episcopacy.[33]

Quite logically, then, and without compromising his principles, Bradshaw could claim that:

so long as it shall please the king and civil state (though to the great derogation of their own authority as we may have occasion here-after to prove) to maintain in this kingdom, the state of the hierarchy or prelacy; We can (in honour to his majesty and the state and in desire of peace) be content without envy to suffer them to enjoy their state and dignity and live as brethren amongst those ministers that shall acknowledge spiritual homage unto their spiritual lord-ships paying unto them all temporal duties of tenths and such like; yea and joining with them in the service and worship of God so far as we may do it without our own particular communicating with them in those humane traditions and rites that in our consciences we judge to be unlawful.[34]

Of course, Bancroft's canons were designed expressly to deny men like Bradshaw the luxury of so qualified a commitment to the national church. But as we have seen, for Bradshaw, at least, they were the occasion only of an interruption in his ministry; the puritan grape-vine had contrived to frustrate the demand for complete conformity and allow Bradshaw to continue his career within the national church.

Certainly there can be no doubting the strength of Bradshaw's allegiance to the church of England. Perhaps it was because his published polemics on conformity and church polity appeared so close to open schism and the advocacy of separation that Brad-shaw spent a good deal of time refuting the separatist position. As well as engaging in a number of disputations and conferences with known separatists, Bradshaw wrote a critique of the dialogue between Smith the Se-baptist and Mr Clifton, after the latter had been won over to the separatist case. Neither work has survived but in 1614 Bradshaw published his *The unreasonablenesse of the separation*. This was a refutation of the works of Francis Johnson who had apparently 'fetched some arguments' from one of Bradshaw's works against conformity.[35] Rather than be tarred with the separatist brush Bradshaw went into print.

Interestingly, he did not repudiate his earlier works high-lighting the deficiencies of the English church. Those polemics, he pointed out, were concerned with only one side of the coin:

Our church assemblies being such as by the laws of the land they ought to be; are so far forth separated from the world; joined together in the communion of the gospel by the voluntary profession of faith etc. and freed from Antichrist as is sufficient to make them true visible churches of Christ, notwithstanding that many things may be wanting to the full and desired perfection of them.[36]

But such imperfection was inevitable.

It is true that light hath no fellowship with darkness nor Christ with Antichrist. Yet there is no light in men in this life but it is mingled with some darkness and the best Christians that are or ever have been since the Apostles' times may be infected with some parts of Antichristianism.[37]

Hence, it was not the existence of abuses that was at stake; merely the exact status and significance of those abuses. For Bradshaw, while many of them were undoubtedly Antichristian in origin, yet they could not 'be said to overthrow though it may somewhat stain the ministry of Christ'.[38] Certainly, merely on the basis of the ceremonies in question, the entire English church could not be written off as simply Antichristian. To begin with, claimed Bradshaw,

our ministry in divers congregations of the land at the least teach not only many excellent points of doctrine. But so much doctrine as is sufficient to the salvation of him that believeth the same; even all the main fundamental points of salvation clearly set down in God's word.[39]

But in addition to that profession of right doctrine, the ministry

opposeth itself professedly to the Pope of Rome as that great Antichrist which directly and expressly renounceth all ecclesiastical homage unto him or any of his professed clergy, that denieth and disputeth against (most effectually) all the main and fundamental points of popery, which opposeth itself to the uttermost of the strength and power thereof to all the professed friends of the Pope and church of Rome, that holdeth and maintaineth all the members thereof to be heretics and idolators and in the state of condemnation and such as no good Christian ought to communicate spiritually withal. That ministry (I say) doth directly war against the beast and against all that worship his image etc.[40]

Bradshaw's close relation to the moderate puritan position is perfectly illustrated by his insistence on doctrine as the main ground of a true church and by his reliance on the anti-papal stance adopted by many puritan divines within the English church. It thus provides eloquent testimony to the role of moderate puritanism in validating the English church's claims to the status of a true church and in providing perhaps the most effective argument against separation.

Moreover, in dealing with the areas most affected by Antichristian dross, Bradshaw drew the distinction between form and content. While the ministers of the word in England may have been called 'priests' and 'deacons', those mere titles could not destroy the essence of the ministry as ordained by Christ.[41] It was, therefore, quite possible to infuse into erroneous or Antichristian forms a properly reformed content. Hence, merely because there was not, within the church, the position or title of doctor or teacher, did not of itself mean that there were not men within that same church exercising precisely that function:

This may reasonably be held that some of our ministers (whether priests or deacons so called or whether parsons, vicars, curates or stipendiaries) are pastors and some teachers that so many of them as have and use the gift, not only of doctrine and instruction but of exhortation are pastors, that those who wanting the power of exhortation and yet have and use the gift of instruction and doctrine are such teachers as he [Johnson] meaneth. And therefore herein also it should be yielded unto him, that it were fit that every congregation should have both these offices and that the teacher should be the pastor's assistant yet it doth not follow but that in want of sufficient men for both these offices in every congregation some may enjoy one and some another.[42]

In the same spirit Bradshaw could observe that

though it should be granted that the Book of Common Prayer in all the parts and parcels thereof is not the true worship of God but containeth in it some devices and inventions of man, yet the true worship of God (notwithstanding) is prescribed in it.[43]

Neither were the dictates of the law to be taken at face value:

The ministry (at least in some places) may be good though the law in general should admit and establish such a one as is bad...for the governors of churches and commonwealths who have the dispensation of laws may in their Christian wisdom and moderation permit a ministry in sundry respects different from that which the laws require...And he cannot be ignorant but that some by their connivency are yet suffered in some points of their ministry to swerve from some observances which the laws require.[44]

Moreover, although subscription was required to a liturgy and canons that were far from perfect, to subscribe was not 'ministerially to teach the errors contained in the said books'. After all, could not the minister

teach doctrine in itself directly contrary to those untruths yea and yet satisfy also the mind of the law which being human and therefore not always perfect, may command that very truth to be taught which being thoroughly followed will destroy some untruths, which the same law also requires?[45]

Similarly, the episcopal form of ordination could be augmented by more godly procedures. For the bishops conferred only the liberty to preach; they did not thrust men into the ministry, but left them 'to be further called or chosen either by the people or those patrons unto whose fidelity the people have committed this charge'.[46] On this view, the two forms, episcopal and puritan, official and unofficial, far from being mutually exclusive, fitted neatly inside one another. There was no contradiction in loyalty to both. Even in the case of episcopacy Bradshaw maintained that there was no necessary contradiction between his position and the status quo. For

though a particular church or congregation may be complete without them [that is 'general visitors or overseers of churches'] it is fit and agreeable to reason and no ways repugnant to God's word that under the supreme magistrate there should be other governors to protect and encourage those ministers and churches which do their duty and to punish those which shall offend.[47]

In other words, strip a prelate of his papal pretensions, his 'iure divino' claims, and all that was left was a royal officer for ecclesiastical affairs and he, of course, need represent no threat to the basic principle of ministerial equality or the status of 'the pastors of particular congregations' as 'the highest ordinary ecclesiastical officers'.[48]

There was, therefore, no necessary contradiction between Bradshaw's view of church government and the present position. As the case of ordination showed, the two forms, puritan and episcopal, merely complemented one another, or rather the puritan version compensated for the shortcomings of the official one.[49] How then, asked Bradshaw, could the godly inside the English church be said

to halt between two opinions when so far only as the truth (in their judgement and opinion) is established by public laws they embrace it acknowledging their subjection to the same laws and contrarily where they judge that the law swerves from the truth they take another course.[50]

Moreover, however imperfect the English ministry might be,

it can never be proved that the admittance of this ministry is a hindrance of a better, but rather it is a means to keep out a worse and a way in time to bring a better, if a better be to be brought in...And if it be as lawful for us to conjecture as for him their general schism and rent from this ministry hath been one main and principal means to uphold it as it is.[51]

There, in a nutshell, was the mainstream puritan response to separatism. That Bradshaw expressed it with such vigour, not only in private conferences, but in print, gives the lie to the seeming radicalism of his earlier pamphlets. It would be unfair to say that, confronted with the consequences of his own principles in the shape of separatism, he had been forced to retrace his steps. There are no direct contradictions between his anti-separatist works and his earlier pamphlets. Indeed, as I have tried to show, they were integrally linked. Bradshaw's insistence on the autonomy of the individual congregation certainly enabled him to stress the congruence of the puritan view of church polity and the contemporary social hierarchy and hence turn aside conformist accusations of puritan subversion. But it also enabled him, by stressing the compatibility of the then unregenerate state of the church and the puritan forms which it contained, to turn aside separatist charges of time-serving and inconsistency.

But it is undeniable that there was a tension between Bradshaw's anti-conformist and his anti-separatist positions. It was the tension experienced, to a greater or lesser degree, by every mainstream puritan ideologue. Having denied himself the middle ground of adiaphora, Bradshaw felt it in its most acute form. However, he never recanted or conformed. The result, to quote his friend Gataker, was that he was

never suffered to continue long quiet in any settled place of more public employment through the envy and malice of some that had a jealous eye in him and the disturbances of him in the work of his ministry set on foot by others ill-affected towards him, but accruing from the same, pursued by some of those who were of greater power and authority in ecclesiastical affairs and could not brook any that did not in all particulars comply with them, as they conceived him not to do.[52]

Bradshaw, then, never returned to the public ministry of the church, but ended his days in the Redich household.

From Chaderton's point of view, this was a sad waste. It deprived the English church of the full services of an able and highly trained minister. There could hardly be a better illustration of the very real practical considerations that underlay theoretical disputes amongst the godly over the issue of subscription. For apart from his radical pamphlets about conformity (and these, as Gataker pointed out, were 'underhand printed and published as they could be secretly got out and dispersed')[53] Bradshaw was the model divine of the moderate puritan (Emmanuel) school. His preaching style was apparently modelled on that of Chaderton. He took part in learned ministerial exercises at Ashby de la Zouche, Repton, and Burton upon Trent (meetings no doubt in the mould of the prophesying outlined by Chaderton and the college exercise at Emmanuel).[54] Similarly he displayed the formal doctrinal interests of the puritan scholar. In 1615 he published his *A treatise of justification*, and Gataker records that he planned a lengthy reply to 'Dutch' Thomson's *Diatribae de amissione et intercissione justificationis et gratiae*.[55] As one would expect with a radical so concerned with the Antichristian remnants still defiling the English church, anti-papal polemic did not bulk large amongst his published works, although a large part of his *A plaine and pithy exposition of the second epistle to the Thessalonians* was devoted to the identification of the Pope as Antichrist.[56] Similarly, with typical pastoral zeal, he spent a great deal of effort in trying to convert Lady Ferrers (Mr Redich's mother-in-law) from popery to true religion.[57] It is, however, in his basically edificational works, largely published after his death by his friend Gataker, that we find the final proof of Bradshaw's place in a study of the evangelical strain of Emmanuel puritanism. Mostly produced during his period in the Redich household, these works centre around the major events in that household – a marriage, a death in the family – and seek to interpret these in

terms of Bradshaw's own brand of Calvinist religion. Taken together with his *A preparation to the receiving of Christ's body
and blood*, these works reveal Bradshaw guiding the individual
believer through the course of his life, constantly reminding him
of the essential limits and constraints of his spiritual condition.[58]
Although they might contain material that could be construed in
an anti-conformist way, these were primarily edificational tracts
designed to bring home, through Bradshaw's exhortatory skill as
a preacher, the existential significance of right doctrine. It was
here, in his role as an ordinary preacher of the word, that
Bradshaw stood closest to the Chaderton tradition. As he had
begun in the Emmanuel tradition, under Chaderton's own tute-
lage, so Bradshaw, bringing the fruits of true religion to the
Redich household, was to end in it.

I 2

Conclusion

This study has tried to trace the outline of a certain evangelical protestant world-view. It was a world-view which united presbyterians like Chaderton with non-presbyterians like Whitaker and, later, establishment moderates like Chaderton with young firebrands like William Bradshaw. On a personal level it was this world-view that held together the various roles – scholar, preacher, theologian, puritan polemicist, administrator – that made up the career of men such as Chaderton, Cartwright or Whitaker. More generally, it served to unite many puritans with the more zealously protestant of the Elizabethan bishops.[1]

The core of this world-view was provided by an all-encompassing concern with the potentially transforming effects of the gospel on both individuals and on the social order as a whole. The gospel, in the form of the word preached, was to be spread by university-trained divines like Chaderton and his pupils at Christ's and Emmanuel. The doctrinal position that lay behind this attitude was uncompromisingly Calvinist.

Thus far, then, the findings of this study might be taken to accord with much recent research which has tended to argue 'puritanism', conceived as a coherent or self-conscious body of opinion, out of existence. It has been replaced, as the central theme in the religious history of the period, by an emphasis on a basic protestant consensus of precisely the sort described above. This approach was developed in studies of the Jacobean and Caroline church and in particular in studies of Arminianism, where a static, even sterile, Calvinist consensus has been invoked as the backdrop against which the really dynamic element in the situation – Arminianism – emerged. This present analysis might be thought simply to transfer such an approach from the early seventeenth to the later sixteenth century.[2] Hence Professor Elton has, quite rightly, cited Chaderton as a man whose 'puritan' opinions on certain subjects were no obstacle to his integration into the Elizabethan establishment. Similarly, in another recent article, he has observed that it was not necessary to be a 'puritan' in order to hate popery.[3]

The existence of a basic doctrinal consensus in the English church, coupled with a certain identity of outlook and interest between moderate puritan divines and certain bishops and influential laymen, undoubtedly served to integrate 'puritans' into the ecclesiastical and secular hierarchies of Elizabethan England. The Elizabethan regime was from the outset protestant, and expressions of protestant zeal doubled quite effectively as expressions of loyalty to that regime. An emphasis on the threat posed by Rome served to underline that point. As this study has sought to demonstrate, this provided puritans like Whitaker and Cartwright with a crucial defence against conformist allegations of puritan subversion.

The extent to which the style of divinity described in this study as 'moderate puritan' was the predominant style current in the Elizabethan church, and one through which individual puritans could insinuate themselves into the Elizabethan establishment, provides a valuable corrective to views of 'puritanism' as an entirely oppositionist force centred on the classis movement and continually teetering on the edge of open separation. But this is not to replace a crude view of an ideologically monolithic 'oppositionist' puritan movement by an equally distorting emphasis on doctrinal consensus and political orthodoxy. On the contrary, this study represents an attempt to transcend the crude dichotomy between conflict and consensus which seems to beset the recent historiography of the early modern period. The false choice of *either* a rigidly defined, party-based conflict or opposition, *or* a conflict-free consensus, has to be refused.[4]

That even presbyterianism, and still less other, less systematic, expressions of puritan dissent, did not resemble some underground resistance movement dedicated to the radical restructuring of Elizabethan society, is undoubtedly true. But that should not lead us to suppress the ambiguity, tension and often sharply critical attitude implicit in the relationship between moderate puritanism and the contemporary status quo. The very fact that a man as respectable as Chaderton could denounce episcopacy as Antichristian and the bishops as corrupt should alert us against any such tendency, as should the even more formally moderate Whitaker's activities in St John's.

If their protestant commitment served to integrate such men into the Elizabethan establishment, it also prompted them to use their positions within that establishment in certain ideologically determined, puritan ways. The assaults on the structure of the liturgy, normally taken to be the defining characteristics of Elizabethan puritanism, were merely the most visible, polemically coherent and divisive forms taken by the general impulse toward further reformation, the infusion of existing structures of authority or discipline with more and more explicitly protestant values and principles. But as the careers of both Chaderton and Whitaker prove, it was possible to pursue that general aim in less contentious, but in the long term no less significant, ways.

But where does all this leave those traditional 'puritan' issues concerning the liturgy and polity of the church? What was their precise status for a man like Chaderton or Whitaker? Given the very strong personal links between mainstream moderates like Whitaker and presbyterians like Chaderton, and the complete congruence between the presbyterian and non-presbyterian elements in the careers of Chaderton or Dering, it would seem that the divide between a presbyterian and a non-presbyterian, or between an out-and-out non-conformist and a moderate semi-conformist, was not necessarily crucial. This is not to argue that the issues involved were trivial. They were not, as Chaderton's longstanding presbyterianism and the immense pains he took to defuse the potentially divisive and disruptive issue of subscription surely demonstrate. But it is to claim that amongst men who recognised the sincerity and zeal of each other's protestantism such divisions were not of prime importance. Certainly this study has sought to prove that in the face of the conformists' repeated attempts to use the issue of conformity and church polity to divide godly opinion, and in particular to separate the moderate, largely non-presbyterian mainstream from the presbyterian left, the unity of godly opinion held firm.[5] For the internal history of puritan opinion, then, these issues are not as crucial as they might at first appear. Rather they represent questions of principle, important in themselves but on which men of good-will and protestant zeal could disagree (and disagree passionately), but whose mere existence was not enough in itself decisively to divide puritan opinion. And it is the continuing links between moderates and presbyterians, even at the close of the 1580s with conformist repression at its height, that in part underwrite the modified view of presbyterianism and its place in the moderate puritan world-view outlined above.[6]

If the core of the moderate puritan position lay neither in the puritan critique of the liturgy and polity of the church nor in a formal doctrinal consensus, where can it be located? It lay in the capacity, which the godly claimed, of being able to recognise one another in the midst of a corrupt and unregenerate world. That capacity in turn rested on a common view of the implications of right doctrine, both for the private spiritual experience of the individual and for the collective experience and activity of the godly community. In short, what was involved in puritanism – and what should prevent modern scholars from seeking to conflate puritan divinity with a formal doctrinal consensus – was the insistence on the transformative effect of the word on the attitudes and behaviour of all true believers. It was this, applied to the public sphere, and particularly to the person of the magistrate and the councillor, that lay behind puritan campaigns for further reformation in church and state and the concomitant attempts to purge the social order of its sins and corruptions. Yet campaigns like these were but one expression or effect of the puritan impulse, an impulse stemming from the experience of true justifying faith and the consequent integration of the individual into the community of the godly and the separation of that community, in the view of its members at least, from the profane and the ungodly.

It has been argued here that the puritan style of practical divinity, and the view of the implications of right doctrine enshrined in it, contained a certain internal spiritual dynamic, a dynamic that forced the believer into a constant struggle to externalise his sense of his own election through a campaign of works directed against Antichrist, the flesh, sin and the world. It is perhaps the basic contention of this study that if puritanism is to be defined at all it must be in terms of that spiritual dynamic. One such externalisation of true belief was to be found in presbyterianism and similar campaigns for further reformation.

But to confuse such campaigns, which were but one expression or product of the basic puritan impulse, with that impulse itself is to confuse the letter with the spirit. It was perhaps the distinguishing mark of the moderate puritan position, as espoused by Chaderton and Cartwright, to avoid precisely such a confusion. The analysis of Elizabethan religious opinion might be greatly clarified if historians were to make a similar effort.

Here the central distinction to make may be that between puritanism seen as an ideological construct – a series of positions or principles, both polemical and edificational, each logically linked with or connected to the others – and puritanism seen as a term to be applied to particular men. It is relatively easy to distinguish a series of distinctively puritan opinions or attitudes to a whole series of issues ranging from certain strict standards of moral discipline to the polity of the church or even the nature of foreign policy. All these opinions were linked: they were linked logically as emanations of the same protestant world-view and also linked practically since, for obvious reasons, they were often espoused by the same men. However, it is important to remember that while it is both possible and legitimate to construct such a thing as a unitary puritan position, the actual positions taken up by individual men need never have corresponded to that model. Different aspects of that over-all position were given different degrees of emphasis by different men in different situations. Through an analysis of a series of divines this study has sought to construct such a model of the puritan position and to establish some of the major features of its internal structure. But it has also sought to distinguish between those features of the puritan world-view essential to its maintenance and those which, although linked to impulses at the centre of that world-view, could yet be dispensed with and still leave the essential elements in a man's puritanism intact. On the present view, presbyterianism was just such a 'peripheral' element. Predicated on precisely the same principles as those which underlay Whitaker's protestantism, it represented an extension of those principles which Whitaker himself found it both conceptually possible and personally necessary to reject. Yet he could do so without losing the respect and admiration of committed presbyterians like Chaderton. By a process of comparison, of sifting and juxtaposing variations on the basic theme of the puritan world-view, this study has attempted to penetrate to the kernel of the puritan position, to identify the opinions, attitudes and impulses essential to establish and maintain a position of respect and acceptance amongst the godly. On this basis it becomes possible to argue that despite the divergences within puritan opinion at any one time and, more importantly, despite the shifts in emphasis over a period of time as different issues moved from the centre to the periphery of puritan concern, puritan opinion nevertheless enjoyed a remarkable degree of continuity and internal coherence throughout the period under discussion. It is possible to argue that after 1590 puritanism, as a nexus of polemical positions concerning the structure of the church designed for public assertion and defence, went into decline. Certainly the rather low-key performance by Chaderton and his colleagues at Hampton Court might suggest as much. But it would surely not be legitimate, on that basis, to claim that puritanism, regarded as a shared body of religious experience, a certain view of the implications of right doctrine and a common perception of the self and the selves of other fellow believers as members of a community of the godly, went into a similar decline. Here the mutual respect, the clear links of thought and feeling betwen Chaderton and avowed radicals like Brightman and Bradshaw should serve to redeem Chaderton from the charge of mere conformity and bring us back to that capacity of the godly to recognise one another in the midst of a corrupt world as one of the central defining characteristics of puritanism.

But this is not to endorse the view that sees a basically 'political' puritanism, centred on the classis movement, superseded during the 1590s by a politically quiescent, pietistic strain of practical divinity. On the present view, that pietistic, personal core had underlain the puritan impulse from the start. The illusion of a fresh undertaking at the end of the century is based on the fact that a certain sort of edificational text became more likely to be printed as the century progressed. But, as the analysis of the manuscript sources in chapter 6 is designed to show, it was precisely that style of divinity that had been prevalent during the previous decades. The removal of presbyterianism from the practical agenda of any puritan movement that wished to retain its place within the national church, firstly by the events of 1589/90 and latterly by the fiasco of Hampton Court, simply allowed puritan divines to give their undivided attention to their role as preaching ministers and practical pastors. Yet such activities had always stood at the centre of their lives. Presbyterianism itself was predicated on the ineffectiveness of the church of England as a proselytising institution. Although the issue of church polity and the conduct of public polemic may dominate the printed works of Thomas Cartwright or Walter Travers, there is no reason to suppose that such issues and activities also dominated their lives in the church as pastors and preachers. Similarly, Laurence Chaderton's St Paul's Cross sermon of 1578, with its emphasis on the role of good works in a true profession of the gospel and as a validation of a true justifying faith, prefigured many themes supposedly typical of the later more pietistic style of puritan divinity.[7]

It is one thing to argue for an experiential basis for any effective definition of, or approach to, puritanism. It is quite another to apply such principles in practice. For hardly ever is the historian in possession of the 'unprocessed' account of religious or personal experience set down in letters or diaries. The most that can be hoped for in many cases is an amalgam of formal doctrine and practical divinity such as that analysed in chapter 6. Moreover, in numerous cases the historian is denied sufficient documentation for even that sort of analysis. However desirable the analysis of puritanism in terms of its personal and inter-personal spiritual core may be, such an analysis is inevitably often impossible and the historian is thrown back on precisely the sorts of formal, public issues which, it has been argued here, are best seen as but symptoms, external signs of the shared religious experience of the godly.

This study through its concentration on a centrally placed group of puritan divines, has sought to circumvent this difficulty. If its conclusions, drawn from a very limited, if relatively well-documented sample, can be accepted, they might provide the basis for an approach to a wider analysis of puritan opinion. In particular they might allow a greater coherence and continuity to be attributed to puritan religion despite the considerable fluctuations in the level of public debate and dispute about issues usually regarded as definitively puritan.

Some idea of the workings of such an approach can be gleaned from the issue of anti-popery. Anti-popery, of course, was hardly a puritan monopoly. However, if the vision of the reality, unity and mutuality of the community of the godly provided the positive aspect of puritan religion, it was balanced by the threat posed to that community by popery. The livelier the sense of that threat, the more sensitive and deep-rooted the perception of the division betwen the community of the godly and a corrupt and potentially popish world.

This provides a peculiarly clear example of an area where puritanism cannot be collapsed into a mere doctrinal consensus. For the doctrinal basis of Elizabethan anti-popery, summed up in the identification of the pope as Antichrist, was common currency. But there was more than one way in which to regard the popish threat and these different attitudes to Rome were in turn re-flections of divergent views of the community of the godly and of its relations with the world and, indeed, of its relations with the national church. The central example of this divergence is provided in the present context by the contrast between William Whitaker's attitude to Rome and that displayed by Whitgift, and to a lesser extent Burghley, during the Everard Digby affair and, later, during the theological disputes of 1595/6. Whitaker's attitude was characterised by a very uncompromising, though implicit, division between godliness and ungodliness (revealed most clearly in his government of St John's) and his willingness to subsume that distinction into that between Christ and Antichrist, true religion and popery. That last tendency comes through clearly in his treatment both of Digby and of his opponents of 1595/6. Clearly, for Whitaker, any lapse from his own strict definition of Calvinist orthodoxy was tantamount to popery.

Other men, like Whitgift or the slightly confused Burghley, took a rather different view of the consequences of the pope's status as Antichrist and the nature of the popish threat. Their attitude was characterised by a relative unwillingness to allow the division between Christ and Antichrist to be so directly trans-ferred from the theoretical sphere of anti-papal polemic to the practical sphere of church or college government. In both the Digby affair and the 1595/6 disputes Whitaker's attempts to assimilate his opponents' position to popery were resisted by Whitgift and Burghley who both demanded rather more stringent doctrinal proof of popery than an inability to fully endorse the Calvinism of William Whitaker.

In formal terms the differences involved here were non-existent. All the parties agreed that the pope was Antichrist. All of them hated popery. Yet they differed in their perception of the implications of that agreement. Whitaker's readiness to assimilate to popery any dissent from his own rigorous standards of moral and doctrinal orthodoxy stemmed from the sensitivity and exclusivity of his view of the community of the godly. It was that, of course, which provided the foundation of his continuing links with more overtly committed puritans like Chaderton and Cartwright. Thus in these incidents we are confronted not merely by a series of disputes between tetchy theologians and dons over the minutiae of doctrinal orthodoxy, but by an implicit dispute over whether or not St John's College, or, indeed, Cambridge University, was to be governed according to puritan principles and assumptions.[8]

What was involved was a clash between two rival views of the implications of right doctrine, or, more accurately, between two divergent views of the necessary relationships between those implications and the the principle of social order. It was not that puritans denied or directly challenged the predominant ideology of hierarchy and degree. Even in their more radical presbyterian moments they could invoke such themes to buttress their own position. However, there was present in their outlook a distinctive view of the relationship required between the need for order and hierarchy and the demands of true religion. Again presbyterianism and related issues provided the clearest and most developed example of this tension. But again this represented merely one product of a general tendency or attitude that underlay the whole puritan position.

Like so much else in puritan thought, this distinctive view of the necessary relationship between the values of true religion and the social order grew from the very roots of the protestant impulse. Having turned their backs on the popish idea of the authority of the church and fathers and on the intercessionary role of the priest, protestants were left with the study of scripture (guided, of course, by properly trained clerics) and the internal testimony of the Spirit attendant upon it as the only source for, and validation of, true belief. This was something which puritans took seriously not merely as a polemical position against Rome but as a guiding principle in their practical divinity. Here is Thomas

Cartwright on the need for intense scriptural study and theological engagement on the part of all believers, no matter how humble:

If (as hath been showed) all ought to read the scriptures then all ages, all sexes, all degrees and callings, all high and low, rich and poor, wise and foolish have a necessary duty therein; of which particularities neither do the scriptures nor ancient writers keep silent. For the scriptures declareth that women and children and that from their infancy that noble and ignoble, rich and poor, wise and foolish exercise themselves in the holy scriptures. And Theodoret liketh well that the points of religion which the Church taught were not only known of doctors and masters but of tailors, smiths, weavers and other artificers; not of men only but of women and the same not only learned but labouring men, sewsters, servants and handmaids; not of citizens alone but of country-folk, ditchers, delvers, neat-herds, and gardeners, disputing even of the Holy Trinity.

Similarly, the scripture was suitable not only for all callings but for all occasions:

being commanded to be talked of both within the house and without; both lying, sitting and walking; a man would think that therein is commanded the exercise of it in all places both table and bench, both boat and barge.[9]

These were hardly sentiments likely to appeal to a conformist worried about the preservation of social order and subordination.

Puritans compounded the offence by denying that distinction between matters of formal divinity, fit only for the discussion of scholars, and questions appropriate for a more popular audience. Cartwright, for instance, denied that there should be any difference between a 'teacher in the school and a pulpit man':

For the doctrine in school is and ought to be the same that is in the pulpit and that in pulpit as exact, absolute and necessary as that in the school. The difference is that in the school it hath not annexed the goad and prick of exhortation as the other hath.[10]

This had particular application to the central doctrine of predestination. 'The secrets of the Lord', conceded Cartwright, 'are to himself.' But there were things 'which are revealed unto us and our children'. These were revealed to man not

to jangle them but to speak, to dispute, to write and to preach of them with all reverence. And if whole books have been written of predestination it is no marvel, it being a principal post of true religion and fear of God especially seeing this pure and wholesome water hath been troubled with the filthy feet of your popish sophisms. And if men have abused these worthy treatises and have drawn poison from whence they might and ought to have sucked nourishment; yet that ought not to stop either the preacher's mouth nor stay the pen of the learned scribe, unless you will have almost all sound doctrine buried in silence, which is any way racked to another use and sense than it is delivered.

'A man is not only not hindered by the preaching of predestination (and to the people) from his duty, but helped that when he glorieth he may glory in the Lord.'[11]

Chaderton made the same point, in a more general context. He vigorously refuted the argument that since obscure or difficult passages in scripture offered occasions of error or heresy, they should be avoided. If men were misled by the word, the fault lay not in any shortcomings inherent in scripture but in 'the corruption of the heart'.[12] This could provide no excuse to confine the word within merely human limits. On the contrary, it should be freely available to all men. Due to the fact of sin this would no doubt lead to corruptions and errors, but that was unavoidable.

The conformist position was markedly different. For them the preservation of order provided a real check on the style and content of a man's preaching. When, at Hampton Court, Bancroft lamented the antinomian consequences of puritan preaching on predestination (although it should be noted that he did not challenge the objective truth of the Calvinist doctrine of predestination that was still predominant in the English church) and even questioned the need for a preaching ministry at all times, he was employing a very different view of the relations between true religion and the social order from that outlined by Cartwright and Chaderton.[13]

Indeed, the puritans went further. We have already seen that on the individual level Chaderton and others regarded a period of upheaval and anguish as a sign of true belief. This view could be transferred quite readily to the collective level, particularly once the need to oppose Antichrist in all his forms had been invoked to lift this imperative from the individual level onto the stage of public policy and political and administrative action.

For, as Cartwright argued, true order was impossible in the presence of popery:

Popery is such a time wherein (as Saloman sayeth) 'the servants ride and the masters go on foot', that is to say wherein commonly the bishop can bite but cannot bark, the pastor can milk but not feed, the priest can mum but not speak, it is needful that in such a case the water should go against the stream, the scholar should teach his master, the sheep control his pastor.[14]

To an extent what was involved here were two distinct and opposed concepts of order. Both employed the language of the conventional ideology of hierarchy and degree, but they differed crucially over the extent to which religious values – for example the radical demands of true religion for a complete and un-compromising break with sin, Satan, the flesh and their agent in history, Antichrist – should be allowed to actually constitute the concept of order. However, the differences between these two approaches to order were not clear-cut. The confusions and convergences between the two are just as important for an understanding of the puritan position as the differences and divergences. Hence, in the passage just cited, Cartwright first equated disorder with popery. That disorder was initially defined in secular terms, as the comparison with the inversion of the roles of master and servant implied. But almost immediately that secular view of disorder was assimilated to a religious one and was implicitly identified with an ecclesiastical view of disorder in which the component parts and roles that made up a true church were seen to be neglected, ignored or confused. We are confronted here, therefore, with a tripartite concept of order. On the first level, order is defined purely in terms of the preservation of the hierarchy of secular society. On the second, that vision is assimilated to one based on the need to preserve a certain view of true religion. The third level required the equation of that second aim with certain specific aspects of ecclesiastical order. The con-formist position involved the identification of certain potential clashes between the first and second levels and the resolution of them broadly in favour of the demands of the first level. This was accomplished by means of practical and theoretical limitations placed on the implications of right doctrine and the central assumptions of the protestant position. These limitations (centred on the concept of things indifferent) served entirely to deny the third level of the view set out by Cartwright, which in its most developed form produced the presbyterian platform.

In contrast, the puritan position assumed a basic congruence between the first and second levels and, in the case of the presbyterians, of all three. It was this assumed congruence that enabled Chaderton and Cartwright to defend presbyterianism, which in conformist eyes represented a massive threat to order, in terms of the conventional ideology of hierarchy and degree. For popery and its legacy within the English church, both in terms of popular irreligion and ignorance and the corruption of its institutional structure, was seen by men like Cartwright and Chaderton to threaten their concept of order at every level.

Hence it was impossible to conceive of a properly stable or ordered society in which any element of popery remained. In other words, puritan zeal inevitably led to tension with contemporary social reality (through its struggle against sin and the flesh) and was finally pushed onto the stage of public policy by the spectre of popery. But since popery and its allied forces of superstition and irreligion had thoroughly penetrated and subverted many of the structures of contemporary society, any attempt to purge the social order of its popish elements would, in the short term at least, appear to subvert the very cause of order in the name of which the process of reformation was being carried out. It was to this paradox that Cartwright was referring in the passage cited above. It remained true, therefore, that despite their undoubted willingness to countenance a certain sort of upheaval on both the personal and collective levels in the struggle for true religion, puritans like Chaderton and Cartwright nevertheless remained wedded to the ideology of order, hierarchy and degree. Contemporary society might appear, on one view, as overgrown with popish corruptions. But beneath those corruptions could be discerned the outline of a properly godly commonwealth. Reformation was conceived as the strengthening of those sound and godly elements. No matter what the disruption involved, therefore, such a process could be justified in terms of order and true hierarchy.

There was, therefore, a real tension at the heart of the puritan position. It has formed no part of the purpose of this study to resolve that tension in favour either of order, consensus commitment to the status quo, or of the radical drive for further reformation and the challenge to conventional concepts of order. It might be argued that this study reveals certain supposed puritans to have been more moderate than has previously been assumed. But it is equally true to say that it has found certain very moderate figures to have been a good deal more radical than they might at first appear. In short, it has implications for the 'moderate', 'anglican' Whitaker as well as the 'radical', 'presbyterian' Chaderton. The intention, then, has not been to remove or resolve the resulting ambiguity and tension from the puritan position as presented here, but to describe and document it. If the result is ambiguous, I would hope that that ambiguity is a function of the nature of the puritan impulse and its relations with the society which sustained it, rather than of any confusion or conceptual inadequacy inherent in the preceding analysis.

Notes

I. INTRODUCTION: LAURENCE CHADERTON AND THE PROBLEM OF PURITANISM

1. For the initial impact of presbyterianism see P. Collinson, 'John Field and Elizabethan puritanism', *Elizabethan government and society: essays presented to Sir John Neale*, ed. S. T. Bindoff, J. Hurstfield and C. H. Williams (London, 1961); also Collinson, *The Elizabethan puritan movement* (London, 1967).
2. Collinson, *Puritan movement*, pp. 388–9; for Johnson's congregation see B.L. Harley Mss 7042, fols. 35–8, 59–64, 204–5; for the situation confronted by Johnson after the collapse of the classis movement see my article 'The dilemma of the Establishment puritan: the Cambridge Heads and the case of Francis Johnson and Cuthbert Bainbrigg', *J.E.H.* 29 (1978).
3. On the vestiarian controversy see J. H. Primus, *The vestments controversy* (Kampen, 1960); Collinson, *Puritan movement*, pp. 71–83. Also see below chapter 3 and chapter 9.
4. J. S. Coolidge, *The Pauline Renaissance in England: puritanism and the Bible* (Oxford, 1970).
5. Travers and Cartwright were the leading presbyterian ideologues of their generation. Certainly Cartwright, after his long controversy with Whitgift in the admonition controversy, had emerged as the leading theoretician of the presbyterian movement and, for polemical purposes at least, the 'representative' precisian divine. For Cartwright see A. F. S. Pearson, *Thomas Cartwright and Elizabethan puritanism* (Cambridge, 1925). For Travers see S. J. Knox, *Walter Travers: paragon of Elizabethan puritanism* (London, 1962).
6. Ward, an undergraduate at Christ's during the late 1580s, became a fellow of Emmanuel in 1596, Master of Sidney Sussex in 1609 and Lady Margaret Professor of Divinity in 1622. He was also one of the English representatives at the

synod of Dort. A noted pluralist, Ward was the friend and correspondent of some of the leading scholars and divines of the period (Bishop Davenant, Archbishop Ussher, Sir Robert Cotton). For Ward see *D.N.B.*

7. H. C. Porter, *Reformation and reaction in Tudor Cambridge* (Cambridge, 1958), chapter 12; I. Breward, The life and theology of William Perkins, 1558–1602', unpublished Ph.D. thesis, Manchester University, 1963, and Breward's introduction to *The works of William Perkins* (Abingdon, 1970).

8. I owe this formulation of the problem to a seminar paper given at the Institute of Historical Research by the late Professor W. J. D. Cargill Thompson.

9. For this see below chapter 10. For a comparison of the position of Chaderton after Hampton Court with that of Thomas Sparke, identical in formal terms but very different in polemical significance, see chapter 8 of my thesis, 'Laurence Chaderton and the Cambridge moderate puritan tradition', unpublished Ph.D. thesis, Cambridge University, 1978.

10. For all this see below chapter 5 where Cartwright's position is compared with that of Robert Some, again identical in formal terms but very different in polemical significance.

11. For this see below, chapter 7.

12. For this see below chapter 11.

13. Collinson, 'A comment: concerning the name puritan', *J.E.H.* 31 (1980), which is a comment on a longer piece by P. Christianson called 'Reformers and the Church of England under Elizabeth I and the early Stuarts', *J.E.H.* 31 (1980).

2. MODERATE BEGINNINGS: THE CASE OF EDWARD DERING

1. P. Collinson, *A mirror of Elizabethan puritanism: the life and letters of 'Godly Master Dering'* (London, 1964), p. 4.

2. Edward Dering and John More, *A briefe and Necessarie Catechisme* (Middelburg, 1590), Dering's Epistle to the Christian Reader, sig. A2v.

3. *Ibid.*, sig. A4.

4. Dering to Burghley dated November 1573, B.L. Lansdowne Mss vol. 17, no. 90, fol. 197v.

5. Dering and More, *Catechisme*, Epistle, sigs. A3v–A4.

6. Dering to Burghley dated November 1573, B. L. Lansdowne Mss vol. 17, no. 90, fol. 198r–v.

7. Dering and More, *Catechisme*, Epistle, sig. A4.

8. Dering to Parker, dated 5 September 1570, B.L. Stowe Mss 743,

no. 1, fols. 4–10v. Dering to Cecil, dated 18 November 1570, B.L. Lansdowne Mss vol. 12, no. 86, fols. 190–1v; Dering, *A sermon preached before the queenes maiestie* (London, 1570).

9. B.L. Lansdowne Mss vol. 12, no. 86, fol. 191v.
10. B.L. Stowe Mss 743, no. 1, fols. 8v–9.
11. Dering to Cecil, dated 18 November 1570, B.L. Lansdowne Mss vol. 12, no. 86, fol. 191r–v.
12. For Dering's letter to Burghley see P.R.O. S.P. 12/85/75, dated 24 March 1572; for his visit to Field and Wilcox see Inner Temple Library Petyt Mss 538/47, fol. 481. John Field and Thomas Wilcox were the authors of the radical presbyterian pamphlet *An admonition to the parliament*. For this see P. Collinson, 'John Field and Elizabethan puritanism', *Elizabethan government and society: essays presented to Sir John Neale*, ed. S. T. Bindoff, J. Hurstfield and C. H. Williams (London, 1961).
13. For the date of the proceedings see Collinson, *Godly Master Dering*, p. 21.
14. For Dering's replies to the articles presented to him in Star Chamber and a further 'Answer unto four articles' see *A parte of a register* (Middelburg, 1593), pp. 73–85. For a manuscript version of the former see Lambeth Palace Library Mss 2550, fols. 170f. For this passage *A part of a register*, pp. 79–80, article 17.
15. B.L. Lansdowne Mss vol. 17, no. 90, fol. 198r–v.
16. Dering to Burghley, dated November 1573, B.L. Lansdowne Mss vol. 17, no. 90, fol. 199.
17. *A parte of a register*, p. 74, article 2; p. 82.
18. *Ibid.*, p. 77, article 11; p. 78, article 15; p. 75, article 7.
19. *Ibid.*, p. 76, article 7.
20. Dering to Burghley, dated November 1573, B.L. Lansdowne Mss vol. 17, no. 90, fols. 199–200r, 197.
21. *Ibid.*, fol. 200. For a similar position more moderately stated and used in a purely anti-papal context see below, chapters 6 and 8.
22. *A parte of a register*, p. 75, article 4.
23. It is significant that Dering's most explicitly presbyterian statements, which provided a gloss on his replies to the articles, were taken not from an official document at all but from a private letter to Burghley.
24. Hence, even in his most overtly presbyterian moments, Dering could write of the bishops: 'we know their doing and our hope is of them as of members of the church. We love as brethren

and honour them as elders...But this I must needs say and freely confess if I were in one of their places I am afraid I should not have been so soon persuaded.' Dering to Burghley, dated November 1573, B.L. Lansdowne Mss vol. 17, no. 90, fol. 200v.

3. CHADERTON'S PURITANISM

1. Laurence Chaderton, *An excellent and godly sermon... preached at Paules Cross* (London, 1580). For a discussion of this sermon see below, chapter 7. For a fuller discussion of the structure and contents of this sermon see my thesis, 'Laurence Chaderton and the Cambridge moderate puritan tradition', unpublished Ph.D. thesis, Cambridge University, 1978, chapter 2, section (a).

2. For these depositions see P.R.O. Star Chamber Depositions 5A 49/34. For Chaderton as Cambridge corresponding secretary see the deposition of John Johnson. For Chaderton as moderator see that of Thomas Stone.

3. See J. Strype, *Annals of the Reformation under Elizabeth* (7 vols., Oxford, 1824), vol. 3, pt. 2, p. 477.

4. B.L. Harley Mss 7042, fols 36r, 59v–60r.

5. Peter Fairlambe, *The recantation of a brownist or a reformed puritan* (London, 1606), sigs. C3 and D3.

6. For Fulke's career see Dr R. J. Bauckham, 'The career and theology of Dr William Fulke, 1537–1589', unpublished Ph.D. thesis, Cambridge University, 1973.

7. Mathew Sutcliffe, *An answere to a certaine libel supplicatiorie* (London, 1592), p. 41, where Sutcliffe alleged that Field published the book against Fulke's will. Quoted in A. F. S. Pearson, *Thomas Cartwright and Elizabethan puritanism* (Cambridge, 1925), p. 273.

8. Dudley Fenner, *A defence of the godlie ministers* (Middelburg, 1587), p. 56. According to Fenner Fulke was 'a learned and deep divine who hath been after Master Jewel and M. Nowel the chiefest defender by writings both in our tongue and in Latin of the truth against the papists'. This illustrates perfectly the sort of prestige which the conduct of a vigorous attack on the papists could earn for a godly divine and shows the role of anti-papal polemic in establishing the essentially respectable nature of the puritan tradition.

9. Laurence Chaderton, *A fruitful sermon, upon the 3, 4, 5, 6, 7 and 8 verse of the 12 chapter of the epistle of St. Paule to the Romanes* (London, 1584), p. 12.

10. *Ibid.*, pp. 12–13.
11. *Ibid.*, p. 18. This doctrine of callings or vocation was a long-standing element in the protestant tradition, starting with Luther, whose 'Berufsethik' was strongly echoed in the works of William Tyndale. It is echoed in the catechism of the Book of Common Prayer where the need 'to do my duty in that state of life unto which it shall please God to call me' is stressed. It is similarly prominent in the Homily of 'Order'. For puritans like Chaderton it played an absolutely central role in controlling the radical tendencies inherent in presbyterianism and, more generally, in the puritan insistence on the need for a strongly personal internalisation of the truths of right doctrine. Like so much else in the puritan tradition it was in many ways summed up in the works of William Perkins, for which see I. Breward, 'The life and theology of William Perkins, 1558–1602', unpublished Ph.D. thesis, Manchester University, 1963, fols. 277f.
12. Chaderton, *A fruitful sermon*, pp. 22–3.
13. *Ibid.*, pp. 26–7. This theme of the corruption and pride of the pharisees as archetypal church leaders was to occur in Chaderton's lectures in the 1590s. See below, this chapter.
14. *Ibid.*, pp. 28–9.
15. *Ibid.*, pp. 29, 33–4.
16. *Ibid.*, p. 34.
17. *Ibid.*, pp. 41–2.
18. *Ibid.*, p. 43. This insistence on the greed and corruption of the rulers of the church bringing corruptions into the church was to form a central theme in Chaderton's lectures of 1590. For which see below, this chapter.
19. For this point see below, chapter 7.
20. Chaderton, *A fruitful sermon*, pp. 51–2.
21. *Ibid.*, pp. 54–5.
22. *Ibid.*, p. 73.
23. *Ibid.*, pp. 45–6.
24. *Ibid.*, pp. 82–3.
25. Chaderton, Paules Crosse, sig. C5. The family of love referred to here by Chaderton was an Anabaptist sect inspired by the life and writings of a Dutch radical, Henry Nicholas. These writings were translated into English and traces of the sect have been found in the England of Elizabeth's reign. Their rather confused mysticism led to a widespread belief that they taught an immoral antinomianism. Certainly in Chaderton's works they appear as a watchword for extremist protestant sectarianism.
26. Chaderton, *A fruitful sermon*, p. 69.

27. *Ibid.*, pp. 69–70.
28. *Ibid.*, pp. 70–2.
29. *Ibid.*, pp. 71–2.
30. *Ibid.*, p. 87.
31. *Ibid.*, p. 56.
32. This image of the unreformed church as a maimed human body was a stock presbyterian conceit. But if it was rhetorically effective it nevertheless left the exact degree of the injury vague. Such ambiguity was central to the moderate position. Hence Cartwright could use the same image in his anti-separatist works to draw the distinction between a mortal injury and a merely severe disablement. According to Cartwright the English church could be likened to a man who had lost a limb: she was seriously injured, even crippled, but her wounds were not fatal.
33. Chaderton, *A fruitful sermon*, pp. 86–7.
34. *Ibid.*, pp. 84–5.
35. *Ibid.*, p. 91.
36. Chaderton, *Paules Crosse*, 'To the Christian reader'. Sentiments such as these probably account for the paucity of Chaderton's own published works.
37. All details about Chaderton's life are taken from William Dillingham's *Life of Chaderton*, first published in Latin in 1700. All quotations and citations are taken from the English translation by E. S. Shuckburgh (Cambridge, 1884). Dillingham, *Life of Chaderton*, p. 14.
38. Dr Williams Library Morrice Mss A, fols. 191f. A partial transcript is printed in *The seconde parte of a register*, ed. A. Peel (2 vols., Cambridge, 1915), vol. 1, pp. 133–4.
39. Samuel Clarke, *A general martyrologie* (London, 1677), pp. 133, 169.
40. Cambridge University Library Baker Mss Mm/1/43, pp. 437–8. For this suggestion concerning Chaderton's co-ordinating role see P. Collinson, *The Elizabethan puritan movement* (London, 1967), p. 126.
41. B.L. Egerton Mss 2812, fol. 28. For a second letter implying that Chaderton had accepted the charge see *ibid.*, fol. 76v.
42. Chaderton was only one referee. John Still, Roger Goad (Provost of King's College, Cambridge), John Knewstubb (the leading Suffolk puritan) and Robert Beaumont were also asked for references. See Ipswich Borough Records; Assembly book 31 Elizabeth – 6 James I Assembly of 4 May, 32 Elizabeth. Quoted in P. Collinson, 'The puritan classical movement in the

reign of Elizabeth I', unpublished Ph.D. thesis, London University, 1957, fol. 1019.

43. In this instance Chaderton was only one amongst many called out to support the puritan candidate for the post. See Castle Museum Colchester, Essex Archaeological Society Mss C43 and C48. For a comprehensive account of the affair see Collinson, 'Puritan classical movement', pp. 598–606.

44. Clarke, *Martyrologie*, p. 169.

45. For details concerning Bradshaw see Clarke, *Martyrologie*, pp. 25f. which includes the 'Life of William Bradshaw' written by his friend and contemporary at Sidney Sussex, Thomas Gataker.

46. For Josiah Nichols, see P. Clarke, 'Josiah Nichols and religious radicalism 1553–1639', *J.E.H.* 28 (1977), 133f.

47. Collinson, *Puritan movement*, p. 166.

48. For Huntingdon see C. Cross, *The puritan Earl* (London, 1966).

49. For these bequests see Emmanuel College, Cambridge, Mss Col. 20. 1.

50. For Cartwright's will see Pearson, *Thomas Cartwright*, pp. 484–5.

51. For this bequest see K. W. Shipps, 'Lay patronage of East Anglian puritan clerics in pre-Revolutionary England', unpublished Ph.D. thesis, Yale University, 1971, fol. 304.

52. For this bequest see Cambridge University Registry Guard Book 95, nos. 1 and 2.

53. All quotations from the college statutes are taken from the translation of the original Latin text by the college librarian, Dr F. H. Stubbings. There is a copy of his translation in Emmanuel College Library. For this passage see Statute 21.

54. *Ibid.*, preface to the statutes.

55. For an exposition of this sermon see above, this chapter.

56. Emmanuel Statutes 11.

57. For this exercise see Emmanuel College, Cambridge, Mss Col. 14. 1, pp. 3–9.

58. J. S. Coolidge, *The Pauline Renaissance in England: puritanism and the Bible* (Oxford, 1970), pp. 23f.

59. This is not to suggest that these were exclusively presbyterian doctrines. On the contrary, they were to be found at the centre of the protestant world-view. As ever, presbyterianism was merely the development of elements shared by the whole spectrum of religious opinion.

60. Emmanuel College, Cambridge, Mss Col. 14. 1. p. 1.

61. Cambridge University Library Mss Mm/2/35, fols. 161f, entry dated 18 January 1605.
62. B.L. Harleian Mss 7033, fol. 98r–v. A paper headed 'Public disorders as touching Church causes in Emmanuel College in Cambridge'. One need only look at William Whitaker's experience at St John's to see what happened when similarly puritan institutions and attitudes were introduced into a college which lacked Emmanuel's basic ideological consensus. For which, see below, chapter 8.
63. The arguments concerning 'things indifferent', or adiaphora as they were called, had already been fully rehearsed during the vestments controversy of Edward VI's reign and the 1560s. For this see J. H. Primus, *The vestments controversy* (Kampen, 1960) and B. J. Verkamp, *The indifferent mean* (Ohio, 1977). For a full discussion of an extended argument conducted entirely in these terms later in the century by Chaderton, see below, chapter 9.
64. The initial enquiry and Cartwright's response are contained in one paper (Dr Williams Library Morrice Mss A, fols. 49–50r; for the same in Latin see Morrice Mss B II, fols. 204–5). Cartwright also seems to have included his latest work, *The rest of the second replie of Thomas Cartwright: agaynst master doctor Whitgift's second answer...* (n.p., 1577), for the comment of the brethren. Their response to that and a letter from Anthony Gilby, both highly critical of Cartwright's modified position, are also in the Morrice Mss A, fol. 135 and BII, fols. 131–4. These documents were printed almost in full in *A parte of a register...* (Middelburg, 1593). The passages cited here are from the printed version since due to wear and tear on the manuscript certain words are no longer legible. It should be noted that Cartwright's position on this issue corresponded almost exactly to that which Bullinger and Peter Martyr, during the 1560s, advised their English brethren to adopt. Cartwright himself cited the support of the 'professors and ministers in Heidelberg' for his position. For all this see Primus, *The vestments controversy*.
65. For Fulke and Whitaker see below, chapter 4.
66. The contrast between radicals and moderates should not be overdrawn. A moderate like Chaderton could still take part in the presbyterian propaganda campaign of 1584 and remain a committed presbyterian for the rest of the decade. But there was a certain difference in approach at stake here.
67. Collinson, *Puritan movement*, p. 248. This summary of the

issue of subscription obviously relies heavily on Professor Collinson's account of the events of 1583/4.

68. For this and a more detailed examination of the moderate position on subscription see chapter 3 of my thesis, 'Chaderton and the Cambridge moderate puritan tradition'.

69. Pembroke College, Cambridge, Mss LC. II. 2. 164, fol. 5v.

70. *Ibid.*, fol. 10v.

71. *Ibid.*, fol. 10v.

72. *Ibid.*, fol. 11r.

73. *Ibid.*, fol. 10r.

74. *Ibid.*, fol. 13r.

75. *Ibid.*, fol. 15v.

76. *Ibid.*, fol. 19v.

77. *Ibid.*, fol. 18r.

78. *Ibid.*, fol. 39r.

79. *Ibid.*, fol. 38r.

80. *Ibid.*, fol. 22v.

81. *Ibid.*, fol. 23r.

82. *Ibid.*, fol. 22v.

83. *Ibid.*, fol. 6r.

84. *Ibid.*, fol. 33r.

85. *Ibid.*, fol. 33v.

86. *Ibid.*, fol. 10r.

87. *Ibid.*, fol. 10r–v (numbered from the back). For Chaderton's view of the interpretation of scripture as a collective exercise see the account of the prophesyings described by him above.

88. *Ibid.*, fol. 25r.

89. *Ibid.*, fol. 9r (numbered from the back).

4. THE MODERATE PURITAN DIVINE
AS ANTI-PAPAL POLEMICIST

1. C. Hill, *Antichrist in seventeenth century England* (London, 1971). Also see R. J. Bauckham, *Tudor apocalypse* (Abingdon, 1978).

2. For an analysis of precisely this use of the rhetoric of Antichrist with particular reference to separatists and radicals, see P. Christianson, *Reformers and Babylon* (Toronto, 1978).

3. William Whitaker, *Ad rationes decem Edmundi Campioni iesuitae...responsio Guilielmi Whitakeri* (London, 1581). This book prompted a reply from Duraeus which was in turn answered by Whitaker in his *Responsionis ad decem illas rationes...defensio contra confutationem Ioannis Duraei scoti,*

presbyteri, iesuitae (London, 1583). A translation of the first work, with passages from the second appended, was produced by a London minister, Richard Stock, and published in 1606 as *An Answere to the ten reasons of Edmund Campion the iesuit* (London, 1606). Hereafter referred to as *Against Campion* (Stock), p. 165.

4. For Fulke, see R. J. Bauckham, 'The career and theology of Dr William Fulke, 1537–89', unpublished Ph.D. thesis, Cambridge University, 1973. For the continuing respect of radicals for moderates in the Fulke/Whitaker school, see my article 'Robert Some and the ambiguities of moderation', *Archiv für Reformationsgeschichte* 71 (1980).

5. All these details about Whitaker's early life are taken from a biography by Abdias Ashton, a protégé of Whitaker's and a fellow of St John's during Whitaker's period as Master. This was printed (in Latin) as an appendix to Whitaker's *Praelectiones...de ecclesia* (Cambridge, 1599). An English translation was published in 1772 together with Whitaker's *Cygnea Cantio: or the swan-song*. Hereafter cited as Ashton, *Life of Whitaker*.

6. *Liber precum publicorum ecclesiae Anglicanae...Latine Graeci editus* (London, 1569).

7. Whitaker, *Catechismus parvus Latine (Alexander Nowell) et Graece (W.W.)* (London, 1574); Nowell, *Christianae pietatis prima institutio* (London, 1578).

8. Ashton, *Life of Whitaker*, p. 6.

9. Whitaker (trans.), *Joannis Jewelli adversus T. Hardingum volumen alterum...conversum in latinum a Guilielmo Whitakero* (London, 1578), Dedicatory Epistle.

10. Ashton, *Life of Whitaker*, pp. 8–9.

11. Whitaker, *Ad rationes decem E. Campioni*, Dedicatory Epistle.

12. The post had been first offered to Fulke, who had refused it, in itself a telling testimony to the dominance of English theology by anti-papal polemic. Bauckham, 'William Fulke', p. 101.

13. Trinity College, Cambridge, Mss B/14/9 p. 118, Whitgift to Neville dated 8 December 1595. For Whitaker's acknowledgement of his debt to Whitgift see his *Adversus Thomae Stapletoni...defensionem* (Cambridge, 1594), Dedicatory Epistle. See also, Ashton, *Life of Whitaker*, p. 10.

14. In two letters to Burghley of 1594/5 Whitaker signed himself as Burghley's chaplain. (See B.L. Additional Mss, 4276, fol. 192, dated January 1594/5 and B.L. Lansdowne Mss vol. 80, no. 10, fol. 26, dated November 1596.) Of Whitaker's books, those

against Campion of 1581, Sanders of 1583, Duraeus of 1583, Rainolds of 1585 and Bellarmine of 1588 were dedicated to Burghley. That against Stapleton of 1594 was dedicated to Whitgift.

15. Whitaker, *Disputatio de sacra scriptura* (Cambridge, 1588), translated by W. Fitzgerald as *A disputation of holy scripture* (Parker Society, Cambridge, 1848). See also a letter to Burghley from Whitaker of August 1583 telling him of the forthcoming publication of his book against Duraeus and of his intention to dedicate it to him. P.R.O. S.P. Dom 12/162/9.

16. Richard Bancroft, *A survay of the pretended holy discipline* (London, 1593), p. 379.

17. *D.N.B.*

18. Dillingham, *Life of Laurence Chaderton*, trans. E. S. Shuckburgh (Cambridge, 1884), p. 9.

19. Will of Richard Culverwell; Somerset House, wills proved in the Prerogative Court of Canterbury, 9 Windsor 1585. I owe this reference to P. Collinson, 'The puritan classical movement in the reign of Elizabeth I', unpublished Ph.D. thesis, London University, 1957.

20. For Whitaker's second marriage, see C. H. Cooper, *Athenae Cantabrigienses* (3 vols., Cambridge, 1861), vol. 2, p. 548. On Whitaker's death Joan again married a puritan, this time Josiah Nichols, the Kentish puritan minister. Her first husband, Fenner, had been a minister at Cranbrook in Kent in the 1580s.

21. For Whitaker's continuing intimacy with Chaderton see a letter from Whitaker to Burghley of 1590, now in St John's College, Cambridge. For Whitaker's departure in 1595, see Cambridge University Library Mss Mm/2/25, fol. 162r.

22. Cambridge University Library Mss Mm/2/25, fol. 162r.

23. H.M.C. *Sidney and D'Lisle Papers*, vol. 2, p. 203.

24. I owe this reference and the more general point about foreign policy to Dr S. L. Adams, 'The protestant cause: religious alliance with the European Calvinist communities as a political issue in England 1585–1630', unpublished D.Phil. thesis, Oxford University, 1973.

25. B.L. Lansdowne Mss vol. 45, no. 58, fol. 125 r–v dated 1 September 1585.

26. *Ibid.*, vol. 43, no. 39, fol. 94, dated February 1584/5; for a similar letter citing Whitaker's services to the church and petitioning Burghley for some unspecified advancement (presumably the mastership of St John's), see *ibid.*, vol. 42, no. 64, fol. 146, dated 1 December 1584. Whitaker took his D.D. in

1587, defending the proposition 'Papa est insignis ille Antichristus'. See J. Strype, *The life and acts of John Whitgift* (3 vols., Oxford, 1822), vol. 1, p. 459.

27. Cambridge University Registry Mandates of Elizabeth I, no. 200.

28. Whitaker, *Responsionis ad decem illas rationes...defensio contra confutationem Ioannis Duraei scoti, presbyteri, iesuitae* (London, 1583), Dedicatory Epistle, p. 4.

29. B.L. Lansdowne Mss vol. 69, no. 54, fol. 123r–v. Whitaker, Goad, Barwell and Chaderton to Burghley, dated 27 February 1591/2.

30. Walter Travers, *A full and plaine declaration of ecclesiasticall discipline owt of the word of God* (Zurich, 1574), pp. 14–15.

31. Walter Travers, *An answere to a supplicatorie epistle of G.T. for the pretended catholiques* (London, 1583), sig. B3. (Hereafter cited as Travers, *Answere*.)

32. *Ibid.*, p. 111.

33. *Ibid.*, pp. 116–17.

34. For instance, see *ibid.*, pp. 141 or p. 285.

35. *Ibid.*, p. 118.

36. *Ibid.*, p. 216.

37. *Ibid.*, p. 216.

38. *Ibid.*, pp. 275–6.

39. *Ibid.*, pp. 285–6.

40. *Ibid.*, p. 287.

41. *Ibid.*, p. 73.

42. *Ibid.*, p. 352.

43. Thomas Cartwright, *A confutation of the Rhemists translations, glosses and annotations on the New Testament* (Leyden, 1618), p. 286. 'If the crow may reproach the swan with blackness you may also charge us with sectary and schismatical names.' 'The name of Christian is our glory as the godly under the law gloried in the name of Jew or Israelite. Of men how godly and learned soever we take no name.'

44. We have already seen that Whitaker's contacts in high places allowed him to assume a pseudo-official status for his works. In chapter 6 we shall examine the style of divinity which he propounded in those works. His assumption that this indeed constituted the official doctrinal position of the English church was to prove central to his conduct (and that of all the Calvinist Heads) during the theological disputes of 1595/6.

45. Cartwright, *A confutation*, sigs. A2–4r.

46. R. G. Usher, *The presbyterian movement in the reign of Queen Elizabeth as illustrated by the Minute Book of the Dedham Classis 1582–9* (Camden Society, 1905), pp. 79–80.

47. P.R.O. S.P. Dom. 12/154/48.
48. For details of Cartwright's career and movements, see A. F. S. Pearson, *Thomas Cartwright and Elizabethan puritanism* (Cambridge, 1925).
49. Anyone in any doubt as to Cartwright's status as the symbol of the movement, for polemical purposes at least, need only refer to the works of Richard Bancroft: 'His [Cartwright's] authority indeed is very great as being in effect the patriarch of them all. Those things that he writeth are almost oracles. Happy is the brother that can come in his company. If he be in prison prayers are made for his deliverance; if he be delivered great thanks are publicly given unto God for the same. If he command, the rest obey; if he relent I think they will all relent.' Bancroft, *A survay*, p. 374.) Whether this is an accurate description of Cartwright's real position in godly circles (which it almost certainly is not) is not the point at issue. For what the passage does provide is solid evidence for Cartwright's symbolic role in much contemporary polemic as the personification of the presbyterian movement.
50. See, for instance, Cartwright, *A confutation*, p. 293 for a presbyterian interpretation of the terms 'bishop' and 'deacon'; as for ceremonies, Cartwright denounced confirmation and the imposition of hands (p. 277), popish interrogatories in baptism (p. 675), the excessive length of popish prayers (p. 292) which had 'in a manner driven preaching out of the Church of God', the very name of priest in its application to any save Christ (p. 662), and the administration of the Lord's Supper, in private, to the sick (p. 142).
51. B.L. Lansdowne Mss vol. 64, no. 17, fol. 57.
52. Cartwright, *A confutation*, p. 249. Although the most obvious, this was not the only way in which Cartwright modified his presbyterianism in *A confutation*. As we have seen with Travers the whole subject of anti-papal polemic entailed a concentration on doctrine as opposed to church discipline, and also on the invisible as opposed to the visible church (for which see the following chapter), both of which seriously modified the radical coherence of the presbyterian position.
53. P. Collinson, *The Elizabethan puritan movement* (London, 1967), p. 236. Peter Baro was a French émigré who had been at Cambridge University since 1573 and had held the Lady Margaret chair of divinity since 1574. During the early 1580s his doctrinal orthodoxy was challenged by a group of divines, led in Cambridge by Laurence Chaderton but aided and

abetted by London-based divines like William Charke and Walter Travers. For an account of this campaign and of the issues at stake in the theological dispute between Baro and Chaderton, see chapter 6 of my thesis, 'Laurence Chaderton and the Cambridge moderate puritan tradition', unpublished Ph.D. thesis, Cambridge University, 1978. Baro was later to become a major protagonist in the theological disputes of 1595/6, for which see above chapter 9, particularly section 3.

54. Thomas Nashe, *Works*, ed. R. B. McKerrow (5 vols., Oxford, 1958), vol. 3, p. 368.

55. Cartwright, *A confutation*, 'From the publisher to the curious reader'.

56. William Fulke, *The text of the New Testament* (London, 1589), Epistle Dedicatory, sig. A2.

57. For the Latin *Acta* of this synod, see B.L. Harleian Mss 7029, fol. 64r–v printed in J. Strype, *Annals of the Reformation under Elizabeth* (7 vols., Oxford, 1824), vol. 3, pt 2, pp. 477–9.

58. Quoted in Pearson, *Thomas Cartwright*, p. 203.

59. Thomas Cartwright, *A brief apologie of Thomas Cartwright against...Mr Sutcliffe...*(Middelburg, 1596), sig. C2. Also B.L. Lansdowne Mss vol. 64, no. 17, fols. 57–8.

60. Bancroft, *A survay*, see p. 379 for his attempt to enlist Whitaker to the conformist case, as discussed above; p. 391 for his similar treatment of Rainolds; p. 392 and p. 395 for an extended attempt to enlist Fulke to the conformist side by quotation from his anti-papal works.

61. *M. Some laid open in his coulers* (Rochelle, 1589) was an anonymous attack (attributed to Job Throckmorton) on Robert Some following his own attack on the separatists and on John Penry. It sought to denounce Some as a puritan renegade who had sold out to the conformists for the sake of his own career. In order to do so it distinguished very sharply between Some's careerism and the protestant principle of men like Whitaker, Chaderton, Fulke, Cartwright and Rainolds. Indeed, Bancroft's own attempts to enlist these men to the conformist side were prompted by this very pamphlet (see *A survay*, p. 374). But the anonymous author did not claim that these moderates were presbyterians, he merely implied that they were men of un-impeachable scholarship, well-affected to the aims and attitudes even of radicals like Penry. Hence Bancroft's efforts to prove that they were not presbyterians, while strictly accurate, were not really to the point. He could prove that they were not presbyterians; he could not prove that they were not puritans.

For an account of the attack on Some, see my article 'Robert Some', *Archiv für Reformationsgeschichte* 71 (1980).

62. Chaderton's name is conspicuous by its absence from both *Dangerous positions* (London, 1593) and *A survay*. At one point in the former work (p. 80) Bancroft named the corresponding secretaries of the movement at Oxford, Cambridge and London, to whom the Northampton classis wrote. He named Travers at London, Gellibrand at Oxford but only 'one at Cambridge'. But Chaderton's name was clearly mentioned in the deposition on which that passage was based. For that and other evidence of Chaderton's involvement in the classis movement see above, chapter 3.

63. Dillingham, *Life of Chaderton*, p. 3.

5. THOMAS CARTWRIGHT: THE SEARCH FOR THE CENTRE AND THE THREAT OF SEPARATION

1. B. R. White, *The English separatist tradition* (Oxford, 1971), p. 94. For relations between Johnson, in his radical presbyterian phase, and moderate administrators like Chaderton see my article 'The dilemma of the Establishment puritan: the Cambridge Heads and the case of Francis Johnson and Cuthbert Bainbrigg', *J.E.H.* 29 (1978).

2. For Chaderton's appeal to the Queen's closest advisers see above, chapter 3.

3. B.L. Harley Mss 7042, fols. 35–8, 59–64, 204–5.

4. This was precisely the response which greeted two anti-separatist works published by Robert Some in 1588 and 1589. Some was a university divine who by the end of the 1580s had risen to become Master of Peterhouse; a man of puritan sympathies in the 1570s and early 1580s, he was later to prove active on the Calvinist side in the theological disputes of 1595/6. Some's printed pamphlets, written as a result of his apparently genuine alarm at the threat of separation, may also have been prompted by a desire for the patronage and preferment which he pursued in the polarised atmosphere of the late 1580s. Certainly his *A godly treatise containing and deciding certaine questions moved of late in London and other places touching the ministrie, sacraments and church* (London, 1588) and his *A godly treatise wherein are examined and confuted many execrable fancies* (London, 1589) received a very hostile reception from John Penry in his *A defence of that which hath bin*

written (London, 1589) and from the anonymous author (Job Throckmorton?) of *M. Some laid open in his coulers* (Rochelle, 1589) in which Some was denounced as a conformist turncoat. For Some's career and opinions and an analysis of this exchange see my article 'Robert Some and the ambiguities of moderation', *Archiv für Reformationsgeschichte* 71 (1980).

5. For Cartwright's leading role in setting out the moderate position on conformity see above. Similarly, for his recruitment as an anti-papal polemicist see above.

6. *Cartwrightiana*, ed. A. Peel and L. H. Carlson (London, 1951), p. 49 and p. 60 for Anne Stubbe's initial letter to Cartwright. Hereafter cited as *Cartwrightiana*.

7. For Some's anti-separatist polemic see above, note 4.

8. *Cartwrightiana*, p. 49.

9. *Cartwrightiana*, p. 75.

10. This applies not just to obvious cases like the published works of the leading precisian and conformist spokesmen, but even to such 'objective' evidence as the Star Chamber Depositions taken from certain members of the classis movement in 1590. For apart from the initial slant inherent in the nature of the questions, each deponent had his own axe to grind: either to protect himself or his friends or, in the case of Thomas Edmunds, to denounce his erstwhile colleagues to the authorities (P.R.O. Star Chamber Depositions 5A 49/34).

11. *Cartwrightiana*, p. 62.

12. *Ibid.*, p. 71.

13. *Ibid.*, p. 73.

14. *Ibid.*, p. 64.

15. *Ibid.*, p. 64.

16. *Ibid.*, p. 53.

17. *Ibid.*, p. 72. Cartwright used this distinction between the personal characteristics of the officer and the divine nature of the office in connection with unpreaching ministers. These, whatever their personal failings, could not detract from the efficacy of the sacraments received at their hands – that came from God.

18. *Ibid.*, p. 65.

19. *Ibid.*, p. 68.

20. *Ibid.*, p. 68.

21. *Ibid.*, p. 54.

22. *Ibid.*, p. 54.

23. *Ibid.*, p. 51.

24. 'endeavouring to our uttermost to a sufficient ministry, I would

think in the mean season, that the good things that they are able to give us may be taken at their hands', ibid., p. 56. That provisional opening phrase sums up the moderates' campaign for reform and its role in sustaining their position within the church. For while that campaign continued there remained the possibility of future change and any accommodation that might be made with a corrupt present was made, by definition, 'in the mean season'. In this way a partially reformed present was redeemed by the prospect of a fully reformed future. It was as the guarantor of that future that the classis movement achieved its central role in the puritan worldview.

25. *Ibid.*, p. 52.
26. *Ibid.*, pp. 66–7.
27. *Ibid.*, p. 67.
28. *Ibid.*, p. 68.
29. *Ibid.*, p. 50.
30. *Ibid.*, p. 70.
31. *Ibid.*, p. 54–5.
32. *Ibid.*, p. 62. There could be no finer example of the importance attached to anti-papal polemic in safeguarding the true church. Without the skills necessary to confute the popish adversary how could the church be sure that it professed the truth?
33. *Ibid.*, pp. 67–8.
34. Professor Collinson has amply demonstrated the role of the universities in forging the personal and ideological links that produced the classis movement. See P. Collinson, *The Elizabethan puritan movement* (London, 1967), pp. 122f.
35. *Cartwrightiana*, p. 62.
36. Thomas Cartwright, *A confutation of the Rhemists translations, glosses and annotations on the New Testament* (Leyden, 1618), sig. B3, where Cartwright had asserted that all men should have direct access to the scriptures 'that the points of religion which the Church taught were not only known of Doctors and Masters...and not of men only but of women and the same not only learned but labouring men, sewsters, servants, and handmaids'. This would not (as the papists alleged) lead to heresy for 'heresy maketh her nest oftener in the breast of the learned and of those that read the Scriptures in the learned tongues than in the common people's heads'. Cartwright denied that 'the spirit of Christ is appropriated to the learned'. For 'God revealed his secrets (for the most part) to the simple and unlearned and...not many wise men nor many noble men

are taught by his spirit'. Evidently what could be freely asserted against the papists had to be heavily qualified when dealing with the separatists. Only by keeping the two contexts constantly in mind can the full subtlety and tension of Cartwright's position be appreciated.

37. This invocation of the authority of the clerical elite was paralleled on a collective level by Cartwright's appeal to the opinion of other reformed churches, all of whom accepted the English church as a true church of God (*Cartwrightiana*, p. 71). 'Which argument if the church's authority albeit it be not so strong as it will enforce yet ought it to stay all sudden and hasty judgements' (*ibid.*, p. 52).

38. For an exposition of this view of the presbyterian platform see above, chapter 3.

39. Cartwright's letter had not been intended for publication. But a copy of it fell into the hands of Robert Browne who printed it along with his own comments in his *An answere to master Cartwright* (London, 1583?), pp. 86–96. For a discussion of the date of this book as well as that of Cartwright's initial letter see A. F. S. Pearson, *Thomas Cartwright and Elizabethan puritanism* (Cambridge, 1925), p. 221.

40. Richard Bancroft, *A survay of the pretended holy discipline* (London, 1593), p. 447.

41. For Some's oblique reference to Cartwright see his *A godly treatise touching the ministrie*, p. 35.

42. For instance see *ibid.*, 'To the Reader'.

43. For all this see my article 'Robert Some', *Archiv für Reformationsgeschichte*, 71 (1980).

6. WILLIAM WHITAKER'S POSITION AS REFLECTED THROUGH HIS ANTI-PAPAL POLEMIC

1. William Whitaker, *Disputatio de sacra scriptura* (Cambridge, 1588) translated by W. Fitzgerald as *A disputation of holy scripture* (Parker Society, Cambridge, 1848), p. 27. Hereafter referred to as *A disputation*.

2. Whitaker, *Praelectiones...de ecclesia* ed. J. Allenson (Cambridge, 1599), p. 429.

3. Whitaker, *A disputation*, p. 415.

4. Whitaker, *An answere to a certeine book, written by M. William Rainolds* (Cambridge, 1585), pp. 187–8.

5. Whitaker, *An Answere to the ten reasons of Edmund Campion*

the iesuit trans. Richard Stock (London, 1606), pp. 122–3. Hereafter referred to as *Against Campion* (Stock).

6. *Ibid.*, p. 216.
7. Whitaker, *A disputation*, pp. 449–50.
8. *Ibid.*, p. 455.
9. Whitaker, *An answere to Rainolds*, preface p. 20.
10. *Ibid.*, pp. 20–1.
11. Whitaker took his D.D. in 1587 and one of the theses he defended in the process was 'Papa est insignis ille Antichristus'. See J. Strype, *The life and acts of John Whitgift* (3 vols., Oxford, 1822), vol.1, p. 459. Also see 'thesis proposita et defensa in Cantabrigiensi academia die comitiorum Anno Domini M.D. LXXXII – Pontifex Romanus est ille Antichristus quem futurum scriptura praedixit', printed in Whitaker, *Ad Nicolai Sanderi demonstrationes . . . responsio Guilielmi Whitakeri* (London, 1583), pp. 223f. The whole book was dedicated to proving that the Pope was Antichrist.
12. Whitaker, *Ad Nicolai Sanderi*, p. 88.
13. Whitaker, *An answere to Rainolds*, pp. 140–1.
14. Whitaker, *Against Campion* (Stock), p. 172.
15. Whitaker, *Ad Nicolai Sanderi*, p. 280.
16. Whitaker, *Against Campion* (Stock), p. 137. Marginal note comprising an extended quotation (in translation from the original Latin) from Whitaker's book against Duraeus. Cartwright agreed completely with Whitaker's account of the Fall and man's complete impotence to work his own salvation. 'The natural corruption which is in us hath blotted out all that beautiful image of God' and 'instead thereof set another deformed and ugly image of ignorance and profanes' (*A confutation*, p. 348). 'We deny not but that we have the natural power to will or nill, choose or refuse, but we deny that by the natural power of our will unreformed and unrenewed we are able to will or choose any good or nill or refuse any sin, especially as it is sin' (*A confutation*, p. 351). Hence Cartwright could write of the Jews that 'although therefore they were lost by their free will yet they could not be saved by their free will'. Like Whitaker, therefore, Cartwright held that concupiscence, even after baptism, was simply sin, adding that 'it causing sin is in itself much more sinful than that whereof it is the cause' (*A confutation*, p. 348). Similarly, like Whitaker, Cartwright dismissed the papist position on these issues, with its insistence on the co-operation of man's free will with God's grace, as simply Pelagian, and their argument that because 'we are

exhorted to put on a new man therefore we have free will to come to good' he described as 'more savouring of Aristotle than of Paul', a contrast that echoes Whitaker's own disparaging remarks on Campion's liking of pagan philosophy as opposed to the methods of true divinity (*A confutation*, pp. 289 and 490).

17. Whitaker, *Against Campion* (Stock), pp. 223–6.
18. *Ibid.*, p. 230.
19. *Ibid.*, p. 254. Marginal note, quoting in translation from the original Latin, from p. 713 of Whitaker's book against Duraeus.
20. For this point see *ibid.*, p. 254, 'at the last day it is no marvel if Christ pronounce the curse of the law against the reprobates who were never freed from the curse'.
21. *Ibid.*, p. 254.
22. *Ibid.*, p. 230. Marginal note, quoting in translation from the original Latin, from p. 603 of Whitaker's book against Duraeus.
23. *Ibid.*, p. 230.
24. *Ibid.*, p. 225. Marginal note, quoting in translation from the original Latin, from p. 586 of Whitaker's work against Duraeus. Cartwright concurred entirely with Whitaker's view of the role of works in man's salvation: 'We willingly yield that between the calling and the reward of life everlasting there must be good works without the which the faith of the gospel which men profess is argued to be a vain and dead faith' (*A confutation*, p. 331). Yet those works were entirely the work of God, created 'when there was no more seed or sparkle of them in our degenerate estate than there was matter subject unto the creation of the world which appeared and was made of nothing' (*A confutation*, p. 489). Moreover, even among the elect good works were imperfect. It was only the imputation of Christ's merits to his elect that allowed God to save so imperfect and sinful a creature as man without contradicting his own perfect justice. Before God men were, therefore, justified by faith alone; it was only before men that they were justified by faith and works. (For the imperfection of works, even amongst the elect, see *A confutation*, p. 331; for the imputation of Christ's merits to the elect, see *A confutation*, p. 333; for the role of works in our justification before men, see *A confutation*, p. 658.)
25. Whitaker, *Against Campion* (Stock), p. 218.
26. *Ibid.*, p. 234. Marginal note quoting, in translation from the original Latin, from p. 626 of Whitaker's book against Duraeus.
27. *Ibid.*, p. 232.
28. *Ibid.*, pp. 234–5.

29. L. Jardine, 'The place of dialectic teaching in sixteenth-century Cambridge', *Studies in the Renaissance* 21 (1974).

30. This addiction to Ramist logic-chopping may well have exercised an influence on the content of late sixteenth-century English Calvinism and in particular may have lain at the root of 'protestant scholasticism', that process whereby the Calvinist position was reduced into an internally coherent and polemically defensible whole. (For this see below chapter 9.) For an instance of this approach in direct conflict with a very different set of attitudes, more self-consciously sensitive to the ambiguities of scripture and more willing to cite the authority of other divines, in short altogether less rationalist, see the account of a doctrinal dispute between Chaderton and Peter Baro, in my thesis, 'Laurence Chaderton and the Cambridge moderate puritan tradition', unpublished Ph.D. thesis, Cambridge University, 1978.

31. As we have already seen, Whitaker had stressed the need for an inner assurance in validating the truths of scripture: 'in order that we should believe anything there is need of the internal infusion of the spirit' (Whitaker, *A disputation*, p. 335).

32. Whitaker, *Praelectiones...de ecclesia*, p. 464.

33. Whitaker, *Against Campion* (Stock), p. 234.

34. See below, chapter 7, for a discussion of puritan practical divinity which, it will be argued, centred around the doctrine of predestination in general and the doctrine of assurance in particular.

35. Whitaker, *Against Campion* (Stock), pp. 195–6. Cartwright held exactly the same position on this matter as Whitaker. Answering the same papist claim that the Calvinists made God the author of sin, he rejected the idea that God merely permitted the sins of the wicked as an offence against 'his wonderful sceptre and government which he holdeth in all the world' (*A confutation*, pp. 31–2). Cartwright also made the same distinction that Whitaker had made between the intentions of the sinner and those of God in willing the sin (*A confutation*, p. 31).

36. The first of these sermons was preached in February and printed as an appendix to Whitaker's *Praelectiones...de conciliis*, ed. J. Allenson (Cambridge, 1600). The second was preached in October at the height of the theological disputes and was printed in Whitaker's *Praelectiones...de ecclesia*. An English translation, *Cygnea Cantio or the swan-song*, was published in 1772. For Whitaker's role in the disputes see below, chapter 9.

37. Whitaker, *Praelectiones...de ecclesia*, p. 37.
38. Whitaker, *An answere to Rainolds*, p. 55.
39. Whitaker, *A disputation*, p. 55. A point maintained in opposition to the popish view of the church as 'the pastors, bishops, councils, pope'.
40. Whitaker, *Praelectiones...de ecclesia*: for the first point, see pp. 159f; for the second, pp. 145f.
41. Whitaker, *Ad Nicolai Sanderi*, pp. 48–9.
42. Whitaker, *Against Campion* (Stock), pp. 84–5.
43. Whitaker, *Praelectiones...de ecclesia*, p. 141.
44. *Ibid.*, p. 151.
45. *Ibid.*, p. 246.
46. Whitaker, *Ad Nicolai Sanderi*, p. 64.
47. Cartwright had taken precisely the same line. He had an extremely exalted view of the sacrament's role in the church and saw the unity of the church as 'perfectly sealed by these two sacraments' (*A confutation*, p. 476). 'There is no promise made unto us of life everlasting in Christ Jesus which is not sufficiently witnessed and assured unto us by these two sacraments of baptism and of the Lord's Supper' (*ibid.*, p. 477). Nevertheless, baptism was 'the seal of righteousness not righteousness itself' (*ibid.*, p. 347). Distinguishing between 'that which the minister doth in every baptism and that our saviour Christ doth' Cartwright reserved the actual salvation of the elect for 'the free working of his Holy Spirit' (*ibid.*, p. 14).
48. For Whitaker's discussion of the marks of the church analysed here see his *Praelectiones...de ecclesia*, pp. 388f.
49. Whitaker, *An answere to Rainolds*, p. 79.
50. *Ibid.*, pp. 80–1.
51. Whitaker, *Against Campion* (Stock), pp. 163–4.
52. Whitaker, *Praelectiones...de ecclesia*, p. 287.
53. Whitaker, *Praelectiones...de conciliis*, p. 87.
54. Whitaker, *Praelectiones...de ecclesia*, p. 287.
55. *Ibid.*, p. 285.
56. *Ibid.*, p. 281.
57. *Ibid.*, pp. 454f.
58. Whitaker, *Praelectiones...de conciliis*, pp. 55–6.
59. *Ibid.*, p. 91.
60. *Ibid.*, pp. 86–7.
61. *Ibid.*, p. 90.
62. *Ibid.*, p. 86. There is a significant difference here between Whitaker's position and that of Cartwright. Whereas Whitaker refused to recognise any cut and dried distinction between

laymen and clerics, Cartwright advanced a far more exclusive view. Certainly Cartwright allowed the right of 'private men' to attend council 'to hear the causes debated and object their doubts and scruples that trouble their peace of conscience', but he reserved the power to regulate such lay attendance, to control the agenda and finally to decide the questions at issue to 'bishops and elders'. Although by 'bishop' Cartwright meant an ordinary minister of the word and an 'elder', according to the presbyterian dispensation, was a layman elected into an ecclesiastical office, there was a certain tension between the exclusive clericalism of Cartwright's presbyterianism and the 'Erastian' realities of the Elizabethan church of which Whitaker's works provide such an accurate reflection. Cartwright, *A confutation*, pp. 294–5.

63. The insistence on the quality of a man's doctrine as the decisive means of validating his position in the church is typical of Whitaker's position. He was continually appealing away from the popish reliance on a visible succession and a man's place in an established hierarchy of ecclesiastical offices to the question of doctrine. Hence, in reply to Bellarmine's insistence on the necessity of episcopal ordination in the creation of a true minister, Whitaker merely asked 'what if the bishops were all Arians as was once the case? Is then ordination by these three bishops still to be retained by us? By no means.' (*Praelectiones...de ecclesia*, p. 287.)

64. Whitaker, *Praelectiones...de conciliis*, pp. 103f.

65. For Whitaker's invocation of Burghley's authority in 1595/6 see below, chapter 9.

66. For Whitgift's resentment of the Heads' attitude to his authority as Archbishop see below, chapter 9.

67. This is not to suggest that these images were entirely independent of contemporary social reality. On the contrary, they were a mixture, a synthesis of the descriptive and the prescriptive.

68. Whitaker, *An answere to Rainolds*, preface, pp. 13–14. In terms of the precisian/conformist debate such an attitude was ambiguous. It could be used either to rebuke puritans for the triviality of their objections to the liturgy or to advocate the reform of such inherently indifferent and insignificant external details in order to avoid offending the godly or the weak in faith. Either way it seems clear that Whitaker did not regard such questions as important.

69. *Ibid.*, preface, p. 9.

70. For Whitaker's reaction to challenges to the orthodoxy of his

doctrinal position see chapters 8 and 9 below on his period as
Master of St John's and the theological disputes of 1595/6.

71. For Cartwright's view that the church may err and yet remain
a true church, see *A confutation*, p. 494; for his definition of
the universal catholic church as 'the company of the elect' see
ibid., p. 495; for his admission that the true church may for a
time 'lie hid' see *ibid.*, p. 520.

7. THEORY INTO PRACTICE:
PURITAN PRACTICAL DIVINITY IN THE 1580S AND 1590S

1. Pembroke College, Cambridge, Mss LC. II. 2. 164. Hereafter cited as Chaderton.

2. North Yorkshire Record Office, Hutton Mss ZAZ. Hereafter cited as Hutton Mss. I owe my knowledge of this to Dr Bill Sheils.

3. Laurence Chaderton, *An excellent and godly sermon...
preached at Paules Crosse* (London, 1580). Hereafter cited as Chaderton, *Paules Crosse*.

4. Chetham Library, Manchester, Mss Mun. A/2/78. Hereafter cited as Ashton. George Estye was a fellow of Caius College, 1584–1600, active on the Calvinist side in the disputes of 1595/6.

5. For Ashton's petitioning against Barrett, see Trinity College, Cambridge, Mss B/14/9, p. 43; for that against Baro, see Cambridge University Registry Guard Book 6, vol. 1, no. 32; for his support of Johnson, see B.L. Lansdowne Mss vol. 61, no. 10; for his support of Alvey see B.L. Lansdowne Mss vol. 79, no. 67, fol. 166 and no. 68, fol. 168. For his collaboration with Bedell, Ward and Gataker see Samuel Clarke, *A general martyrologie* (London, 1677), p. 250.

6. Ashton, p. 70.

7. Chaderton, fol. 32.

8. Ashton, p. 198, 'The course of nature giveth place to God's will'.

9. *Ibid.*, p. 67.

10. *Ibid.*, p. 70.

11. *Ibid.*, p. 93.

12. *Ibid.*, p. 105.

13. *Ibid.*, p. 129.

14. Chaderton, fol. 12v (numbered from the back).

15. Chaderton, *Paules Crosse*, sigs. E5v–6.

16. Chaderton, fol. 14v.

17. *Ibid.*, fol. 6r (numbered from the back).
18. Ashton, p. 66.
19. Chaderton, fols. 17v–18r.
20. *Ibid.*, fol. 2v and fol. 32.
21. Chaderton, *Paules Crosse*, sig. F2v; Hutton Mss pp. 107 and 120. For the doctrine of providence see K. V. Thomas, *Religion and the decline of magic* (London, 1971), pp. 78–112. For a discussion of its central role in the lives of the puritan laity see A. J. Fletcher, *A county community in peace and war: Sussex 1600–1660* (London, 1975), pp. 66f.
22. Ashton, p. 72.
23. *Ibid.*, p. 76.
24. *Ibid.*, p. 30.
25. *Ibid.*, p. 68.
26. Chaderton, fol. 2v.
27. Ashton, p. 18.
28. Chaderton, fol. 1.
29. Ashton, p. 56.
30. *Ibid.*, p. 47.
31. Chaderton, fol. 3.
32. Ashton, p. 21.
33. *Ibid.*, p. 45.
34. *Ibid.*, p. 88.
35. *Ibid.*, p. 45.
36. *Ibid.*, p. 54.
37. *Ibid.*, p. 106.
38. *Ibid.*, p. 142.
39. *Ibid.*, p. 16.
40. *Ibid.*, p. 49.
41. Chaderton, fol. 12v.
42. *Ibid.*, fol. 9v (numbered from the back).
43. *Ibid.*, fol. 10r (numbered from the back).
44. Ashton, p. 140.
45. *Ibid.*, p. 104.
46. Chaderton, *Paules Crosse*, sig. A8.
47. *Ibid.*, sig. F2r–v.
48. Ashton, p. 104.
49. Chaderton, fol. 41v.
50. *Ibid.*, fol. 23.
51. *Ibid.*, fol. 23.
52. Chaderton, fol. 8v.
53. *Ibid.*, fol. 22.
54. *Ibid.*, fol. 27v.

55. *Ibid.*, fol. 18r.
56. *Ibid.*, fol. 4r–v.
57 *Ibid.*, fol. 21v.
58. Ashton, p. 101.
59. *Ibid.*, p. 58.
60. *Ibid.*, p. 101.
61. *Ibid.*, p. 159.
62. *Ibid.*, p. 159.
63. *Ibid.*, p. 101.
64. Chaderton, *Paules Crosse*, sig. C3r–v.
65. *Ibid.*, sigs. G2v–3.
66. *Ibid.*, sigs. F6v–7.
67. Chaderton, fol. 30r.
68. *Ibid.*, fol. 22r.
69. *Ibid.*, fol. 18r.
70. *Ibid.*, fol. 25v.
71. *Ibid.*, fol. 42r.
72. *Ibid.*, fol. 2r.
73. *Ibid.*, fol. 1r.
74. Ashton, p. 251.
75. *Ibid.*, p. 122.
76. *Ibid.*, p. 204.
77. Chaderton, fol. 16v.
78. *Ibid.*, fol. 8v. (numbered from the back).
79. Ashton, p. 107.
80. Chaderton, fol. 1.
81. *Ibid.*, fols. 40v–41r.
82. *Ibid.*, fol. 11v.
83. Ashton, p. 89.
84. *Ibid.*, p. 97.
85. *Ibid.*, p. 129.
86. *Ibid.*, p. 99.
87. *Ibid.*, p. 164.
88. *Ibid.*, p. 153.
89. *Ibid.*, p. 118.
90. *Ibid.*, p. 142.
91. *Ibid.*, p. 31.
92. *Ibid.*, p. 192.
93. *Ibid.*, p. 75.
94. *Ibid.*, p. 157.
95. *Ibid.*, p. 110.
96. *Ibid.*, p. 40.
97. *Ibid.*, p. 86.

98. *Ibid.*, p. 19.
99. *Ibid.*, p. 47.
100. *Ibid.*, p. 43.
101. *Ibid.*, p. 272.
102. *Ibid.*, pp. 150–1.
103. *Ibid.*, p. 189.
104. *Ibid.*, p. 246.
105. *Ibid.*, p. 32.
106. *Ibid.*, p. 38.
107. *Ibid.*, p. 85.
108. *Ibid.*, p. 73. Interestingly Ashton added one caveat: 'To some elected Princes is due not simple obedience but respective homage as the Emperor King Philip in Flanders was styled Earl of Flanders and ought to be a protector not an oppressor.' Hence Ashton was able to reconcile his own defence of the cause of obedience and still support the Dutch revolt against the papist Spaniards.
109. Chaderton, fol. 8v (numbered from the back).
110. Ashton, p. 98.
111. Chaderton, fol. 27r.
112. Ashton, p. 169.
113. *Ibid.*, p. 169.
114. *Ibid.*, p. 218.
115. *Ibid.*, p. 189.
116. *Ibid.*, p. 150.
117. *Ibid.*, p. 189.
118. *Ibid.*, p. 113.
119. *Ibid.*, p. 233.
120. *Ibid.*, p. 184. These faults of ambition and pride provide the secular counterpart to the pharisees. In all three instances the basic model was that of a stable hierarchy of orders and offices perverted and overthrown through the sins of ambition and pride.
121. Chaderton, *Paules Crosse*, sig. C5r–v. Ashton also held that 'widows, orphans and strangers' were to be provided for (Ashton, p. 206) and exhorted the magistrate 'to execute justice in the morning and deliver the oppressed out of the hands of the oppressor' (Ashton, p. 111).
122. Chaderton, *Paules Crosse*, sig. F2v.
123. *Ibid.*, sig. F3.
124. Ashton, p. 61.
125. *Ibid.*, p. 210.
126. *Ibid.*, p. 210.

127. *Ibid.*, p. 204.
128. *Ibid.*, p. 204.
129. *Ibid.*, p. 252.
130. *Ibid.*, p. 151.
131. Chaderton, fol. 40r.
132. Hutton Mss, p. 124.
133. *Ibid.*, pp. 111–12.
134. *Ibid.*, pp. 126–8.
135. *Ibid.*, pp. 137 and 125 for denial of Satan leading to atheism.
136. *Ibid.*, p. 141.
137. Ashton, p. 157.
138. *Ibid.*, p. 113.
139. *Ibid.*, p. 120.
140. *Ibid.*, p. 181.
141. *Ibid.*, p. 90.
142. *Ibid.*, p. 80.
143. *Ibid.*, p. 181.
144. Chaderton, fol. 42r–v.
145. Hutton Mss, p. 137.
146. P. Collinson, ' "A magazine of religious patterns": an Erasmian topic transposed in English protestantism' in D. Baker (ed.), *Studies in church history* (Oxford, 1977), vol. 14.
147. Ashton, p. 224. It is typical of the tension and ambiguity of the moderate position that precisely this same text, used here by Ashton as a model of zeal, should have provided Chaderton with a central proof text in his arguments in favour of conformity in 1604/5.
148. *Ibid.*, p. 87.
149. For a discussion, from a slightly later period, of the open-ended nature of the puritan concept of idolatry see J. Sears Magee, *The godly man in Stuart England* (Yale, 1976), pp. 71–6.
150. Ashton, p. 122; Chaderton, *Paules Crosse*, sig. A8.
151. Hutton Mss, pp. 129–30.
152. To be precise, while the individual's victory over his spiritual enemies came with death and his final union with God through Christ in heaven, the ultimate defeat of Antichrist and the ultimate division between the righteous and the wicked would only be achieved with the second coming of Christ and then the day of judgement.
153. See Ashton, p. 225, where it is asserted that while the efficient cause of election is God's love, the final cause is 'that thou might serve him and give him glory in doing his commandments'. 'Certa est electio in praedestinatis … Electi a primis

mundi fundamentis (Rev. 17.8, 2 Tim. 2 . . .) Electi non possunt decipi, reliqui facile (Matt. 24.2, 1 Thess. 2, Rev. 13).' Also see Ashton, p. 214. Chaderton's position on predestination as it was couched in these lectures will emerge subsequently.

154. See above, this chapter.
155. Ashton, p. 217.
156. For this point see H. C. Porter, *Reformation and reaction in Tudor Cambridge* (Cambridge, 1958), pp. 344f.
157. Ashton, p. 73.
158. *Ibid.*, p. 102.
159. *Ibid.*, p. 42.
160. Chaderton, fols. 9v–10r.
161. Ashton, p. 73.
162. *Ibid.*, p. 145; for the same assertion see Chaderton, fol. 15r.
163. Ashton, p. 83.
164. Chaderton, fol. 32v.
165. Ashton, p. 83.
166. *Ibid.*, p. 62.
167. *Ibid.*, p. 143.
168. *Ibid.*, p. 135.
169. Hutton Mss, p. 111.
170. *Ibid.*, p. 134.
171. *Ibid.*, p. 136.
172. Chaderton, fol. 32v.
173. Hutton Mss, p. 135.
174. Chaderton, fol. 38r.
175. Hutton Mss, p. 136.
176. Ashton, p. 249.
177. Chaderton, fol. 41r–v.
178. *Ibid.*, fol. 14r.
179. *Ibid.*, fol. 14r.
180. *Ibid.*, fol. 30r.
181. *Ibid.*, fol. 11v (numbered from the back).
182. Chaderton, *Paules Crosse*, sigs. G4r–G5r.
183. Hutton Mss, p. 116.
184. Ashton, p. 277.
182. Chaderton, *Paules Crosse*, sigs. G4r–G5r.
186. *Ibid.*, sig. E3r.
187. *Ibid.*, sig. E1r.
188. Chaderton, fol. 41v.
189. Ashton, p. 75.
190. *Ibid.*, p. 80.
191. Chaderton, fol. 2r.

192. Ashton, p. 249.
193. *Ibid.*, p. 80.
194. Chaderton, fol. 40v.
195. Chaderton, *Paules Crosse*, sig. D5v–D7v.
196. *Ibid.*, sig, D3.
197. Ashton, p. 177.
198. Chaderton, fol. 6v (numbered from the back).
199. Porter, *Reformation and reaction in Tudor Cambridge*, p. 399f.
200. Chaderton, fol. 29r.
201. Ashton, p. 79.
202. Chaderton, fol. 19r.
203. *Ibid.*, fol. 20v.
204. Ashton, p. 79.
205. *Ibid.*, p. 79.
206. Chaderton, fol. 12v.
207. Ashton, p. 244.
208. Chaderton, fols. 12v–13r.
209. Hutton Mss, p. 133.
210. Chaderton, fol. 42r.
211. *Ibid.*, fol. 28v.
212. *Ibid.*, fol. 24r.
213. *Ibid.*, fol. 6v (numbered from the back).
214. Ashton, p. 13.
215. *Ibid.*, p. 225.
216. Chaderton, fol. 9v (numbered from the back).
217. For instance see B. G. Armstrong, *Calvinism and the Amyraut Heresy* (Madison, 1969), or J. S. Bray, *Theodore Beza's doctrine of predestination* (Neukopp, 1975). The most recent and fullest application of such an approach to English puritan thought is R. T. Kendall, *Calvin and English Calvinism to 1649* (Oxford, 1979). Dr Kendall examines similar material to that discussed here and addresses many of the same issues. His main concern, however, is with a theological evaluation of what he terms 'experimental predestinarianism'. I am neither qualified nor concerned to make that sort of theological value judgement. Where Dr Kendall's approach is analytical and critical, mine is merely descriptive. It represents an attempt to make sense of the way in which puritan preachers used and presented certain doctrines in the pulpit. While such an analysis may shed some light on Dr Kendall's approach, for a theologically sophisticated and critical account of these issues the reader is referred to Dr Kendall's monograph.

8. WILLIAM WHITAKER AT ST JOHN'S:
THE PURITAN SCHOLAR AS ADMINISTRATOR

1. B.L. Lansdowne Mss vol. 50, no. 38, fol. 82, Howland to Burghley, 27 June 1586.
2. *Ibid.*, no. 65.
3. Cambridge University Registry Mandates of Elizabeth I, no. 200.
4. T. Baker, *History of St John's College, Cambridge*, ed. J. E. B. Major (2 vols., Cambridge, 1869), vol. 1, p. 180.
5. Cambridge University Registry Guard Book 93, no 8, paper headed 'our master's answers to the reasons which we gave of our petitions'.
6. Cambridge University Registry Guard Book 93, no. 6.
7. *Ibid.*, 93, no. 6.
8. For Digby's version and Whitaker's response to it see B.L. Lansdowne Mss vol. 57, no. 78, fols. 175f. For Digby's fullest statement see B.L. Harleian Mss 7039, fols. 97–9.
9. B.L. Lansdowne Mss vol. 57, no. 78, fol. 178, section headed 'causes considered in proceeding against Mr Digby', complaints 9, 10, 11; Cambridge University Registry Guard Book 93, no. 6, complaints 1, 2, 3 and 10.
10. B.L. Harleian Mss 7039, fol. 157r–v.
11. B.L. Lansdowne Mss vol. 57, no. 78, fol. 178.
12. *Ibid.*, fol. 177r–v. Digby's offence *was* trivial. He was charged not even with refusal to pay his commons but merely with sitting down to dinner with his bill unpaid.
13. B.L. Harleian Mss 7039, fol. 161r–v; *ibid.*, fol. 158 for the formal judgement of the college visitors.
14. B.L. Lansdowne Mss vol. 57, no. 71, fol. 162.
15. *Ibid.*, no. 72, fol. 161.
16. *Ibid.*, no. 70, fol. 160.
17. Whitaker to Burghley, dated 26 October 1590, now in St John's College Library.
18. For all this see my article, 'The significance of the Elizabethan identification of the pope as Antichrist', *J.E.H.* 31 (1980).
19. B.L. Lansdowne Mss vol. 57, no. 41, fol. 100.
20. *The Eagle* (St John's College magazine) 27, p. 22.
21. Cambridge University Registry Guard Book 93, no. 8.
22. *Ibid.*, suggestion no. 5.
23. *Ibid.*, suggestion no. 4.
24. *Ibid.*, suggestion no. 24.
25. *Ibid.*, suggestions nos. 7 and 8.

26. *Ibid.*, suggestion no. 17.
27. *Ibid.*, suggestion no. 9.
28. *Ibid.*, suggestion no. 19.
29. *Ibid.*, suggestion no. 14.
30. K. L. Spunger, *The Very Learned Dr William Ames* (Illinois, 1972), p. 23.
31. Cambridge University Registry Guard Book 6, vol. 1, nos. 36 and 37.
32. Here the names of Daniel Munsay and Henry Alvey spring to mind. Both had pressed for and welcomed Whitaker's election as Master and were subsequently to take a consistently puritan line. For earlier puritan activity in St John's see H. C. Porter, *Reformation and reaction in Tudor Cambridge* (Cambridge, 1958), pp. 119f. Of the Suffolk ministers whose university careers have been traced by Professor Collinson thirty out of eighty-one came from St John's, including their leader, John Knewstubb, twice candidate for the mastership of St John's. See P. Collinson, *The Elizabethan puritan movement* (London, 1967), p. 128. In seeking to make the college into a puritan seminary Whitaker was in a sense only trying to return it to its original state.
33. Cambridge University Registry Guard Book 6, vol. 1, no. 35.
34. *Ibid.*, complaints 2, 3, 15.
35. Cambridge University Registry Guard Book 93, no. 2. This account is by an opponent of Whitaker's but nevertheless accords closely with another by Whitaker himself of his own conduct during an election to the post of college president. See below, this chapter.
36. Cambridge University Registry Guard Book 6, vol. 1, no. 35, complaint 38.
37. Cambridge University Registry Guard Book 6, vol. 1, no. 35, complaints 6 and 40; also Cambridge University Registry Guard Book 93, no. 7.
38. Cambridge University Registry Guard Book 93, no. 7.
39. Cambridge University Registry Guard Book 6, vol. 1, no. 35, complaint 43.
40. Cambridge University Registry Guard Book 93, no. 14.
41. *Ibid.*, no. 2.
42. *Ibid.*, no. 3.
43. *Ibid.*, no. 8, paper headed 'our master's answers to the reasons which we gave of our petitions'.
44. *Ibid.*, no. 10.
45. B.L. Harleian Mss 7039, fols. 163–4.

46. For these accusations see B.L. Lansdowne Mss vol. 79, no. 61, fols. 158f, section headed 'particular exceptions against Mr Alvey', six fellows to Burghley, 14 December 1595.
47. *Ibid.*, no. 61.
48. Cambridge University Library Mss Mm/2/25, fol. 161v.
49. For all this see B.L. Lansdowne Mss vol. 79, no. 61, fols. 154f.; *ibid.*, no. 69, fol. 170, dissident fellows to Burghley. For those in favour of Alvey, *ibid.*, no. 68, fol. 161 and *ibid.*, no. 62, fol. 156.
50. 'Life of John Bois' by Anthony Walker printed in D. Peck, *Desiderata curiosa* (2 vols., London, 1732–5), vol. 2, p. 44.
51. Whitaker to Burghley, 26 October 1590, letter in St John's College Library.
52. P.R.O. Star Chamber Depositions 5A 49/34, depositions of Henry Alvey, William Perkins, Thomas Barber, Thomas Stone and John Johnson; Collinson, *Puritan movement* (London, 1967), pp. 401–3.
53. Both these letters are now in St John's College Library.
54. B.L. Lansdowne Mss vol. 63, no. 86, fol. 211.
55. *Ibid.*, no. 93, fol. 225.
56. *Ibid.*, no. 92, fols. 223–4.
57. Whitaker to Burghley, letter in St John's College Library.
58. B.L. Lansdowne Mss vol. 63, no. 91, fol. 221, Heads to Burghley.
59. A visitation was in the air and Whitaker was worried by the prospect; see B.L. Lansdowne Mss vol. 63, no. 93, fol. 225 and the letter to Burghley in St John's College Library.
60. Knox to Burghley, letter in St John's College Library.
61. B.L. Lansdowne Mss vol. 63, no. 95, fol. 229, Palmer to Burghley, dated 5 November 1590.
62. Knox to Burghley, letter in St John's College Library.
63. Whitaker to Burghley, letter in St John's College Library.
64. Knox to Burghley, letter in St John's College Library.
65. Whitaker to Burghley, letter in St John's College Library.
66. Knox to Burghley, letter in St John's College Library.
67. Whitaker to Burghley, letter in St John's College Library.
68. B.L. Lansdowne Mss vol. 79, no. 69, fol. 170, dissident fellows to Burghley, December 1595.
69. *Ibid.*
70. B.L. Lansdowne Mss vol. 79, no. 61, fols. 154f.
71. *Ibid.*, no. 69, fol. 170.
72. *Ibid.*, no. 61, fol. 155.
73. Whitaker to Burghley, letter in St John's College Library.

74. For the moderate puritan position in the 1590s see my article 'The dilemma of the Establishment puritan: the Cambridge Heads and the case of Francis Johnson and Cuthbert Bainbrigg', *J.E.H.* 29 (1978).
75. Neile's letter is quoted in Baker, *History of St John's College*, Cambridge, vol. 1, p. 182, fn. 4; Dr Porter refers to the 'sinister fact' of Alvey's rise to power and of an 'Alvey party' in the college. He subscribes to the view that Whitaker was 'a scholar and a busy one' and hence did not know what was going on in the college. Porter, *Reformation and reaction in Tudor Cambridge*, pp. 200–2.

9. THE THEOLOGICAL DISPUTES OF THE 1590S

1. Barrett had been at Trinity as an undergraduate, matriculating there as a pensioner in February 1579/80, he proceeded B.A. in 1584/5. He was subsequently made a fellow of Caius and it was as such that he preached the sermon discussed here for the degree of B.D.
2. For details of the sermon, see Barrett's first retraction, drawn up by the Heads as a point by point rebuttal of his initial statement. Cambridge University Registry Guard Book 6, vol. 1, no. 33, printed in Strype, *The life and acts of John Whitgift* (3 vols., Oxford, 1822), vol. 3, pp. 317–19. The original is in Latin; there is a translation in T. Fuller, *History of the University of Cambridge*, ed. M. Prickett and T. Wright (London, 1840). The above translation and paraphrase are my own. For the date of the sermon, see Cambridge University Registry Guard Book 6, vol. 1, no. 39. The Heads' objection to Barrett's use of the term 'Calvinist' is significant. The implication was that all that was at stake here was the opinion of one man and his followers. But in their own eyes the Heads were not followers of any merely human authority, but the guardians of true religion as vouchsafed by God to man in scripture. Cartwright had made a similar point against the papists, denying all party labels in favour of the simple term 'Christian'. Similarly, the Heads' reference to foreign divines as 'lights and ornaments of *our* church' was indicative of their essentially international conception of the reformed church, a conception which was to bring them into conflict with the more narrowly nationalist attitudes of Whitgift.
3. H. C. Porter, *Reformation and reaction in Tudor Cambridge* (Cambridge, 1958), p. 378.

4. William Whitaker, *Praelectio habita Februarii 27 Anno. Dom.* 1594/5 printed in his *Praelectiones...de conciliis*, ed. J. Allenson (Cambridge, 1600). The sermon was preached before a distinguished audience which included the Earl of Essex. Whitaker's sermon was also printed in 1613 by Anthony Thysius, professor of divinity at Harderwijk, together with Peter Baro's *Summa trium de praedestinatione sententiarum*, in which Baro denied absolute predestination in both its supra- and sublapsarian forms. It was, according to Thysius, Baro's heresy that provoked Whitaker into this sermon 'adversus universalis gratiae assertores'. I owe this reference to the kindness of Dr N. R. N. Tyacke. On Baro's theological position see Porter, *Reformation and reaction in Tudor Cambridge*, pp. 376f.

5. Whitaker, *Praelectio*, pp. 5–6, for this distinction between God's antecedent and consequent wills. This was a stock point of dispute with the papists and indeed had been a familiar talking point in the long mediaeval debate of free will and predestination and one which Luther had discussed in his *De servo arbitrio of* 1525. I owe this point to Professor E. G. Rupp.

6. Whitaker, *Praelectio*, p. 9, for Whitaker's criticism of this position and pp. 9–10 for his citation of Augustine and Aquinas.

7. *Ibid.*, pp. 11ff.

8. *Ibid.*, pp. 12–15.

9. B.L. Lansdowne Mss vol. 66, no. 56, fol. 114.

10. For Whitaker's clash with Digby see above, chapter 8.

11. From an account of the proceedings against Barrett in a letter from the Heads to Whitgift. The sessions were attended by Some, Goad, Jegon, Tyndall, Whitaker, Barwell, Chaderton, Preston and Clayton. Trinity College, Cambridge, Mss B/14/9, p. 38.

12. *Ibid.*, pp. 42–3.

13. *Ibid.*, pp. 33–6.

14. *Ibid.*, pp. 17–20. Heads to Whitgift, dated 12 June 1595.

15. *Ibid.*, pp. 1–4. Whitgift to Heads, dated 19 June 1595.

16. *Ibid.*, pp. 3–4.

17. *Ibid.*, p. 1.

18. *Ibid.*, pp. 9–10, Whitgift's letter of protest at Burghley's volte-face following Some's intervention. For the Heads' letter citing Some as their emissary see *ibid.*, p. 23.

19. For the Heads' decision to defy Whitgift see a letter from Richard Clayton, Master of Magdalene, to Whitgift lamenting the Heads' decision 'to justify all their former proceedings in

all points both for the manner thereof and the whole doctrine in the retraction; and in all these matters they will be their own judges immediately under Her Majesty and in no case acknowledge any authority your Grace hath any way in these causes over them either to determine what the doctrine is of the church of England or otherwise howsoever but stand peremptorily upon their privileges which they take to be a sufficient warrant for all their dealings', *ibid.*, p. 25, dated 7 July 1595.

20. *Ibid.*, p. 27. Heads to Whitgift.
21. *Ibid.*, p. 21. Whitaker to Whitgift, dated 13 June 1595.
22. *Ibid.*, pp. 47–50. Whitaker to Whitgift.
23. For Whitaker's favourable response to Francis Johnson in his clash with the university authorities in 1589 see my article, 'The dilemma of the Establishment puritan: the Cambridge Heads and the case of Francis Johnson and Cuthbert Bainbrigg', in *J.E.H.* 29 (1978).
24. B.L. Lansdowne Mss vol. 80, no. 10, fol. 26 .
25. For Whitaker's machinations during the Digby affair see above, chapter 8.
26. Trinity College, Cambridge, Mss B/14/9, p. 48.
27. Some had first preached a sermon denouncing Barrett, for which Barrett had caused him to appear before the Consistory. Having been exonerated there by his Calvinist allies (Duport, Goad, Tyndall, Barwell and Chaderton, all of whom signed a letter to Whitgift defending Some, *ibid.*, pp. 30–2, dated 16 July, 1595) he had been called to Lambeth. There, according to Whitgift, he had been 'in friendly sort reasoned with by myself and some one or two other'. But on his return to Cambridge he had preached another sermon, this one highly critical of Whitgift himself. It compared the Archbishop to 'Annas, Caphas, John, Alexander and all the rabble of the commission about the High Priest' (*ibid.*, pp. 5–8. Whitgift to Heads, dated 11 July 1595).
28. *Ibid.*, pp. 5–8. Whitgift to Heads, dated 11 July 1595.
29. *Ibid.*, pp. 30–1. Heads to Whitgift, dated 16 July 1595.
30. *Ibid.*, pp. 55–8. Heads to Whitgift, dated 11 July 1595.
31. *Ibid.*, p. 59.
32. *Ibid.*, pp. 61–4, for Barrett's answers to Whitgift's interrogatories and *ibid.*, pp. 65–9 for Whitaker's comments.
33. *Ibid.*, pp. 13–16. Whitgift to Heads, dated 30 September 1595.
34. *Ibid.*, p. 13.
35. *Ibid.*, pp. 71 and 14.

36. *Ibid.*, pp. 14–15.
37. *Ibid.*, pp. 13–14.
38. *Ibid.*, p. 15.
39. *Ibid.*, p. 80.
40. For Barrett's second retraction, drawn up by Whitgift, see Trinity College, Cambridge, Mss B/14/9, pp. 75–6.
41. Porter, *Reformation and reaction in Tudor Cambridge* (Cambridge, 1958), pp. 364–75.
42. For instance, see Basil Hall's article 'Calvin against the Calvinists' in *John Calvin*, ed. G. E. Duffield (Abingdon, 1966). Also see H. D. Forster's article 'Liberal Calvinism', *Harvard Theological Review*, 16 (1923), which although primarily concerned with the Synod of Dort, deals with the whole question of Calvin's relations with his 'followers'. Also see F. J. Shriver, 'The ecclesiastical policy of James I: two aspects: puritanism 1603–5: the Arminians 1611–25', unpublished Ph.D. thesis, Cambridge University, 1967, for a discussion of the relationship between Arminianism and the Calvinist tradition. Now see R. T. Kendall, *Calvin and English Calvinism to 1649* (Oxford, 1979). Much of this literature tends to blame Beza for destroying the ambiguity and tension in Calvin's thought which, it is claimed, stemmed from Calvin's sensitivity to the subtleties of scripture. See T. H. L. Parker, *Calvin's New Testament commentaries* (London, 1971), pp. 26–88, where Calvin's attitude to scripture is favourably compared with a more dogmatically based hermeneutic, founded on a new methodology of topics and commonplaces, which began with Erasmus and was taken up by Melancthon, Bullinger and Bucer. At present this whole matter is a subject of considerable scholarly debate but for the present purpose it is enough simply to note the existence of a difference between Calvin and his later followers.
43. In this paragraph I have attempted to summarise, inevitably rather crudely, the views of other scholars. This process of systematisation, sometimes called 'protestant scholasticism', has been discussed in Hall's article cited above, as well as by Breward in his introduction to *The works of William Perkins* (Abingdon, 1970). Also see Breward, 'The life and theology of William Perkins, 1558–1602', unpublished Ph.D. thesis, Manchester University, 1963. Also see Kendall, *Calvin and English Calvinism to 1649*; J. S. Bray, *Theodore Beza's doctrine of predestination* (Neukopp, 1975); B. G. Armstrong, *Calvinism and the Amyraut Heresy* (Madison, 1969). For the quotation from Breward see *The works of William Perkins*, p. 86. Also

J. P. Donnelly, 'Italian influences on the development of Calvinist scholasticism', *Sixteenth Century Journal* 7 (1976).

44. Trinity College, Cambridge, Mss B/14/9, p. 14.

45. John Whitgift, *Works* (3 vols., Parker Society, Cambridge, 1851–3), vol. 1, pp. 260–1.

46. Hutton had come up to Cambridge in 1546, becoming a fellow of Trinity in 1555. At Cambridge he became one of Grindal's chaplains and Lady Margaret Professor of Divinity in 1561, succeeding his patron Grindal as Master of Pembroke Hall the following year. (For this see *D.N.B.*) He took a moderate line on the issue of conformity and together with Whitgift and other Heads he signed the famous letter to Burghley asking him as Chancellor of the University to moderate the enforcement of conformity there. (For the text of this letter, see J. Strype, *The life and acts of Matthew Parker* (London, 1711), Appendix book 3, no. 39, pp. 69–70. Also P. Collinson, 'The "nott conformytye" of the young John Whitgift', *J.E.H.* 15 (1964).) But unlike Whitgift, Hutton remained true to his moderate principles. Hence, while Whitgift took up the cudgels against the presbyterians, Hutton went north to become dean of York. His preferment was accordingly slower than that of Whitgift: it was not until 1589 that he was appointed Bishop of Durham and only in 1595 was he elevated to the archiepiscopal see at York. For Hutton see my article 'Matthew Hutton: a puritan bishop?', *History*, 64 (1979).

47. Hence in 1600 Whitgift could write to Hutton warning him in case the younger, more precise sort should 'say that zeal is quenched in you and that you dote in your old age, as it pleaseth some here to say of me; and yet peradventure, when we are gone, they will wish us alive again' (B.L. Stowe Mss 1058 fol. 239v.).

48. The disputes were first mentioned in passing by Whitgift in a letter dated 19 August 1595. Allusive references to doctrinal points central to the disputes as well as to 'the retraction' suggest that Hutton was already fully familiar with events in Cambridge (see B.L. Stowe Mss 1058, fol. 236). Of Hutton's extant letters dealing with the disputes, one, dated October 1595, was printed in 1613 in the preface to Hutton's *Brevis et dilucida explicatio*...and another, dated March 1595/6, is in Trinity College, Cambridge. Trinity College, Cambridge, Mss B/14/9, p. 151.

49. Trinity College, Cambridge, Mss B/14/9, pp. 151f. and 149.

50. *Ibid.*, pp. 149–50.

51. *Ibid.*, pp. 149–50.
52. Lambeth Palace Library Mss 2550, fols. 132f.
53. *Brevis et dilucida explicatio verae, certae et consolationis plenae doctrinae de electione, praedestinatione et reprobatione* was the full title of Hutton's tract and the heading under which the entire collection appeared. The other works included in it were *De justificationis coram deo et fidei justificantis perseverantia non intercisa* by Laurence Chaderton; *Tres quaestiones* by Robert Some; *De praedestinatione disputatio opposita quibusdam non tantum e pontificiis recentioribus sed e protestantis transmarinis quorum error in ecclesiam Anglicam influere coeperat* by Andrew Willett and *De certitudine salutis et perseverantia sanctorum non interrupta* by George Estye, who had been one of the deponents against Barrett in 1595. Of the contributors, the only two still alive in 1613 were Chaderton and Willett. Chaderton, therefore, was the last survivor of those who had been actively involved in the disputes. Given that the whole purpose was to present those disputes as a Calvinist victory and draw a parallel between the situation in Cambridge in the 1590s and more recent events in the Netherlands (to stop the spread of the Arminian heresy to England), and given the presence of a manuscript draft of Hutton's treatise amongst Chaderton's papers, it seems very likely that it was Chaderton who acted as editor and collator for the book as it appeared in 1613. The book's status as a piece of covert Calvinist polemic is seen most clearly in the preface. There the comparison with the Low Countries was explicitly made and a long account of the 1595/6 disputes appended which presented them as a straight Calvinist victory. Great play was made with Hutton's Calvinism and the opinion of Whitgift was assimilated to that of his archiepiscopal colleague (hence the publication of Hutton's letter to Whitgift of October 1595). The Lambeth Articles were printed in full, complete with a Calvinist gloss made up of extended quotes from the works of Augustine and Ambrose (recalling Hutton's own emphasis on patristic rather than modern reformed authorities). Finally, to bring things up to date, Perkins was enlisted through his influence on Playfere and Willett and Davenant of Cambridge, and Rainolds and Holland of Oxford were cited as proponents of the same cause. This volume was edited by Anthony Thysius and provided the companion volume to his reprint of Baro's *Summa trium de praedestinatione sententiarum* and Whitaker's 1595 *concio ad clerum*.

54. Trinity College, Cambridge, Mss B/14/9, p. 80.
55. The original draft put forward by Whitaker has been printed in *Articuli Lambethani* (London, 1651). These can be compared to the text finally approved by Whitgift (printed in Strype, *John Whitgift*, vol. 2, p. 280. Throughout the following discussion I have followed Dr Porter's translations from the original Latin in his *Reformation and reaction in Tudor Cambridge*, p. 371, and pp. 365–6.
56. Hall, 'Calvin against the Calvinists' in Duffield, *John Calvin*.
57. Porter, *Reformation and reaction in Tudor Cambridge*, p. 370.
58. Lambeth Palace Library Mss 2550, fols. 164f.
59. William Barlow, *Sum and substance of the conference* printed in E. Cardwell, *A history of conferences and other proceedings connected with the Book of Common Prayer, 1558–1690* (Oxford, 1840), p. 185.
60. R. Buick Knox, *James Ussher, Archbishop of Armagh* (Cardiff, 1967), p. 18.
61. Porter, *Reformation and reaction in Tudor Cambridge*, p. 376.
62. Trinity College, Cambridge, Mss, B/14/9, p. 121. Vice-Chancellor and Heads to Whitgift, dated 13 December 1595.
63. *Ibid.*, p. 130. Goad to Whitgift, dated 13 January 1596.
64. *Ibid.*, p. 117. Cecil to Whitgift.
65. Whitaker had sent Burghley a copy of his sermon dealing with the issues in dispute (later published posthumously as *Cygnea Cantio* in 1599) in November, together with a covering letter trying to enlist Burghley's support for the Heads' case and telling him of the forthcoming meeting at Lambeth. B.L. Lansdowne Mss, vol. 80, no. 10, fol. 26; Whitaker to Burghley, dated 19 November, 1595.
66. Trinity College, Cambridge, Mss B/14/9, pp. 127–8. Letter from Tyndall to Whitgift dated 19 December 1595. This comparison between the justice of God and the justice of temporal rulers was also used by Baro against the Calvinists. There may, therefore, have been contact between Baro and Burghley even at this early date, although the earliest extant letter dates from the following February. (B.L. Lansdowne Mss, vol. 80, no. 69, fol. 172. Baro to Burghley dated 9 February 1596.)
67. For this account of the meeting between Tyndall and Whitaker and Burghley, see Trinity College, Cambridge, Mss B/14/9, pp. 127–8. Tyndall to Whitgift, dated 19 December 1595.
68. T. Fuller, *The church history of Great Britain*, ed. J. S. Brewer (6 vols., Oxford, 1845), vol. 5, p. 226.
69. Trinity College, Cambridge Mss B/14/9, pp. 118–20.

70. *Ibid.*, pp. 124–5. Baro to Whitgift, dated 13 December 1595.
71. *Ibid.*, p. 135. Whitgift to Goad, dated 15 January 1596.
72. *Ibid.*, pp. 130–4. Goad to Whitgift, 13 January 1596.
73. Jacobus Arminius, *Works*, trans. and ed. J. and W. Nichols (3 vols., London, 1825–75), vol. 1, p. 91.
74. Baro set out his position in a series of letters to Whitgift. Of these, the first (upon which this paragraph is based) was dated 13 December 1595. Trinity College, Cambridge, Mss B/14/9, pp. 124–5.
75. *Ibid.*, pp. 135–6.
76. *Ibid.*, p. 136.
77. *Ibid.*, pp. 137–8. Vice-Chancellor and Heads to Whitgift, dated 29 January 1596. For Baro's account of the same proceedings, see ibid., pp. 139–40. Baro to Lancelot Andrewes, dated 20 January 1596.
78. *Ibid.*, pp. 107–16 for depositions; and *ibid.*, pp. 137–8 for the outcome.
79. *Ibid.*, pp. 95–100. Baro to Whitgift, dated 27 January 1596, is an example of this.
80. For Goad's initial letter to Burghley, see B.L. Lansdowne Mss, vol. 80, no. 58. Goad to Burghley, dated 29 January 1596. For Burghley's reply, see Trinity College, Cambridge, Mss B/14/9, p. 129.
81. Trinity College, Cambridge, Mss B/14/9, pp. 139–40. Baro to Lancelot Andrewes, dated 20 January 1596.
82. *Ibid.*, pp. 95–100. Baro to Whitgift, dated 27 January 1596.
83. *Ibid.*, pp. 157–9. Baro to Whitgift, dated 4 February 1596.
84. *Ibid.*, pp. 160–1. Baro to Whitgift, dated 22 March 1596.
85. Porter, *Reformation and reaction in Tudor Cambridge*, p. 386.
86. Cambridge University Library Mss Mm/1/35, p. 349.
87. *Ibid.*, p. 356. Jegon to Whitgift. For Playfere's later robust defence of Calvinist orthodoxy against John Overall, see H.M.C. *Marquis of Salisbury*, vol. 10, pp. 211–12.
88. For this see Cambridge University Registry Guard Book 90, nos. 22–32 and Cambridge University Library Mss Mm/1/35, pp. 365–6.
89. Cambridge University Library Mss Mm/1/35, pp. 365–6. Jegon, Tyndall, Chaderton, Barwell and Montague to Burghley, 18 March 1598.
90. *Ibid.*, p. 365. Bancroft to Jegon, 12 March 1598.
91. Cambridge University Registry Guard Book 90, no. 29; Cambridge University Library Mss Mm/1/35, p. 366. Jegon to Whitgift, 18 March 1598.

92. Cambridge University Registry Guard Book 90, no. 32.
93. Cambridge University Library Mss Mm/1/35, pp. 365–6.
94. The university was under close scrutiny for any sign of precisian disorder at this time. For a letter from William Barlow, another of Whitgift's hard line conformist protégés, to Jegon, communicating the Archbishop's disapproval of a commencement question concerning popery and foreign policy and also of the master of Sidney Sussex's desire to take his doctorate early (according to Barlow a typically puritan assault on academic propriety), see *ibid.*, p. 367.
95. Cambridge University Library Mss Gg/1/29, fol. 104r–v.
96. H.M.C. *Marquis of Salisbury*, vol. 10, p. 211.
97. *Ibid.*, vol. 10, p. 211.
98. *Ibid.*, vol. 10, p. 241.
99. See Dr N. R. N. Tyacke's article, 'Puritanism, Arminianism and counter revolution', *The origins of the English Civil War*, ed. C. Russell (London, 1973).
100. For Baro's letter to Andrewes, see Trinity College, Cambridge, Mss B/14/9, pp. 139–40; for his letter to Hemmingius, see Arminius, *Works*, vol. 1, p. 91. Hemmingius was a Danish Lutheran divine who played a leading role in the reaction against the Calvinism of Beza and others. Baro had quoted his opinion at length in his earlier clash with Chaderton. See Cambridge University Registry Guard Book (Miscellanea), vol. 15, no. 55, in argument six from Baro's long treatment of the first 'Quaestio' (unpaginated).
101. Cambridge University Registry Guard Book 6, vol. 1, nos. 24 and 25.
102. Rudd was bound over by Jegon to appear before the High Commission on 28 April 1597 (*ibid.*, no. 27). For the letters to Whitgift complaining of Rudd's behaviour, see Cambridge University Library Mss Mm/1/35, pp. 348–51.
103. For this letter, see Cambridge University Library Mss Mm/1/35, p. 373.
104. Their position was virtually identical to that produced by the Johnson and Bainbrigg affair of 1589 for which see my article 'The dilemma of the Establishment puritan', *J.E.H.* 29 (1978).

10. CONFORMITY: CHADERTON'S RESPONSE
TO THE HAMPTON COURT CONFERENCE

1. See P. Collinson, *The Elizabethan puritan movement* (London, 1967), pp. 448f.
2. The terms in which Chaderton's argument was conducted were anything but new. They had been set long before, during the earlier controversies over vestments and subscription. For these, see above, chapter 3 and chapter 3 of my thesis, 'Laurence Chaderton and the Cambridge moderate puritan tradition', unpublished Ph.D. thesis, Cambridge University, 1978. For a systematic account of these earlier disputes see J. H. Primus, *The vestments controversy* (Kampen, 1960). The novelty in the situation stemmed from Chaderton's readiness to set out his position in detail; a readiness which was almost certainly a function of the collapse of presbyterianism, and the far greater polemical freedom this allowed Chaderton in handling the issue of subscription.
3. Lambeth Palace Library Mss 2550, fol. 51v.
4. *Ibid.*, fol. 52v.
5. *Ibid.*, fol. 53r.
6. *Ibid.*, fol. 53r.
7. *Ibid.*, fol. 53r–v.
8. *Ibid.*, fols. 53v–54r.
9. *Ibid.*, fol. 54v.
10. *Ibid.*, fol. 55r.
11. *Ibid.*, fol. 55v.
12. *Ibid.*, fol. 55v.
13. *Ibid.*, fol. 56r.
14. *Ibid.*, fol. 56r–v.
15. *Ibid.*, fol. 57r.
16. *Ibid.*, fol. 57v.
17. *Ibid.*, fol. 58r–v.
18. *Ibid.*, fol. 58r.
19. *Ibid.*, fol. 58v.
20. *Ibid.*, fol. 58v.
21. *Ibid.*, fol. 58v.
22. *Ibid.*, fol. 54r.
23. *Ibid.*, fols. 58v–59r.
24. *Ibid.*, fol. 60r.
25. This paragraph is based on chapter 9 of my thesis, 'Laurence Chaderton', which should be consulted for a fuller analysis of the conference from the viewpoint of the moderate puritan.

Also see F. J. Shriver, 'The ecclesiastical policy of James I: two aspects: puritanism 1603–5: the Arminians 1611–25', unpublished Ph.D. thesis, Cambridge University, 1967. Also M. H. Curtis, 'Hampton Court Conference and its aftermath', *History* 46 (1961).

26. For the anti-puritan repression following the conference see S. B. Babbage, *Richard Bancroft and puritanism* (London, 1962).
27. Lambeth Palace Library Mss 2550, fols. 1r and 2v.
28. *Ibid.*, fol. 1r.
29. *Ibid.*, fol. 2r.
30. *Ibid.*, fol. 7r–v. 'A brief resolution of Joshua 22 from v. 16–34 by way of dialogue'.
31. *Ibid.*, fol. 1r.
32. *Ibid.*, fol. 1v.
33. *Ibid.*, fol. 2r.
34. *Ibid.*, fol. 3r–v.
35. *Ibid.*, fol. 4v.
36. *Ibid.*, fol. 5r.
37. *Ibid.*, fol. 4v.
38. *Ibid.*, fol. 176r. Letter from Brightman to Chaderton, dated 10 January 1604/5.
39. *Ibid.*, fol. 176r.
40. *Ibid.*, fol. 176v.
41. *Ibid.*, fol. 176r.
42. *Ibid.*, fol. 176r.
43. *Ibid.*, fol. 176r.
44. *Ibid.*, fol. 176r. As a marginal comment Chaderton added, 'no poison but sin whose filthiness is not from outward but only from within'.
45. *Ibid.*, fol. 176v.
46. For Brightman's 'congregationalism' see *D.N.B.* and W. Lamont, *Godly Rule* (London, 1969), pp. 51, 72.
47. Lambeth Palace Library Mss 2550, fol. 177r–v, for Chaderton's detailed treatment of Brightman's citations from scripture.
48. For an exchange between a moderate (Robert Some) and a radical (John Penry) which was not maintained on such a gentlemanly level, due mainly to Some's desire to denounce Penry as a crypto-separatist, see my article 'Robert Some and the ambiguities of moderation', *Archiv für Reformationsgeschichte* 71 (1980).
49. Lambeth Palace Library Mss 2550, fol. 13v.
50. *Ibid.*, fol. 11r. From a paper headed 'an examination of 14 reasons seeming to prove that the cross and surplice are unlawful'.

51. *Ibid.*, fol. 13v.
52. *Ibid.*, fol. 2v.
53. *Ibid.*, fol. 46r. In a paper headed 'The surplice is lawful', fols. 40–9.
54. *Ibid.*, fol. 43r.
55. *Ibid.*, fol. 11r.
56. *Ibid.*, fol. 10v.
57. *Ibid.*, fol. 11v.
58. The most famous example here is John Burgess who was deprived in the aftermath of Hampton Court, having refused to subscribe on grounds identical to those set out by Chaderton. For Burgess, see Babbage, *Richard Bancroft and puritanism*, pp. 166–74 and 381–6.
59. Lambeth Palace Library Mss 2550, fol. 28r. From a letter from Chaderton to Ezekiel Culverwell, rector of Great Stanbridge, 27 January 1608.
60. *Ibid.*, fol. 60r.
61. *Ibid.*, fol. 28r.
62. *Ibid.*, fol. 28r.
63. *Ibid.*, fols. 28v–29. In the margin Chaderton had added, 'thus is plainly answered the first question to wit that such ministers in our church as are thus qualified may (iure divino) judge whether these ceremonies be expedient. Now in that the convocation admitteth non presbyters to this judgement and omiteth many presbyters id factum est jure humano seu et veteri consuetudine non bona. Yet that which is there done must not be condemned of any nor contentiously disobeyed. But what is well determined must be thankfully acknowledged and what otherwise determined must be charitably interpreted (as much as in man lieth) or else excepted against with weight of reason and without all disgrace of person and bitterness of speech.'
64. *Ibid.*, fol. 28v.
65. *Ibid.*, fol. 28v.
66. *Ibid.*, fol. 29r–v.

11. WILLIAM BRADSHAW: MODERATION IN EXTREMITY

1. See above, chapter 3. All information concerning Bradshaw's career is taken from Samuel Clarke, *A general martyrologie* (London, 1677), 2, 'The lives of thirty-two English divines', pp. 25f: 'The life and death of Master William Bradshaw'.
2. *Ibid.*, p. 44.
3. William Bradshaw, *English puritanisme containinge the maine*

opinions of the rigidest sort of those that are called puritanes in the realme of England (Amsterdam, 1605), p. 1.

4. Bradshaw, *A treatise of divine worship* (Amsterdam, 1604), p. 1.
5. *Ibid.*, p. 25.
6. Bradshaw, *A Treatise of the nature and use of things indifferent* (Amsterdam, 1605), p. 20.
7. Lambeth Palace Library Mss 2550, fol. 45.
8. *Ibid.*, fol. 46v.
9. Bradshaw, *A proposition concerning kneeling in the very act of receiving* (Amsterdam, 1605), p. 23.
10. Bradshaw, *Treatise of things indifferent*, p. 21.
11. Bradshaw, *Treatise of divine worship*, pp. 21–2.
12. Bradshaw, *A myld and iust defence of certeyne arguments* (n.p. 1606), pp. 44–5.
13. See the above work, for example, where the 'conformitans' are charged with 'divers points of popery', p. 139; and ibid., p. 123, where the bishops are accused of depriving preachers merely for confuting 'the popish doctrine of other'.
14. Bradshaw, *A plaine and pithy exposition of the second epistle to the Thessalonians* (London, 1620), p. 104. This work was published posthumously by Gataker from Bradshaw's notes.
15. Bradshaw, *A triall of subscription by way of a preface unto certaine subscribers: and reasons for lesse rigour against non-subscribers* (Middelburg, 1599), p. 7.
16. Bradshaw, *A short treatise of the crosse in baptisme* (Amsterdam 1604), p. 24.
17. Bradshaw, *Treatise of divine worship*, p. 40.
18. Bradshaw, *Treatise of the crosse*, p. 9.
19. Bradshaw, *Triall of subscription*, sig. A2v.
20. *Ibid.*, sig. A5v.
21. Bradshaw, *Twelve general arguments, proving that the ceremonies are unlawful printed in Several treatises of worship and ceremonies* (London, 1660), p. 76.
22. Bradshaw, *Triall of subscription*, sig. A6r–v.
23. Bradshaw, *English puritanisme*, p. 13. 'They [the puritans] hold that there are not by any divine institution in the word any ordinary national, provincial or diocesan pastors or ministers under which the pastors of particular congregations are to be subject as inferior officers.'
24. This still allowed Bradshaw to denounce at length the abuses of the present ecclesiastical courts as a far greater encroachment on the rights and powers of lay society than his system. Congregational discipline was to be spiritual and brotherly,

not 'giving the least personal reproaches or threats' but 'only by denouncing the judgements of God against him to terrify him and move him to repentance' (*ibid.*, pp. 26–7). There was to be no inquisition into private matters, no collection of backstairs gossip (*ibid.*, p. 25), no oath ex officio to force a man to testify against himself (*ibid.*, p. 29). The defendant's case was always to be fully heard before the sentence was passed (*ibid.*, p. 28), and only 'evident and apparent crimes' were to be tried (*ibid.*, p. 25). In cases of heresy the judges not only had to prove that the defendant held the opinion in question but also had 'to prove directly unto him that it is an error by the word of God and that it deserveth such a censure before they do proceed against him' (*ibid.*, p. 28).

25. For the powers of the king in causes ecclesiastical see *ibid.*, pp. 32f.
26. Bradshaw, *Twelve generall arguments*, pp. 58–9.
27. Certainly Bradshaw conceded that the king was subject to the spiritual jurisdiction of the church to the same extent 'as the meanest subject in the kingdom'. Yet 'this subjection is no more derogatory to his supremacy than the subjection of his body in sickness to physicians can be said to be derogatory' (*English puritanisme*, p. 33). In a later work he added that the king ought not to be subject to 'the ecclesiastical censures of any churches, church officers or synods but only to that church and those officers of his own court and household unto whom...he shall of his own freewill subject and commit the regiment of his soul' (*A protestacion of the king's supremacie* (Amsterdam, 1605), p. 7).
28. Bradshaw, *English puritanisme*, pp. 11–12.
29. *Ibid.*, p. 35.
30. In the present context Bradshaw's position is being seen primarily as an extension or development of the moderate puritan position adopted by men like Chaderton and Cartwright during the 1580s. Given his personal links with both men such an approach seems justified. But there was more at stake here than a likely personal influence. Bradshaw's position (like Chaderton's) was a response to the ambiguities and demands of the position of the puritan divine committed to the idea of a national church yet alienated by that institution's acknowledged faults and corruptions. Bradshaw's position was further modified by the fate of the presbyterian movement and the practical success experienced by the godly in infusing the corrupt structure provided by the national church with the values of true

religion. Certainly Bradshaw was to cite precisely that success in his anti-separatist works (for which see below) in a manner highly reminiscent of Cartwright's dealings with Harrison and Anne Stubbe. Such a position was all the easier to sustain if the true church did not need the superstructure of synods and classes which the English church clearly lacked and which even the classis movement had failed to provide over a sustained period. For all this see P. Collinson, 'Towards a broader understanding of the dissenting tradition' in *The dissenting tradition*, ed. R. Cole and M. E. Moody (Ohio, 1975). But Bradshaw represents not just a fitting coda for the study of late sixteenth-century puritanism but the start of Perry Miller's 'non-separatist congregationalism'; the roots perhaps of Independency itself. See P. Miller, *Orthodoxy in Massachusetts* (Gloucester, Mass., 1965), chapter 4; also K. L. Sprunger, *The Very Learned Dr William Ames* (Illinois, 1972), pp. 37, 192–3, where Bradshaw is associated with Ames, Parker, Henry Jacob and Paul Baynes as a proponent of 'non-separating congregationalism'. For some critical comments on Miller's position which still point out the considerable continuities between Bradshaw's views on church polity and those of the independents, see Collinson in Cole and Moody.

31. For instance, Bradshaw, *A myld and iust defence*, p. 58: 'This discipline (if we might have equal hearing) we could easily free from all such imputations as whereby it is commonly disgraced by the adversaries thereof with princes and nobles. Yea we could plainly and truly show the same to be nothing prejudicial but very helpful both to all royal authority and also to nobility; yes, better agreeing with the one and the other than all other inventions of men for ecclesiastical government whatsoever.'

32. For Bradshaw's recourse to this rather vague but nevertheless symbolically potent idea of a protestant church incorporating all the reformed churches of Europe, see above. In all this Bradshaw obviously based his position on the assumptions and emphases regarding the unity of the church and the relationship between the visible and invisible church put forward by Whitaker, *ibid.*, p. 57.

33. For a further exposition of the compatibility of Bradshaw's views with the actual state of the English church, see above, this chapter.

34. Bradshaw, *A protestacion of the king's supremacie*, p. 21.

35. For Bradshaw's anti-separatist activities see Clarke, *Martyrologie*, pt 2, p. 56.

36. Bradshaw, *The unreasonablenesse of the separation* (Dort, 1614), sig. Hv.
37. *Ibid.*, sig. Cr–v.
38. *Ibid.*, sig. B3v.
39. *Ibid.*, sig. I3r–v.
40. *Ibid.*, sig. N4.
41. *Ibid.*, sig. Bv. and O4r–v. where it was argued 'that the calling, entrance administration and maintenance of many (at the least) that are called into ecclesiastical offices is in very effect and substance the same that Christ hath appointed'.
42. *Ibid.*, sigs. D3v–D4.
43. *Ibid.*, sig. P2.
44. *Ibid.*, sigs. Bv–B2.
45. *Ibid.*, sig. I4.
46. *Ibid.*, sigs. H2–H3.
47. *Ibid.*, sig. Gv.
48. *Ibid.*, sig. D3v.
49. *Ibid.*, sigs. H2v–H3. 'They may acknowledge a further calling than that of the prelates and yet not therein renounce the calling received from the prelates, but rather ratify the same.'
50. *Ibid.*, sigs. H3v–H4.
51. *Ibid.*, sig. G.
52. Clarke, *Martyrologie*, pt 2, p. 25.
53. *Ibid.*, p. 55.
54. *Ibid.*, p. 55.
55. *Ibid.*, p. 55. Also see Bradshaw, *A treatise of justification* (London, 1615).
56. Bradshaw, *Plaine and pithy exposition*.
57. Clarke, *Martyrologie*.
58. See Bradshaw, *A preparation to the receiving of Christ's body and blood* (London, 1617); also *A meditation of man's mortalitie* (London, 1621) and Bradshaw, *A marriage feast* (London, 1621). Both of these last two works were published posthumously by Thomas Gataker from Bradshaw's notes.

12. CONCLUSION

1. For instance, see my article 'Matthew Hutton: a puritan bishop?', *History* 64 (1979).
2. C. Russell, *Parliaments and English politics 1621–29* (Oxford, 1979), pp. 25–32. N. R. N. Tyacke's seminal article, 'Puritanism, Arminianism and counter-revolution' in *The origins of the*

English Civil War, ed. C. Russell (London, 1973) has been invoked by Russell and others to support such a view.

3. G. R. Elton, 'England and the Continent in the sixteenth century', *Studies in Church History* Subsidia 2, (1979); Elton, 'Parliament in the sixteenth century: functions and fortunes', *Historical Journal* 22 (1979).

4. For this revisionist position see P. Christianson, 'Reformers and the Church of England under Elizabeth I and the early Stuarts', *J.E.H.* 31 (1980). But also see P. Collinson, 'A comment: concerning the name puritan', *J.E.H.* 31 (1980).

5. On this see my article, 'Robert Some and the ambiguities of moderation', *Archiv für Reformationsgeshichte* 71 (1980).

6. This is not to deny the considerable ideological and polemical purchase exerted on the puritan position by the conformists. For one incident in which conformist tactics succeeded in dividing puritan opinion and in which the mediating activities of moderate puritan divines failed to avert a confrontation and the loss of at least one godly minister to separatism, see my article, 'The dilemma of the Establishment puritan: the Cambridge Heads and the case of Francis Johnson and Cuthbert Bainbrigg', *J.E.H.* 29 (1978).

7. This idea of a divide between a 'political' puritanism and a quietest, ethical puritanism is to be found in W. Haller, *The rise of puritanism* (New York, 1938).

8. The preceding paragraphs represent a précis of my article 'The significance of the Elizabethan identification of the pope as Antichrist', *J.E.H.* 31 (1980).

9. Thomas Cartwright, *A confutation of the Rhemists translations, glosses and annotations on the New Testament* (Leyden, 1618), sig. B3. Whitaker made the same point, albeit in rather less colourful language, in his *Disputatio de sacra scriptura* (Cambridge, 1588), translated by W. Fitzgerald as *A disputation of holy scripture* (Parker Society, Cambridge, 1848).

10. Cartwright, *A confutation*, sig. Cv.

11. *Ibid.*, p. 359.

12. Pembroke College, Cambridge, Mss LC. 2. 164 fols. 27v and 25v.

13. E. Cardwell, *A history of conferences and other proceedings connected with the Book of Common Prayer 1558–1690* (Oxford, 1840), pp. 180–1, 191–2.

14. Cartwright, *A confutation*, sig. B3.

Bibliography

MANUSCRIPT SOURCES

British Library

Additional Mss 4276 (letters of sixteenth-century divines including William Whitaker)

Egerton Mss 2812 (letter book of Edward, Lord Zouche)

Harleian Mss 7028–50 (volumes 1–23 of the Baker manuscript)

Harley Mss 7042 (depositions from members of Francis Johnson's London separatist congregation)

Lansdowne Mss

Stowe Mss 743 (miscellaneous letters)

Stowe Mss 1058 (containing letters to and from Matthew Hutton)

Cambridge University Library

Mss Gg/1/29

Mss Mm/1/35–53 (volumes 24–42 of the Baker manuscript)

Mss Mm/2/25 and Mm/2/35 (notes and memoranda by Samuel Ward)

Cambridge University Registry Guard Book 6 (contains material from religious cases in the consistory court)

Cambridge University Registry Guard Book 90 (contains material on St Catharine's College)

Cambridge University Registry Guard Book 93 (contains material on St John's College)

Cambridge University Registry Guard Book 95 (contains material on Emmanuel College)

Cambridge University Registry Guard Book (Miscellanea) vol. 15 (papers relating to Chaderton's dispute with Peter Baro in 1583)

Cambridge University Registry Mandates of Elizabeth I

Cambridge Colleges

Emmanuel Col. 14. 1 (first college order book)

Col. 20. 1 (a book listing benefactors of the college)

Pembroke LC. II. 2. 164 (notes for a series of lectures by Laurence Chaderton of 1590; also some notes from lectures by William Perkins)

St John's Two letters to Burghley (one from Whitaker, the other from Eleazor Knox, both dealing with the dispute of 1590 over an alleged presbytery in the college)

Trinity B/14/9 (a letter book containing material about the 1595/6 theological disputes)

Chetham Library, Manchester
Mss Mun. A/2/78 (commonplace book of Abdias Ashton)

Inner Temple Library
Petyt Mss

Lambeth Palace Library
Mss 2550 (a volume of papers, many of them by or relating to Laurence Chaderton)

North Yorkshire Record Office
Hutton Mss ZAZ (notes taken by a student at St John's during the 1590s from lectures by many leading puritans, Chaderton, Perkins and Estye amongst them)

Public Record Office
Star Chamber Depositions 5A 49/34 (depositions taken from several presbyterian divines in 1590)

There is also some material scattered through the State Papers Domestic for Elizabeth I's reign

Dr Williams Library
Morrice A and B comprising 'A seconde parte of a register'

PRINTED SOURCES

A parte of a register... (Middelburg, 1593)

Arminius, Jacobus *Works* trans. and ed. J. and W. Nichols (3 vols., London, 1825–75)

Bancroft, Richard *A survay of the pretended holy discipline* (London, 1593)
    Dangerous positions (London, 1593)

Baro, Peter *Summa trium de praedestinatione sententiarum...* (Harderwijk, 1613)

Bradshaw, William *A triall of subscription by way of a preface unto certaine subscribers; and reasons for lesse against non-subscribers* (Middelburg, 1599)

A treatise of divine worship (Amsterdam, 1604)

A shorte treatise of the crosse in baptisme (Amsterdam, 1604)

A proposition concerning kneeling in the very act of receiving (Amsterdam, 1605)

Twelve generall arguments, proving the ceremonies are unlawfull in *Several treatises of worship and ceremonies* (London, 1660)

A treatise of the nature and use of things indifferent (Amsterdam, 1605)

A protestacion of the king's supremacie (Amsterdam, 1605)

English puritanisme containinge the maine opinions of the rigidest sort of those that are called puritanes in the realme of England (Amsterdam, 1605)

A myld and iust defence of certeyne arguments (n.p., 1606)

A treatise of justification (London, 1615)

The unreasonablenesse of the separation (Dort, 1614)

A preparation to the receiving of Christ's body and blood (London, 1617)

A plaine and pithy exposition of the second epistle to the Thessalonians (London, 1620)

A meditation of man's mortalitie (London, 1621)

A marriage feast (London, 1621)

Browne, Robert *An answere to master Cartwright* (London, 1583?)

Cartwright, Thomas *The rest of the second replie of Thomas Cartwright; agaynst master doctor Whitgift's second answer...* n.p., 1577)

A brief apologie of Thomas Cartwright against...Mr Sutcliffe... (Middelburg, 1596)

A confutation of the Rhemists translations, glosses and annotations on the New Testament (Leyden, 1618)

Cartwrightiana (ed. A. Peel and L. H. Carlson, London, 1951)

Chaderton, Laurence *An excellent and godly sermon...preached at Paules Crosse* (London, 1580)

A fruitful sermon, upon the 3, 4, 5, 6, 7 and 8 verse of the 12 chapter of the epistle of S. Paule to the Romanes (London, 1584)

Clarke, Samuel *A general martyrologie* (London, 1677)

Dering, Edward *A sermon preached before the queenes maiestie* (London, 1570)

Dering, Edward and More, John *A briefe and necessarie catechisme* (Middelburg, 1590)

Dillingham, William *Life of Laurence Chaderton* (transl. E. S. Shuckburgh, Cambridge, 1884)

Fairlambe, Peter *The recantation of a brownist or a reformed puritan* (London, 1606)

Fenner, Dudley *A defence of the godlie ministers* (Middelburg, 1587)

Fulke, William *The text of the New Testament* (London, 1589)

Hutton, Matthew *Brevis et dilucida explicatio verae, certae et consolationis plenae doctrinae de electione, praedestinatione et reprobatione* (Harderwijk, 1613)

Nashe, Thomas *Works* (ed. R. B. McKerrow, Oxford, 1958)

Peck, Francis *Desiderata curiosa* (2 vols., London, 1732–5)

Penry, John *A defence of that which hath bin written* (London, 1589)

Some, Robert *A godly treatise wherein are examined and confuted many execrable fancies* (London, 1589)

  A godly treatise containing and deciding certaine questions moved of late in London and other places touching the ministrie, sacraments and church (London, 1588)

Sutcliffe, Mathew *An answere to a certaine libel supplicatorie* (London, 1592)

Throckmorton, Job (?) *M. Some laid open in his coulers* (Rochelle, 1589)

Travers, Walter *A full and plaine declaration of ecclesiasticall discipline owt of the word of God* (Zurich, 1574)

  An answere to a supplicatorie epistle of G. T. for the pretended catholiques (London, 1583)

Whitaker, William *Catechismus parvus Latine* (*Alexander Nowell*) *et Graece* (*W.W.*) (London, 1574)

  Christianae pietatis prima institutio (by Alexander Nowell. Greek translation by Whitaker) (London, 1578)

  Joannis Jewelli adversus T. Hardingum volumen alterum... conversum in latinum a Guilielmo Whitakero (London, 1578)

  Ad rationes decem Edmundi Campioni iesuitae...responsio Guilielmi Whitakeri (London, 1581)

  Responsionis ad decem illas rationes...defensio contra confutationem Ioannis Duraei scoti, presbyteri, iesuitae (London, 1583) (Whitaker's work against Campion along with extended passages from his defence against Duraeus was translated by Richard Stock as *An Answere to the ten reasons of Edmund Campion the iesuit* (London, 1606))

  Ad Nicolai Sanderi demonstrationes...responsio Guilielmi Whitakeri (London, 1583)

  An Answere to a certeine booke written by M. William Rainolds (Cambridge, 1585)

  Disputatio de sacra scriptura (Cambridge, 1588) (The Parker Society published a translation of this work by W. Fitzgerald under the title *A disputation of holy scripture* (Cambridge, 1848))

Adversus Thomae Stapletoni...defensionem (Cambridge, 1594)

Praelectiones...de ecclesia ed. J. Allenson (Cambridge, 1599) (The contains a life of Whitaker by Abdias Ashton as well as the text of Whitaker's last public sermon under the title *Cygnea Cantio*)

Praelectiones...de conciliis ed. J. Allenson (Cambridge, 1600) (This contains Whitaker's *Praelectio habita Februarii 27 Anno. Dom. 1594/5*)

Whitgift, John *Works* (3 vols., Parker Society, Cambridge, 1851–3)

Index

349

Printed in the United Kingdom
by Lightning Source UK Ltd.
121618UK00001B/129/A